Black Americans and the White Man's Burden
1898–1903

BLACKS IN THE NEW WORLD

August Meier, Series Editor

Willard B. Gatewood, Jr.

BLACK AMERICANS
and the
WHITE MAN'S BURDEN
1898-1903

UNIVERSITY OF ILLINOIS PRESS

Urbana   Chicago   London

LIBRARY OF CONGRESS CATALOGING IN PUBLICATION DATA

Gatewood, Willard B.
   Black Americans and the white man's burden, 1898–1903.

   (Blacks in the new world)
   Bibliography: p.
   Includes index.
   1. United States—History—War of 1898—Public
opinion. 2. United States—History—War of 1898—Negro
troops. 3. Negroes—History—1877–1964. 4. Philippine
Islands—History—Insurrection, 1899–1901. I. Title.
II. Series.
E721.G27   973.8′9   75-9945
ISBN 0-252-00475-2

For
Robert Gunn Crawford
friend and scholar

Take up the White Man's burden—
  Send forth the best ye breed—
Go, bind your sons to exile
  To serve your captives' need;
To wait, in heavy harness,
  On fluttered folk and wild—
Your new-caught, sullen peoples,
  Half-devil and half-child.

—Rudyard Kipling,
The White Man's Burden
(1899), stanza 1

Preface

America's overseas expansion at the close of the nineteenth century has been the subject of a voluminous and varied historical literature. In addition to broad interpretative works concerned with the origins, nature, and implications of the new imperialism, numerous monographs and essays have concentrated on more specific aspects of the topic. Despite wide differences in approach and emphasis, most of these studies at least touch upon the relationship between imperialism and racism. For some scholars, in fact, the nation's embrace of an imperialistic policy played an important role in transforming the "Mississippi plan" of race relations into the American Way. Perhaps more acutely than other Americans, Negro citizens at the time were conscious of the domestic ramifications of overseas expansion. This study attempts to chart their responses to and their role in the quest for empire between 1898 and 1903. I hope it contributes another dimension to the existing literature on America's imperialistic endeavors and provides some insight into what Negroes themselves perceived as the impact of such enterprises upon their place in American society.

Confronted by a rising tide of prejudice and discrimination in the 1890's, Negro Americans increasingly emphasized self-help, group loyalty, and racial solidarity. Their heightened race consciousness was nowhere more evident than in their responses to the imperialistic activities of Western nations, especially the United States, among darker races at the turn of the century. No less than whites, blacks voiced a variety of opinions regarding the nation's involvement in Hawaii, Cuba, Puerto Rico, and the Philippines. Some opposed it as an expression of Anglo-Saxon supremacy and as a perverted ordering of national priorities which would further undermine the already precarious condition of black citizens; others enthusiastically embraced the New Manifest Destiny in the belief that Negroes would reap a rich and variegated harvest from colonies in the Caribbean and Pacific. But whether Negro Americans supported or opposed overseas expansion, the perspective from which they viewed the nation's outward thrust was substantially different from that of whites. Threatened by a proliferation of legal and extralegal Jim Crow devices, they responded to the Spanish-American War and the establishment of the new empire within the context of their own deteriorating status. Although their plight as an oppressed colored minority within a white-dominated society may well have sharpened their perception of the discrepancies between the rhetoric and realities of imperialism, it scarcely simplified their task of formulating a consistent attitude toward such a policy.

Convinced that racism pervaded the thought of many whites, anti-imperialists as well as imperialists, few were ever wholly reconciled to the arguments of either. Throughout the 1890's Negroes became increasingly aware of the contradiction inherent in a foreign policy of intervention and expansion justified on the grounds of helping the less fortunate. They consistently argued that charity begins at home, or at least it ought to. Although they were reluctant to oppose a policy of imperialism when it came to be identified with the party of Lincoln, their traditional allegiance to Republicanism by no means insured their unqualified endorsement of the nation's colonial experiments.

The vacillation and ambiguity which characterized many Negro Americans' reaction to overseas expansion stemmed in large measure from the dilemmas which it posed for them. On one hand, American military intervention in Cuba, Puerto Rico, and the Philippines appeared to provide opportunities for them to demonstrate their patriotism on the battlefield and thereby enhance their status within American society. On the other hand, as a disadvantaged people desirous of sharing more equitably the rights and privileges of first-class citizenship, they tended to identify racially and ideologically with the colored societies threatened by imperialism. The conflict between the desire to promote their own self-interest and their sympathy for the aspirations of their colored cousins overseas resulted in a potpourri of ambivalent, often contradictory, attitudes which are treated in this volume.

Numerous individuals and institutions provided invaluable assistance in the preparation of this study. I am particularly indebted to librarians and archivists at the University of Arkansas, University of Georgia, Duke University, University of North Carolina, Library of Congress, National Archives, North Carolina State Department of Archives and History, Indiana University, Ohio Historical Society, St. Louis Public Library, New York Public Library (Schomburg Collection), Atlanta University, Alabama Department of Archives and History, United States Army Military History Collection (Carlisle Barracks, Pennsylvania) and Indiana State Library. A grant from the American Philosophical Society greatly facilitated my research. The suggestions and criticisms made by August Meier, Benjamin Quarles, and Louis R. Harlan were always perceptive and extraordinarily helpful. Two of my colleagues, James S. Chase and Randall B. Woods, who also read the manuscript, gave me the benefit of their wise counsel. Emma Lou Thornbrough shared with me information concerning T. Thomas Fortune's mission to the Philippines; L. G. DeLay called my attention to pertinent items in the Nebraska State Historical Society's collections which otherwise would have been overlooked; Louis R. Harlan was generous in providing guidance in regard to materials in the Booker T. Washington Papers. Barbara Lineberger, who typed and retyped the manuscript, displayed extraordinary patience and an uncanny ability to decipher my copy. A special debt of gratitude is due Ann Lowry Weir of the University of Illinois Press for her conscientious editorial assistance. My wife, Lu Brown Gatewood, maintained a constant interest in the project and is in large measure responsible for its completion.

W.B.G.

Contents

One

Overseas Expansion and the Black American: The Setting

Until the Indian problem is settled in the West and the South is made, forced, compelled to live up to the constitutional provision according to equal and exact justice to all citizens in its borders, we shall have no time to look after the disorders provoked by the turbulent and lawless elements of sister governments.

—*New York Age,* July 11, 1891

When it is remembered that the majority of the Cuban insurgents and soldiers are colored people, this unanimity of demand [for Cuban independence] on the part of the press of the country can hardly be understood, unless it be that the Cuban blacks are to pull the chestnuts out of the Spanish fire for the benefit of the Cuban and American whites. Cuba is extremely near our Southern border and everybody knows that the South is wedded to the doctrine of "white supremacy."

—Kansas City *American Citizen,*
October 4, 1895

American life underwent a spectacular transformation during the years between Robert E. Lee's surrender at Appomattox Courthouse and Theodore Roosevelt's charge up San Juan Hill. No American, regardless of occupation, status, or color, escaped the pervasive impact of the economic revolution of the late nineteenth century. The emergence of a new industrial and urban society substantially altered the traditional ideas of democracy and reshaped or redefined issues which attracted public concern. The proliferation of factories and machines was accompanied by the organization of giant corporations and the rise of a new power elite whose gospel of wealth came to assume the status of a folk faith. The same Social Darwinism invoked to justify the privileged position of the new elite served as a rationale for Anglo-Saxon supremacy and as a vindication of overseas expansion. Nothwithstanding the existence of glaring inequities in the standard of living, the regular recurrence of economic crises, and the loud protests of labor and agrarian reformers, the dominant mood of the era was one of indomitable optimism and supreme confidence.

The harsh realities of life, however, acted as a powerful deterrent to such confidence among those whose complexion placed them outside the Anglo-Saxon family. Among such Americans, the largest single group was the black citizenry. For Negro Americans the late nineteenth century, and especially its final decade, was a time of shattered hopes and thwarted aspirations. Although the materialistic, Social Darwinist orientation was not without influence in the black community, Negroes, probably more than any other citizens, had little reason to believe in the authenticity of Horatio Alger's success motif. In an age of rising expectations they encountered a degree of social segregation, political disfranchisement, educational discrimination, and economic exploitation experienced by no other segment of the American population. Even in the struggle waged by labor and reform groups against the dominant economic forces, "Negroes appeared to be among the losers." [1] Excluded from the American Dream and denied opportunities to achieve the full height of manhood, the black citizen had to wage a persistent battle for self-identity and self-esteem in a society dominated by those who viewed him either as a harmless child or as a fiendish beast. But whether child or beast, he belonged to an inferior race. The prestigious *Encyclopaedia Britannica,* in its American edition of 1895, invoked the authority of science to validate its assertion that "the inherent mental inferiority of blacks" was "an inferiority which is even more marked than their physical differences." [2]

In 1890 black Americans entered what one Negro scholar has

1. August Meier, *Negro Thought in America, 1880–1915: Racial Ideologies in the Age of Booker T. Washington* (Ann Arbor: University of Michigan Press, 1963), p. 23.
2. Lewis H. Carlson and George A. Colburn, eds., *In Their Place: White America Defines Her Minorities, 1850–1950* (New York: John Wiley and Sons, 1972), p. 98.

termed "the vale of tears." [3] The promise of Reconstruction lay in shambles; constitutional amendments designed to protect the rights of black citizens had become largely inoperative through a succession of anti-egalitarian decisions by the federal courts. The virtual disappearance of the moral idealism which had characterized the abolitionist movement and the indifference of the Republican party toward the black man's rights removed most restraints against the institutionalization of crude negrophobia. All the while, white supremacy polemicists formulated elaborate theories of black degeneracy which not only provided a rationale for the proliferation of legal and extralegal Jim Crow contrivances, but also served as apologies for the increasing instances of lynching and other forms of racial violence.[4] Nor was the virulent racism of the 1890's confined to the states of the old Confederacy. The nation, in fact, had acquiesced in the southern solution to the Negro Question. In 1890 Congressman Henry Cabot Lodge's "force bill," which was designed to protect the Negro's exercise of suffrage in the South, failed because the Republicans gave higher priority to economic issues and intersectional harmony.[5] The Lodge bill marked the last effort by a federal administration to protect Negro voting rights in the South until the passage of a civil rights act sixty-seven years later. "We have made friends with the Southerners," William Graham Sumner noted. "They and we are hugging each other. . . . The Negro's day is over. He is out of fashion." [6]

In the 1890's, as in other periods when Negroes were "out of fashion," they moved from an emphasis upon politics, agitation, and assimilation toward a philosophy emphasizing self-help, group loyalty, race pride, and industrial education. This philosophy, which marked a shift in tactics rather than in ultimate aims, culminated in the message of Booker T. Washington of Tuskegee

3. Benjamin Brawley, *A Social History of the American Negro* (New York: Macmillan, 1921), p. 297.

4. George M. Frederickson, *The Black Image in the White Mind: The Debate on Afro-American Character and Destiny, 1817–1914* (New York: Harper and Row, 1971), pp. 228–282.

5. Stanley P. Hirshson, *Farewell to the Bloody Shirt: Northern Republicans and the Southern Negro, 1877–1893* (Bloomington: Indiana University Press, 1962), pp. 200–235.

6. Quoted in David Healy, *U.S. Expansionism: The Imperialist Urge in the 1890's* (Madison: University of Wisconsin Press, 1970), p. 41.

Institute, the principal spokesman of black America by the time of Frederick Douglass's death in 1895. The question of a race leader continued to prompt considerable discussion in the Negro community after that date, and numerous individuals aspired to the title. But Washington, a man who publicly eschewed politics and articulated a philosophy acceptable to whites, ultimately emerged as the most influential black man in the United States. Many whites interpreted the emergence of Washington to mean that Negroes had abandoned their quest for full citizenship.

In analyzing the differences between Douglass and Washington, a perceptive black contemporary noted that the "two men are in part products of their own times but are also natural antipodes." In the age of moral idealism Douglass had for a half-century functioned as a bold and fearless leader of heroic proportions, inspiring his people by voicing their highest aspirations. Coming to prominence in "an age of merchant princes" when legalized racism was well underway, Washington assumed the role of an accommodationist willing to accept "the best terms which he thinks it possible to secure" and inclined to tell the white world what it was disposed to listen to, rather than what it needed to hear. A social pacifist who accepted segregation as the price of racial harmony, he employed the rhetoric of optimism, materialism, and Social Darwinism so fashionable in the acquisitive society of the late nineteenth century in elaborating upon economic self-help, initiative, and racial solidarity as the means by which Negroes could achieve their constitutional rights. His emphasis upon the acquisition of property and high moral character, coupled with vague, ambiguous references to ultimate goals, prompted whites to mistake his means for his ends. By neither avowing nor disclaiming "in distinctive terms a single plank in the platform of Douglass," Washington encouraged whites to believe that he accepted "their estimate of the Negro's inferior place in the social scheme," at the same time exasperating blacks who desired from him "a definitive statement upon questions of vital concern." [7]

7. Kelly Miller, "Washington's Policy," in Hugh Hawkins, ed., *Booker T. Washington and His Critics: The Problem of Negro Leadership* (Boston: D. C. Heath, 1962), pp. 49–54.

But the wizard of Tuskegee was a man of many faces, adept at adjusting his tactics to fit the occasion and the audience. However accommodating or obsequious he may have appeared in public, his secret campaigns against disfranchisement, peonage, and Jim Crow were scarcely the actions of a man who acquiesced in the prevailing racial system.[8]

Not all Negroes committed to Washington's formula of economic uplift emulated his circumspect, accommodationist tactics: what he did secretly to defend Negro rights they were likely to do publicly. For example, the militant editor of the *New York Age,* T. Thomas Fortune, combined the self-help formula of his friend from Tuskegee with the protest tradition of Douglass.[9] Clearly, the emergence of Washington did not bring an end to black protest any more than it terminated the black man's interest in politics. Even Washington, who in his famous Atlanta Address of 1895 disparaged the involvement of Negroes in politics, became in time a black Warwick who distributed patronage, constructed political alliances, and served as confidant to presidents.

The themes of group loyalty, race pride, and self-help which reached maturity in the 1890's and were incorporated into the doctrine of Booker T. Washington produced within the Negro community a kind of ethnocentrism or black nationalism. As August Meier has observed, this ethnocentrism, which emphasized support for Negro enterprises and the cultivation of pride in black history, "implied that Negroes should remain a distinctly separate group in American society but that they should also enjoy the rights of citizenship." In fact, for Washington and those who embraced his policy of conciliation and gradualism, "the separatist ideology functioned both as a mechanism of accommodation to American racism and as a device for overcoming it." [10] While an appeal to racial consciousness was a standard ingredient in the tactic of accommodationism, the most militant form of

8. For a biographical interpretation of Washington, see Louis R. Harlan, "Booker T. Washington in Biographical Perspective," *American Historical Review*, LXXV (October, 1970), 1581–99; Louis R. Harlan, "The Secret Life of Booker T. Washington," *Journal of Southern History*, XXXVII (August, 1971), 393–416.

9. Meier, *Negro Thought in America*, pp. 167, 226.

10. *Ibid.*, p. 167; August Meier, Elliott Rudwick and Francis L. Broderick, eds., *Black Protest Thought in the Twentieth Century* (Indianapolis: Bobbs-Merrill, 1965), p. xxv.

black nationalism in the late nineteenth century was expressed
by Henry M. Turner, a well-known bishop in the African Methodist Episcopal Church.[11] An indomitable emigrationist whose
style and rhetoric had little in common with those of the accom-
modationists, Turner led a back-to-Africa movement which attracted considerable support among marginal black farmers in
the South early in the 1890's. Although black citizens in general
applauded Turner's bold assault on racism in the United States,
relatively few actually migrated to Africa even at the height of
his black nationalist movement. The Negro middle class in particular failed to share Turner's pessimism about the future of
black citizens in America. The progress of the race in the quarter-
century since Emancipation, more evident from the perspective
of the black middle class than for those black Southerners still in
quasi-slavery, was sufficient to keep alive the hope of ultimately
sharing equitably in the American Dream. Notwithstanding the
rising tide of violence and repression which prompted some Negro
Americans to embrace emigration, the prevailing view within the
articulate black community in the years following Washington's
Atlanta Compromise was that black citizens should "work out
their own destiny" within the United States.[12]

Even though the message of Tuskegee represented a summation
of trends in Negro thought that had become dominant by 1895,
black Americans continued to exhibit widely diverse responses to
their deteriorating status. These responses ranged from obsequious toadyism to the highly vocal rage of the disesteemed. A complex of circumstances that existed in the late 1890's helps explain
the fluidity and variation that characterized the ideological views
voiced by Negroes. At the time Washington was still in the process of consolidating his position as the foremost spokesman of
black America. Because his power had not yet reached its zenith,
there was less risk involved in diverging from the Tuskegee line.

11. See J. Minton Batten, "Henry M. Turner: Negro Bishop Extraordinary,"
Church History, VII (September, 1938), 231–246.
12. See Edwin S. Redkey, *Black Exodus: Black Nationalist and Back to Africa
Movements, 1890–1910* (New Haven: Yale University Press, 1969); Edwin S. Redkey,
"The Flowering of Black Nationalism: Henry McNeal Turner and Marcus Garvey,"
in Nathan I. Huggins, Martin Kelson, and Daniel M. Fox, eds., *Key Issues in the
Afro-American Experience*, 2 vols. (New York: Harcourt Brace Jovanovich, 1971),
II, 108–115.

Furthermore, the mounting sense of crisis which gripped black Americans prompted a frantic search for alternatives which neither conformed to Washington's formula nor indicated much concern for ideological consistency.

The oppressive atmosphere of the late 1890's which quickened the Negro's awareness of belonging to a "nation within a nation" and encouraged an emphasis on racial separatism also accentuated what W. E. B. Du Bois described as the sense of twoness present among all black citizens; as Americans and as Negroes, they possessed "two warring ideals in one dark body." [13] Several years before Du Bois became identified as Washington's principal adversary, he pointed up the dilemma posed by the anomalous position of Negroes in American society. "What, after all, am I?" he asked in 1897. "Am I an American or am I a Negro? Can I be both? Or is it my duty to cease to be a Negro as soon as possible and be an American? If I strive as a Negro, am I not perpetuating the very cleft that threatens and separates Black and White America?" [14] The hesitation and doubt spawned by such self-questioning during the closing years of the nineteenth century made those years "a time of vacillation and contradiction for the American Negro." [15] The response of black citizens to the expansionist trends in American foreign policy during this era dramatized the vacillation and contradiction born out of their unreconciled strivings.

Because black Americans were preoccupied in the 1890's with their own struggles for full citizenship, they devoted relatively little attention to foreign affairs.[16] The principal exceptions were incidents involving either Negro citizens from the United States or colored peoples elsewhere. For example, the episode in American diplomacy which perhaps elicited the most interest among black citizens prior to 1897 was the so-called Waller affair. In 1891 President Benjamin Harrison appointed a prominent black Republican from Kansas, John L. Waller, as American consul

13. W. E. B. Du Bois, *The Souls of Black Folk: Essays and Sketches* (Chicago: A. C. McClurg, 1931), p. 3.
14. W. E. B. Du Bois, *The Conservation of the Races* (Washington: American Negro Academy, 1897), Occasional Papers, No. 2, p. 11.
15. *Ibid.*, pp. 11–12.
16. See the conclusions in Elsie M. Lewis, "The Political Mind of the Negro, 1865–1900," *Journal of Southern History*, XXI (May, 1955), 201–202.

to Madagascar. Upon retiring from that post in January, 1894, Waller remained in Madagascar with a "view to establish relations in trade between that country" and the United States. In time, he received from the native rulers a large land concession on which to develop rubber and timber resources. His activities aroused the hostility of French authorities who were then in the process of extending their control over the island. With the arrival of French troops in December, 1894, they proclaimed martial law and placed all postal dispatches under surveillance. Early the following year, after confiscating letters written by Waller, the French arrested him for conspiring to undermine their authority. Tried and convicted by a military tribunal, the ex-consul was sentenced to twenty years in prison.[17]

Negro Americans in particular were outraged by what they considered the high-handed treatment of an American citizen by a foreign power. The incident also provided ample opportunity for them to express their hostility toward European imperialistic ventures which reduced independent colored nations to colonial status. For months the editorial columns of black journals throughout the United States were filled with comments on the Waller case.[18] George L. Knox, a black businessman and editor in Indianapolis, organized a successful campaign to raise funds to secure Waller's release. Many Negroes came to believe that the administration of President Grover Cleveland would have acted more promptly and vigorously if the American citizen "rotting in the Marseilles prison" had been white rather than black.[19] Prodded into action by the protests of black citizens as well as others critical of his handling of the case, President Cleveland referred to the Waller affair in his annual message to Congress in December, 1895, and promised a prompt and satisfactory settle-

17. Katheryn R. Nickles, "The Case of John L. Waller," *Ozark Historical Review*, I (Spring, 1972), 21–30; see also *Papers Relating to the Foreign Relations of the United States, 1895* (Washington: Government Printing Office, 1896), pp. 251–396; *New York Age*, May 9, 1891.

18. *The Freeman* (Indianapolis), September 28, October 12, 19, 26, November 2, 30, December 7, 1895, January 4, 18, March 7, 1896; *The Afro-American* (Baltimore), August 10, October 28, 1895; *Washington Bee*, September 14, 28, 1895; *The Enterprise* (Omaha), February 29, 1896; *The Gazette* (Cleveland), April 27, May 4, June 8, 22, July 13, 20, October 26, 1895.

19. Indianapolis *Freeman*, October 13, November 30, December 7, 1895; Cleveland *Gazette*, June 22, July 13, August 31, 1895.

ment of it. Early the following year, through the combined efforts of the president and various American diplomats, the French government was persuaded to release Waller from prison, where he had remained for almost a year.[20]

Throughout the 1890's the racial consciousness of black Americans was especially evident in the attention they lavished upon the affairs of black nations in Africa and the West Indies. In fact, Liberia, Haiti, and the Dominican Republic were the most durable topics of their concern with foreign affairs until the Cuban question assumed preeminence late in the decade. The historic relationship between the American Colonization Society and Liberia, as well as the visits to the United States of the Liberian pan-African propagandist Edward W. Blyden and the prominence of Bishop Turner's emigration schemes, sustained the interest of Negro Americans in the affairs of this West African republic. In his *School History of the Negro Race in America,* published in 1891, Edward A. Johnson claimed that the success of black people in Liberia offered proof of "what the race can do under favorable circumstances." [21] Of no less importance to them were developments among the black peoples of the West Indies, especially in the two Negro republics, Haiti and the Dominican Republic. As in the case of Liberia, American diplomatic and consular posts in these Caribbean nations came to be used as patronage rewards for politically influential Negro citizens.[22]

Frederick Douglass, who in 1889 became the third Negro American to serve as minister to Haiti, participated in the unsuccessful negotiations aimed at securing for the United States a lease on the Haitian port of Môle-Saint-Nicolas. Whites who held him responsible for the failure of the negotiations "accused him of permitting his identity with the Negro people of Haiti to interfere with his duty as an American minister." [23] His biographer points out that Douglass endorsed the lease for the same reasons that he

20. Nickles, "The Case of John L. Waller," pp. 29–30.

21. Redkey, *Black Exodus,* pp. 47–72; Edward A. Johnson, *School History of the Negro Race in America from 1691 to 1890* (Chicago: W. B. Conkey, 1891), p. 89.

22. See James A. Padgett, "Diplomats to Haiti and Their Diplomacy," *Journal of Negro Hisory,* XXV (July, 1940), 265–330.

23. Philip S. Foner, *The Life and Writings of Frederick Douglass,* 4 vols. (New York: International Publishers, 1955), IV, 137; see also *State Capital* (Springfield, Ill.), August 22, 1891.

favored American annexation of the Dominican Republic in the early 1870's. In both instances Douglass argued that the presence of "Saxon and Protestant civilization" would promote political stability and material progress among blacks in the Caribbean. A somewhat different interpretation by other scholars suggests that while Douglass faithfully executed his diplomatic instructions during the negotiations regarding the Môle lease, he nonetheless sought to protect "the interests of a country of the same race as his own." [24] Whatever the nature of Douglass's role, Negroes in the United States followed closely every development in American-Haitian relations.

Their reactions indicated the extent to which their own ethnic dualism affected their perception of issues in foreign policy, especially when a colored nation was involved. In 1891, for example, a Negro journalist in St. Paul credited the racist expressions of a white American lieutenant in Port-au-Prince with bringing about the failure of the Môle negotiations. "Color prejudice," he concluded, "has prevented the United States from securing the Môle St. Nicolas as a coaling station." [25] All the while the *New York Age,* which occasionally expressed concern over the influx of West Indian Negroes into New York, was hostile to any suggestion that the United States should annex Haiti; however, its editor was even more severe in his condemnation of anti-annexationists who argued that acquisition of the black republic would "increase our inferior and mongrel population." [26]

In 1897, when Germany broke off relations with Haiti and dispatched ships to Haitian waters, Negroes in the United States demanded that the State Department take as strong a stand as it had against Britain in the Venezuelan boundary controversy. Although the German-Haitian affair was ultimately settled peaceably through the mediation of the American minister in Port-au-Prince, some black citizens were not satisfied that the United States had acted with appropriate promptness or firmness in

24. Benjamin Quarles, *Frederick Douglass* (Washington: Associated Publishers, 1948), pp. 317–322; Rayford W. Logan, *The Diplomatic Relations of the United States with Haiti, 1776–1891* (Chapel Hill: University of North Carolina Press, 1941), p. 457; Myra Himelhoch, "Frederick Douglass and Haiti's Môle St. Nicolas," *Journal of Negro History,* LVI (July, 1971), 161–180.

25. *The Appeal* (St. Paul), May 28, 1891.

26. *New York Age,* March 3, June 13, 27, July 11, 18, August 1, 22, September 5, 1891.

dealing with Germany.[27] In explaining the difference between the position assumed by the United States in the Venezuelan dispute of 1895 and the Haitian affair two years later, a black Democratic editor in Omaha declared: "The skin of the average Haytien is quite dark. That of the average Venezuelan approaches in lightness the complexion of the dominant class of this country. See?" [28]

Although the appointment of diplomatic and consular officers for the Negro republics in the Caribbean invariably sparked lively discussions among black Americans, their interest in Haiti and the Dominican Republic involved considerably more than the distribution of diplomatic patronage. These nations stood as symbols of Negro self-government in the western hemisphere. As the Haitian commissioner at the Columbian Exposition at Chicago in 1893, Frederick Douglass delivered an eloquent address which defined the meaning of Haiti for all people of African ancestry. "The freedom that has come to the colored race the world over," he declared, "is largely due to the brave stand taken by the black sons of Haiti ninety years ago. When they struck for freedom, they builded better than they knew. Their swords were not drawn . . . simply for themselves alone. They were linked and interlinked with their race, and striking for freedom, they struck for the freedom of every black man in the world." The editor of the Omaha *Enterprise* boasted in 1896: "Hayti has maintained her nationality without invoking the intervention of any other power. Strong in natural resources and love of patriotism, her citizens have been her defense." [29] The national heroes of the West Indian republics such as Toussaint L'Ouverture occupied places of prominence in the black Americans' pantheon of "freedom fighters." [30] In 1891 a Negro in San Marcos, Texas, found a ready market for life-size portraits of L'Ouverture among his

27. *Appleton's Annual Cyclopaedia and Register of Important Events of the Year 1897* (New York: D. Appleton, 1898), pp. 381–392; Indianapolis *Freeman*, November 27, December 4, 11, 18, 1897; see also Harriet Gibbs Marshall, *The Story of Haiti* (Boston: Christopher Publishing, 1930), p. 108.

28. *The Afro-American Sentinel* (Omaha), December 18, 1897.

29. Frederick Douglass, "Lecture on Haiti," in Foner, *Life and Writings of Douglass*, IV, 484; *Omaha Enterprise*, February 1, 1896.

30. For example, a Negro weekly newspaper in Salt Lake City serialized a feature on "Toussaint L'Ouverture and the Republic of Hayti" in 1897. See *The Broad Ax* (Salt Lake City), April 3, 10, 17, 24, May 1, 8, 15, 1897; see also E. Johnson, *School History of the Negro Race*, pp. 186–189.

neighbors. He assured the Dominican president Ulises Heureaux that there were "fully 5000 well-to-do farmers in this section who would willingly emigrate to San Domingo if they knew the true condition of the country." The black Texan was "anxious to get out of Texas" because of the growing anti-Negro sentiment there, represented by the recent enactment of a separate coach law.[31] Despite such talk about emigration and the sporadic attempts of Heureaux to entice black Americans to settle in his country, few actually took up residence in the Negro republics of the Caribbean. Racial sentiment might forge a bond between them and the peoples of these nations, but black Americans, regardless of their plight in the United States, could scarcely expect to find respite in Haiti or the Dominican Republic.

Though sensitive to criticism of the instability and turbulence that characterized these West Indian republics, Negroes in the United States nonetheless recognized that such a state of affairs did little to enhance their own struggle for full citizenship. "It is a matter of serious regret," a Negro editor in Ohio commented in 1889, "that Hayti seems destined to periodic revolution; that a government of Negroes is unable to maintain its equilibrium; that the old story that Negroes are incapable of self-government comes very near being verified in the political life of the little island." [32] Three years later, during the discussion of the Lodge election bill, black spokesmen found themselves having to combat the notion that federal protection of the Negro's voting rights would turn the South "into another Hayti." [33] For black Americans, then, Haiti was at once a liability and a symbol of hope: on the one hand, its backwardness and instability were cited by American white supremacists as evidence that black citizens could not be entrusted with full civil rights; on the other, its very existence was proof that a Negro republic could survive in a hostile world dominated by powerful white nations. Although black Americans might regret the lack of material progress and popular democracy

31. Sumner Welles, *Naboth's Vineyard: The Dominican Republic, 1844–1924*, 2 vols. (New York: Payton and Clarke, 1928), I, 467.

32. Cleveland *Gazette*, January 5, 1889.

33. *New York Age*, May 9, 1891; see also *ibid.*, June 13, 27, 1891; Rayford W. Logan, *The Great Betrayal of the Negro from Rutherford B. Hayes to Woodrow Wilson* (New York: Collier Books, 1965), p. 77.

which characterized Haiti, they were inclined to view such conditions as a temporary phase in the nation's evolutionary development. "While we deplore this sad condition of things [in Haiti]," a well-known black editor remarked, "we are by no means despairing of Negroes in Hayti, or Negroes in America." [34] Black Americans believed that Haiti should be left "alone to work out her mission for the children of Africa in the New World and to fulfill her destiny among the Nations of the Earth." [35] Archibald Grimké, a Harvard-educated attorney and the son of a wealthy South Carolina planter who served as consul in the Dominican Republic from 1894 to 1898, probably expressed the prevailing sentiment of black citizens when he declared, a few years later, that if stability in this black republic required either the emergence of another strong man or the introduction of American rule, Dominicans should by all means choose the former. In Grimké's view the "colorphobia" which was certain to accompany the American flag constituted a far greater evil than political instability.[36]

During much of the 1890's Negro citizens tended to focus on specific incidents in American diplomacy (such as the Waller case) which had obvious racial implications, rather than upon the larger questions of policy. But those who did note the nation's increasing international complications voiced reservations about the direction of American foreign policy. For them, the question was one of perverted national priorities. In 1892 a black editor in Kansas City stated the issue when he pointed out that the U.S. government could lavish attention on "the seals in the icy waters of Alaska" and spend millions to "protect a few sailors in the waters of South America" but was unable to find any means to protect the lives and property of its own Negro citizens "within the shadow of the Capitol." [37] For T. Thomas Fortune, any policy

34. Cleveland *Gazette*, January 5, 1889. *New York Age* (July 18, 1891) responded to criticism of Haiti by declaring: "White men are seldom unjust to themselves. They are more rarely just to black men."

35. E. Don Carlos Bassett, "Should Haiti Be Annexed by the United States?" *Voice of the Negro*, I (May, 1904), 198; see also T. Thomas Fortune, "Haytian Revolutions," *ibid.* (April, 1904), 138–142; *New York Age*, June 27, 1891.

36. Archibald Grimké, "The Dominican Republic and Her Revolutions," *Voice of the Negro*, I (April, 1904), 133–138.

37. Indianapolis *Freeman*, October 12, 1895; *American Citizen* (Kansas City), March 11, 1892.

of intervention or expansion justified on the grounds of helping the less fortunate constituted the grossest hypocrisy as long as the United States allowed its own black minority to be subjected to violence and repression. He declared in 1891:

> If the advice of the newspapers . . . was followed, our Government would throw the Monroe Doctrine to the bow-wows and go in for conquering and absorbing all the little independent republics in South America and the West Indies. But the people of the United States will submit to no such policy of conquest and absorption. They have as much as they can manage at home. Until the Indian problem is settled in the West and the South is made, forced, compelled to live up to the constitutional provision of according equal and exact justice to all citizens in its borders, we shall have no time to look after the disorders provoked by the turbulent and lawless elements of sister governments.[38]

Such an attitude, which appears to have been shared by most black Americans, helps explain their reaction to the general drift of American diplomacy.

Insofar as black citizens did concern themselves with expansionist trends in foreign policy, they concentrated on issues involving other peoples of color. The crisis with Chile in 1891 and the Venezuelan boundary dispute in the middle of the decade were largely ignored in the black community, but the question of American annexation of Hawaii prompted considerable discussion because Negro citizens identified with the aspirations of non-Anglo-Saxon native islanders. Their sympathy lay with the "Hawaii for Hawaiians" movement of Queen Liliuokalani, rather than with the provisional republic established on the islands by white Americans. Frederick Douglass condemned what he termed the "unwarrantable intermeddling" of Americans in Hawaiian affairs, also accusing the annexationists of employing fraud and chicanery in deposing the native monarch. "The stories afloat to blacken the character of the Queen," he wrote, "do not deceive me."[39] A black editor in Washington suspected that cartoons in

38. *New York Age,* July 11, 1891; see also Indianapolis *Freeman,* March 14, 1896.
39. Frederick Douglass to Caesar Celso Moreno, March, 1894, in Foner, *Life and Writings of Douglass,* IV, 490; see also *Washington Bee,* September 2, November 11, 1893, January 6, 1894; Omaha *Enterprise,* June 19, 1897; Cleveland *Gazette,* July 1, 1893. For the opposition of white Americans to Hawaiian annexation, see

white newspapers depicting the Queen as a "thick lip and unrefined Negress" were indicative of the status which Hawaiians would be assigned if they came under the protection of the American flag.[40] Harry C. Smith, the outspoken editor of the Cleveland *Gazette* and veteran crusader for the civil rights of black people in Ohio, was more direct in his opposition to the annexation movement. In his view, the brown people of the Hawaiian Islands would forfeit their freedom by submitting to American rule because they would be subjected to precisely the same discriminatory treatment accorded colored people already living in the United States. Voicing similar sentiments, W. S. Scarborough, a well-known Negro scholar at Wilberforce University, pointed out that the fate of Hawaiians under American control should be obvious, since "no race or class has any standing in the United States except the Anglo-Saxon." Scarborough, in fact, was opposed to all forms of expansion and annexation which did not "imply . . . equality of races."[41] Those Negroes who expressed their views regarding the annexation of Hawaii appeared to approve President Cleveland's opposition to what they termed the "Hawaiian steal."[42]

By 1897, when McKinley submitted a new Hawaiian annexation treaty to the Senate, the black community had begun to exhibit a great interest in the general question of overseas expansion. Negro spokesmen who opposed the ratification of the treaty claimed that the prompt recognition of the provisional republic had been tantamount to "racial recognition which to say the least is very small business for our government to be in. . . ." They maintained that the United States could ill afford to assist in making Hawaii "an American plantation of Claus Spreckels," the sugar baron who was erroneously held responsible for plotting the overthrow of the government "of the dark faced natives."[43] A Negro editor in Omaha concluded that "a grosser piece of in-

E. Berkeley Tompkins, *Anti-Imperialism in the United States: The Great Debate, 1890–1920* (Philadelphia: University of Pennsylvania Press, 1971), pp. 27–119.

40. *Washington Bee,* November 25, 1893.

41. Cleveland *Gazette,* April 22, July 1, 1893.

42. *Washington Bee,* December 9, 1893; *Afro-American Advocate* (Coffeyville, Kans.), April 7, 1893.

43. *The Broad-Axe* (St. Paul), July 17, 1897.

justice was never perpetrated against a weak people." [44] Among
those Negroes concerned about "the policy of widening the borders of the country," there was some feeling that such a policy
might be inaugurated more appropriately in Cuba, where "the
experiment of a colonial policy" was less likely to encounter "so
many complications." [45] But the prevailing view appeared to oppose any annexation scheme which would exploit darker races or
deny the fulfillment of their national aspirations. McKinley's
treaty was generally looked upon as providing legal sanction for
the sugar trust to engage in exploitation of the Hawaiian natives,
whose government had already been usurped by a group of white
American adventurers.[46]

The debate over imperialism touched off by the Hawaiian
question became more intense with the outbreak of a revolt
against Spanish rule in Cuba in 1895. The insurrection rekindled
black Americans' interest in Cuban affairs in general, and in its
colored population in particular. A quarter-century earlier, during the Ten Years War (1868–78) when Cuba tried unsuccessfully
to gain its independence, Negro citizens had been outspoken in
their support of the rebel cause. A group of well-known black
Americans including Henry Highland Garnet, Frederick Douglass, and John Mercer Langston petitioned President Grant to
extend belligerent status to the Cuban rebels. Since an independent Cuba came to mean the emancipation of 400,000 Afro-Cuban
slaves, black Americans were all the more concerned about the
outcome of the rebellion. In outlining an appropriate attitude for
Negro Americans to assume toward the Cuban struggle, John M.
Langston in 1873 suggested that they should concern themselves
with more than the mere abolition of slavery on the island. "Especially let the colored American realize that wherever humanity
struggles for National existence and recognition," he declared,
"there his sympathies should be felt, and his word and succor inspiring, encouraging and supporting." [47]

The broader vision enunciated by Langston became evident
among black Americans in their response to the Cuban crisis in

44. Omaha *Enterprise*, June 19, 1897.
45. Indianapolis *Freeman*, July 3, 1897.
46. *Illinois Record* (Springfield), November 6, 1897.
47. Quarles, *Frederick Douglass*, pp. 284–286.

1895, when slavery was no longer an issue. Blacks were quick to emphasize their racial kinship with a large segment of the Cuban population, and to equate the Cubans' fight for independence with their own struggle for first-class citizenship. They endorsed American intervention in Cuba for precisely the same reasons that they opposed it in Hawaii: intervention in Hawaii thwarted the national aspirations of the dark-skinned natives, while intervention in Cuba promised to end the autocratic rule of Spain and pave the way for an independent, democratic regime which Negro Americans consistently envisioned as a black republic.[48]

The Cuban revolt against Spain had scarcely gotten underway when Negroes in the United States began to describe it as a black man's war. Their accounts identified most of the rebel leaders as men of color. Of these, none achieved greater esteem among Americans than the mulatto general Antonio Maceo, whose exploits received full coverage in the Negro press. Maceo, said one editor, was the type of leader "around whom the aspiring young Negro may twine his brightest hopes for the future." [49] By 1896 Negroes throughout the United States had taken up the cry, "All hail Cuba Libre!" A mass meeting of black citizens in Chicago expressed sympathy for the revolutionary spirit in Cuba and pledged support to the cause of Cuban independence. Dr. Allen A. Wesley, a black physician in that city who carried on a regular correspondence with Maceo, was an outspoken advocate of war with Spain to free Cuba from the harsh program instituted by General Valeriano Weyler. While serving as a surgeon on Maceo's staff, another Negro physician, Dr. L. A. Hinds of South Bend, Indiana, sent home reports regarding the illustrious general and his "army of colored men" which circulated widely in the Negro American community.[50] A Negro editor in Parsons, Kansas, ex-

48. Cleveland *Gazette*, May 11, 1895; Indianapolis *Freeman*, June 22, August 3, September 7, 14, 1895; Baltimore *Afro-American*, December 14, 1895.

49. Cleveland *Gazette*, May 11, November 2, 1895, March 14, 1896; Omaha *Afro-American Sentinel*, February 22, 1896; Indianapolis *Freeman*, March 7, April 11, July 25, August 7, 1896, October 31, 1897; *Parsons Weekly Blade* (Parsons, Kans.), May 2, 1896. For a history of the Cuban Revolution between 1895 and 1899, with special attention devoted to Maceo, see the first volume of Philip S. Foner, *The Spanish-Cuban-American War and The Birth of American Imperialism*, 2 vols. (New York: Monthly Review Press, 1972).

50. Omaha *Enterprise*, November 16, 1895; Cleveland *Gazette*, March 14, 1896, May 14, 1898.

tolled the virtues of Maceo and condemned the barbarities of Weyler, demanding that President Cleveland quit hedging on the question of American aid to the Cuban insurgents.[51]

With increasing frequency black spokesmen demanded that the United States intervene in Cuba with a view toward achieving the same ends which the "friendly interposition" of France brought about during the American Revolution. The goal was not to acquire a colony, but to "restore peace without compromising the liberty and independence of the Cuban people."[52] The death of General Maceo late in 1896, which the Negro press described as another instance of Spanish treachery, served to increase their clamor for American intervention. One black journalist noted that, judging from the shouts of "On to Cuba" emanating from the Negro community upon the news of Maceo's death, over 50,000 black Americans could be readied on a moment's notice for military service on the island.[53] But in spite of all the jingoistic clamor, there were occasional discordant notes. The role of the United States in Hawaii apparently prompted some Negroes to have misgivings about the outcome of intervention in Cuba. Others tempered their enthusiasm for the Cuban struggle by referring to the sorry plight of black citizens in the United States and questioning whether black Americans should devote their energies to oppressed peoples elsewhere as long as they themselves were oppressed. The editor of a black midwestern weekly thought it ironic that Negroes in various northern cities should be convening mass meetings to demonstrate sympathy for the beleaguered Cubans when their own kinsmen were being lynched in Georgia. "A wise practical rule is to free yourselves," he advised, "and then possibly you may be able to assist in giving freedom to others."[54]

Following the inauguration of President McKinley in March, 1897, Negroes who had anticipated American intervention in Cuba as soon as Cleveland was out of office grew increasingly impatient with the failure of the new president to assume a more

51. *Parsons Weekly Blade*, May 2, December 12, 19, 1896, January 9, 1897.
52. Omaha *Enterprise*, May 19, 1897.
53. *Washington Bee*, December 19, 1896; *Parsons Weekly Blade*, December 19, 1896; Indianapolis *Freeman*, September 5, 1896.
54. Omaha *Enterprise*, November 16, 1895.

decisive policy. McKinley's inaction appeared all the more incomprehensible to them in view of his effort to annex Hawaii. Several Negro Republicans reminded the president that Cuba was far more important to the security of the United States than the distant Hawaiian Islands with their "hot smoldering mountains." [55] One Negro observer perplexed by McKinley's course claimed that there was "a mysterious something" lurking "way down deep in the bosom of the administration" which accounted for its "Fabian policy" toward Cuba. After considerable thought, he concluded that the "mysterious something" was actually race prejudice. He noted that while in Hawaii the monarchy of the "dark-skinned natives" had been replaced by a lily-white provisional republic, the success of the revolution in Cuba would produce quite different results in terms of racial dominance. In the observer's opinion, McKinley feared that an independent Cuba would mean granting "the black natives the same respect and rights they accord white natives." [56] Other black Americans were inclined to be more generous toward President McKinley and predicted that in time he would formulate a wise and just policy. A useful argument in explaining the apparent absence of a clearcut policy focused on the pressures applied on the administration by American financial interests unwilling for the nation to become involved in the Cuban crisis until they had disposed of their Spanish bonds.[57]

From the beginning of the Cuban rebellion, however, most black Americans tended to look upon the island as a racial utopia. In fact, Cuba was widely depicted as a land in which color prejudice was virtually nonexistent. The popular concept of Cuba's racial conditions embraced by black Americans indicated that they, no less than other citizens, were prone to harbor romantic notions about the island.[58] Undoubtedly the rising tide of prejudice and repression in the United States accounted in large part for their idealized view of racial practices on the island. Whatever their source, such views stimulated considerable discussion regarding Cuba as a haven for Negro Americans anxious to escape

55. Indianapolis *Freeman*, July 3, 1897.
56. Omaha *Enterprise*, June 26, 1897.
57. *Colored Citizen* (Topeka, Kans.), January 27, 1898.
58. Cleveland *Gazette*, March 14, 1896.

the oppressive atmosphere in the United States. As early as 1896 a prominent Nebraska Negro suggested that American aid to the Cuban rebels could be viewed as a step toward solving the nation's race problem, because Negro citizens were certain to emigrate in large numbers to a place "where the Negro is not discriminated against." Cuba was such a land, and its proximity to the United States made emigration to the island far more feasible than to Africa.[59] The idea of Cuba as an inviting field for emigration persisted for some years and inspired a wealth of rhetoric from those in search of ways to alleviate the suffering of blacks in the United States. But Cuban emigration schemes, like those of Bishop Turner, ran counter to the mainstream of Negro thought. Suggestions that an exodus of black Americans to Cuba would follow the overthrow of Spanish rule prompted one Negro editor in 1896 to declare that "the ordinary colored man has no desire to leave for Cuba or any other country." [60]

By 1898 Negro citizens had become caught up in the national discussion concerning overseas expansion. Even though their rhetoric occasionally resembled that of white American expansionists, few were ever wholly captivated by the imperialist mystique. In fact, the ideological context in which Negroes viewed the issues raised by the Cuban crisis and the movement to annex Hawaii was substantially different from that of white citizens. The color and racial composition of the peoples affected by expansion were significant to both whites and blacks, but the black citizens' concern for the darker races of these islands bore little resemblance to the views of whites who spoke in terms of "the white man's burden" and "our little brown brothers." As members of a racial minority increasingly subjected to discrimination and violence in the United States, Negro Americans easily identified and sympathized with the struggles for national existence by the oppressed colored peoples of Hawaii, Cuba, and other islands. Their perspective on American expansion which, as one Negro editor noted, was rooted "in the wrongs we have suffered at home" [61] bred a persistent skepticism toward the altruistic rhetoric used to justify

59. Omaha *Enterprise*, February 1, 1896; see also Kansas City *American Citizen*, December 25, 1896; Cleveland *Gazette*, October 30, 1897.
60. Omaha *Enterprise*, February 1, 1896.
61. Cleveland *Gazette*, October 13, 1900.

such a policy. More than any other segment of the population, Negroes had cause to be critical of an imperialistic course launched in the name of humanity by a nation so enamored of white supremacy. After all, the doctrine of Anglo-Saxonism had served as a rationale for restricting the liberties of black citizens. Although the experience of Negroes made them wary of the sophistries invoked by imperialists, it scarcely simplified their task of formulating a coherent response toward expansionism. Indeed, the prospect of taking up the "white man's burden" spawned a succession of contradictory emotions and attitudes that dramatized the meaning of Du Bois's reference to "two warring ideals in one dark body." ⎯⎯

Two

The Negro in the Impending Crisis

The interests involved in the issues of the war are important with the Afro-American as with anyone else, because however much proscribed . . . in the exercise of his personal and political immunities, his rights per se are as sacred and dear to him as any other citizen. As much as we abominate the terrible injustice done the Afro-American under his own government yet we must never lose sight of the fact that this country and government are his rightful and inalienable heritage.

—Cleveland *Gazette*, March 20, 1898

With the sinking of the U.S.S. *Maine* in Havana Bay on February 15, 1898, war between the United States and Spain no longer appeared remote. For Americans, the destruction of the battleship assumed a symbolic quality much like the siege of the Alamo and the firing on Fort Sumter. The quickened martial fervor found expression in the slogan, "Remember the Maine!" A naval court of inquiry directed to investigate the explosion which sank the ship and resulted in the death of 260 members of its crew reported that a submarine mine caused the disaster, but it was "unable to obtain evidence fixing the responsibility for the destruction of the Maine upon any person or persons." The American people had little difficulty identifying the culprit, however; the prevailing view was that the sinking of the *Maine* was the work of Spanish officials. The popular reaction contained an assortment of emotional and ideological strains which Walter Millis identified as the nation's "new nationalistic pride," restlessness, self-confidence, aggressiveness, and "celebrated humanitarianism." [1] A little more than two months after the explosion in Havana Bay the United

1. Walter Millis, *The Martial Spirit: A Study of Our War with Spain* (Boston: Houghton Mifflin, 1931), p. 107.

States was at war with Spain. By early June, 1898, an army assembled at Tampa stood ready to launch an invasion of Cuba.

Even though black Americans were powerless to influence the direction of official policy, their response to events during the critical weeks between the sinking of the *Maine* and the actual mobilization for war underscored their belief that an armed conflict with Spain would have significant consequences for their own future. For three years prior to the destruction of the *Maine* black citizens had called for American aid to the Cuban insurgents in a way that would neither disturb the peace of the United States nor compromise the Cubans' goal of independence. But the prospect of a full-fledged war raised by the *Maine* affair marked something of a turning point in the attitude of Negro Americans. Notwithstanding their racial and ideological sympathies with their "liberty-loving kinsmen" in Cuba, their primary consideration in contemplating a war with Spain concerned the effect of such a conflict upon their own status. Calvin Chase of the *Washington Bee* spoke for much of the black community when he remarked: "The United States may play the coward in the Maine explosion . . . but whether it does or not the American negro must look to his own interest and protection." [2] But the ideological difficulties posed by the prospect of war were nowhere more graphically demonstrated than in the ambivalent editorial position of Chase's own newspaper. ⌡

Like other Americans, Negroes in general viewed the sinking of the *Maine* as a barbarous act perpetrated by the Spanish government.[3] A few Democrats and Populists were highly critical of President McKinley for "sending one great war vessel into a hostile port without an invitation." [4] But regardless of political affiliation, Negroes expressed outrage at what they termed a Spanish insult to the nation's honor. Whether they thought the insult sufficient to warrant a war with Spain depended largely upon their response to the question posed by a black editor in Topeka, Kan-

2. *Washington Bee,* March 5, 1898.

3. *Iowa State Bystander* (Des Moines), February 18, 1898; see also Wayne Eubank to John P. Green, April 2, 1898, John P. Green Papers, Western Reserve Historical Society, Cleveland, Ohio.

4. See Salt Lake City *Broad Ax,* March 19, 1898; Topeka *Colored Citizen,* February 24, 1898.

sas, who asked, "Amid all the excitement of war . . . the idea arises as to what figure we cut in all this?" [5] Despite his abhorrence of war, Booker T. Washington was convinced that if the United States were forced to battle Spain, Negro Americans would be prepared to participate. Such a conflict, he argued, would offer them a chance "to render service to our country that no other race can," because, unlike whites, they were "accustomed" to the "peculiar and dangerous climate" of Cuba. In mid-March, 1898, Washington informed Secretary of the Navy John D. Long that in the event of war he would be happy to assume responsibility for recruiting "at least ten thousand loyal, brave, strong black men in the south who crave an opportunity to show their loyalty to our land and would gladly take this method of showing their gratitude for the lives laid down and the sacrifices made that the Negro might have his freedom and rights." Though noncommittal in regard to Washington's offer, Secretary Long expressed admiration for the patriotic spirit manifested by his letter.[6]

Pro-war elements within the black community found a military confrontation with Spain desirable because, in their view, it would bestow substantial benefits upon Negro Americans. A few emphasized that a war over Cuba would diminish the color prejudice of white Americans by bringing them into direct contact with a predominantly colored culture. Others maintained that "freedom of the colored people of Cuba" would "have a healthy influence in bringing better conditions for our race in general." But more typical of the arguments advanced to justify black support for war were those of a Negro resident of Los Angeles who wrote:

> As in all other cities the Negro is discussing his attitude toward the government in case of war. Shall he go to war and fight for his country's flag? Yes, yes, for every reason of true patriotism, it is a blessing in disguise for the Negro. He will if for no other reason be possessed of arms, which in the South in the face of threatened mob violence he is not allowed to have. He will be

5. Topeka *Colored Citizen,* March 10, 1898.
6. Booker T. Washington to John D. Long, March 15, 1898, John D. Long to Booker T. Washington, March 18, 1898, Booker T. Washington Papers, Manuscript Division, Library of Congress.

trained and disciplined. He will be generously remunerated for his service. He will get much honor. He will have an opportunity of proving to the world his real bravery, worth and manhood.[7]

The principal theme of those Negroes who favored war was that the black man's participation in the military effort would win respect from whites and therefore enhance his status at home. For the first time since the Negro secured citizenship, they argued, he had an opportunity to prove his loyalty to the flag and to win military recognition. Opposition either to war or to territorial expansion was likely to play into the hands of those bent upon nullifying the last vestiges of the Fourteenth and Fifteenth Amendments. Hence, many black Americans rationalized that the loyalty and patriotism of their race was on trial.[8] A respected black minister in Brooklyn, Dr. J. M. Henderson, claimed that "unpatriotic utterances" emanating from the black community were being used by some whites as evidence that Negroes were incapable of functioning as responsible citizens. In his own opinion, for Negroes "to denounce America and disclaim any concern for the flag" indicated that blacks had "failed to respond to influences of American civilization." [9]

The whole question of the black man's patriotism received a thorough airing as war with Spain became imminent. Those Negroes who viewed such a conflict as a means of ameliorating the plight of their race took the position that the United States was as much the country of the black man as of the white man, and for black Americans to assume that they "had no country to fight for" was to repudiate the heritage of their forefathers who "labored, toiled, fought, bled and died to perpetuate" the ideals of the Declaration of Independence. Moreover, such an assumption could only serve to remove all hope of ultimately sharing in the

7. *The Tribune* (Savannah), April 3, 1898; *The Colored American* (Washington), March 19, 1898; St. Paul *Broad-Axe*, March 3, 1898; "Los Angeles Letter," in Indianapolis *Freeman*, April 23, 1898.
8. Washington *Colored American*, April 9, 1898; *Washington Bee*, April 30, 1898; Salt Lake City *Broad Ax*, April 23, 1898; Cleveland *Gazette*, April 23, 30, 1898; Edward A. Johnson, *History of Negro Soldiers in the Spanish-American War and Other Items of Interest* (Raleigh: Capital Publishing, 1899), pp. 207–216.
9. Indianapolis *Freeman*, May 14, 1898.

rewards of full citizenship.[10] The pro-war advocates also marshaled historical evidence to demonstrate that black people had never been lacking in patriotic fervor. Typical of their efforts was a paper delivered by Bishop W. B. Derrick of the African Methodist Episcopal Church at a meeting in Baltimore early in March, 1898, which described "the bravery of colored Americans as soldiers and sailors in the wars of the republic." [11] Such appeals invariably concluded by pointing out that thirty-three Afro-American seamen had died in the *Maine* explosion. The implication was clear: to avenge the sinking of the *Maine* was to avenge the deaths of these thirty-three brothers. Failure to "Remember the *Maine*" was to countenance dishonor to the race as well as to the nation.

Among the influential Negroes to speak out in favor of a war, none was more severe in his arraignment of the anti-war forces than D. Augustus Straker, formerly an important political figure in South Carolina who had migrated to Detroit and achieved prominence in legal circles. Invoking the names of Crispus Attucks, Peter Salem, and other black patriots, Straker called upon all black Americans to display the same patriotism that had characterized their response to "every national crisis" in the past and to close their ears to the rhetoric of those who cast doubt upon "the patriotism of the race." Negroes, he declared, must be made to realize that a war with Spain over Cuba might well be the means to "end our race troubles." [12] John P. Green, a prominent black Republican in Ohio allied with Senator Mark Hanna, had no doubt that a military conflict would bring about "the rise of the Negro in the estimation of the Anglo-Saxon." While Harry C. Smith of the Cleveland *Gazette* was more restrained in his analysis of the effect of a war upon black citizens, he did insist that a willingness by Negroes to do their full duty in the event of a military conflict would at least reaffirm their "claims to equal liberty and protection" and ratify "more surely the blessings of free gov-

10. Des Moines *Iowa State Bystander,* May 20, 1898; see also Cleveland *Gazette,* March 5, 19, 26, 1898.

11. *The Ledger* (Baltimore), March 12, 1898; for similar sentiments by Bishop Abram Grant of the same church, see Cleveland *Gazette,* May 14, 1898.

12. Indianapolis *Freeman,* April 23, 1898; see also D. Augustus Straker, *A Trip to the Windward Isle, or Then and Now* (Detroit: Press of James A. Stone and Co., n.d.), pp. 7–9, 107–109.

ernment to ourselves and to posterity." [13] Expressing a similar
theme in an address at the First Baptist Church in Washington,
Dr. Frank J. Webb also reminded Negroes that true patriots did
not seek to redress grievances, no matter how great, during a moment of national crisis; he counseled only scorn for "the traitorous thoughts" abroad in the black community.[14] Even though
black citizens might have little reason to love America, the editor
of the Denver *Statesman* concluded, they loved liberty and "Negroes everywhere will choose to fight under Liberty's banner." [15]

Occasionally appearing alongside the appeals to patriotism were
references to the possibility of postwar emigration by black Americans to Cuba, which scarcely seemed consistent with the idea that
a war with Spain would result in racial justice at home. The island continued to be depicted as a place where no race prejudice
existed. Whether or not there was a war between the United
States and Spain, the Cuban republic was certain to be established
and would "create openings for the colored American." In extolling the advantages of Cuba as a haven for oppressed blacks,
the Topeka *Colored Citizen* pointed out that it possessed much
fertile land, a congenial climate, a racially mixed population, and
a society in which merit rather than color determined one's status.
"It will be well to organize now," the *Colored Citizen* advised,
and get there [Cuba] before American prejudice gets rooted." [16]
Undoubtedly such references to emigration betrayed a certain underlying skepticism on the part of those who defended a war with
Spain in terms of its beneficent consequences for black Americans.

One of the most articulate proponents of war and expansionism
who rarely manifested any such skepticism was Edward E. Cooper,
editor of the *Colored American,* a weekly published in Washington, D.C. Described as "the best all-around newspaperman the
colored race has yet produced," Cooper had been associated with
two Negro newspapers in Indianapolis before launching the *Colored American* in 1893. As a reward for his labors in behalf of
the Republican ticket during the presidential campaign three

13. George A. Myers to John P. Green, July 19, 1898, Green Papers; Cleveland *Gazette*, March 5, 1898.
14. Indianapolis *Freeman*, April 14, 1898.
15. Quoted in Topeka *Colored Citizen*, March 17, 1898.
16. *Ibid.*, March 31, 1898; see also *The World* (Indianapolis), April 2, 1898.

years later, he was appointed an assistant inspector of streets in Washington. Always careful to cultivate the socially and politically prominent Negroes in the nation's capital, he also courted the favor of Booker T. Washington [17]—in fact, his journalistic enterprise came to depend largely upon subsidies provided by Tuskegee. Nevertheless, he was a resourceful editor whose paper was generally regarded as a potent influence in molding black sentiment. Because the *Colored American* enjoyed such prominence in black journalism by 1898, its editorial position regarding "the Negro in the impending crisis" constituted at least one significant expression of opinion within the Negro community.

From the beginning Cooper viewed the Cuban crisis as a providential occurrence which promised to inaugurate something of a millennium for black Americans. In the event of war, therefore, Negroes should demonstrate the same "true blue variety" of patriotism that had characterized their position "from Bunker Hill on." The black citizen, he argued, was "an American in inspiration, thought and action" even though he felt "very keenly the humiliating slights put upon him by the unreasoned prejudice against his color." "The question now pressing for an answer," Cooper wrote in mid-March, 1898, "is will the dominant forces, the Anglo-Saxon people, be grand enough to rise in their might and unloose themselves from the bondage of prejudice." [18] He thought so. In his view, a war to liberate Cuba and its large colored population would serve to dissipate the prejudice of white Americans and bring about a full recognition of the rights and privileges hitherto denied black citizens in the United States. His optimism rested on the assumption that such a war would usher "in an era of good feeling the country over, and cement the races into a more compact brotherhood through a perfect unity of purpose and patriotic affinity." The humanitarian concern for the oppressed Cuban, according to Cooper, was certain to prompt a "quickened sense of duty toward one another at home," and a "loftier conception of the obligations of government to its hum-

17. See I. Garland Penn, *The Afro-American Press and Its Editors* (Springfield, Mass.: Willey, 1891), pp. 338–339; Henry F. Kletzing and William Crogman, *Progress of a Race, or the Remarkable Advance of the Afro-American* (Atlanta: J. L. Nichols, 1897), pp. 569–571; D. W. Culp, *Twentieth Century Negro Literature* (Atlanta: J. L. Nichols, 1902), pp. 464–465.
18. Washington *Colored American,* March 19, 1898.

blest subject." In short, the nation's commitment to a "broad, high purpose" would go far toward eliminating America's race problem. But Cooper conceded that deviation from this high purpose would alter, if not negate, the beneficent effects of America's crusade upon black citizens at home as well as the colored people struggling against Spanish tyranny. The nation's commitment, he concluded, ruled out the annexation of either Cuba or Hawaii unless the inhabitants of these islands requested it. For Cooper, annexation was "of doubtful expediency at present." [19]

The arguments of Cooper and others who believed that a war with Spain would promote the welfare of black Americans encountered strong opposition from a highly vocal antiwar element. Several ministers who achieved considerable notoriety in the white press for what were described as their "traitorous expressions" set the tone of this opposition. One of these was the Reverend D. C. Gaddie of Louisville, who told his congregation: "I would rather take a gun and kill an American citizen than to aid the Americans in a war with Spain." [20] Even more explicit was the pronouncement of the Reverend W. R. Gullins of Farmville, Virginia. He insisted that if the United States got into war, the fighting ought to be reserved for those "brave lynchers" whose acts of violence and murder went unpunished in a country that boasted to the world of its love of liberty and justice. "Must the Negro fight?" he asked. "For what? Fight to bring other Negroes [in Cuba] under the flag that has never as yet protected those who are already here?" [21] Monroe Dorsey, editor of the *Parsons Blade* in Kansas, emphatically denied that either the *Maine* disaster or the conditions in Cuba necessitated a war with Spain. In his view, the cause of Cuban independence could best be served simply by lending moral and material assistance to the insurgent forces. Like the clergymen, the Kansas editor was highly dubious of any direct American involvement in a country where blacks constituted such a large portion of the population.[22]

The black opponents of war denied that an armed conflict with

19. *Ibid.,* March 19, 26, April 2, 9, 16, 1898.
20. Springfield *Illinois Record,* March 12, 1898; see also *Augusta Chronicle* (Augusta, Ga.), March 8, 1898.
21. *Richmond Reformer* quoted in Indianapolis *World,* May 14, 1898.
22. *Parsons Weekly Blade,* April 16, 1898.

Spain would do anything to achieve racial justice. On the contrary, it would distract national attention from the outrages committed against Negro citizens at home and allow them to go unnoticed while Americans concentrated their humanitarian energies on Cuba.[23] Indeed, according to the *Washington Bee,* Negroes in the United States were "as much in need of independence as Cuba is." [24] A young black man in Iowa vividly expressed one point of view among Negroes when he declared: "I will not go to war. I have no country to fight for. I have not been given my rights." [25] Even Negroes who disagreed with such expressions understood only too well the conditions which prompted them. For whites who criticized black citizens for being indifferent patriots, the Indianapolis *Freeman* defined patriotism as meaning "a home to protect that protects the individual in return"—a definition intended to explain why Negroes displayed so little patriotic fervor when "all the country is agog with war fever." [26]

One of the most articulate antiwar spokesmen among Negroes was John Mitchell, Jr., of the *Richmond Planet.* Born of slave parents in 1863, Mitchell attended a primary school conducted by a Baptist minister and later studied at the Richmond Normal School. In 1884 he assumed editorial direction of the *Planet,* which he transformed within a few years into an outspoken advocate of the black man's rights. Twice elected president of the Afro-American Press Association in the 1890's, the young editor waged a frontal assault upon lynchings, disfranchisement, and segregation. While winning plaudits for his boldness as a journalist, Mitchell was also achieving considerable influence in religious, fraternal, and political circles. His tenure as a member of the Richmond City Council from 1888 to 1896 marked the height of his personal involvement in politics, but for many years he was an important figure among black Republicans in Virginia.[27]

Even though Mitchell had lost some of his zeal as a defender of Negro rights by 1898 and had begun to acquiesce in the approach

23. *Ibid.,* April 9, 1898.
24. *Washington Bee,* March 5, 1898.
25. Des Moines *Iowa State Bystander,* May 20, 1898.
26. Indianapolis *Freeman,* March 19, 1898.
27. On Mitchell's career, see Penn, *The Afro-American Press and Its Editors,* pp. 183–187; Meier, *Negro Thought in America, 1880–1915,* pp. 231–232.

of Booker T. Washington, he still possessed enough of the crusading spirit to use the columns of the *Planet* to expose what he considered the colossal hypocrisy of a war with Spain over Cuba in particular and the policy of expansion in general. As an editorial critic of the war, his newspaper surpassed even George A. Dudley's *American Citizen* of Kansas City, which early took the position that "human life at home . . . should be protected before reaching out to protect others." [28] Also convinced that "charity begins at home," Mitchell argued that the financial and military resources which would be required to relieve Cubans of Spanish tyranny could be more appropriately used to relieve black Americans of their oppression and poverty. To employ military force in behalf of Cuba was, in his opinion, to fly in the face of the racial mores of white Americans and to extend to people of color abroad a degree of protection denied colored citizens at home. If indeed the American leaders had a genuine humanitarian interest in Cuba, Mitchell suggested that they prove it by calling upon other nations to assist the United States in ridding the island of Spanish rule. Suspicious of American motives, he scoffed at all the rhetoric about a crusade for humanity and informed the readers of the *Planet* that it was nothing more than a subterfuge for the spirit of conquest which had gripped the nation's political leaders and the greed of capitalists bent upon exploiting Cuban resources. In view of the color prejudice of white Americans, Mitchell early concluded that colored Cubans would find American rule even more oppressive than that of the Spaniards. Although he was sympathetic with the desire of Cubans for freedom and independence, he predicted that American intervention would thwart such aspirations and that the colored inhabitants of the island would find themselves progressing from "the frying pan into the fire." [29]

Mitchell's position, like that of other black opponents of war with Spain, was determined largely by his view of national priorities. The belief that a solution to the race problem in the United States took precedence over any involvement in the Cuban crisis was strengthened by a tragedy which occurred in Lake City, South

28. Kansas City *American Citizen*, January 14, 1898.
29. *Richmond Planet*, April 16, 23, 1898.

Carolina, within two weeks after the sinking of the *Maine*. From the beginning of his term as postmaster at Lake City, Frazier B. Baker, a black Republican, had encountered opposition from whites. The lengths to which they were prepared to go in preventing Negro officeholding were demonstrated on February 22, 1898, when a mob set fire to Baker's house and shot at members of his family as they tried to escape. Baker and his infant son were killed. Since a federal official had been subjected to mob action, Negroes "thought now the federal government could step in and punish the perpetrators of this outrage" without having the case lost in the docket of some state court.[30] The black citizens of Chicago sent Ida Wells Barnett, the well-known anti-lynching crusader, to Washington to press for vigorous and prompt action by the attorney general. After some weeks Mrs. Barnett realized that her mission had little chance of success because of intense excitement over the prospects of a war with Spain. Her failure underscored the contention of antiwar spokesmen within the Negro community that a conflict with Spain would distract attention from the crisis confronting black Americans.[31] A black editor in Lexington, Kentucky, suggested that if "Remember the Maine" was "the white man's watch-word," then "remember the murder of postmaster Baker . . . should be the Negro's." [32]

Although some Negroes were "content to allow the Baker incident to sleep until the war scare is over," [33] John Mitchell demanded immediate action, especially in providing governmental relief for Baker's widow and children. For him, the attention to the Baker case could not be postponed, because it had a bearing on the whole issue of imperialism. He argued that the tragedy at Lake City was sufficient reason to question the wisdom of an expansionist policy which would affect the lives of colored people in Cuba and elsewhere. "Tell us no more about a war with Spain,"

30. On the Baker affair, see George B. Tindall, *South Carolina Negroes, 1877–1900* (Columbia: University of South Carolina Press, 1952), pp. 255–256.

31. Ida B. Wells, *Crusade for Justice: The Autobiography of Ida B. Wells,* ed. Alfreda M. Duster (Chicago: University of Chicago Press, 1970), pp. 252–254.

32. *Lexington Standard* quoted in Cleveland *Gazette*, August 17, 1898; see also Indianapolis *Freeman*, February 26, March 5, 1898; *Washington Bee*, March 19, 1898; Springfield *Illinois Record*, March 5, 1898; Kansas City *American Citizen*, February 24, 1898.

33. Indianapolis *Freeman*, April 2, 1898.

he declared, "discourse no longer upon the beauties of the 'Pearl
of the Antilles' (Cuba), sing no more the song of annexation of
the 'garden spot of the Pacific' (Hawaii). We can defend none of
these if we cannot protect our own citizens [living] within forty-
eight hours' ride of the national capital." [34]

Other black opponents of war persisted in the belief that the
"hot-headed war ranters" could do infinitely more good by addressing themselves to the plight of black citizens in the South
than they could "in trying to force President McKinley into declaring war with Spain." Although antiwar spokesmen invariably
expressed the hope that Cubans would gain their freedom, they
were nonetheless convinced that American soldiers should be kept
at home to combat the racial violence which was disturbing the
domestic peace of the United States.[35] The argument that the
United States should attend to the "Spaniards" within its own
boundaries before tackling those elsewhere expressed a view which
Negroes, regardless of their attitude toward Cuba, found hard to
resist. Ralph W. Tyler, a prominent Ohio black man, confided to
a friend that he would not fight for the United States "as long as
the nightmare of Lake City remains undispelled." Cyrus D. Bell,
an influential black Nebraskan, further pointed out that there
"was good reason . . . to doubt that even the starvation of the re-
concentradoes in Cuba betokens any greater degree of cold blooded
brutality on the part of the Spaniards than has been exhibited
time and again by the whites of countless Southern communities
toward their colored neighbors." For all their cruelty, so the argument ran, the Spaniards at least had not fastened upon Cuba a
system of racial discrimination comparable to that in the United
States.[36]

The opponents of war viewed with utter contempt those "colored would-be heroes" so quick to make offers of their brawn and
valor. Such offers smacked too much of "groveling sycophancy,"
an attitude which could only have adverse effects upon the status
of black people. Calvin Chase reminded Negroes that "fidelity is

34. *Richmond Planet,* February 26, 1898.
35. *Parsons Weekly Blade,* April 9, 1898; *Weekly Call* (Topeka), June 25, 1898.
36. Ralph W. Tyler to George A. Myers, May 4, 1898, George A. Myers Papers,
Ohio Historical Society, Columbus; Omaha *Afro-American Sentinel,* April 30, 1898;
see also Kansas Ciy *American Citizen,* February 24, 1898.

at times an expression of race weakness." [37] According to John Mitchell, there was every reason why Negroes should not take up arms. Because "Negro haters have declared that this is a white man's country," he argued, white men ought to be willing to sacrifice their lives in a war to avenge the *Maine*. Mitchell further asserted that if the black man was not "good enough to exercise the right of franchise," then certainly he was not "good enough to exercise the right to enlist in the service of the United States." To deny the right to vote, he insisted time and again, was to remove the obligation to fight. Mitchell and other black opponents of war also warned Negroes against being deceived by those whites who, appearing as the friends of black men, favored their enlistment in military service. Such whites, they argued, were motivated by sentiments no more noble than those which prompted them to advocate disfranchisement. In brief, "Negro haters" had undergone no sudden change in attitude, and they desired to put Negro soldiers "in the lead" to "suffer the loss of life," so that white Americans could reap whatever benefits a war with Spain was likely to produce.[38]

Antiwar spokesmen also denied emphatically that black citizens had any obligation to prove themselves by responding to a call to arms. They contended that the valor and loyalty of Negroes had been amply demonstrated in every war in which the United States had been involved, from the American Revolution on. To counteract the notion that Negroes would promote "the progress of the race" by flocking to the colors in case of a conflict with Spain, the antiwar elements called attention to the barren results of their participation in previous wars. "Hence while we may be loyal and patriotic, while our blood may boil for revenge upon those Spanish brutes who have spared neither woman nor child in their diabolical butchery," Calvin Chase explained, "yet common sense and experience ought to teach that severe silence becomes us." He found it scarcely becoming for Negroes to promote what was certain to be a Jim Crow war resulting in a Jim Crow empire which would leave colored Americans as well as the colored population of Cuba in a more oppressed condition than ever.[39]

37. *Washington Bee*, March 19, 1898.
38. *Richmond Planet*, March 26, April 2, 23, 1898.
39. *Washington Bee*, March 19, 1898.

The polarization of opinion regarding a war with Spain represented by Edward E. Cooper and John Mitchell did not characterize the response of black Americans in general. Few were as overtly pessimistic as Mitchell, and even fewer were as optimistic as Cooper. Most black citizens probably favored peace, but because they could never reconcile their belief that charity ought to begin at home with their desire for the freedom of the dark-skinned rebels of Cuba, their utterances revealed a complex of ambivalent attitudes toward the Cuban crisis, themselves, their status, and the role they should play in a war with Spain. A resolution by the Fraternal Union of America, a Negro organization meeting in Omaha, expressed the sentiment of many blacks when it called for Cuban independence "peaceably, if possible, by force if necessary." [40] The ambivalence was even more apparent in the musings of John Lay Thompson, a Negro lawyer and editor in Des Moines. "While we do not favor war," he declared, "yet we think the time is ripe for the United States to free Cuba and get indemnity for the destroying of our vessel." [41]

The deliberations of a prestigious Negro study club in Washington two weeks following the *Maine* disaster provided insight into black citizens' response to the question of American intervention in Cuba. At its regular meeting on February 27, 1898, the Congressional Lyceum first heard an eloquent address on "The Means of Our Advancement" by Henry P. Cheatham, a black North Carolinian appointed recorder of deeds in the District of Columbia by President McKinley. But Cheatham's remarks prompted far less interest than a resolution calling upon the United States to "recognize the revolutionists of Cuba" with a view toward aiding the Cuban people in their struggle to become "an independent nation." Immediately Calvin Chase, the volatile editor of the *Bee* who alternately condemned the war mongers and called upon Negroes to respond patriotically, offered an amendment which read: "That the United States do not recognize the independence of Cuba until the said states are able to protect all American citizens in their civil and political rights." A "prolonged and deafening applause" greeted his amendment; after a spirited debate, it was adopted by a vote of fifty-seven to five. Then, in

40. Omaha *Afro-American Sentinel,* April 2, 1898.
41. Des Moines *Iowa State Bystander,* April 1, 1898.

a coup de grace, Chase succeeded in having the resolution as amended laid on the table.[42] By their action the members of the Lyceum indicated that, no less than other black citizens, they were beset by conflicting emotions and attitudes concerning an appropriate response to the Cuban crisis.

Regardless of their attitude toward America's involvement in a war, most Negroes believed that if a military conflict materialized, it was their civic obligation to offer their services—an obligation they would fulfill, provided they could do so in a way that would enhance rather than degrade their status. Though they hoped that a display of patriotism would help dissipate racial prejudice against them, they were never free of misgivings about the outcome of a war, either in its effects upon them or upon their colored kinsmen in Cuba. R. B. Montgomery, editor of a black weekly in Milwaukee, came as near as anyone in expressing the attitude of most Negroes when he wrote:

> The weight of war on the general country does not make the burdens of race more tolerable, and if they [Negroes] should refuse to engage in the struggle the burden will not in any degree lessen. It is highly probable that out of the nation's necessity will spring the race's opportunity and from between the dragon teeth of cruel war may be wrung concessions that years of sulking could never bring about. At least it is the Negro's business to be on the safe side.[43]

Even the most jingoistic rhetoric expressed by blacks rested on the assumption that Negro Americans could not afford to risk being on any other side.

While Negro citizens debated their appropriate response in case of war, the United States moved closer to a break with Spain. On April 11, 1898, President McKinley sent a message to Congress recommending intervention in Cuba. In a lengthy critique of the message, the antiwar *American Citizen* of Kansas City concluded that it "lacked the fervor and zeal of righteous convictions in the cause of momentous consequences." [44] John Mitchell in the *Richmond Planet* maintained that the presidential statement demon-

42. *Washington Bee,* March 5, 1898.
43. *Wisconsin Weekly Advocate* (Milwaukee), July 9, 1898.
44. Kansas City *American Citizen,* April 15, 1898.

strated nothing as clearly as the fact that "every excuse for interfering has been removed, every reason for war swept away." [45] On
the contrary, Edward Cooper's *Colored American* undoubtedly reflected the sentiment of the black political elite based in Washington by commending McKinley's "calm and dispassionate" message
and claiming that it left Congress no alternative but to declare
war.[46] On April 19, 1898, Congress responded to the president's
recommendation by recognizing Cuban independence and disclaiming any intention to annex the island. Such action, which
tended to corroborate the arguments of the pro-war advocates concerning a crusade for humanity and justice, seems to have been
effective in arousing greater enthusiasm among those Negroes who
were lukewarm toward a military conflict over Cuba.

On April 22, 1898, the Navy began to establish a blockade
around Cuban ports, and the next day President McKinley issued
a call for 125,000 volunteers. Finally, on April 25, Congress voted
a war resolution which declared that a state of war between Spain
and the United States had existed since April 21. The official declaration of war was the signal for black citizens to close ranks and
do "their full duty." The time for debate was over. Even such
outspoken opponents of war as the *Richmond Planet* and Kansas
City *American Citizen* counseled their readers to support the war.
"The wisdom of it is questioned," John Mitchell declared. "However, all loyal citizens must do their duty." [47] Like other antiwar
spokesmen, he emphasized that acquiescence did not signify any
change of heart regarding the desirability or need of a war with
Spain. Mitchell predicted that those black citizens who counted
upon a display of valor to bring about lasting benefits to their
race were pursuing a "vain hope." Since "self respect, education
and wealth" were the prerequisites for elevating the status of black
citizens, he urged Negroes to work and accumulate money "while
the white folks are fighting." [48]

Within a few days after the official declaration of hostilities, a
delegation of prominent black politicians who claimed to represent

45. *Richmond Planet*, April 16, 1898.
46. Washington *Colored American*, April 16, 1898.
47. *Richmond Planet*, April 30, 1898; see also Kansas City *American Citizen*,
April 22, 1898.
48. *Richmond Planet*, May 7, 1898.

every state and territory in the nation called upon President McKinley at the White House to pledge the support of 9,000,000 Negro citizens for the war effort. The delegation, headed by P. B. S. Pinchback, a former lieutenant governor of Louisiana who occupied the status of an elder statesman among Negroes, included Judson Lyons, register of the treasury; Henry P. Cheatham, recorder of deeds in the District of Columbia and formerly a congressman from North Carolina; and Cheatham's brother-in-law George H. White of North Carolina, the lone black member of Congress. The president reportedly was moved by the "Patriotic Address" read by Pinchback. The document recited the black man's role in all previous wars, beginning with Attucks in the Revolution, and concluded with the promise that Negro citizens would uphold that tradition for loyal service in the war with Spain.[49] The action of Pinchback and his delegation drew considerable criticism from such antiwar journals as the *Washington Bee* and from black Democrats who described them as "a little coterie of politicians" without a constituency who presumed to speak for all black Americans.[50]

Of those who defended the Pinchback committee, none was more eloquent than Edward E. Cooper. Others might consider the black man's display of patriotism as expedient without expecting any improvement in his status to result from it, but Cooper persisted in the belief that there was "nothing but good in this war for the black people of America or Cuba, and of the world at large." When Calvin Chase of the *Washington Bee* spoke of the "impudent obtrusiveness" of Pinchback and his committee, Cooper responded by elaborating upon the benefits which a war would bestow upon Negroes. He refused to accept the view that the war was merely "a white man's quarrel" and reminded his readers that not only would a military victory over Spain constitute a triumph for the "mulatto people" of Cuba, but it would also bring about an "enlarged sphere for the social and commercial activities

49. Washington *Colored American*, April 30, 1898. The Cleveland *Gazette* (April 14, 1906) quoted Maceo as saying: "Annexation [of Cuba] to the United States? I would never consent to it. No white man will ever reduce me to the level of an Alabama Negro."

50. *Washington Bee*, April 30, 1898; *The American* (Coffeyville, Kans.), May 7, 1898.

of the dark-hued races" everywhere. Of more immediate concern, he pointed out, was the salutary effect of the war upon race relations within the United States, a theme pursued by the *Iowa State Bystander* and other pro-war black newspapers. Reiterating his belief that racial animosities would disappear as white and blacks united in a common cause to liberate Cuba, Cooper urged Negroes to respond to the president's call for volunteers so that "the Negro's manhood is placed directly in evidence." By taking up arms, he reasoned, the black American would not only "emphasize his title to all the privileges of citizenship but would also gain the respect of whites and augment his own self-esteem." As he viewed the situation, the black man was "on trial," and nothing less than an enthusiastic rallying to the flag would put him in a position to share in the potentially rich harvest of overseas expansion.[51]

Cooper undoubtedly represented the prevailing sentiment among the black political elite residing in Washington, but support for the war in particular and for expansion in general by other Negroes, even at the peak of patriotic fervor, was substantially less enthusiastic. More typical perhaps was the attitude of George A. Myers of Cleveland, who served as Senator Hanna's liaison with the black community in Ohio. Although Myers did not publicize his reservations about a war with Spain, he confided to a friend: "I am not very enthusiastic over the 'war question.' I am under the opinion that the country should demonstrate its ability to protect the citizens within its own domain, especially when some are a part and parcel of the government—(Baker at Lake City, S.C.) before interfering with other governments about the treatment of their subjects, plainly speaking that we should 'first cast the mote out of our own eye.' "[52] Myers's friend and political associate, Jere A. Brown, who took a similar view toward a war to liberate Cuba, admitted that his "patriotism was 'kind of weak' by the treatment we receive at the hands of the general government as to protecting us in our rights at home. . . ."[53]

Nevertheless, the response of black men to the president's call for volunteers indicated that Pinchback and his committee had not

51. Washington *Colored American,* April 30, 1898.
52. George A. Myers to John P. Green, May 3, 1898, Green Papers.
53. Jere A. Brown to John P. Green, April 14, 1898, *ibid.*

misread black opinion. Thousands of Negroes throughout the nation offered their services as volunteers, but whether in the North or South, their offers were made on the condition that they were to receive "every right and privilege accorded to any other American citizen." As one black attorney in Chicago put it, Negroes expected "to fight, not cook." [54] Monroe Dorsey of the *Parsons* (Kansas) *Blade* declared: "Now is the time to make Uncle Sam toe the mark and show his colors." [55] Even Cooper reminded President McKinley of his debt to black voters and urged him to intervene personally to insure equitable treatment for those Negro Americans who volunteered for military service. "We are not more anxious to be shot or killed than any other class," he concluded, "but the principle of military and civil recognition is at stake, and we wished to be called . . . to bear the nation's burdens as well as its joys." [56]

54. *Chicago Tribune,* May 22, 1898; for similar sentiments, see *Washington Bee,* April 30, 1898.
55. *Parsons Weekly Blade,* April 23, 1898.
56. Washington *Colored American,* May 28, 1898.

Three

Laurels for the Race

X

We used to think the negro didn't count for much—
Light fingered in the melon patch and chicken yard,
  and such:
Much mixed in point of morals and absurd in point of
  dress,
The butt of droll cartoonists and the target of the press;
But we've got to reconstruct our views on color, more or
  less,
Now we know about the Tenth at La Quasina [*sic*]!
                        —B. M. Channing, "The Negro Soldier"

During April and May, 1898, while the War Department labored feverishly to mobilize a large army of regulars and volunteers, questions of strategy and war aims underwent frequent revision. The movements of the Spanish fleet altered American campaign plans in the Caribbean, but finally on May 26, 1898, as a result of a council of war at the White House, the decision was made to shift the proposed campaign from Havana to eastern Cuba and Puerto Rico. In the meantime, on May 1, 1898, Commodore George Dewey's easy victory over the small Spanish naval force in Manila Bay had opened up a new front. Although it appears that naval strategists originally viewed pressure on the Philippines as a means of inducing Spain to withdraw from Cuba, President William McKinley ordered an invasion of the islands. By mid-June two large armies of American troops were en route to battlefields halfway around the world from each other: General Wesley Merritt's Eighth Army Corps sailed from San Francisco on May 25 and arrived in Manila thirty-six days later; the Fifth Army Corps under

General William R. Shafter left Tampa on June 14 and anchored off the coast of Cuba a week later.[1]

Among the first troops readied for service in Cuba were the four black regiments of the regular army. The mere sight of these soldiers marching off to war momentarily united the Negro community behind the war effort. Even those who still possessed serious misgivings about a war with Spain were reluctant to say or do anything that would detract from the pride and hope inspired by the mobilization of the black regulars. Organized shortly after the Civil War, the black regiments—the Twenty-fourth and Twenty-fifth Infantry, and the Ninth and Tenth Cavalry—had been stationed on the western frontier throughout most of their existence. All commissioned officers of these units were white men, except for a few chaplains who were never allowed command positions. Although some white officers looked upon assignments with black troops as undesirable and tried to escape the disadvantage of being associated with them, most white commanders of the Negro regiments were protective of their men and actually sensitive to any display of prejudice toward them.[2] As for the black soldiers themselves, they were convinced that all Negro Americans were "more or less affected by their conduct in the army." Such a sense of racial responsibility helps explain why the Negro troops consistently maintained "a record for good service"—a record marred by few instances of alcoholism and desertion, the two major problems of the army in the late nineteenth century.[3] The contribution of the black regiments to the pacification and protection of the West won for them an enviable reputation. By 1890 they had become elite units of the army. The black cavalrymen in particular were famous

1. For these developments see Graham A. Cosmas, *An Army for Empire: The United States Army in the Spanish-American War* (Columbia: University of Missouri Press, 1971), pp. 73–82, 102–130.

2. For treatment of the black soldiers of the regular army see Arlen L. Fowler, *The Black Infantry in the West, 1869–1891* (Westport, Conn.: Greenwood Publishing, 1971); Horace Mann Bond, "The Negro in the Armed Forces of the United States prior to World War I," *Journal of Negro Education*, XII (Summer, 1943), 263–287; L. D. Reddick, "The Negro Policy of the United States Army, 1775–1945," *Journal of Negro History*, XXXIV (January, 1949), 9–29; Jack D. Foner, *The United States Soldier between Two Wars: Army Life and Reforms, 1865–1898* (New York: Humanities Press, 1970), pp. 128–146.

3. Fowler, *Black Infantry in the West*, pp. 87, 97, 137.

for their exploits in the Indian wars. Popularly known as "Buffalo soldiers," they attracted "a good deal of interest and not a little envy" among other troops.[4]

Although the record of the black regulars was a source of racial pride among Negroes, their spokesmen persistently protested against their assignment to isolated forts west of the Mississippi River and their exclusion from the cadre of commissioned officers. T. Thomas Fortune of the *New York Age* crusaded for the establishment of a colored artillery unit primarily because such a unit would be located in the East. "We want an artillery unit," Fortune declared, "so we can come back to civilization and show the whites how to soldier." [5] In March, 1898, Congressman George H. White sponsored a bill which provided for a Negro artillery unit.[6] But all such efforts proved futile. By the outbreak of the Spanish-American War there were still no black artillerymen, nor were there any black commissioned officers except a few chaplains and Lieutenant Charles Young, a Negro graduate of West Point, who was on detached service as professor of military science at Wilberforce University. All Negro soldiers remained in the West. The stationing of a troop of the Ninth Cavalry at Fort Myer, Virginia, in 1891, as a reward for its part in the successful Pine Ridge campaign against the Indians touched off such opposition among whites in the area that the experiment was abandoned and the troop returned to its western camp.[7] Not until the Spanish-American War were the Negro regiments pulled out of the West and sped to camps in the South in preparation for the invasion of Cuba.

As early as March, 1898, the commanding general of the army recommended that the Twenty-fifth Infantry be transferred to stations in the South.[8] Since military authorities, as well as many Negroes, operated on the assumption that black men possessed a natural immunity to the climate and diseases of the tropics, the black soldiers in the West were among the first troops actually

4. John Bigalow, Jr., *Reminiscences of the Santiago Campaign* (New York: Harper and Brothers, 1899), p. 16.

5. *New York Age*, December 23, 1889.

6. Washington *Colored American*, March 19, 1898.

7. *New York Age*, March 21, May 9, 1891.

8. Marvin E. Fletcher, "The Negro Soldier and the United States Army, 1891–1917" (Ph.D. dissertation, University of Wisconsin, 1968), p. 158.

mobilized for service in Cuba.[9] Even before the official declaration
of war, the Negro regiments stationed at various posts in Utah,
Montana, and other states in the West had been transferred to
camps at Chickamauga Park, Georgia, and Key West, Florida.[10]
The soldiers welcomed their new assignments as evidence that they
would "all eventually land in Cuba," where a demonstration of
"their soldierly qualities" was certain to win new respect for their
race. Julius F. Taylor, a black Democratic editor in Salt Lake City
who had been highly critical of the clamor for war, was greatly impressed by the outpouring of patriotic sentiment and display of
goodwill which attended the departure of black infantrymen from
nearby Fort Douglas. A large, racially mixed crowd lined the
streets of Salt Lake City to bid farewell to the men of the Twenty-
fourth Infantry. Even those whites who had vigorously protested
the stationing of black troops at Fort Douglas two years earlier
seemed, for the moment at least, to have rid themselves of racial
prejudice. The soldiers themselves were happy, as Taylor noted,
not only because their new assignment held the prospect for winning new laurels in Cuba, but also because it would remove them
from a place that had at times been acutely color conscious. Ironically, in view of their later experiences in the South, the soldiers
hoped that their new location "would be more congenial to them
and their families." [11]

As the troops of the four Negro regiments traveled eastward
aboard flag-draped trains, they were greeted all along their route
by crowds of well-wishers, both black and white. Even the antiwar
editor of the Kansas City *American Citizen* conceded that the sight
of these black soldiers "going forth to die for their country" kin-
dled "the sparks of patriotism that have lain dormant for years." [12]
In describing the reception accorded the black troops, George W.
Prioleau, a black chaplain of the Ninth Cavalry, wrote: "All the
way from northwest Nebraska this regiment was greeted with

9. For expressions of this sentiment, see Russell A. Alger to Garret A. Hobart,
July 2, 1898, Senate Document No. 334, 55 Cong., 2 sess., p. 1; *The Daily Picayune*
(New Orleans), May 15, 17, 1898.
10. "Record of Events," Regimental Returns of the Regular Army, Twenty-
fourth and Twenty-fifth Infantry Regiments, April–June, 1898, Record Group 94,
National Archives.
11. Salt Lake City *Broad Ax*, April 23, 1898.
12. Kansas City *American Citizen*, April 22, 1898.

cheers and hurrahs. At places where we stopped the people assembled by the thousands. While the Ninth Cavalry band would play some national air, the people would raise their hats, men, women and children would wave their handkerchiefs, and the heavens would resound with their hearty cheers. The white hand shaking the black hand." [13] But as Prioleau also pointed out, the cheering stopped abruptly as the troop trains crossed into Kentucky and Tennessee. Thereafter Negroes on hand to greet the soldiers were not allowed to approach the train. The few whites present viewed the scene either in surly silence or in wonder. Sergeant Horace B. Bivins of the Tenth Cavalry, who had entered military service upon leaving Hampton Institute in 1887, noted that as black soldiers "neared the South the demonstrations became less fervent" and much to the astonishment of many soldiers, especially those born and reared outside the South, all waiting rooms in the railroad stations were segregated.[14] Sergeant Frank W. Pullen of the Twenty-fourth Infantry was impressed by the contemptuous attitude of white Southerners. "It mattered not if we were soldiers of the United States, and going to fight for the honor of our country," he wrote, "we were 'niggers' as they called us and treated us with contempt." Enraged by reports regarding the treatment of Negro soldiers in the South, F. J. Loudin of Fisk University wrote a friend that he longed "to hear that the Spanish fleet has cast anchor off Charleston, New Orleans, Savannah and a few more of those hell holes and is pouring in lead and iron so they [whites] will know that the great day of His wrath is upon them." [15]

Upon their arrival at Chickamauga Park and Key West, the black regulars served notice upon white civilians that they expected to be treated like other soldiers and would not submit docilely to indignities of any kind. They took shots "at some whites who insulted them" and forced the railway company to abandon the Jim Crow arrangements on the train between Chickamauga Park and Chattanooga. Saloons and cafes which refused

13. George W. Prioleau to H. C. Smith, May 13, 1898, in Cleveland *Gazette*, May 21, 1898.
14. Herschel V. Cashin *et al.*, *Under Fire with the Tenth Cavalry* (New York: F. Tennyson Neely, 1899), pp. 61–62.
15. Sergeant Major Frank W. Pullen, Jr., quoted in Johnson, *Negro Soldiers in Spanish-American War*, p. 36; F. J. Loudin to J. P. Green, May 14, 1898, Green Papers.

service to black soldiers risked being wrecked. In Key West, where two companies of the Twenty-fifth Infantry were stationed, a black noncommissioned officer was arrested and jailed for refusing to surrender his revolver to a white sheriff. Upon hearing of the outrage, twenty-five black soldiers descended upon the jail and demanded the surrender of their comrade at the point of bayonet. The sheriff complied with their demand within the five minutes allowed him. In Chattanooga a similar incident almost occurred on April 23, when a member of the Tenth Cavalry was jailed for disorderly conduct. Only the arrival of a detachment of the provost guard prevented his comrades from storming the jail. On occasion Negro regulars also interceded in behalf of black civilians who in their opinion were being mistreated by white policemen. For example, a group of armed infantrymen prevented the arrest of a Negro woman on the streets of Chattanooga because they claimed she was being bullied.[16]

Publicity about such incidents, especially in the southern press, provoked diverse reactions. John Mitchell of the *Richmond Planet* applauded the black soldiers for asserting their rights; when a black sergeant was jailed in Key West for failure to surrender his sidearms to the local sheriff, Mitchell insisted that the sergeant was merely standing up for his constitutional rights.[17] On the other side, the Memphis *Commercial Appeal* and the *Washington Post* agreed with those white citizens of Chattanooga who likened the Negro regulars to drunken ruffians swaggering through their city at will. The Memphis newspaper suggested that if the "colored troops don't behave any better in Cuba than they did in Chattanooga the army had better lose them in the Gulf of Mexico."[18] But the Chattanooga *Daily Times,* a persistent defender of the black troops, claimed that their behavior scarcely warranted all the sensational accounts about their lawlessness. The *Times* was inclined to believe that they were no more lawless than white troops stationed at Chickamauga, an opinion shared by the *Charleston*

16. *The Daily Times* (Chattanooga), April 21, 23, 24, 25, 26, 27, 28, 29, 1898. On the black regulars in Key West, see William J. Schellings, "Key West and the Spanish-American War," *Tequesta,* XX (1960), 25–26; *Leslie's Weekly,* LXXXVI (May 12, 1898), 298.

17. *Richmond Planet,* April 30, 1898.

18. *Commercial Appeal* (Memphis), quoted in Chattanooga *Daily Times,* April 30, 1898; *Washington Post,* April 27, 1898.

News and Courier. In fact, the *News and Courier* maintained that Negro troops ought to be "kindly treated and not subjected to any unusual show of antipathy," because they were "good soldiers and the government needs good soldiers just now." [19]

During the first two weeks in May, 1898, all black units of the regular army (including the two companies of the Twenty-fifth Infantry originally sent to Key West) arrived at Tampa, the port selected as the best suited for embarkation to Cuba. During the next month of what was called "the rocking chair period," over 4,000 Negro troops were among the invasion army concentrated in the area around Tampa. Chaos and confusion prevailed in every quarter, and as Frank Freidel has noted, the "logistics snarl was too complicated" for the commander, General William R. Shafter, to unravel.[20] At Tampa as at Chickamauga the Negro units continued to receive an influx of new recruits, because the War Department had ordered all regiments to have three battalions of four companies, which meant an additional 750 men for each regiment. The arrival of so many raw recruits only compounded the confusion at the embarkation point. The Negro troops of the Twenty-fourth and Twenty-fifth Infantry pitched camp at Tampa Heights, and the Ninth Cavalry was located nearby. But when the Tenth Cavalry arrived, it could find no suitable camping-ground and was ordered to Lakeland along with several white cavalry units.[21]

Scarcely had the first companies of black soldiers arrived in the Tampa area when white civilians began to lodge complaints against them. Gilson Willets recalled that whites came "into Tampa from all points in Florida, rush to the recruiting tents, catch one glimpse of the 'nigger' soldiers, and flee." [22] Indicative of the atmosphere was the hostile attitude of the local press. Within a few days after the arrival of the Negro troops, the *Tampa Morning Tribune* reported: "The colored troops are splendid horsemen and show off to great advantage. The colored infantrymen stationed in Tampa and vicinity have made themselves very offensive to the people of the city. The men insist upon being treated as

19. Chattanooga *Daily Times*, April 25, 1898.
20. Frank Freidel, *The Splendid Little War* (Boston: Little, Brown, 1958), p. 49.
21. Cosmas, *An Army for Empire*, p. 113; Bigalow, *Reminiscences*, p. 33.
22. Gilson Willets, *The Triumph of Yankee Doodle* (New York: F. Tennyson Neely, 1898), p. 106.

white men are treated and the citizens will not make any distinction between the colored troops and the colored civilians." [23]
While the *Tribune* treated the rowdiness of white soldiers with
tolerance or levity, it viewed similar behavior by Negroes as evidence of their immunity to military discipline. Almost daily from
the time they arrived until they departed for Cuba, the local press
gave front-page coverage to every incident involving Negro troops.
Sensational accounts of "rackets" and "riots" by "these black ruffians in uniform" appeared regularly in dailies throughout the
South.[24]

White citizens in Tampa, disturbed by "the insults and men-
dacity perpetrated by the colored troops," demanded that the city
provide them greater police protection against so many undisciplined black soldiers "with criminal proclivities." Although the
new recruits obviously did not display the same degree of discipline as the veterans, there was little inclination by whites to
accord either a semblance of the tolerance shown white soldiers.
Negro troops resented what they interpreted as deliberate attempts to malign them and to cast aspersions upon the distinguished record which they had compiled during the Indian wars
in the West.[25] In a letter to a friend, a black infantryman in
Tampa declared:

> Prejudice reigns supreme here against the colored troops. Every
> little thing that is done here is chronicled as Negro brazenness,
> outlawry, etc. An ordinary drunk brings forth scare headlines in
> the dailies. Some of our boys were refused a drink at one of the
> crackers' saloons . . . and they politely closed him up. That was
> put down as a "nigger riot" and the commanding general was
> appealed to in the interest of the "respectable white citizens." [26]

From the beginning the Negro troops in the Tampa area made it
clear that they had no intention of submitting to the discriminatory treatment accorded black civilians.

The black soldiers in Lakeland, no less than those in Tampa,
were convinced that they had been stationed in the midst of "a

23. *Tampa Morning Tribune*, May 5, 1898.
24. *Ibid.*, May 7, 10, 12, 1898.
25. *Ibid.*, May 10, 12, 18, 1898; *The Florida Times-Union and Citizen* (Jacksonville), May 13, 1898.
26. "Letter from Tampa," in *The Ledger* (Baltimore), June 4, 1898.

hotbed of rebels." Within a few days after their arrival in Lakeland, the Negro cavalrymen demonstrated their unwillingness to abide by local racial customs. Angered by the refusal of the proprietor of Forbes Drug Store to serve one of their comrades at the soda fountain, a large group of armed black soldiers returned to the store and to a barbershop next door. When the white barber yelled obscenities at a Negro trooper who requested a shave, they "shot up the barbershop." Moving into the streets, where a sizable crowd had assembled, the soldiers began to fire indiscriminately and to threaten anyone who challenged them. Joab (Abe) Collins, a white civilian in the crowd, was killed. Although Collins had been hurling insults at the troops, his death was apparently caused by a stray bullet. Several white officers of the Tenth Cavalry arrived on the scene and finally quieted the disturbance. After an investigation, they turned over two black cavalrymen, James Johnson and John Young, to local authorities for trial.[27] Although the incident gave the Tenth Cavalry a bad name and inspired numerous reports of misconduct by the black soldiers, Corporal John Lewis later explained that the shooting of "Collins, the white bully" was an "act of Providence" because it taught the white people of Lakeland to respect black men in uniform.[28] However, whatever respect they displayed was clearly based upon fear rather than upon any basic change in racial views.

Accurate information about clashes involving Negro troops in the Florida camps was all the more difficult to obtain because of the War Department's rigorous censorship of all telegraphic news involving military personnel. It appears, however, that such clashes usually resulted either from insults by whites or from attempts by black soldiers to break segregation barriers. The mere sight of smartly dressed, precision-drilled Negro soldiers was sufficient to arouse envy and hostility among some whites; animosity toward black troops was even more evident whenever they were placed in positions to exercise authority over white soldiers. White citizens protested loudly, for example, when Negroes on military patrol duty arrested white soldiers.[29] Regularly taunted by epithets such

27. *Tampa Morning Tribune*, May 18, 19, 21, 25, 1898; Springfield *Illinois Record*, June 11, 25, 1898; Bigalow, *Reminiscences*, pp. 36–37.

28. John E. Lewis to editor, Springfield *Illinois Record*, June 25, 1898.

29. *Florida Times-Union and Citizen* (Jacksonville), May 31, 1898; Charles Johnson Post, *The Little War of Private Post* (Boston: Little, Brown, 1960), p. 56.

as "all niggers look alike to me," the black soldiers quickly concluded that nowhere was anti-Negro prejudice more virulent than in Florida. In time they also came to understand that such prejudice was by no means confined to whites from the South. A committee of city officials from Philadelphia who were in Tampa to inspect Pennsylvania volunteers publicly expressed concern about the "continual fighting" between white and black soldiers which they blamed upon "the insolence of the negroes who were trying to run Tampa." [30] In the opinion of black soldiers, racism even pervaded the gospel dispensed to the troops by Dwight L. Moody and other northern evangelists. "Dwight Moody is here galore," a Negro soldier wrote home, "but the colored boys care nothing for his color prejudiced religion." [31]

Those black troops unaccustomed to the racial mores of the South were appalled at the humiliating treatment to which all Negroes were subjected. They expressed utter dismay at learning that some business establishments in Tampa refused to allow Negroes to make purchases across the same counters as whites. Saloons and cafes which insisted upon maintaining the color line became the special targets of the black soldiers' ire, and several were forced to close "to prevent bloodshed." [32] John Bigalow, the white captain of a black cavalry unit, claimed that the white Floridians' lack of subtlety in race relations was the principal cause of friction with the black troops. He insisted that if whites treated colored soldiers with civility, "however much they might discriminate against them," there would be little trouble. Whether or not his analysis was correct, there seems to have been little inclination for white merchants to accept his substitute, "we don't deal with colored people," for their more customary "we don't sell to damned niggers." Regular encounters with such prejudice solidified the determination of black troops to force whites to respect them as soldiers and as men.[33] A Negro soldier in Tampa

30. *Atlanta Constitution,* June 13, 1898. For a complimentary account of the black soldiers' discipline, see W. J. Rouse, "The United States Colored Regulars," *New York Times Magazine,* June 5, 1898, pp. 4–5.
31. "Letter from Tampa," Baltimore *Ledger,* June 4, 1898.
32. George W. Prioleau to H. C. Smith, May 13, 1898, in Cleveland *Gazette,* May 21, 1898; see also *Tampa Morning Tribune,* May 13, 1898; Washington *Colored American,* August 20, 1898.
33. Bigalow, *Reminiscences,* pp. 36–37.

wrote a friend: "Our fellows think it is h— to have to fight in defense of people who are so prejudiced. They are determined to make these crackers 'walk Spanish' while here or else be treated as men." [34] Commenting on the racial customs he had witnessed in the South, Chaplain Theophilus G. Steward of the Twenty-fifth Infantry remarked: "A glorious dilemma that will be for the Cuban negro, to usher him into the condition of the American negro." [35]

The black troops were obviously in a more favorable position than others of their race to insist upon equitable treatment. They possessed arms and whatever legal protection was inherent in their uniforms, and they existed in sufficient numbers to risk forceful action against their detractors. Yet their display of restraint was perhaps more remarkable than their occasional use of force to combat discrimination and to retaliate against insults. At least one factor which helped prevent more frequent and violent reactions on their part was their feeling of being on trial and the conviction that their actions had consequences for all black Americans.[36] Because of this belief, Negro soldiers were all the more resentful of what they considered the sensational and distorted publicity lavished upon everything they did.

Nothing so clearly dramatized the paradox and incongruity bred by racial prejudice as the experience of the men of the Twenty-fourth Infantry in charge of Spanish prisoners during their transfer from Tampa to Fort McPherson, Georgia. In several towns along the route crowds of whites gathered, presumably to view the Spaniards; but the center of their attention and the target of their insults and taunts were the Negro soldiers. A Catholic priest from Atlanta who was granted permission to minister to the Spaniards at Fort McPherson concisely expressed the sentiments of those disturbed by the appearance of black soldiers in a position of authority over white men, even though such men were prisoners of war. "It is an outrage," the priest declared, "that white men [Spaniards] have been subjected to the humiliation of having

---

34. "Letter from Tampa," Baltimore *Ledger,* June 4, 1898.
35. Quoted in *The Nation,* LXVI (May 5, 1898), 335.
36. See Fowler, *Black Infantry in the West,* p. 97; Savannah *Tribune,* December 3, 1898.

negro guards over them." [37] Such venting of prejudice by white Americans, according to Chaplain George W. Prioleau of the Ninth Cavalry, served to emphasize the hypocrisy involved in the American crusade in behalf of Cuba, a nation whose population was predominantly colored. "Talk about fighting and freeing poor Cuba and of Spain's brutality," the black chaplain observed, "is America any better than Spain?" [38] The recognition of such hypocrisy which became evident in the expressions by Negro soldiers in Florida clearly had a psychological impact. The restraint of these troops in the face of continued discrimination and insults wore increasingly thin.

On the eve of the army's embarkation for Cuba, Tampa was the scene of one of the most serious racial clashes to occur in a military encampment during the Spanish-American War. Known as the Tampa riot, this disturbance on the night of June 6, 1898, climaxed the tension that had been steadily mounting for over a month. The arrival in the city of large contingents of free-wheeling white volunteer regiments only served to worsen the situation. Although the War Department's heavy-handed censorship of military news made it difficult to ascertain the details of the riot, the story ultimately seeped through the censor and appeared in the nation's press. Letters from black soldiers in Tampa published in Negro newspapers presented their version of the affair. Apparently the riot was triggered by a group of intoxicated white volunteers from Ohio who decided to have some fun with a two-year-old Negro boy. The child was snatched from his mother by a white soldier, who entertained his comrades by holding him in one hand and spanking him with the other. Then, held at arm's length with his head down, the child served as a target for several soldiers to demonstrate their marksmanship. Presumably the winner was the soldier who sent a bullet through a sleeve of the boy's shirt. Having had their fun, the soldiers returned the dazed child to his hysterical mother. Already angered by an accumulation of outrages, the black troops of the Twenty-fourth and Twenty-fifth

37. Quoted in Savannah *Tribune,* May 21, 1898; see also Omaha *Afro-American Sentinel,* May 7, 1898.

38. George W. Prioleau to H. C. Smith, May 13, 1898, in Cleveland *Gazette,* May 21, 1898.

Infantry regiments viewed the behavior of the Ohio volunteers as anything but sporting; in fact, the incident set them off on a wild, destructive rampage. They stormed into the streets firing their pistols indiscriminately, wrecking saloons and cafes which had refused to serve them, and forcing their way into white brothels.[39] Apparently they clashed not only with white civilians but also with white soldiers. The reaction of the *Tampa Morning Tribune* to reports that soldiers had outraged white prostitutes was ironic in view of its disregard for the legal rights of Negroes. "While these women are of the lowest type," the *Tribune* editorialized, "the law gives them protection." [40]

The provost guard and the Tampa police tried in vain to restrain the rioters. Finally, troops from the Second Georgia Volunteer Infantry, a white regiment, were assigned the job of restoring order. The relish with which the Georgia soldiers performed the task was equaled only by their deadly efficiency. Near daybreak on the morning of June 7 the riot was quelled. The *The Tampa Morning Tribune* published highlights of the disturbance, but it came to regret the publicity given the affair, apparently out of fear that it would reflect adversely upon the city. The newspaper later denied that there had been any riot and classified as "sheer rot" reports that the streets of Tampa "ran red with negro blood." [41] Yet twenty-seven black troops and several white Georgia volunteers from Tampa, all with serious wounds, were transferred to the hospital at Fort McPherson near Atlanta, suggesting something more than a routine disturbance.[42]

Despite the sketchy nature of the news reports, the disturbance in Tampa played into the hands of whites who objected to the use of Negro troops in the war with Spain. White Southerners and other Americans contended that the decision to mobilize black troops was a serious error because it made the Negro "forget his place" and presume "that he has changed or benefitted his social

39. For several somewhat different versions of the Tampa riot, see *Atlanta Constitution*, June 12, 13, 1898; *Augusta Chronicle*, June 11, 1898; *Tampa Morning Tribune*, June 8, 1898; Cleveland *Gazette*, June 25, July 2, 1898; *Richmond Planet*, June 18, 1898.
40. *Tampa Morning Tribune*, June 8, 1898.
41. *Ibid.*, June 8, 25, 1898.
42. *Atlanta Constitution*, June 11, 1898.

condition by wearing a blue coat and carrying a gun." The *Atlanta Constitution* argued that the Tampa affair clearly demonstrated that "army discipline has no effect on the negro." "There was no need to send Negro troops to Cuba," the *Constitution* concluded, "and now to send them, after this event, is criminal." [43] The *Arkansas Gazette* of Little Rock agreed with the *Washington Post*'s contention that Negro troops should either be pulled out of the South or sent as an advance guard to Cuba, since "their presence and insolence has a pernicious influence among the negro population" of the region.[44] Other white Southerners who objected to the use of black soldiers were nevertheless uneasy about sending only whites off to war, lest the Negroes at home seize the opportunity to stage a mass uprising in their absence. A white editor in South Carolina resolved the dilemma by suggesting that all Negro soldiers be sent "to the Philippines where it would be 'kill Dick, kill devil' between them and the Malays." [45]

If the Tampa riot allowed whites to vent their prejudice against black troops, it served to magnify the misgivings of those Negroes who had never been enthusiastic about the war. The black press generally accepted without question reports that the streets of Tampa "ran red with negro blood" and that "many Afro-Americans were killed and scores wounded." Convinced that the white press had unjustly blamed black troops for precipitating the disturbance, Negro newspapers hastened to point out that the unbelievably crude behavior of white volunteers had been the source of trouble and condemned the "slaughter of black troops" by the Georgia regiment as "inhuman and uncalled for." "Spaniards have done about as badly at times with Cubans," a Negro editor in Cleveland observed, "and the country is waging war with the former because of it. Our door sill seems to be equally as bloody, at least the Southern half." [46] Other Negroes who speculated about the meaning of the Tampa riot were no less concerned about the display of prejudice by northern white soldiers than about the

43. *Ibid.*, June 11, 12, 1898. The *Constitution* declared that in view of "the wild and demoniac conduct of the negro regulars at Tampa" they should be "ordered back to the Indian reservations" lest they "assault white Cubans."

44. *Arkansas Gazette* (Little Rock), April 30, 1898.

45. *The State* (Columbia, S.C.), June 13, 1898.

46. Cleveland *Gazette*, June 25, July 2, 1898; Savannah *Tribune*, July 2, 1898; *Richmond Planet*, June 18, 1898.

slaughter perpetrated by the Georgia troops. They were particularly disturbed by the fact that white volunteers from Ohio had caused the fracas, and that white soldiers from Michigan had openly expressed disappointment that a Georgia unit, rather than themselves, had been chosen "to get the niggers." [47]

Within a week after the riot, the troops in Tampa embarked for Cuba. Except for a few contingents of new recruits which remained in Florida, the Negro regiments formed a part of the invasion force; the color line was rigidly maintained, despite the confusion which attended the departure from Tampa. A white officer of the Tenth Cavalry tried to arrange for his men to eat in local restaurants before sailing for Cuba. The typical response to these inquiries was voiced by a lady proprietor who refused on the grounds that "to have colored men eat in her dining room would ruin her business." [48] Even on board the transports arrangements were made for the segregation of the black soldiers, who were usually assigned to the lowest decks. On at least one vessel the color line was maintained by placing white troops on the port side and the men of the Twenty-fifth Infantry on the starboard side.[49]

The American invasion force of about 17,000 men which left Tampa on June 14, 1898, arrived at Daiquiri on the southeastern coast of Cuba seven days later. The "Buffalo soldiers," other dismounted cavalry regiments of the regular army, and a single volunteer outfit known as the Rough Riders made up the Cavalry Division commanded by General Joseph Wheeler. The two black infantry regiments which were brigaded with various white units belonged to the First and Second Divisions, under the commands of generals Jacob F. Kent and Henry W. Lawton, respectively. The invasion itself was attended by almost as much confusion as characterized the scene at Tampa. Under cover of fire provided by the navy, troops from the transports anchored in the waters near Daiquiri scrambled onto the rocky beach after battling an unusually rough surf. They gained control of the area between Daiquiri and Siboney without opposition from the Spaniards. The

47. *Augusta Chronicle,* June 11, 1898.
48. Bigalow, *Reminiscences,* p. 50.
49. Fletcher, "Negro Soldier and the United States Army," p. 195.

black cavalrymen, who were among the first to get ashore, were kept busy unloading the transports and repairing the road from Siboney to Santiago. Along with men from the Twenty-fifth Infantry, they also served as scouts and patrols and as guards for the supply base at Siboney. Corporal C. D. Kirby, a black trooper on guard duty at the supply depot, achieved an enviable reputation among his comrades for intercepting two Spaniards who slipped into the restricted area on a dark, moonless night.[50]

The first battle of the Cuban campaign took place on June 24, 1898, at Las Guasimas,[51] a juncture in the road from Siboney to Santiago marked by a clump of guasima trees. The responsibility for precipitating this controversial engagement rested with the plucky ex-Confederate, General Joseph Wheeler. The fighting at Las Guasimas was done largely by the First and Tenth Cavalry of the regular army and by the Rough Riders. The Ninth Cavalry, dispatched from Siboney as soon as news of the battle reached there, arrived only after the Spaniards were in retreat. The soldiers of the Twenty-fifth Infantry who marched off to reinforce the American lines at Las Guasimas got lost and ultimately wound up where they had started. The Negro troopers of the Tenth Cavalry, who had been held in reserve when the battle began, moved to the front with their Hotchkiss guns and attacked the Spaniards at what was considered their most impregnable point. The men of Troops B and I in particular won praise from white commanders, whose reports concerning Las Guasimas repeatedly referred to their gallantry, "perfect coolness," and "fine discipline."[52] Sergeant Major Edward L. Baker of the Tenth Cavalry recorded in his diary following the Las Guasimas engagement: "The First U.S. Cavalry and Rough Riders were unstinted in

50. Theophilus G. Steward, *The Colored Regulars in the United States Army* (Philadelphia: A.M.E. Book Concern, 1904), pp. 116–122; "Records of Events," Regimental Returns, Twenty-fourth and Twenty-fifth Infantry, June, 1898; C. D. Kirby to Mrs. Charles Kirby, in Springfield *Illinois Record*, August 27, 1898.

51. On the battle of Las Guasimas, see Freidel, *Splendid Little War*, pp. 75–89; Cashin, *Under Fire with the Tenth Cavalry*, pp. 79–80; Steward, *Colored Regulars*, pp. 122–141.

52. *Annual Report of the War Department for the Fiscal Year Ending June 30, 1898*, House Document No. 2, 55 Cong., 3 sess., pp. 347–349; hereafter cited as *Annual Report of the Department of War, 1898*; James M. Guthrie, *Camp-Fires of the Afro-American; Or, the Colored Man as a Patriot* (Philadelphia: Afro-American Publishing, 1899), pp. 687–688.

extolling the qualities of their brothers in arms, the Tenth U.S. Cavalry." [53] A black infantryman who witnessed the battle claimed that without the "smoked Yankees" of the Tenth, "the Rough Riders would not have dislodged the Spaniards by themselves." [54] When the white commander of Troop B (Tenth Cavalry) was, in his own words, "unfortunate enough to lose the troop," his place was taken by a black noncommissioned officer, John Buck, who led the unit in an assault that contributed significantly to the defeat of the Spaniards. Sergeant Buck was probably the first Negro soldier to assume command of a troop or company during the Cuban campaign, but before the end of the war similar performances by black noncommissioned officers became common.[55] Black Americans both in and out of military service concluded that if Negro soldiers made efficient commanders under combat conditions, they were entitled to be relieved of restrictions which prevented them from receiving commissions in the regular army.

Following the victory at Las Guasimas, the Tenth Cavalry buried the dead and tended to the needs of the wounded. The main body of the army moved forward and camped in the vicinity of Savilla and El Pozo in preparation for an assault on Santiago. While awaiting orders to advance, the men foraged for food and battled the heat, rain, and insects. The Twenty-fourth Infantry, which was the last regiment to land at Daiquiri, finally moved to the front two days after the battle at Las Guasimas. By June 30 most of the Negro regulars were encamped with the invasion force a few miles from the village of El Caney and near the San Juan Heights, where the Spaniards were busy strengthening their fortifications.[56]

At the time one contingent of black soldiers was engaged in a dangerous mission in southwestern Cuba, far removed from the action around Santiago. Sailing from Florida on June 21, 1898, with several companies of Cuban soldiers which had been concentrated at Tampa, a detachment of Troop M of the Tenth Cavalry finally succeeded in landing at Jucaro; there they made contact

53. "Diary of E. L. Baker, Sergeant-Major, Tenth U.S. Cavalry," in Steward, *Colored Regulars*, p. 260.
54. Quoted in Johnson, *Negro Soldiers in the Spanish-American War*, p. 43.
55. Steward, *Colored Regulars*, pp. 135–136, 138–139.
56. *Ibid.*, pp. 150–151; Cashin, *Under Fire with the Tenth Cavalry*, pp. 84–90.

with the Cuban insurgent army under General Maximo Gomez. Isolated from other American forces for about three months while they fought with the Cubans, the black cavalrymen under Lieutenant Carter P. Johnson participated in several notable engagements, including the capture of El Hebro, and won particular distinction for staging a daring rescue operation on June 30, 1898, at Tayabocoa. Four privates who took part in the mission received Congressional Medals of Honor. Having sustained only one casualty, the men of Troop M rejoined their regiment in September.[57]

In the meantime, beginning on July 1, 1898, troops of all four black regiments participated in the bloody struggle which opened the way for the conquest of Santiago. The battles at El Caney and San Juan Hill [58] made the encounter at Las Guasimas appear as a minor skirmish. Among the first troops to arrive at the Spanish fortification at El Caney were the men of the Twenty-fifth Infantry. With a yell "which would have done credit to a Comanche Indian," the black infantrymen seemed oblivious to the "perfect hailstorm of bullets," the blazing July sun, and the barbed-wire entanglements as they charged the blockhouses.[59] A white lieutenant of the Twenty-fifth declared that "it was at El Caney, 'the Hornet's Nest,' that our colored Regulars fought and won." [60] Writing home after the victory at El Caney, a black sergeant noted with pride that the "coolness and bravery that characterized our fathers in the '60's have been handed down to their sons of

57. E. N. Glass, *History of the Tenth Cavalry* (Tuscon: Acme Printing, 1921), pp. 32–33; Cashin, *Under Fire with the Tenth Cavalry*, pp. 175–176; Irvin H. Lee, *Negro Medal of Honor Men* (New York: Dodd, Mead, 1967), pp. 90–94. The indiscretions of Lt. Johnson while drunk are chronicled by N. G. Gonzales of the Columbia *State*, who traveled with Gomez's army; see Columbia *State*, September 26, October 7, 1898.

58. The account of the black regulars' role at El Caney and San Juan Hill is drawn largely from Steward, *Colored Regulars*, pp. 150–220; Cashin, *Under Fire with the Tenth Cavalry*, pp. 89–134; John H. Nankivell, *History of the Twenty-fifth Regiment of the United States Infantry, 1869–1926* (Denver: Smith-Brooks, 1927), pp. 73–84; William G. Muller, *The Twenty-fourth Infantry: Past and Present* (n.p., 1923); *Annual Report of the Department of War, 1898*, pp. 328–334, 347–349, 434–439, 704–710; Allan Keller, *The Spanish-American War: A Compact History* (New York: Hawthorn Books, 1969), pp. 149–170.

59. Johnson, *Negro Soldiers in the Spanish-American War*, pp. 47–49; see also Andrew S. Draper, *The Rescue of Cuba: An Episode in the Growth of Free Government* (Boston: Silver Burnett, 1899), p. 103.

60. James A. Moss, *Memories of the Campaign of Santiago* (San Francisco: Mysell and Rollins, 1899), p. 41.

the 90's." And if anyone still doubted "the fitness of the colored soldier for active field service," he referred them to the white commanders who had witnessed their performance at the "Hornet's Nest." [61]

While the men of the Twenty-fifth Infantry were demonstrating their prowess as combat soldiers at El Caney, the other three Negro units, the Twenty-fourth Infantry and the Ninth and Tenth Cavalry, were participating in the assault upon the Spanish entrenchments atop San Juan Heights. Finding himself in command of an assortment of infantrymen and cavalrymen, including his own Rough Riders and Negro troops, Colonel Theodore Roosevelt led the charge up the ridge. Sergeant George Berry, a thirty-year veteran of the Tenth Cavalry, planted the colors of the Third Cavalry as well as those of his own regiment on San Juan Hill. "If it had not been for the Negro cavalry," declared a corporal in Roosevelt's volunteer outfit, "the Rough Riders would have been exterminated." [62] No less dramatic was the performance of the Twenty-fourth Infantry, located on the extreme left of the American line in the attack on the Spanish stronghold. A black infantryman who stormed San Juan Heights under a barrage of Spanish bullets described his comrades as "an angry mob" oblivious to the death and destruction around them. Many officers were either killed or wounded; as Corporal John R. Conn of the Twenty-fourth noted, "there was no organization recognized." In the disorder of the San Juan assault the command of black troops often fell to black noncommissioned officers, whose performance could scarcely have been more effective. Indeed, all those who witnessed the battle of San Juan Hill agreed with the assessment of the correspondent Richard Harding Davis, who declared that "the negro soldiers established themselves as fighting men" in that engagement.[63]

61. Sergeant M. W. Saddler to the Editor, July 30, 1898, in Indianapolis *Freeman*, August 27, 1898.

62. Steward, *Colored Regulars*, p. 243; Johnson, *Negro Soldiers in the Spanish-American War*, p. 85; see also *The Santiago Campaign: Reminiscences of the Operations for the Capture of Santiago de Cuba in the Spanish-American War, June and July, 1898* (Richmond: Williams Printing, 1927), pp. 421–423.

63. John R. Conn to Mrs. J. W. Cromwell, August 24, 1898, in *The Evening Star* (Washington), September 17, 1898; Steward, *Colored Regulars*, pp. 201–202; Richard Harding Davis, *The Cuban and Porto Rican Campaigns* (New York:

On July 3, 1898, while American troops "dug in" atop San Juan Heights, a truce was arranged which remained in effect until July 10. When on the latter date the Spaniards refused the terms of surrender proposed by General William R. Shafter, the armistice came to an end and the assault on Santiago began. Lieutenant John J. Pershing of the Tenth Cavalry recalled that "the battle raged with the same old fury as of those early July days; shells and bullets whistled violently for a few moments, but the enemy's fire gradually died away and was silenced." The exchange of fire ceased on July 11, and the Spanish army formally surrendered six days later.[64]

By the time of the surrender, war had lost much of its glamour for the victorious American troops. A black infantryman wrote to his sister after the Santiago campaign, saying that it "seemed almost impossible that civilized men could so recklessly destroy each other." [65] A seasoned veteran of the Tenth Cavalry who had assisted in burying bodies "badly eaten by vultures" assured a friend that he hoped "to see no more war." He also noted that "nearly all the officers have played out and gone" and that the enlisted men, exhausted, hungry, and "almost naked," were suffering from inadequate supplies of medicine, food, and drinking water. Diseases and fevers were rampant. In describing the condition of the troops, a black cavalryman claimed that many of his comrades were so emaciated that they were barely recognizable. But even though the climate and diseases of Cuba had taken a frightful toll among Negro soldiers, he pointed out, their condition was immeasurably better than that of the white troops who were dying "like sheep." "It only goes to show beyond a doubt," the black soldier concluded, "that the colored troops can stand more hardships than the whites under any condition." [66]

Charles Scribner's Sons, 1904), p. 244; see also John B. Atkins, *The War in Cuba: The Experiences of an Englishman with the United States Army* (London: Elder, Elder, 1899), pp. 129–130.

64. From a lecture by Lt. John J. Pershing reprinted in Steward, *Colored Regulars*, pp. 195–216. For a brief account of Pershing's attitude toward black soldiers, see Richard O'Connor, *Black Jack Pershing* (Garden City: Doubleday, 1961), pp. 42, 44–50.

65. John R. Conn to Mrs. J. W. Cromwell, August 24, 1898, in Washington *Evening Star*, September 17, 1898.

66. Sergeant J. C. Pendergrass to R. Anderson, July ?, 1898, in Springfield *Illinois Record*, September 3, 1898; "Member of Tenth Cavalry," *ibid.*, September 10, 1898.

Black seamen, though less conspicuous than their brethren in the army, took part in all important naval engagements and shared fully in the war's privations. Because most of the 2,000 Negroes in the wartime navy served as cooks, stewards, gunner's mates, machinists, firemen, and coal-passers, they had few opportunities to attract public attention for individual feats of heroism. Among those who did receive such recognition were Elijah B. Tunnell, a cook aboard the *Winslow*; one of the first casualties after the declaration of war, he became known as a "second Attucks." John Jordan, a gunner's mate on Dewey's flagship, was credited with firing the first shot in the battle of Manila Bay. The only black sailor to win the Navy Medal of Honor was Robert Penn, a fireman on the U.S.S. *Iowa* who had abandoned the tobacco fields of his native Virginia and joined the Navy in the hope of finding a better life. On July 20, 1898, as the *Iowa* lay off the coast of Cuba, an explosion ripped through one of its boiler rooms, trapping a coal-passer. In rescuing the severely injured seaman, Penn displayed a fearlessness and skill that awed his fellow crewmen. Four months later the Negro fireman was awarded the navy's highest honor "for intrepidity at the risk of his own life above and beyond the call of duty." But such acts of heroism and occasional recognition did little to improve the Negro sailor's chances for advancement. According to a veteran black seaman, Negroes in the navy were at the mercy of officers "through whose veins . . . runs the poisonous blood of Negrophobia." [67]

The expedition to Puerto Rico following the conquest of Santiago involved few troops and relatively little resistance from the Spaniards. In Puerto Rico the Americans were greeted by a wildly enthusiastic native population. If in any respect the Spanish-American War deserved to be labeled a "splendid little war," it was for the campaign between July 25 and August 14, 1898, that extended American control over Puerto Rico. Although only one Negro unit (Company L of the Sixth Massachusetts Volunteer Infantry) participated in that campaign, individual Negro soldiers attached to other regiments, as well as black sailors and teamsters,

67. Cleveland *Gazette*, May 28, 1898; Nicholas H. Campbell, "The Negro in the Navy," *Colored American Magazine*, VI (May–June, 1903), 406–413; Benjamin Quarles, *The Negro in the Making of America* (New York: Collier Books, 1969), p. 179; Lee, *Negro Medal of Honor Men*, pp. 53–55.

took part in it.[68] A black regular writing from the city of Ponce described the island as "the first place in my life I have been and found no distinction in color." William C. Payne, a cabin steward who arrived in Puerto Rico aboard the U.S.S. *Dixie,* wrote home extolling the economic opportunities which awaited enterprising black Americans in that island as well as in Cuba. In his opinion, Negroes in the United States should lose no time in preparing to take up residence in these islands where they would find the people, climate, and soil so congenial to their advancement.[69] The publicity given to such reports in the black press helps explain why so many Negroes in the South attempted to sign up for the labor force recruited by the government to assist in the postwar reconstruction of Cuba. Late in July, 1898, for example, the large number of black laborers from South Carolina who boarded the *Uto* for Santiago left little doubt that "they were happy to be leaving Charleston" for a place which promised greater opportunities for personal freedom and economic advancement.[70]

Although reports of economic possibilities in the Caribbean aroused the interest of many Negro Americans, their primary concern was the effect which the performance of black soldiers in the Santiago campaign would have upon the status of black people in the United States. The soldiers themselves anticipated that their role in rescuing Cuba from Spanish rule would "create in the mind of the whole country a stronger belief in the possibilities of the race." With the exception of men like John Mitchell, who saw "not a ray of visible hope upon the horizon of the future" for either "the dark skinned inhabitants" of Cuba or the United States, most black editors were inclined to believe that the brave deeds performed by the "sons of Ham" on the battlefield not only would open the way for black soldiers to obtain commissions in the regular army, but also would move all black Americans closer to being "clothed with all the inalienable rights of citizenship." [71] In the

68. George H. Braxton, "Company 'L' in the Spanish-American War," *Colored American Magazine,* I (May, 1900), 19–25; Frank E. Edwards, *The '98 Campaign of the Sixth Massachusetts, U.S.V.* (Boston: Little, Brown, 1899), pp. 76–280.

69. The letters are reprinted in Willard B. Gatewood, Jr., *"Smoked Yankees" and the Struggle for Empire: Letters from Negro Soldiers, 1898–1902* (Urbana: University of Illinois Press, 1971), pp. 53–55, 60–61; see also W. C. Payne, *The Cruise of the U.S.S. Dixie* (Washington: E. C. Jones, 1899).

70. Columbia *State,* July 27, 1898.

71. Springfield *Illinois Record,* May 28, July 9, 1898; *Richmond Planet,* August 20, 1898.

wake of the victory at Santiago, a black editor in Wichita voiced the most extravagant hopes of Negro Americans when he declared that the war with Spain meant more to the black man "than anything since the morning stars sang together." "It will," he concluded, "shape his destiny as a citizen and bring him up to the full measure of a man the world over." [72] However, neither the struggle of black men to join the volunteer army nor the postwar fate of the black regulars justified such robust optimism.

72. *The Tribune* (Wichita), July 23, 1898.

Four

Embattled Non-Combatants

There should be no color line in patriotism. Americans cannot afford to set an example in bad manners.

—Washington *Colored American,*
May 14, 1898

A man would be a very big fool to show patriotism for a government that says she does not want a people, not even to die in defense of a righteous cause, on account of color.

—*Washington Bee,* May 28, 1898

While an invasion force made up primarily of regular soldiers assembled at Tampa, thousands of Negro civilians indicated that they were prepared to do their full duty in the war with Spain. Recruiting stations became crowded with black men who, desiring to enter the army, sought to take advantage of the order by the War Department requiring the four Negro regiments of the regular army to expand to maximum strength. The immediate and positive response of black Americans to President McKinley's call for 125,000 volunteers on April 23, 1898, seemed to contradict earlier references to them as "indifferent patriots." Pride in the black regulars stationed at Tampa, and especially in their performance a few weeks later on the battlefields of Cuba, sustained their enthusiasm even in the face of conditions which scarcely encouraged patriotic ardor. "The colored soldiers are at the front," Calvin Chase announced on the same day that President McKinley issued his call for volunteers, "and thousands of valiant colored men are only waiting for Uncle Sam to say 'Come on boys' and a howling response will be forthcoming." [1] Like other Americans, Negroes interpreted the president's call as such a message.

In response to the presidential announcement, black citizens

1. *Washington Bee,* April 23, 1898.

throughout the United States convened mass meetings which heard eloquent appeals for displays of black patriotism and passed resolutions calling upon government officials to allow black men "to share in the defense of the flag." [2] Such gatherings usually marked the beginning of campaigns to organize, on an informal basis, all-black volunteer units ranging in size from single companies to full regiments. Leaders in the black community opened recruiting stations, and as soon as enough men were enrolled for a company, battalion, or regiment, they elected officers and began drill practice while awaiting acceptance into the volunteer army. In most instances black leaders found it far easier to recruit volunteers than to have them accepted for service on terms considered consistent with the self-respect and rights of Negro citizens.

Whether a state possessed a large or small Negro population, its black citizens were determined to be represented in the volunteer army. Negro citizens in Iowa, Kansas, and California organized single companies of volunteers,[3] while the Committee on Organization of Afro-American Volunteers in New York, under the leadership of T. Thomas Fortune and T. McCants Stewart, a Negro attorney, promised to raise a full regiment. In Alabama a group of prominent Negroes from Mobile and Birmingham, including the well-known black banker W. R. Pettiford, set out to organize a battalion. Two Negro businessmen in Little Rock, John E. Bush and J. H. Sykes, used their influence in persuading black Arkansans to "sign up" for volunteer service, and Henry Demas, an important black Republican in New Orleans, served as a kind of coordinator for the enlistment efforts undertaken by Negroes throughout Louisiana. But whether in New York City, Milwaukee, or some obscure hamlet in the Mississippi delta, Negroes who responded to the call to arms almost without exception insisted that as soldiers they expected to share in "a reasonable and just distribution both of the honors and emoluments of patriotic devotion." [4] Writing two years later about the efforts of black citizens

2. Little Rock *Arkansas Gazette,* April 27, 1898; Milwaukee *Wisconsin Weekly Advocate,* May 7, 1898.
3. Indianapolis *Freeman,* May 7, 1898; Des Moines *Iowa State Bystander,* May 6, 1898; Topeka *Colored Citizen,* April 28, 1898.
4. *New York Times,* June 23, 1898; *The Age-Herald* (Birmingham), April 23, 24, 26, 30, 1898; Little Rock *Arkansas Gazette,* April 26, 27, 28, 30, 1898; New Orleans *Daily Picayune,* May 22, 24, 1898.

to gain recognition in the volunteer army, Booker T. Washington noted that they were "subjected to very great and mortifying disappointment." [5]

Their disappointment resulted from a complex of factors which appeared to provide what Washington called a "stone wall" barrier against black volunteers. In calling for 125,000 volunteers, President McKinley established a quota for each state and stipulated that preference be given to existing National Guard units; he left governors with broad authority over such matters as selecting the militia units to be mustered into federal service and commissioning their officers. In the heat of patriotic enthusiasm, numerous groups, including Negroes, diverse ethnic groups, and bands of aged Civil War veterans, as well as established militia units, clamored for recognition in the volunteer service. The task of a governor was complicated by the fact that frequently the number seeking admission to military service far exceeded the quota established for his state. In some instances politics, rather than strictly military considerations, determined the manner in which a state responded to the presidential call.[6] For Negroes, the most serious problem at the moment was related to the request that states give preference to existing National Guard units in filling their quotas.

In 1898 relatively few states possessed either all-black or racially integrated militia organizations. In most states of the South, where a majority of Negroes lived, their representation in the National Guard had undergone substantial reductions within the previous twenty years. Typical in this respect was North Carolina; by the time of the Spanish-American War, the force of black militiamen had been reduced from two battalions in the 1880's to a single company, the Charlotte Light Infantry with only forty men and officers.[7] Although a few states in the South had disbanded all

5. Booker T. Washington, *A New Negro for a New Century* (Chicago: American Publishing House, 1900), p. 28.

6. For the background to the first call for volunteers, see Cosmas, *Army for Empire*, pp. 107–110, 114–115.

7. Frenise A. Logan, *The Negro in North Carolina, 1876–1894* (Chapel Hill: University of North Carolina Press, 1964), pp. 203–204; see also "History of the State Guard," in *Annual Report of the Adjutant General of the State of North Carolina for the Year 1901* (Raleigh: Edwards and Broughton, 1902), Appendix, pp. 116–124.

black militia units, several (including Georgia, Virginia, and Alabama) retained sizable contingents of black troops on their militia rosters. Georgia had three battalions and six unattached companies, all of which consistently received superior ratings from the state's inspector general. The ranking black militia officers in the state were Colonel John Deveaux of Savannah, a prosperous businessman and editor who was prominent in the Republican party of Georgia, and Colonel Floyd H. Crumbley of Atlanta, a merchant and real estate dealer who had formerly been a sergeant major in the Tenth Cavalry of the regular army.[8] Virginia's black militiamen were organized into battalions under the command of two widely respected black men, Major William H. Johnson and Major Joseph B. Johnson.[9] Alabama possessed a battalion of black troops which by 1898 was maintained only at skeletal strength. That it had survived at all was due in large measure to efforts of its Negro commander, Reuben R. Mims of Mobile, an employee of the post office who was well known in church and fraternal as well as political circles.[10]

In spite of a nationwide movement to reform and expand militia forces in the late nineteenth century, those in many southern states continued to show signs of decay and neglect. The reports of adjutants general in the South during the 1890's were filled with references to the state of disintegration existing in the white regiments, and to the inadequacy of militia funds. If the white units received little financial support from state legislatures, Negro militiamen received even less. To a great extent, in fact, they depended upon private contributions for the purchase of equip-

8. *Report of the Adjutant General of the State of Georgia from January 1, 1899 to October 17, 1900* (Atlanta: George W. Harrison, 1900), pp. 5–6, 8, 13. Savannah *Tribune* (April 23, 1898) provided a remarkably detailed account of the black militia because its editor John Deveaux was the ranking black officer in the militia.

9. For a history of the black militia in Virginia, see William Henry Johnson, *History of the Colored Volunteer Infantry in Virginia, 1871–1899* (Richmond: n.p., 1923); *Report of the Adjutant General of Virginia for the Year 1897* (Richmond: Superintendent of Public Printing, 1897), pp. 37–39; Jack P. Maddex, *The Virginia Conservatives, 1867–1879: A Study in Reconstruction Politics* (Chapel Hill: University of North Carolina Press, 1970), pp. 192–193.

10. *Biennial Report of the Adjutant General of Alabama, 1898* (Montgomery: Romer Printing, 1898), pp. 2–3, 72; *Huntsville Gazette* (Huntsville, Ala.), December 22, 1894; Roster of Officers, Alabama State Troops, Department of Archives and History, Montgomery, Ala.

ment and arms. John H. Deveaux repeatedly complained about the discrimination practiced in the allocation of militia funds in Georgia.[11] Nor was any effort made to conceal the special status of the black militiamen. They were not brigaded with white regiments and, in the case of Virginia, their officers "reported directly to and received orders directly from the Office of Adjutant General." In Georgia the military code made "the colored officer always junior to the white officer regardless of their relative rank." [12] Throughout the South there was a growing feeling that Negro militia units were superfluous. The adjutants general of Georgia and Virginia agreed that it was "hard to conceive the circumstances under which they [Negro militiamen] would be useful." [13] When the rising tide of racism in the 1890's strengthened the opposition of whites to the retention of black units in the National Guard, their existence became a source of embarrassment to state officials. The unwillingness of state authorities in the South to call out Negro militiamen in times of civil disturbances left little for them to do other than to drill and parade during Emancipation Day celebrations.

The all-black militia units which existed in states outside the South were neither numerous nor immune to the influence of racial prejudice. In some states, of course, the Negro population was too small to support such organizations. At least two states (Maine and Nebraska) where few Negroes lived apparently made no effort to enforce the color line within their militias, but the racially mixed units from these states usually included no more than a half-dozen black men. Even so, their appearance in the volunteer army during the Spanish-American War prompted considerable comment.[14] A different arrangement in Massachusetts allowed a black company with a complete roster of black officers as a part of an otherwise all-white regiment. This unit, known as Company L of the famous Sixth Massachusetts Infantry, claimed to be the old-

11. Savannah *Tribune,* August 7, 14, December 11, 1897.
12. *Report of the Adjutant General of Virginia, 1897,* pp. 38–39.
13. *Ibid.; Report of the Adjutant General of Georgia, 1899–1900,* p. 13.
14. *The Post-Dispatch* (St. Louis), June 5, 1898; Gerald H. Early, "The Negro Soldier in the Spanish-American War" (Master's thesis, Shippenburg State College, 1970), p. 42.

est black military organization in the United States.[15] In states such as New York and Kansas, where the Negro population was large enough to support all-black militia units, the efforts of black citizens to gain representation in the National Guard had been conspicuously unsuccessful. When Negroes in New York sought admission to the volunteer army in 1898, they were told that since the state possessed no black militia companies, their request could not be honored. Confronted by an angry delegation representing the Committee on Organization of Afro-American Volunteers, Governor Frank S. Black expressed regret that the color line had traditionally excluded Negroes from New York's militia but explained that the organization of all-black National Guard units required funds which he did not possess at the time.[16]

In spite of constitutional provisions in Ohio and Indiana which appeared to restrict service in the National Guard to white males, both states allowed all-black units. By 1898 such units occupied a separate status in relation to the regimental structure. Ohio's black militia battalion, the Ninth Battalion Infantry, maintained a rather precarious existence from the early 1880's until 1897, when Charles W. Fillmore [17] of Springfield, a well-known black Republican who at the time held a minor post in the office of the secretary of state, was appointed commander with the rank of major. Fillmore reorganized the battalion and secured the services of Lieutenant Charles Young, the black West Point graduate then detailed to Wilberforce University, to instruct his men in military science and tactics.[18] Unfortunately for Fillmore, his relationship

15. John W. Cromwell, *The Negro in American History* (Washington: American Negro Academy, 1941), p. 59; Miles V. Lynk, *The Black Troopers, or the Daring Heroism of the Negro Soldiers in the Spanish-American War* (Jackson, Tenn.: Lynk Publishing House, 1899), pp. 103–104; see also Edwards, *The '98 Campaign of the 6th Massachusetts*; Braxton, "Company 'L' in the Spanish-American War," 19–25.

16. *New York Times*, June 23, 1898; *New York Daily Tribune*, June 23, 1898.

17. For a sketch of Fillmore, see "Major Charles W. Fillmore: Promoter of the Economy Fire Insurance Company," *Colored American Magazine*, XII (April, 1907), 310–312.

18. Pauli Murray, *State Laws on Race and Color* (Cincinnati: Women's Division of Christian Service, Methodist Church, 1950), p. 352; *Ohio State Journal* (Columbus), April 24, 1898; *Annual Report of the Adjutant General of Ohio, 1891* (Springfield: Springfield Publishing Co., 1892), pp. 430–433; *Annual Report of the Adjutant General of Ohio, 1896*, p. 8; *Annual Report of the Adjutant General of Ohio, 1897*, pp. 69–73, 111–117.

with the battalion was seriously jeopardized by two controversies which erupted in the election year of 1897. Both involved Republican governor Asa S. Bushnell, who had commissioned Fillmore as a major in the militia, and adversely affected his reputation among the state's black electorate. The governor's handling of a lynching which occurred in Urbana, Ohio, in June, 1897,[19] aroused a storm of protest; black citizens threatened political reprisal in the forthcoming election. Although Bushnell was reelected in November, the Urbana affair seriously eroded his popularity with black voters.[20] At the same time a senatorial campaign brought to a climax a complicated Republican factional struggle between the forces of Senator Joseph B. Foraker, with whom Bushnell was allied, and those of the Cleveland industrialist Marcus A. Hanna, himself a candidate for the Senate.[21] Black Republicans, already hostile to Bushnell because of the Urbana lynching, now accused him of complicity in a plot to prevent the election of Hanna, whom they described as a "great friend of the race." Hanna's election early in January, 1898, was an occasion for rejoicing among anti-Bushnell blacks.[22] Caught in the crossfire of these political developments, Fillmore for a time attempted to retain favor with both Hanna and Bushnell. In an effort to combat any ill will which Bushnell entertained against blacks for their opposition during the gubernatorial campaign, he offered the Ninth Battalion as an escort for the governor in the inaugural parade. But upon learning that such a gesture would be greeted with "jeers and hisses" from Negro citizens, Fillmore withdrew the offer on the grounds that he could not subject his militiamen to such ostracism. This act marked the beginning of a prolonged controversy between him and the governor; it jeopardized the

19. See *Annual Report of the Adjutant General of Ohio, 1897*, pp. 18–31; *Appleton's Annual Cyclopaedia of the Year 1897*, p. 651; Willard B. Gatewood, Jr., "Ohio's Negro Battalion in the Spanish-American War," *Northwest Ohio Quarterly*, XLV (Spring, 1973), 55–59.

20. Cleveland *Gazette*, June 12, July 3, 10, 31, August 14, 21, September 4, October 16, 23, 1898.

21. See Everett Walters, *Joseph Benson Foraker: Uncompromising Republican* (Columbus: Ohio History Press, 1948), pp. 135–140; Herbert Croly, *Marcus Alonzo Hanna: His Life and Work* (New York: Macmillan, 1912), pp. 239–241, 251, 256; Philip D. Jordan, *Ohio Comes of Age, 1873–1900* (Columbus: Ohio State Archeological and Historical Society, 1943), pp. 308–312.

22. Cleveland *Gazette*, October 23, 1897, January 15, 29, 1898.

status of the Ninth Battalion at the moment when the United States went to war with Spain.[23]

Negro militiamen in Indiana suffered an even more serious misfortune on the eve of the war. The state had two separate black militia companies, organized in 1882 and 1885 respectively, which on several occasions had acquitted themselves "with honor" during civil disturbances in the 1890's. The senior black officer in Indiana's National Guard was Captain Jacob M. Porter, a messenger in the Indiana National Bank of Indianapolis and a veteran of the Civil War.[24] Early in April, 1898, as war with Spain became imminent, Porter and a group of leading black citizens in Indianapolis sought to have the separate status of the militia companies removed and the units incorporated into the regular regimental structure of the state's military force. Otherwise the black militiamen believed that they would have little chance of being called into volunteer service in case of war. Republican governor James A. Mount took the opposite view but promised to work toward increasing the two companies to battalion strength if Negroes would abandon efforts to eliminate the separate status of black militiamen. Some Negroes interpreted the governor's proposition as a subterfuge to deprive blacks of any opportunity to serve their country on the same terms as other citizens. A series of protest meetings, coupled with black Democrats' noisy condemnation of the governor, transformed the dispute into a heated controversy that resulted in the mustering out of the two militia companies, leaving Indiana Negroes without representation in the National Guard by the time war was officially declared.[25]

For a quarter of a century prior to the outbreak of the war with

23. Columbus *Ohio State Journal*, January 8, May 3, 8, 11, 12, 1898; Cleveland *Gazette*, January 15, 29, 1898; Washington *Colored American*, May 7, 1898; Charles W. Fillmore to George A. Myers, April 16, 1898; R. W. Tyler to George A. Myers, May 14, 1898, Myers Papers.

24. Emma Lou Thornbrough, *The Negro in Indiana: A Study of a Minority* (Indianapolis: Indiana Historical Bureau, 1957), p. 250n; Clifton J. Phillips, *Indiana in Transition: The Emergence of an Industrial Commonwealth, 1880–1920* (Indianapolis: Indiana Historical Bureau and Indiana Historical Society, 1968), p. 65; *The Journal* (Indianapolis), April 2, 1898.

25. Indianapolis *Journal*, March 4, April 2, 9, 1898; Indianapolis *Freeman*, April 9, 23; Indianapolis *World*, April 9, 16, 23, 1898; James A. Mount to Robert B. Bagby, April 26, 1898, Correspondence of James A. Mount, Archives Division, Indiana State Library.

Spain, Negroes in Illinois had maintained military bodies either on an informal basis or as part of the state militia. Early in the 1890's after the last all-black unit had been dropped from the militia roster by an economy-minded legislature, Negroes in Chicago initiated a movement that ultimately resulted in the organization of a black battalion. The unit was accepted into the Illinois National Guard in 1895 largely through the efforts of John C. Buckner, a black Republican member of the legislature.[26] Buckner served as commanding officer of the Ninth Battalion (Colored) until early in 1898, when clashes between him and Governor John R. Tanner led to his replacement as major by John R. Marshall. Buckner's friends accused the governor of "playing politics" with the militia in an effort to pave the way for his election to the Senate. Not even Booker T. Washington's commendation of Marshall, an alumnus of Hampton Institute and the foreman of a large construction company in Chicago, could dispel persistent rumors to the effect that Buckner's successor was a mere political flunky of Governor Tanner, who enjoyed neither the respect nor the confidence of most black people in the state.[27] As in Indiana and Ohio, the black militia unit in Illinois was beset by controversy and uncertainty by the time President McKinley issued his first call for volunteers.

In 1898 conditions in neither the North nor the South augured well for Negroes bent upon acquiring "the honors and emoluments" bestowed upon those who displayed "patriotic devotion." In most states black militia organizations occupied a status which offered slight hope that they would be shown any preference in organizing the volunteer army. Furthermore, the size of black militia units posed additional obstacles. Negroes usually belonged to separate or unattached battalions and companies, and unless a state's quota included units of less than regimental strength, their admission would require consolidation of black and white units to form mixed regiments. Few governors were willing for white

26. W. T. Goode, The "Eighth Illinois" (Chicago: Blakely Printing, 1899), pp. 5–16, 25–26, 65–69; Springfield Illinois Record, July 23, 1898.
27. Members of the State Project of the Works Project Administration of the State of Illinois, "Camp Lincoln," Journal of the Illinois State Historical Society, XXXIV (September, 1941), 292–294; Springfield Illinois Record, November 13, 1897, January 15, March 19, May 7, 21, 1898; Southern Workman, XXVII (October, 1898), 200.

and black soldiers to be brigaded together, much less to tolerate racially mixed regiments. Governor Tanner of Illinois expressed a common sentiment when he explained that the amalgamation of black units with a white regiment would be "unsatisfactory to all parties concerned." [28] Other governors who opposed such amalgamation cited the example of the regular army, which restricted Negroes to all-black regiments under white officers.[29] Since the War Department shared the racial attitudes prevailing in the larger white society, it provided little encouragement to Negro volunteers, at least not until political and military circumstances prompted a different course. In fact, black Americans came to believe that the War Department, especially Adjutant General Henry C. Corbin, was primarily responsible for their failure to receive equitable treatment.[30]

The use of Negroes as volunteer soldiers sparked a lively discussion among white Americans; their attitudes ranged from a kind of paternalistic indulgence to resolute opposition. White Americans usually commended the patriotic enthusiasm displayed by black citizens but often explained their eagerness to enter military service either in terms of their desire for financial betterment or their innate love of uniforms and parades. Some whites conceded, however, that "the colored men of the country are willing to enlist . . . under circumstances" that white men would consider intolerable.[31] And a few, such as a white editor in Mobile, sympathized with the desire of black volunteers to have a voice in the selection of their officers.[32] But most white citizens who believed that black Americans were entitled to representation in the volunteer force were unwilling to advocate anything more than a limited use of Negro volunteer soldiers under the command of white officers.

From the beginning even this view was challenged by those whites opposed to the enlistment of Negro volunteers on any terms. The Negro, they claimed, was immune to military disci-

28. *Chicago Tribune,* April 28, 1898.
29. Indianapolis *Journal,* April 2, 9, 1898; *Arkansas Gazette,* May 3, 1898.
30. Cromwell, *The Negro in American History,* pp. 58–59.
31. New Orleans *Daily Picayune,* June 3, 1898; Birmingham *Age-Herald,* May 27, 1898; Milledge Lockhart, "The Colored Soldier in the South," *New York Times Illustrated Magazine,* XLVII (August 14, 1898), 7.
32. *The Daily Register* (Mobile), May 31, 1898.

pline, and the blue uniform of the volunteer would only make him "impudent and tyrannical in his dealings with white men." To confirm such opinions they pointed to the disturbances in Chattanooga and Tampa involving Negro soldiers of the regular army, insisting that if black regulars with years of training were still given to outbursts of brutish behavior, black volunteers would certainly be more inclined to "sully the uniform of the United States Army." [33] Another oft-cited reason for opposing the enlistment of Negro volunteers found expression in the Memphis *Commercial Appeal*'s argument that military experience would "have a demoralizing effect on them when they return." [34] White Americans came to the conclusion that the basic motive which prompted Negroes to enter the volunteer service was the hope of acquiring "their ideal of freedom." [35] But if that ideal was "social equality," the *New York Times* declared, it might as well be abandoned, because "all sensible men" had long ago dismissed as foolish any scheme which attempted to establish "social equality between the races . . . by forcing them to associate." [36] In an editorial addressed to Negroes, the *Washington Post* described as "childish cant" all "the talk of insults and striking back" emanating from "a lot of self-appointed colored leaders" whose only qualification was their bumptiousness and whose only possible achievement was mischief for the Negro race. "The war will go right along whether the colored warriors join the army or stay at home," the *Post* concluded, "and if we send a million fighting men to the front, there will remain several other millions to preserve order at home and attend to any 'trouble' the disgruntled colored leaders may see fit to make." [37]

For many white Southerners the issue was not quite that simple. Some feared that unless Negroes were called upon to "shoulder their part of the fighting" another generation of white males in the South would be decimated by war. The New Orleans *Daily Picayune* maintained that black men, properly disciplined by

33. *Arkansas Gazette*, April 30, 1898; *Augusta Chronicle*, June 11, 1898; *Atlanta Constitution*, June 14, 1898; *Washington Post*, April 27, 1898.
34. Quoted in the Baltimore *Ledger*, May 7, 1898.
35. Birmingham *Age-Herald*, January 3, 1899.
36. *New York Times*, July 13, 1898.
37. *Washington Post*, May 26, 1898.

white officers and kept in all-black units, could perform efficiently as soldiers in the tropical climate of Cuba.[38] Other whites manifested less concern about the fate of young white men in the tropics than about the unprotected civilian white population at home. They were uneasy about sending only whites off to war lest Negroes at home seize the opportunity to make trouble, but they were unwilling to allow Negroes to become volunteers on their own terms. Some whites took seriously predictions that there would be a general "uprising of the black man" in the South as soon as the white militiamen were engaged elsewhere. "While our husbands and brothers are fighting for Cuban freedom," a white woman in Virginia asked, "who is going to protect our homes from the desperate negro?" [39]

The same question troubled Governor Atkinson of Georgia. Although the governor persistently rejected requests by Negro militiamen for admission to the volunteers, he was nonetheless concerned about mustering in so many white National Guard units for fear that the state would be without adequate means to "quell riots and maintain order." [40] Such fears led to the organization of a corps of Home Guards [41] to perform militia functions for the duration of the war. According to a black editor in Savannah, the organizers of these quasi-military units endeavored "to make it appear that in case of any large percent of the white citizens being called to the front that a certain class of colored people will take advantage of it and create trouble." The Savannah editor viewed the Home Guards as little more than "white cappers" endowed with the authority of the state.[42]

Despite all their patriotic rallies and enlistment efforts, Negroes were ignored by most governors in filling quotas under the first call for volunteers. In Arkansas, Texas, Louisiana, and Mississippi, black citizens who tendered the services of volunteer companies were "given to understand that colored men were not acceptable,

---

38. New Orleans *Daily Picayune*, May 15, 17, June 11, 1898.
39. *Washington Bee*, May 21, 1898.
40. Chattanooga *Daily Times*, April 25, 1898.
41. New York and Ohio also organized temporary wartime militias to replace those units mustered into the volunteer army, but there is no evidence that Negroes viewed these temporary organizations as a threat to their security.
42. Savannah *Tribune*, April 30, 1898.

in fact not wanted." [43] The sponsors of black volunteers in Tennessee succeeded only in obtaining a promise from Governor Robert Taylor to "attend to colored troops" as soon as he had taken care of white militiamen. When the governor of New York failed to accept volunteers recruited by the Committee on Organization of Afro-American Volunteers, the patriotic rallies sponsored by black citizens in the state quickly gave way to protest meetings. T. Thomas Fortune appealed the case of black New Yorkers directly to the White House. The black company of volunteers organized in Des Moines by E. S. Willets, formerly of the Twenty-fifth Infantry, received such ambiguous advice from Republican governor Leslie Shaw that Iowa's Negroes became discouraged. In Indiana black citizens continued to denounce Governor Mount for forcing the two Negro companies out of the militia on the eve of the war and made it plain that they intended to use whatever political pressure they could muster in gaining their reinstatement.[44]

But as Negroes elsewhere soon learned, membership in the militia by no means insured admission to the volunteer army. Only in Massachusetts did the entry of black militiamen into the volunteer service take place without controversy. The acceptance of the Sixth Massachusetts meant that its all-black Company L became the first Negro unit to enter the volunteer army. Commenting on the distinctive character of the company, and especially on the fact that it possessed a complete roster of black officers, the *New York Times* promised that "its course throughout the present difficulty with Spain will be watched with interest." Unlike those in Massachusetts, the black militiamen in Georgia received no recognition in filling the state's quota.[45] Despite the existence of a relatively large black militia force, Governor Atkinson of Georgia "acted as if there were no colored troops" in his state. When he summoned militia officers to Atlanta to discuss the state's quota, "no colored commander was invited," not even the

43. *Arkansas Gazette,* May 18, 1898; New Orleans *Daily Picayune,* May 15, 17, June 11, 1898; W. J. Porter to R. B. Hawley, May 4, 1898, William McKinley Papers, Manuscript Division, Library of Congress.

44. Kansas City *American Citizen,* May 20, 1898; Robert A. Lanier, Jr., "Memphis Greets the War with Spain," *West Tennessee Historical Society Papers,* XVIII (1964), 50–51; *New York Times,* June 23, 1898; Des Moines *Iowa State Bystander,* May 6, 1898; Indianapolis *World,* April 23, June 18, 1898.

45. *New York Times,* May 17, 1898.

two Negro colonels.[46] The state officials of Illinois were not as callous in responding to the question of Negro volunteers; however, the result was the same—the Negro militia battalion in the state was not selected for volunteer service under the first call. But the noisy protests voiced by the politically significant black electorate in Illinois were not lost upon Governor Tanner. In the event of a second call for volunteers, he promised that the state would have a full regiment "officered from colonel down by colored men." [47]

Quite to the contrary, black militiamen in South Carolina and the District of Columbia received no such commitment. Although South Carolina encountered considerable difficulty in mustering in its quota of volunteers, Governor W. H. Ellebre resolutely refused to mobilize black troops. He ignored the entreaties of the black militiamen as well as the offers made by Thomas W. Miller, Robert Smalls, and other prominent Negroes who desired to lead the "black sons of South Carolina" into war against Spain. In fact, the Negro militiamen in Charleston were disarmed and their weapons shipped to Columbia for use by whites in the volunteer army. Shortly afterward, a white editor noted that "all their [Negroes'] talk and bluster about their willingness to go to the front seems to have counted for nothing." Even though the cause of the First Separate Colored Battalion in the District had the support of the black press and of Negro Republican office-holders concentrated in Washington, its efforts to win a place in the volunteer army were of no avail. The battalion consisted largely of Civil War veterans, including several recipients of the Medal of Honor, and its members felt strongly that its rejection was a reflection upon their "loyalty and efficiency." [48]

In the first call three states other than Massachusetts ultimately included black volunteer units within their quotas. All three— Ohio, North Carolina, and Alabama—possessed black militia organizations, but the decision to utilize Negro troops in filling their

46. Savannah *Tribune*, April 30, 1898; see also *New York Daily Tribune*, June 24, 1898.

47. *Chicago Tribune*, April 28, 1898; Springfield *Illinois Record*, May 21, 1898.

48. Constance M. Green, *The Secret City: Race Relations in the Nation's Capital* (Princeton: Princeton University Press, 1967), pp. 130–131. For the Negro militia in South Carolina, see George B. Tindall, *South Carolina Negroes, 1877–1900* (Columbia: University of South Carolina Press, 1952), pp. 286–288; Columbia *State*, May 5, 14, June 18, 1898.

quotas resulted largely from unusual circumstances existing in those states. In Ohio the muster in of the state's black battalion took place in the aftermath of a political struggle which left the commission of Major Fillmore insecure and a sizable segment of the Negro voters alienated from Governor Bushnell. The acceptance of the Ninth Battalion appears to have been based upon two considerations: it was an efficient military organization, and its selection might mollify black hostility toward Bushnell, thereby enhancing his standing with the Negro electorate. Although Bushnell actually called the Ninth Battalion into service, many Negroes preferred to give credit to Senator Mark Hanna. Their explanation was that Bushnell acted only in response to pressure from the War Department which had been exerted at the request of Hanna. What is certain, however, is that Bushnell had no intention of permitting Fillmore to retain command of the battalion, even though a majority of the men in the battalion as well as numerous black civilians signed petitions requesting that the major remain in command. The petitioners were not so much concerned about the personal fate of Fillmore as they were about the possibility that a white commander might replace him. Finally, after the black militia had been officially mobilized, Governor Bushnell acted on the matter: he relieved Fillmore of his command and refused to allow him to remain with his battalion in any capacity, "even as a private." In his place the governor chose Charles Young, who was commissioned on May 13, 1898, as major of the Ninth Ohio Battalion, U.S.V. The choice of Young proved universally popular with black Ohioans, whose battalion enjoyed the distinction of being the only black volunteer unit under the command of a black graduate of West Point.[49]

The role of politics was even more clear-cut in North Carolina, where Negro voters had figured significantly in the election of Republican Daniel L. Russell as governor in 1896. Although the state had only one black militia company, Negroes in a half-dozen

49. Columbus *Ohio State Journal*, May 3, 8, 11, 12, 14, 15, 20, 21, 1898; Cleveland *Gazette*, May 21, 1898; see also Wendell P. Dabney, *Cincinnati's Colored Citizens: Historical, Sociological and Biographical* (Cincinnati: Dabney Publishing, 1926), pp. 125–127. For examples of numerous petitions from blacks requesting Bushnell to enlist additional Negro troops, see George W. Shanklen to Asa Bushnell, June 30, 1898, and J. H. Brownwell to Asa Bushnell, July 16, 1898, Asa Bushnell Papers, Ohio Historical Society, Columbus.

towns had hastily organized groups of volunteers and offered their services to the governor. Black citizens insisted that in filling the state's quota of volunteers, they should be recognized "in accord with their voting population." They also impressed upon the governor their desire to have black officers. Fully aware of his obligations to black voters in the past and anxious to retain their support in the future, Governor Russell first attempted to persuade the War Department to expand the state's quota so that he could accept a full regiment of black volunteers. When his request was rejected, Russell enlisted the support of the state's senators, Populist Marion Butler and Republican Jeter C. Pritchard, as well as its black Republican congressman George H. White, in an effort to work out some arrangement whereby black volunteers could be recognized. The War Department finally agreed to allow North Carolina to furnish a battalion of infantry in lieu of the battery of artillery prescribed by the state's quota. While the white Democratic press, led by Josephus Daniels's Raleigh *News and Observer,* railed against "these Republican maneuvers," Governor Russell on April 27, 1898, authorized the creation of a black infantry battalion with a complete roster of black officers. The major in command was James H. Young, a leading black Republican and editor of the Raleigh *Gazette,* who functioned as a liaison between Russell and his black constituents. Negroes throughout the United States applauded Governor Russell for his courageous action in extending official recognition to the Negroes of his state and suggested that the governors of New York, Illinois, and Indiana would do well to follow his example.[50]

In Alabama, meanwhile, Governor Joseph F. Johnston proved receptive to Negroes' demands for representation in the volunteer forces. A Civil War veteran and leader of the progressive faction of Alabama's Democratic party, Johnston had been first elected in 1896 and was nominated for a second term three days before President McKinley issued his first call for volunteers.[51] Because Ne-

50. Willard B. Gatewood, Jr., "North Carolina's Negro Regiment in the Spanish-American War," *North Carolina Historical Review,* XLVIII (October, 1971), 372–375.

51. For Governor Johnston's career and the political situation in Alabama, see Sheldon Hackney, *From Populism to Progressivism in Alabama* (Princeton: Princeton University Press, 1969).

groes still exercised political leverage in Alabama, they were likely
to receive at least a hearing from an incumbent governor facing
reelection. But Governor Johnston's inclination to accept Negro
volunteers appears to have been inspired less by political considerations than by calculations regarding the present and future demands on the state's relatively small militia force. Alabama's
quota consisted of two regiments and a battalion of infantry; but
because the total infantry organizations in the state militia consisted of only three white regiments and a colored battalion, and
because a second call for volunteers appeared imminent,[52] Johnston "decided, against popular opinion in his state, to raise colored troops." But he was not willing to defy public opinion to the
extent of placing Negro officers in command of the battalion of
black volunteers. Major Reuben R. Mims and other Negro officers
in the militia were replaced by whites from socially prominent
families. To command the battalion, the governor selected Robert
L. Bullard, a native of the state and a West Point graduate who
at the time was a captain in the regular army. Despite promises
of fair treatment from Bullard and other officers, Negroes were
reluctant to enter the volunteer service under white officers. As a
result, filling each of the four companies of the black battalion to
a capacity of eighty men took place, according to Major Bullard,
"very, very slowly."[53]

The fact that only four states accepted Negro volunteers under
the president's first call scarcely fulfilled the grandiose promises
made by those pro-war advocates in the black community who
spoke in terms of the "rich harvest" to be reaped by the demonstration of "patriotic devotion." Indeed, their extravagant calculations about thousands of black volunteers organized into several
regiments, as well as their speculation about the appointment of a
Negro general,[54] found little confirmation in the first call for volunteers. The experience of most Negroes who offered their services under the first call led them to dismiss such talk as mere
twaddle. Expressing the disappointment felt by black Americans,

52. *Biennial Report of the Adjutant General of Alabama, 1898,* pp. 2–3, 12–13;
Birmingham *Age-Herald,* April 29, 30, May 1, 1898.
53. Robert L. Bullard Diary (MS in the Robert L. Bullard Papers, Manuscript
Division, Library of Congress), pp. 81–83, 86–87; Birmingham *Age-Herald,* April 30,
May 27, 28, 1898; Mobile *Daily Register,* May 31, 1898.
54. *Washington Bee,* April 30, 1898.

the Kansas City *American Citizen* declared: "Since our contempt-ible rejection . . . our patriotic lamp, which was full of ambition, zeal and devotion, has exploded, and a spirit of supreme disgust overwhelms it." [55] Even Edward Cooper's *Colored American* ad-mitted that "the discrimination against the colored soldiers" had become "plainly marked." Such discrimination, a black remarked, had caused Negroes in his state of Indiana "to stand aloof from the enlistment idea." [56] But Monroe Dorsey of the *Parsons Blade* reminded Negroes that their services would be needed before the war ended, and he encouraged them to persist in efforts to win admission to the volunteer army on the same terms as other Amer-icans. "Though one man is turned down," he wrote, "another one steps up and asks for the same thing. One prominent Negro after another has organized troopers and tendered their services . . . only to be refused, but others are going right over the same ground. Some of them will get through the gates by and by." [57] That black volunteers had gotten through the gates in Ohio, North Carolina, Massachusetts, and Alabama was sufficient reason to believe that others would be accepted if the president issued a second call.

Much of the controversy about accepting black volunteers re-volved around the question of officers. The War Department raised few objections to Negro volunteers per se, and indeed ac-cepted as scientific fact the idea that Negroes were peculiarly suited for service in tropical climates. But the department, as well as state authorities, argued that military efficiency required placing white officers in charge of Negro troops. Typical were the ideas expressed by Major Bullard of the Alabama battalion, himself a career army officer. He believed that white officers were necessary to turn the innate qualities of Negroes to military advantage, be-cause black soldiers had no respect for officers of their own color. In his opinion, no black officer could overcome "the lack of manly pride" common to all black soldiers or restrain effectively their "susceptibility to . . . passions." [58] Expressing a less sophisticated

55. Kansas City *American Citizen*, May 20, 1898.
56. Washington *Colored American*, May 14, 1898; *The Recorder* (Indianapolis) quoted in the Coffeyville *American*, May 28, 1898.
57. *Parsons Weekly Blade*, May 21, 1898.
58. Robert L. Bullard, "The Negro Volunteer: Some Characteristics," *Journal of the Military Service Institution*, XXIX (July, 1901), 29–39; see also Charles J. Crane, *The Experiences of a Colonel of Infantry* (New York: Knickerbocker Press, 1923), p. 255.

version of the same attitude, a white editor in Texas claimed that
white officers were necessary because Negro troops had to "be held
in check like . . . cattle lest they break out and devour white soldiers and commit other crimes." [59] Negroes dismissed such reason-
ing as the product of irrational race prejudice and insisted that as
long as the military forces of the United States segregated black
men into all-black units, these units were entitled to black officers. In 1898 few black Americans took issue directly with the
principle of segregation; rather, their objections focused on the
practice of placing white officers in command of black soldiers,
which eliminated their principal means of sharing in the honors
and emoluments of military service.

The nationwide campaign to have all black volunteers commanded by black officers originated with John Mitchell in Virginia. Although Negroes elsewhere often included a demand for
black officers as one of the conditions for participating in the volunteer forces, it was Mitchell who most forcefully articulated that
demand and transformed it into a national slogan. His concern was
first aroused by the manner in which state officials responded to
the question of accepting Virginia's two black militia battalions as
a part of the state's quota under the first call for volunteers. Governor J. Hoge Tyler, a Democrat, was willing to accept the black
militiamen on two conditions: first, the War Department must
expand the state's quota specifically to include the black battalions; second, these units were to be mustered in under white
officers. The War Department rejected the first condition, and the
black militiamen the second. Mitchell enlisted the aid of prominent Negroes throughout Virginia in opposing any effort that, in
his words, would deprive black militia officers of the "honors to
which they are justly entitled." He argued that the organization of
Negro soldiers into units presupposed "separate officers," and that
any decision to place white officers over black soldiers was altogether inconsistent with white Americans' objections to "race mixing." For him, the duty of state and federal officials was plain:
Virginia's two militia battalions should be organized into a regiment with the senior black officer, Major Joseph B. Johnson, placed
in command with the rank of colonel. Mitchell counseled Negroes

59. *The Herald-Echo* (Mexia, Texas) quoted in *Richmond Planet,* July 16, 1898.

in the state to accept nothing less as a condition for serving in the volunteer army.[60]

With the same sledge-hammer style that characterized his earlier opposition to the war, in his widely circulated weekly Mitchell mounted an editorial campaign to have all Negro volunteer units placed under the command of Negro officers. His slogan was "no officers, no fight." John W. Cromwell, a black attorney and journalist in Washington, assured the Richmond editor that the black man's self-respect forbade any other course. The well-known Negro columnist John E. Bruce, who wrote under the pen name of Bruce Grit, was certain that Mitchell's slogan would find a sympathetic response "in the breast of every Negro who has a spark of manhood in his anatomy."[61] Negro newspapers throughout the United States endorsed the "no officers, no fight" policy and urged their readers to follow the example set by the black militiamen in Virginia by refusing to enter volunteer service unless they could do so under "their own officers." "It is an insult," the Kansas City *American Citizen* declared, "to tell us that we are incapable of holding the rank of an officer—no officers, no soldiers is our motto and we are loyal too."[62] In Iowa and Missouri when Negro volunteer companies were not allowed to choose their own officers, they "positively refused to go under a white captain."[63]

Although the overwhelming majority of Negroes applauded Mitchell's stand and made the "no officers, no fight" slogan a condition for their enlistment in the volunteer army, a few black spokesmen considered such an approach "too extreme." The editor of the *American Eagle,* a Negro weekly in St. Louis, objected

60. Willard B. Gatewood, Jr., "A Negro Editor on Imperialism: John Mitchell, 1898–1901," *Journalism Quarterly,* XLIX (Spring, 1972), 46–47; a useful collection of quotations from the black press on the "no officers, no fight" campaign is found in George P. Marks, ed., *The Black Press Views American Imperialism, 1898–1900* (New York: Arno Press, 1971), pp. 33–50.

61. *Richmond Planet,* June 11, 18, 1898.

62. Kansas City *American Citizen,* June 18, 1898.

63. Des Moines *Iowa State Bystander,* June 17, 1898; *Parsons Weekly Blade,* July 2, 1898. Negroes applauded the action of the Gilmer Rifles, a company of black volunteers in Alabama, which, according to news stories, "mutinied" rather than serve under white officers. What actually happened, however, scarcely deserved to be called a mutiny. Upon surrendering his command to a white officer, the black captain advised all those in his company who would not give "cheerful obedience" to white officers to "say so at once." Twelve men stepped forward and were allowed to return home. See Mobile *Daily Register,* May 30, 1898.

to any attempt by black citizens to correct "one public wrong by committing another public wrong." [64] Edward Cooper agreed, and though critical of "the narrowness of the army directors," he urged Negroes to continue to volunteer their services without relaxing their agitation for selecting their own officers. George L. Knox of the Indianapolis *Freeman*, while disappointed that so few states had allowed Negro officers, warned that it was both unpatriotic and impolitic for Negroes "to strike back in a time so disadvantageous." Knox believed that racial discrimination and segregation would end "only in a revolution in the sentiment of the country as a whole," and that attempts to wring concessions from the government in a time of national emergency would merely postpone such a revolution.[65]

Even more outspoken in opposition to the "no officers, no fight" proposition was the Baltimore *Ledger*, which was "thoroughly convinced that such a course and attitude would certainly not prove an advantage . . . to the race." The *Ledger* agreed, of course, that competent Negroes should receive commissions, but it maintained that when no such colored men were available, as was often the case, Negroes should accept white officers "instead of becoming sulky and displaying a spirit of insubordination." Attaching conditions to one's patriotism was itself a questionable practice; more important, according to the Baltimore paper, was the fact that insubordination and threats of political reprisal alienated whites, including those who traditionally befriended black citizens. "We cannot afford," the *Ledger* concluded, "to lose the sympathy and active support of a single faithful and true Anglo-Saxon friend of the race." [66]

Such rhetoric was anathema to John Mitchell, who considered it the worst form of toadyism. In answering his critics, he discussed the extraordinary nature of the Spanish-American War, which in his opinion marked a radical departure from American tradition. He insisted that the nation's honor was not at stake, nor was the government in peril; the conflict was simply a "war of conquest" waged in defiance of the Constitution. Mitchell, however, did not

64. *American Eagle* (St. Louis) quoted in *Richmond Planet*, May 28, 1898.
65. Washington *Colored American*, May 28, 1898; Indianapolis *Freeman*, May 28, 1898.
66. Baltimore *Ledger*, June 11, 1898.

rest his case upon constitutional considerations alone. Racial justice and the self-respect of black people were, as usual, of primary importance. Angered and frustrated by black critics of his "no officers, no fight" campaign, he condemned their accommodationist attitude as worthy only of cowards and degenerates. In his opinion his critics had adopted a position that could only serve to perpetuate the racial caste system of the United States. At one point Mitchell exploded: "A race of people who, denied the right of suffrage, outraged, butchered, with their rights ruthlessly trampled upon . . . that would kiss the hand that smites and begs the privilege of dying for their oppressors is degenerate indeed." [67] If the black press reflected black opinion with any degree of accuracy, most Negro Americans fully agreed with Mitchell's assessment. By a practical application of his ideas, they attempted to obtain greater recognition in the volunteer army under the president's second call.

While black citizens throughout the United States impressed upon state and local officials their desire to have black officers in charge of black volunteer units, black Republicans in Washington worked feverishly to secure federal action that would overcome the widespread discontent among Negroes. Among those most active in the cause were Pinchback, Lyons, Cheatham, and John R. Lynch, formerly a power in Mississippi politics and at the time a minor official in the Treasury Department. Lynch was an old acquaintance of President McKinley, having known him when both men were members of the House of Representatives. From time to time the proud and defiant James Lewis of New Orleans, a Civil War veteran and important black Republican in Louisiana, assisted these men, who individually and collectively attempted to use whatever influence they possessed in persuading congressmen and members of the McKinley administration to make it possible for Negroes to receive commissions in the volunteer forces.[68] At the same time a host of black citizens with previous military experience anticipated that the federal government would enlist vol-

67. *Richmond Planet*, May 7, 21, 28, June 11, 25, 1898.

68. Indianapolis *Freeman*, May 21, 1898; *Washington Bee*, May 21, 1898; Washington *Evening Star*, May 30, 1898; Christian A. Fleetwood to William McKinley, June 14, 1898, Christian A. Fleetwood Papers, Manuscript Division, Library of Congress.

unteer regiments in addition to those furnished by the states and pressed their individual claims upon the War Department. One of these was Christian A. Fleetwood, a fifty-eight-year-old veteran of the Civil War and holder of the Medal of Honor, who in 1898 was employed in the Records and Pensions Office of the War Department. A major in the District of Columbia National Guard, Fleetwood presented himself as an example of a black man with the experience and competence necessary to hold a commission in the volunteer army.[69]

Of those Negroes who waged campaigns for personal preferment, few received so much publicity and support in the black community as Henry O. Flipper, the first Negro graduate of West Point who had been courtmartialed and dismissed from the army in 1882. Black Americans generally agreed with Flipper's contention that his dismissal was the result of prejudice on the part of his commanding officer, Colonel William R. Shafter. The revival of interest in the Flipper case called attention to the role of Shafter at a critical juncture, because Flipper's former commanding officer was at the time the general in command of the invasion force concentrated at Tampa. In the view of some black observers, Shafter personified the anti-Negro prejudice that pervaded the whole officer corps of the army. But Flipper's main concern in 1898 was to clear up his record so that the War Department would act favorably on his offer to serve in the volunteer army.

Employed as a civil and mining engineer in the West, Flipper was in Washington in 1898 as a consultant in a claims case. While he was in the city, rumors abounded to the effect that McKinley planned to combine companies of black volunteers from various states into a federally sponsored regiment with black officers. The *Washington Post* even printed a story claiming that the regiment would be under the command of Flipper as colonel and Charles Young as lieutenant colonel. Encouraged by such reports, Flipper sought out prominent Negroes in Washington whose influence would be useful in clearing his record. Register of the Treasury Judson Lyons promised to get him "right back into the Army." Nothing came of the promise, and Flipper returned to the mining

69. Christian A. Fleetwood to John R. Lynch, June 7, 1898, William G. Moore to Russell A. Alger, May 7, 1898, Fleetwood Papers; *Washington Bee*, April 30, 1898.

frontier of the Southwest an embittered, defeated man. His bitterness was directed at Lyons and other black political figures in Washington as much as anyone else, because he believed they had merely played him for a "sucker and bled him to the limit" with their requests for money to cover expenses involved in exerting what Flipper concluded was their nonexistent influence upon federal officials in his behalf.[70]

But Flipper's cynical assessment of the Negro politicians in Washington scarcely did justice to their efforts to win greater recognition for black volunteers. Their entreaties at least called the attention of the McKinley administration to the widespread agitation among Negroes. Their activity alone, however, did not account for the consideration which the issue received from policy makers. As important, or perhaps more so, in bringing about an increase in the number of Negro volunteers was the War Department's calculation of future military needs for service in tropical climates.[71] Numerous bills specifically providing for the organization of black volunteer troops were introduced in Congress in April and May, 1898, but none managed to get out of committee. Nor was Congressman George H. White any more successful in securing additional representation for Negroes in the regular army. However, Representative John A. T. Hull of Iowa, the influential chairman of the House Military Affairs Committee, was only too well aware of the demands of Negro citizens because of a group of his own black constituents seeking admission to the volunteer army. Hull was sympathetic to their demands and welcomed the opportunity to assist in getting passed S.R. 4468, a bill approved by the War Department and enacted on May 10, 1898, which provided for the enlistment of 10,000 volunteers who were immune to "diseases incident to tropic climates." [72]

Calvin Chase later claimed that the idea of ten "immune" regiments of infantry recruited directly by the federal government in

70. Henry O. Flipper, *Negro Frontiersman: The Western Memoirs of Henry O. Flipper,* ed. Theodore D. Harris (El Paso: Texas Western College Press, 1963), pp. vi–ix, 37–41; Washington *Colored American,* May 7, 1898; Cleveland *Gazette,* May 28, 1898; Springfield *Illinois Record,* May 21, 1898.

71. See Fletcher, "The Negro Soldier and the U.S. Army," pp. 229–230.

72. *Ibid.,* pp. 230–232; *Congressional Record,* 55 Cong., 2 sess., pp. 4730–41, 5366, 6188, 6219, 6401, 6652, 6689, 6734, 6753; Des Moines *Iowa State Bystander,* June 3, 1898; Cosmas, *Army for Empire,* pp. 134–136; *Washington Post,* May 10, 1898.

addition to the state volunteer units originated with a black man, James Lewis. According to Chase's account, Colonel Lewis sold the idea to the House Military Affairs Committee with the intention that all ten regiments would be composed of black soldiers under black officers. Although Lewis undoubtedly supported the "immune" concept and used whatever influence he possessed in having it enacted into law, it scarcely seems probable that his role was as significant as Chase indicated, particularly in view of the fact that the War Department consistently assumed that black men were peculiarly fitted for service in tropical climates. Regardless of the origin of the proposal, the departmental decision to designate only four of the "immune" regiments as black units caused some Negroes such as Chase to charge that black Americans had again been deceived by military authorities.[73]

However, the number of regiments allocated to blacks prompted less controversy than the decision regarding their officers. The War Department decided that in the four all-black "immune" regiments Negroes could hold commissions as lieutenants, but that all other commissions were to be held by whites. The arrangement was a compromise between the department's idea that Negroes made good soldiers only if commanded by whites and the vociferous demand within the black community for Negro officers. The compromise was altogether unsatisfactory for those who adopted the "no officers, no fight" slogan. Congressman George H. White conferred twice with President McKinley in an effort to have him remove restrictions against colored officers in the "immune" regiments, but his visits to the White House were no more successful than those to the War Department by Lewis and Pinchback.[74]

A sense of outrage pervaded much of the Negro community. T. Thomas Fortune pointed out that when black citizens demanded the right to hold commissions in the volunteer army, they did not restrict their aspirations to the lowest possible commission but intended that all ranks should be open to black men. In his view the establishment of a "deadline" beyond which "Afro-Americans cannot go" was an insult.[75] O. M. Wood, the principal

73. *Washington Bee,* September 17, 1898.
74. Topeka *Colored Citizen,* July 14, 1898; Cleveland *Gazette,* July 16, 1898.
75. Quoted in the Cleveland *Gazette,* July 16, 1898.

of L'Ouverture School in St. Louis who had earlier denounced the governor of Missouri for refusing to accept black officers under the first call, was outraged that the federal government should engage in the same kind of discrimination. He claimed that the real purpose for establishing the "deadline" against Negro officers was to provide "fat positions" for whites who "would not be accepted by soldiers of their own race." Since no self-respecting black man would volunteer for service in the "immunes," he predicted, the four federal regiments would be composed only of "dregs of negrodom" whose officers would come from a comparable stratum of white society.[76]

The Negro press, with few exceptions, characterized the strictures against Negroes holding any commissions above that of lieutenant "as a phase of race discrimination that the Negroes of this country were not prepared to expect from the present Republican administration." Convinced that Negroes had a right to expect more from an administration which they had helped to elect, John Mitchell suggested that black voters take note of the fact the "President McKinley and his advisers are against us" and vote accordingly in the next election.[77]

Increasingly Negroes came to view the volunteer army as an exercise in politics and race prejudice rather than in patriotism. Some accused McKinley of "running the war for political buncombe;" therefore Negroes were being ignored because there was "too much political pull against them." It was the height of irony, others pointed out, that McKinley should lavish so many honors upon ex-Confederates whom he appointed generals and colonels in the volunteer army while he was willing to recognize only with lieutenancies the claims of black men who had served beside him during the Civil War.[78] Edward E. Cooper, who as usual was "loath to adversely criticize or embarrass an administration" which Negroes "helped to call into power," nonetheless felt obligated to question the justice of the War Department's policy regarding

76. Springfield *Illinois State Record*, June 25, 1898; see also St. Louis *Post-Dispatch*, June 28, 1898.

77. *Industrial Messenger* (Knoxville) quoted in Washington *Colored American*, July 2, 1898; Cleveland *Gazette*, July 16, 1898.

78. Springfield *Illinois Record*, June 25, 1898; Topeka *Colored Citizen*, May 26, 1898; Savannah *Tribune*, June 25, 1898; Topeka *State Ledger*, June 9, 1898.

black officers for the "immune" regiments. Like others, Cooper was all the more concerned because black citizens, having largely abandoned any hope of fair treatment by state officials, now confronted the prospect of comparable discrimination at the hands of the federal government.[79] Negro spokesmen suggested that if the appointment of volunteer officers was to be "a kind of son-of-prominent-men affair," the president should at least recognize the claims of certain black men, notably Charles R. Douglass, the son of Frederick Douglass, whose military experience and family background entitled him to share in the honors distributed by the War Department. Failure to obtain either adequate recognition for Douglass, Fleetwood, and other prominent "sons of the race" or the removal of restrictions on black officers in the "immune" regiments heightened the frustrations of black Americans and prompted their more frequent references to political reprisals against the Republican party. "The present war," the editor of a black weekly in Kansas lamented, "has served to accentuate the Negro's peculiar position more than anything else could. It is being made very plain now that he is first a Negro then a citizen or a soldier as the case may be." [80]

The hostile reaction of Negro citizens to the arrangements regarding the four black "immune" regiments elicited at least a measure of concern among white Republicans. Representative Hull of Iowa was careful to inform Negroes in his state that he was in no way responsible for the restrictions against black officers. On the contrary, he claimed to have worked closely with Congressman White in an attempt to persuade McKinley "to have all colored officers for all colored regiments." According to Hull, the President alone could authorize such an arrangement.[81] As the responsibility for the "deadline" against black officers came to be placed exclusively upon the White House, the McKinley administration took steps to counteract the growing hostility of black voters. The War Department, for example, publicly denied that it had established an inflexible policy regarding Negro officers. Privately, Secretary of War Russell Alger stated that as a rule "men of color" were not to be commissioned above the rank

79. Washington *Colored American,* July 2, 1898.
80. *Ibid.,* June 11, July 2, 1898; Coffeyville *American,* June 11, 1898.
81. Des Moines *Iowa State Bystander,* June 17, 1898.

of lieutenant, but he conceded that "possibly the captains might be colored if suitable men . . . could be found." [82] Adjutant General Corbin informed Henry Demas, whose black volunteers in Louisiana objected strenuously to white officers in the "immune" regiments, that "any assembly of protest against the action of the War Department is not advisable and should be discouraged in every way possible as it can only have injurious results." [83]

While the ambiguous statements emanating from the War Department allowed friends of the McKinley administration within the black community to place a more favorable interpretation upon its stand regarding black officers, the president himself enlisted the aid of John R. Lynch and other Negro officeholders in an effort to soften the criticism of his administration among black citizens and to win their approval of his policy regarding the "immunes." Then, in June, 1898, McKinley made Lynch a paymaster of the volunteers with the rank of major—an appointment received with considerable enthusiasm.[84] Even John Mitchell conceded that the president had at last begun to extend proper recognition to "the Afro-American contingent." [85] Shortly afterward, the president won additional praise from Negroes by endorsing Secretary Alger's recommendation that Congress provide 25,000 colored troops to be recruited from the nation at large. "In view of the special adaptability of colored troops for service under the conditions of a tropical climate," Alger wrote, "the passage of this bill is regarded as very important. . . ." Although Congress failed to act upon the secretary's recommendation, Negroes were inclined to interpret it as evidence that the administration was attempting to extend "due recognition to the race." [86]

Even more important in improving McKinley's image among

82. Russell A. Alger to James A. Mount, May 28, 1898, Mount Correspondence.

83. Henry C. Corbin to Henry Demas, June 8, 1898, Document File #114616, Records of the Adjutant General's Office, Record Group 94, National Archives; hereafter cited as Adjutant General's Records with appropriate document number.

84. Christian A. Fleetwood to John R. Lynch, June 7, 1898, Fleetwood Papers; John Roy Lynch, *Reminiscences of an Active Life: The Autobiograph of John Roy Lynch,* ed. John Hope Franklin (Chicago: University of Chicago Press, 1970), pp. 399–406.

85. *Richmond Planet,* July 2, 1898.

86. Russell A. Alger to Garrett A. Hobart, July 2, 1898, in Senate Document No. 334, 55 Cong., 2 sess., p. 1; Cleveland *Gazette,* July 9, 1898; Washington *Evening Star,* July 7, 1898.

black citizens was the pressure he applied upon the states to accept more Negroes under the second call for volunteers. On May 26, 1898, two weeks after the passage of the law authorizing the organization of the "immune" regiments by the federal government, his call for 75,000 additional volunteers went out to the states. In an effort to have sound military policy prevail over mere "patronage-mongering," the War Department required states to fill their quotas under the second call by bringing to full strength existing volunteer units before offering any new ones for federal service. In the case of North Carolina, however, both President McKinley and Secretary Alger made it clear to the Republican governor that they desired a black regiment from the state although they could not "say so officially." [87] Other states such as Virginia, where black militiamen desired to join the volunteer army provided they could retain "their own officers," were informed that the president had "expressed particular anxiety to give colored men an opportunity to enter service." [88]

Under the second call for volunteers, seven states responded by mustering in Negro units. Ohio added a fourth company to its black battalion,[89] while North Carolina and Alabama raised their black volunteer forces to regimental strength. Governor Russell, anxious to satisfy the demands of his Negro constituents in North Carolina, welcomed the opportunity to muster in a black regiment with a complete roster of Negro officers. The Third North Carolina Infantry, under the command of Colonel James H. Young (whom the Democratic press persisted in describing as "Jim Young of chocolate hue and resplendent regimentals"), figured prominently in the rhetoric of the white supremacy campaign waged by the Democrats in the summer and fall of 1898.[90] In Alabama the second call for volunteers touched off much speculation as to how the state would fill its quota of two additional battalions of infantry. Because of the requirement that each existing volunteer company be expanded to a maximum of 106 men,

87. J. C. L. Harris to Daniel L. Russell, May 5, 1898, Daniel L. Russell to Marion Butler, June 11, 1898, Daniel L. Russell Papers, North Carolina Department of Archives and History, Raleigh.

88. *Report of the Adjutant General of Virginia, 1898–1899*, p. 48.

89. *Correspondence Relating to the War with Spain. . . ,* 2 vols. (Washington: Government Printing Office, 1902), I, 621.

90. See Gatewood, "North Carolina's Negro Regiment," 377–379.

state officials doubted that enough whites would be recruited to make up two battalions. The possibility of raising a single battalion of whites seemed more realistic, but as one observer noted, "it might happen that the white battalion would be detailed to join the negro battalion now in camp . . . [and] this would occasion all sorts of entanglements." Apparently to avoid such entanglements and to ensure adequate recruits to fill Alabama's quota, Governor Johnston decided to expand the black battalion organized under the first call to a full regiment, known as the Third Alabama, U.S.V. Those Alabamians who protested "against any more negroes being called out" undoubtedly took comfort in the fact that all commissioned officers were white except a black Presbyterian minister who served as chaplain with the rank of captain. Governor Johnston and the regimental commander, Colonel Bullard, took pride in what they called their "fine husky regiment of negroes" and determined to make it a model unit.[91]

While Ohio, North Carolina, and Alabama expanded their existing black volunteer forces under the second call, four other states mustered in Negro units for the first time. One of these was Illinois; there Governor Tanner, sensitive to the political implications of the clamor among black citizens for recognition in the volunteer army, moved promptly to fulfill his earlier promise to organize an all-black regiment. The governor authorized the recruitment of enough men to raise the state's black militia battalion to regimental strength. Major Marshall, who had succeeded Buckner as commander of the battalion early in May, 1898, was placed in charge of the recruitment campaign. His task was complicated by the fact that many Negroes resented what they considered Tanner's shabby treatment of Buckner and suspected that Marshall was merely being used to raise a black regiment which would ultimately be commanded by white officers. Despite such misgivings among Negroes, Marshall succeeded in raising the quota for an all-black regiment in record time. On June 18, 1898, Governor Tanner designated the regiment as the Eighth Illinois

91. *Biennial Report of the Adjutant General of Alabama, 1898*, p. 13; Birmingham *Age-Herald*, May 27, June 1, 2, 10, 24, 1898; Mobile *Daily Register*, June 21, 1898; Bullard Diary, pp. 89–90; see also Willard B. Gatewood, Jr., "Alabama's 'Negro Soldier Experiment,' 1898–1899," *Journal of Negro History*, LVII (October, 1972), 342–344.

Infantry, with a complete roster of Negro officers—including Marshall, who was commissioned colonel. For the moment Negroes in Illinois appeared to close ranks behind the new regiment and to accept the appointment of Marshall as a necessary sacrifice to obtain a goal of greater significance than granting Buckner the honor of being placed in command.[92] Once the regiment was safely under the direction of those loyal to Tanner and his faction of the state's Republican party, the governor worked diligently to fulfill the black troops' desire to go to Cuba. "I shall never rest," he declared, "until I see this regiment—my regiment—on the soil of Cuba, battling for the right and for their kinsmen." [93] Whatever Tanner's motives, his concern for the Eighth Illinois was not without tangible political results: his popularity within the black community soared, and some Negroes even went so far as to describe the governor as "a second Lincoln." [94]

In neighboring Indiana the Republican administration of Governor Mount was concerned about the widespread discontent among Negro voters caused by the mustering out of the state's two black militia companies on the eve of the war. When the second call for volunteers was issued, Mount telegraphed Senator Charles W. Fairbanks: "Political situation makes it imperative that Indiana [be] represented at the front by Colored men." [95] The governor and the senator worked feverishly to gain the War Department's approval for their plan to organize a black battalion commanded by black officers. Despite their efforts, however, Indiana was allowed to muster in only two companies of Negro volunteers which were to be attached to the Eighth Infantry, one of the immune regiments under Colonel Eli Huggins.[96] When Colo-

92. Goode, "Eighth Illinois," pp. 39–40; Springfield Illinois Record, June 25, 1898; Chicago Tribune, June 18, 19, 1898.

93. Chicago Tribune, July 10, 1898; Springfield Illinois Record, July 16, 1898.

94. Springfield Illinois Record, July 23, 28, 1898. For a more detailed account of the formation of the Eighth Illinois, see Willard B. Gatewood, Jr., "An Experiment in Color: The Eighth Illinois Volunteers, 1898–1899," Journal of the Illinois State Historical Society, LXV (Autumn, 1972), 293–305.

95. James A. Mount to Charles W. Fairbanks, May 28, 1898, Charles W. Fairbanks Papers, Lilly Library, Indiana University, Bloomington.

96. James A. Mount to Charles W. Fairbanks, June 1, 1898, James A. Mounts to Charles W. Fairbanks, June 3, 1898, ibid.; Charles W. Fairbanks to James A. Mount, June 3. 1898, Mount Correspondence; Indianapolis Journal, May 28, 29, 30, June 1, 2, 3, 1898.

nel Huggins and the War Department indicated that they would accept "but two companies with white captains only," Senator Fairbanks and Governor Mount appealed directly to the White House in an effort to remove the restrictions against colored men being commissioned as captains of the companies. Impressed by their entreaties, President McKinley modified the War Department's regulations concerning Negro officers, and Indiana's two companies were mustered into federal service on July 15, 1898, under black captains, Jacob M. Porter and John J. Buckner, who had previously commanded the black units of the state militia.[97] Although the Indiana companies became "attached" to the Eighth Infantry, U.S.V., early in September, they did not become an integral part of this immune regiment—an unusual arrangement which allowed them to retain their identity as state organizations within a unit sponsored by the federal government without regard for state boundaries. In the opinion of the War Department, the Indiana companies, like other volunteer outfits, were inspired more by political than by military considerations, a view corroborated by the correspondence between Senator Fairbanks and Governor Mount regarding its organization.[98]

Another governor who proved receptive to the agitation among Negroes for recognition under the second call for volunteers was John W. Leedy of Kansas, who was anxious to bolster his declining political fortunes by courting Negro voters. A Populist elected in 1896 on a Populist-Democratic fusion ticket, Leedy was in serious political trouble by the time of the Spanish-American War. Not only had he been unable to overcome the effects of the Democratic-Populist defeat in the national elections of 1896, but his administration had also been plagued by internal dissension. Facing re-

97. Charles W. Fairbanks to James A. Mount, June 4, 1898, H. C. Corbin to James A. Mount, June 8, 1898, Charles W. Fairbanks to James A. Mount, June 10, 1898, Mount Correspondence; James A. Mount to William McKinley, June 6, 1898, Records of the Adjutant General, #91750.

98. H. C. Corbin to James A. Mount, August 29, 1898, Mount Correspondence; Indianapolis *Freeman*, September 3, 10, 1898; "Report of an Inspection of Company A and B, 1st Indiana by Lt. Col. Marion Maus," Appendix 7, in Army War College, "The Colored Soldier in the United States Army" (typescript, U.S. Army Military History Collection, Carlisle Barracks, Pa.), pp. 32–34. For a more detailed account of the Indiana companies, see Willard B. Gatewood, Jr., "Indiana Negroes and the Spanish-American War," *Indiana Magazine of History*, LXIX (June, 1973), 115–139.

election in the fall of 1898, he needed desperately to regain the support of those elements such as Negroes who had become estranged from populism. Unlike other governors, Leedy ignored the War Department's instructions in regard to giving preference to organized militia units in filling volunteer quotas. In fact, he by-passed the state's National Guard units and recognized instead those volunteer units organized by citizens throughout the state. Since there were no black units in the Kansas militia, the governor's decision won almost universal praise among Negroes.[99]

By the time of the second call, black Kansans had organized a sufficient number of companies to constitute a two-battalion regiment which Leedy readily accepted as part of the state's quota. Fully aware of the Negro demand for a full slate of black officers, he resisted pressure from within his administration to place whites in command of the black regiment and commissioned twenty-nine Negro officers for the new Twenty-third Kansas, U.S.V. As regimental commander with the rank of lieutenant colonel, Leedy chose James Beck, a black Populist who held a minor post in his administration. If Leedy's decision to muster in a black regiment was designed to enhance his standing among Negroes, it appeared for the moment at least to have been highly successful. Even those black citizens who had become disenchanted with populism conceded that he was "a pretty fair one after all" and had dared to do "what many a governor would have been too cowardly to do." [100]

Political considerations apparently figured less prominently in the Virginia Democratic governor's decision to mobilize the state's black militiamen under the second call for volunteers. Governor Tyler was scarcely in a position to ignore President McKinley's wishes regarding the use of black militiamen because of the general state of disintegration which characterized Virginia's National Guard in 1898 and the apathetic response of whites for volunteer

99. On Leedy and the political situation, see O. Gene Clanton, *Kansas Populism: Ideas and Men* (Lawrence: University Press of Kansas, 1969), pp. 207–209; Walter T. K. Nugent, *The Tolerant Populists: Kansas Populism and Nativism* (Chicago: University of Chicago Press, 1963), pp. 190, 191, 203, 204. On Kansas Populism and Negroes, see William H. Chafe, "The Negro and Populism: A Kansas Case Study," *Journal of Southern History*, XXXIV (August, 1968), 402–418.

100. Topeka *Colored Citizen*, May 26, June 2, June 23, 1898; *Parsons Weekly Blade*, June 25, 1898; Topeka *State Ledger*, June 25, 1898; Willard B. Gatewood, Jr., "Kansas Negroes and the Spanish-American War," *Kansas Historical Quarterly*, XXXVII (Autumn, 1971), 305–307.

service. In short, the fact that three white regiments had already been mobilized under the first call for volunteers meant that the state needed to utilize its two Negro militia battalions in the second call. Clearly, however, the question of whether Negroes should be used in filling the state's quota posed a dilemma for many white Virginians. On one hand, they opposed placing Negroes in military positions which would cause them to "forget their place." On the other, they did not relish the prospect of having only white soldiers sacrificed on the battlefield. But the real source of controversy concerned the commissioning of Negro officers. Although the white press agreed that Negro volunteers "could be handled much more effectively by white officers," the black militiamen insisted upon retaining their own officers. In fact, the men agreed to be mustered in only on the condition that they would have Negro officers. The *Richmond Planet* refused to budge on its "no officers, no fight" proposition, and its editor John Mitchell offered rebuttals to every objection raised in the white press regarding black officers.[101]

Although Governor Tyler authorized the two Negro majors of the militia, William H. Johnson and Joseph B. Johnson, to recruit additional men to organize a black regiment, he frankly admitted that he was perplexed as to the proper course regarding the appointment of officers. The need to utilize the black militiamen, and the demand for black officers which they made as a condition for service, left him little latitude in acting in accordance with those Virginians who demanded that all officers be white men. Interestingly enough, Tyler at one point took a legalistic position and argued that compliance with such demands would be a violation of the Fourteenth Amendment. Whatever his constitutional scruples, however, the governor sought to pacify his white critics by proposing a compromise which would allow Negroes to hold commissions as company and battalion officers and a white man to serve as commander of the regiment. The plan seemed to quiet the fears of most white Virginians, while Negroes accepted it reluctantly as the best they could secure without stronger support from the Republican administration in Washington for a

101. Richmond *Dispatch*, June 5, 18, 1898; Richmond *Enquirer*, June 11, 1898; *Richmond Planet*, June 4, 11, 25, 1898; *Report of the Adjutant General of Virginia, 1898–1899*, pp. 47–50; Johnson, *Colored Volunteer Infantry in Virginia*, pp. 47–49.

complete roster of Negro officers. As finally organized, the black regiment, designated as the Sixth Virginia, U.S.V., contained all black officers except Richard C. Croxton, a thirty-two-year-old native white Virginian and graduate of West Point who was appointed as commander with the rank of lieutenant colonel, and Dr. Allen Black, the surgeon of the first battalion. With the mustering in on August 9, 1898, of a company from Norfolk, the formation of the Sixth Virginia was complete. Even though Negroes had acquiesced in the governor's scheme for staffing the regiment, they were never satisfied with the arrangement or free of suspicions about Colonel Croxton. John Mitchell served notice that the white colonel would be watched closely for any evidence of racial discrimination.[102]

At the same time that the states were organizing units of black volunteers, the War Department was busy recruiting men for the four immune regiments—the Seventh, Eighth, Ninth, and Tenth Infantry—to be composed of Negroes. Although the law establishing these regiments had originally envisioned the recruitment of men from swampy areas who supposedly were immune to malaria, the concept was soon abandoned in practice; the black immune regiments ultimately included companies from the hill regions of the south as well as from such northern states as New Jersey.[103] In fact, the whole idea of immunity came in for considerable ridicule. Negroes in particular resented the idea that they were any more immune to "fever, hot weather, foul air, bad stenches and hard work" than any other Americans and claimed that while they were anxious to take up arms, they desired to do so "on the same footing as the rest." [104] The southern white press criticized the concept of immunity only as it applied to the six white regiments organized under the immune act; its validity in regard to Negroes was seldom questioned. In a facetious editorial on Negro immunes which revealed much about the white Southerner's attitude regarding the admission of black men into the volunteer army, the Raleigh *News and Observer* claimed that after an intensive

102. *Richmond Planet,* July 2, 1898; Richmond *Dispatch,* June 8, 1898; Willard B. Gatewood, Jr., "Virginia's Negro Regiment in the Spanish-American War," *Virginia Magazine of History and Biography,* LXXX (April, 1971), 199–200.
103. Fletcher, "The Negro Soldier and the U.S. Army," pp. 230–232; *Washington Bee,* July 23, 1898; *New York Times,* May 25, June 26, 1898.
104. N. C. Bruce to the Editor, May ?, 1898, *The News and Observer* (Raleigh), May 22, 1898.

search it had finally discovered what really "made a negro immune" in military terms. According to the editor, black candidates for commissions as lieutenants in the immune regiments were asked: "In case you are accepted, will you expect to eat with white officers or to be on social equality with them?" Only those who answered in the negative "were declared immune and were accepted." [105]

Despite such crude jesting at the expense of the black immunes, the federally sponsored regiments provided the only opportunity for many Negroes to participate in the crusade against Spain. Those black companies organized at the outbreak of the war and refused admission to the volunteer army under state quotas had largely abandoned any hope of enlisting until the War Department was authorized to organize the immune regiments. Those companies which had maintained their organization often enlisted in a body in one of the immune outfits. For example, three companies of black volunteers from Arkansas traveled to St. Louis, where they joined companies from Missouri, Iowa, Ohio, and other states to form the Seventh Infantry, U.S.V., better known as the Seventh Immunes. Because the governor of Georgia continued to ignore the black National Guardsmen in his state, a large number resigned from the militia to join the Tenth Immunes. A company of black volunteers from Houston which had been refused admission to military service by the governor of Texas journeyed to New Orleans in order to join the Ninth Immunes. The Ninth, however, was made up primarily of black Louisianans originally recruited by Henry Demas and included members of several of the most prominent black families in the state. Although Negroes resented the restrictions which prevented them from holding commissions above the rank of lieutenant in the immunes, recruiters rarely encountered difficulty in filling regimental quotas. Ultimately 4,000 Negroes enlisted in the four immune regiments.[106]

The mobilization of black volunteers was the signal for Negro

105. *Ibid.*, June 21, 1898.
106. Allan S. Peal to Asa Bushnell, July 18, 1898, John Booth to William McKinley, June 18, 1898, Bushnell Papers; *Arkansas Gazette*, June 12, 13, 18, July 14, 1898; St. Louis *Post-Dispatch*, June 28, July 11, 19, 1898; *Augusta Chronicle*, June 22, July 8, 10, 17, 26, 1898. For an account of the Negro immunes, see W. Hilary Coston, *The Spanish-American War Volunteer* (Middleton, Pa.: Mount Pleasant Printery, 1899); Lockhart, "The Colored Soldier in the South," 7; Crane, *Experiences of a Colonel of Infantry*, pp. 257–274.

women to participate in the war effort. Some delivered patriotic addresses and published essays encouraging black soldiers to do their full duty. Typical was Ida Wells Barnett, who "eagerly assisted in the movement to get the Eighth Regiment mobilized" and remained in Springfield as long as the Illinois volunteers were encamped there. Like other black women at the Springfield camp, she performed a variety of chores ranging from clerical work to nursing duties in the camp hospital. Almost every black unit had its ladies' auxiliary made up of female relatives and friends of the soldiers. Such organizations sponsored various fund-raising activities in order to supply the volunteers with special foods, clothing, and luxury items. The ladies' auxiliary of the Eighth Illinois, for instance, raised over $1,000 which was used to purchase canned peaches and other delicacies for the regiment while it was on duty in Cuba. But perhaps Negro women made their most notable contributions as nurses. In July, 1898, Mrs. A. M. Curtis, wife of the chief surgeon at the Freedman Hospital in Washington and an active member of the Red Cross Society, was commissioned by the War Department to recruit "contract nurses" for duty in Cuba. In her search for women who were supposedly immune to the tropical fevers of the island, she set up headquarters in New Orleans and enlisted the aid of Colonel James Lewis in recruiting twenty-five nurses. Other black women, including the well-known settlement house worker Victoria Earle Matthews, volunteered their services in the fall of 1898 to minister to the fever-stricken veterans of the Cuban campaign who had been sent to the hospital camp at Montauk Point, Long Island.[107]

By the late summer of 1898, Negroes' struggle for the right to participate in the volunteer army in capacities other than those "in the culinary departments" had produced tangible results. Over 10,000 black men had been mustered into the volunteer forces, and of the 259 who held commissions, two were full colonels. While the two types of black volunteer units—state organizations and the federally sponsored immunes—were in the process of being formed, news arrived from Cuba describing the heroism

107. Wells, *Crusade for Justice*, p. 254; Springfield *Illinois Record*, August 5, October 29, 1898; Little Rock *Arkansas Democrat*, July 19, 20, 1898; Washington *Colored American*, July 20, 1898; Cleveland *Gazette*, January 28, 1899.

and gallantry of the Negro soldiers in the regular army. The volunteers, inspired by the exploits of the regulars, were anxious to emulate their example and thereby "make a new era for the Negro race." [108] Because President McKinley had authorized an assault on Havana, their opportunities for combat appeared to be unlimited. But such prospects virtually disappeared with the signing of the armistice on August 12, 1898, by which Spain agreed to evacuate both Cuba and Puerto Rico. Only the black volunteers in the Sixth Massachusetts who took part in the Puerto Rican campaign actually engaged in combat. Others could hope only to serve as occupation troops.

108. Springfield *Illinois Record,* May 28, 1898.

Five

Victory's Shadows

We opine that in the great act of complete conciliation between north and south that the Negroes will not be ground
to dust between the upper and nether millstone of national
cohesion.

—Indianapolis *Freeman,* July 23, 1898

But there remains one other victory for the Americans to
win—a victory as far-reaching and important as any that
occupied our army and navy. We have succeeded in every
conflict except in the effort to conquer ourselves in the
blotting out of racial prejudices. We can celebrate the era
of peace in no more effectual way than by a firm resolve on
the part of the northern men and the southern men, black
and white men, that the trenches which we together dug
around Santiago shall be the eternal burial place of all
which separates us in our business and civil relations.

—Booker T. Washington
Speech, Chicago Peace Jubilee
October, 1898

By mid-August, 1898, as the last Negro volunteers were being
mustered in, the sick and exhausted troops in Cuba began to
arrive at Montauk Point, Long Island, to rest and recuperate before being assigned duty elsewhere. "Never before," a Negro
chaplain declared, "had the people seen an army of stalwart men
so suddenly transformed into an army of invalids." But he hastened to point out that "the colored troops arrived from the front
in as good condition as the best." [1] Though shocked by the physi-

1. Steward, *Colored Regulars in the United States Army,* p. 227. Victoria Earle
Matthews, the founder of a Negro settlement house in New York, visited Montauk
Point and was appalled by the black regulars' stories about the indignities they
suffered in Cuba at the hands of their white officers, especially Colonel E. H. Liscum
of the Twenty-fourth Infantry; see Cleveland *Gazette,* January 28, 1899.

cal appearance of both black and white soldiers, most observers were no less impressed by the esprit de corps and self-confidence so evident among the Negro troops. John Bigalow, Jr., a white captain in the Tenth Cavalry, was certain that the record of the Negro regiments in Cuba had enhanced "the self-respect and stimulated the aspirations" of all colored citizens, civilians as well as soldiers.[2] After listening to the Negro veterans of the Cuban campaign talk of "their exploits as they set about the tent doors polishing their sabres," a white journalist who visited Montauk Point concluded: "This is the talk of men who believe in themselves and are not ashamed of their color; heroes as good as any in the land." [3]

Nor were the black soldiers engaging in idle boasts. Tangible evidence of their heroism was provided by the twenty-six Certificates of Merit and the five Congressional Medals of Honor bestowed upon them for their performance in Cuba.[4] But their qualities as soldiers were by no means limited to dramatic feats in combat. The promptness with which the Twenty-fourth Infantry accepted the assignment to work in the yellow fever hospitals at Siboney after eight other regiments refused it was what one white officer described as "the crucial test of the mettle of men." It was a task that the black infantrymen performed with compassion and efficiency in spite of being called "niggers" occasionally by some white soldiers working at the hospital.[5] In short, the conduct of the Negro troops, whether in combat or in the yellow fever hospitals, tended to confirm Colonel Roosevelt's contention that they belonged to "an excellent breed of Yankee." [6]

Throughout the Santiago campaign, however, Negro civilians as well as the soldiers themselves expressed considerable dissatisfaction with the treatment accorded the black regiments by the white press. They contended that the dispatches of correspondents in Cuba consistently slighted the exploits of the Negro regulars.

2. Bigalow, *Reminiscences of the Santiago Campaign*, pp. 36–37.

3. Cleveland Moffett, "Stories of Camp Wikoff," *Leslie's Weekly*, LXXXVII (October 13, 1898), 287.

4. Lee, *Negro Medal of Honor Men*, pp. 90–94; Steward, *Colored Regulars*, pp. 280–281; *Twin City American* (Minneapolis–St. Paul), May 4, 1899.

5. Fletcher, "The Negro Soldier and the U.S. Army, 1891–1917," pp. 217–219; Steward, *Colored Regulars*, pp. 223–225.

6. Washington *Colored American*, October 16, 1898.

Reese Turner, a black resident of Pratt City, Alabama, voiced a common sentiment when he complained that the contribution of Negro soldiers had been all but ignored by white editors bent upon giving full credit for the military victory to the Rough Riders and other white troops.[7] Negroes feared that the black soldiers would be denied the place in history to which their sacrifices on the Cuban battlefield entitled them. Unless the distortions of contemporary records were corrected, they argued, future generations of black Americans would have little reason to take pride in the role of their ancestors in the war with Spain.[8] But almost as disturbing as the journalistic neglect of the black soldiers was the anonymity and patronizing tone that characterized even the favorable notices they received in the white press. Calvin Chase castigated the white newspapers for treating black soldiers as "nameless beings" and for identifying a man who distinguished himself in battle only as "a negro soldier." [9]

The concern over the coverage of the black soldiers' activities by the white press reached a climax in the wake of the battle of San Juan Hill. Like other Negro Americans, Dr. J. M. Henderson of Brooklyn's Bethel A.M.E. Church believed that news reports of that engagement had so totally disregarded the crucial role played by the Tenth Cavalry that some kind of action was necessary. Fully aware of the precarious financial condition of most black newspapers, he suggested that Negro editors pool their resources to employ their own war correspondent. Edward E. Cooper of the *Colored American* took up the proposal and attempted to marshal support for it by arguing that a black correspondent in the war zone would help Negro soldiers obtain the public recognition their deeds warranted without subjecting them to "patronizing charity." Failure to agree upon the individual for the post and "the abrupt ending of the war" put "a quietus on the scheme to appoint an official war correspondent for the Negro press." [10] But black soldiers compensated in large part for the absence of a Negro military reporter. Convinced that their performance entitled

---

7. Reese Turner to the Editor, Salt Lake City *Broad Ax*, August 13, 1898.

8. Springfield *Illinois Record*, August 13, 1898.

9. *Ibid.*, August 27, 1898; Savannah *Tribune*, December 3, 1898; *Washington Bee*, July 23, September 10, 1898.

10. Washington *Colored American*, July 16, August 6, 1898.

them to a prominent place in the historical record of the Spanish-American War, they bombarded the black press with communications detailing their role in the Santiago campaign.[11] "If our war reporters would only give credit where credit is due," a Tenth Cavalryman wrote a black editor, "there would be no need writing these poorly composed lines that your readers might know of the deeds . . . [of] their dear ones. . . ."[12] And Sergeant M. W. Saddler of the Twenty-fifth Infantry maintained that black soldiers were "coming up unrepresented" unless they themselves provided written records of their experiences.[13] A few white editors conceded that Negroes had a legitimate complaint and the *Springfield Republican* described as "shameful" the extent to which the distinguished record of black troops in Cuba had been ignored by whites.[14]

With the return of the army from Cuba, however, the Negro soldier came in for his share of popular acclaim. Stories of his exploits which often dominated conversations among the troops at Montauk Point quickened popular interest in the black veterans, and for a few brief weeks they enjoyed the status of national heroes. Interviews by white reporters provided data about the "sable heroes" for Sunday supplements of big city newspapers, while politicians and churchmen came to include references to the valor of Negro troops in their patriotic orations. Those black soldiers invited to parade in the victory celebrations and Peace Jubilees held in various cities invariably received thunderous ovations.[15] Citizens of both races in all sections of the country extolled the combat record of the Negro regulars. Even white Southerners, despite an inclination to be patronizing, admitted that blacks had performed well in Cuba. A white soldier in Santiago wrote his

11. For a sample of these letters, see Gatewood, "*Smoked Yankees*," pp. 47–97.
12. *Ibid.*, p. 77.
13. *Ibid.*, p. 55.
14. Cashin *et al.*, *Under Fire with the Tenth Cavalry*, pp. 159–161; Cleveland *Gazette*, July 30, 1898.
15. Hiram Thweatt, *What the Newspapers Say of the Negro Soldier in the Spanish-American War* (Thomasville, Ga.: n.p., n.d.); Brawley, *Social History of the American Negro*, pp. 309–310; Mifflin W. Gibbs, *Shadow and Light: An Autobiography* (Washington: n.p., 1902), pp. 288–294; *Southern Churchman* quoted in Baltimore *Ledger*, August 6, 1898; for a perceptive treatment of the black soldier in contemporary fiction, see Perry E. Gianakos, "The Spanish-American War and the Double Paradox of the Negro American," *Phylon*, XXVI (Spring, 1965), 34–49.

relatives in Georgia: "The negro soldiers down here are a fine lot of men, big and strong, and make fine soldiers. Their marching is perfect and they bear themselves well and *keep in their place.* I have no idea we will have any trouble with them." [16] But no one was more impressed by the black soldiers than the Spaniards who had confronted them in combat. A Spanish officer who took part in the battle of Las Guasimas recalled: "What terrified our men was the huge American negroes. We saw their big black faces through the underbrush and they looked like devils. They came forward under our fire as if they didn't the least care about it." [17]

In the weeks immediately following the American military victory in Cuba a succession of stories about specific acts of heroism performed by Negro troops achieved wide circulation. One of these which appeared in several versions and remained popular for many years related how black cavalrymen saved Colonel Roosevelt and his Rough Riders from annihilation. One version placed the rescue at Las Guasimas, another at El Caney, and a third at San Juan Hill. At the time, regardless of the version in which it appeared, the story encountered no contradiction, least of all from the Rough Riders.[18] In fact, their references to the performance of Negro soldiers tended to substantiate such claims. A Rough Rider whose father had served with Mosby's Rangers asserted that while he was not "a negro lover," honesty compelled him to admit that black soldiers had "saved the day" in the Battle of San Juan Hill.[19] In 1906, when Roosevelt as president dismissed a battalion of Negro infantrymen for their alleged involvement in the Brownsville Affray, he was forcefully reminded of his earlier debt to black soldiers. Senator Nathan B. Scott of West Virginia claimed that "if it had not been for the gallant and courageous action of the Tenth Regiment of Cavalry at the battle of San Juan we might not now have the privilege of having in the White House that brave soldier and 'square deal' and patriotic president of ours." The remark prompted Roosevelt, for the first

16. Quoted in *Augusta Chronicle,* September 23, 1898; see also Henry Watterson, *The History of the Spanish-American War* (New York: n.p., 1898), p. 217.

17. Quoted in "The Negro as a Soldier," *New York Tribune Illustrated Supplement,* August 24, 1898, p. 4.

18. Steward, *Colored Regulars,* pp. 132–133.

19. Johnson, *Negro Soldiers in the Spanish-American War,* p. 85.

time, to deny that his regiment had been saved by the Tenth Cavalry.[20]

In the fall of 1898, however, visitors at Montauk Point were invariably struck by what one described as "the great prestige which has come to the negro through the recent fighting." For the moment at least the old barriers at lunch counters and canteens in the camp had disappeared as a result of "those feats of heroism performed by our colored troops on San Juan Hill." The sentiment of the whole army, according to one journalist, was summed up in the expression: "God bless the nigger!" [21] Stephen Bonsal, the well-known war correspondent who covered the Cuban campaign, claimed that he was "not the only man who had come to recognize the justice of certain Constitutional amendments in the light of the gallant behavior of the colored troops." In his view the "service of no four white regiments could be compared with those rendered by the colored regiments." [22]

Although the commendation of Negro soldiers by whites proved both brief and illusory, their role in the Cuban campaign remained a source of pride for black Americans for many years. The black warriors at Las Guasimas, El Caney, and San Juan Hill took their places alongside Crispus Attucks, Peter Salem, and others in the pantheon of Negro American military heroes. In Negro homes pictures and plaques depicting the charge at San Juan occupied places of honor. Books which celebrated the deeds of black soldiers in Cuba found a ready market. Hundreds of poems ranging from the polished verse of Paul Laurence Dunbar to the crude rhymes of unknown poets extolled the exploits of Negro troops. Of these perhaps the most popular was a lengthy poem entitled "The Charge of the Nigger Ninth." [23] Stories and editorials related to the gallantry of black soldiers dominated the columns of many Negro newspapers. The attitude of the black press was succinctly stated by a Negro editor in Iowa who declared that "the

20. John D. Weaver, *The Brownsville Raid* (New York W. W. Norton, 1970), p. 121.

21. Moffett, "Stories of Camp Wikoff," 286–287.

22. Stephen Bonsal, *The Fight for Santiago* (New York: Doubleday and McClure, 1899), pp. 299–300.

23. For samples of this poetry, see Cashin *et al.*, *Under Fire with the Tenth Cavalry*, pp. 274–284; Johnson, *Negro Soldiers in the Spanish-American War*, pp. 55–58.

South is proud of Roosevelt, the North is proud of Hobson, and we are proud of the colored troops, the heroes of the day." [24]

Although Negro citizens were unanimous in lavishing praise upon the black soldiers who participated in the Santiago campaign, they continued to disagree regarding the ultimate effects of the war upon the status of black people in American society. Those who had argued that a war with Spain would bestow substantial benefits upon the race interpreted the commendation of the Negro regulars by whites and the progress of the movement to enlist black volunteer outfits under black officers as a vindication of their position. A prominent black editor in Baltimore, for example, concluded a tribute to the black veterans of the Santiago campaign with the observation that the war was bringing "much good to the American Negro, as well as to our cousins in Cuba, Manila, Hawaii and elsewhere." For him, the United States was but an instrument of God in "realizing more and more the great fact of Universal Brotherhood." The appointment of black volunteer officers by the governors of Virginia and North Carolina and the laudatory references to the black regulars by such ex-Confederates as General Joseph Wheeler were cited as evidence that the war was liberating white Southerners "from the tyranny of senseless color prejudice." [25] Even those rarely inclined to an optimistic view of the future briefly succumbed to the idea that the black man's "loyalty to the republic in its hour of need" would result in a larger measure of racial justice. According to Charles E. Hall of the *Illinois Record,* the "beclouded horizon" was finally clearing; black Americans stood on the brink of realizing their full rights as first-class citizens.[26]

Of those convinced that the "war was bringing in its train a host of benefits to the American black man," none interpreted events in the summer of 1898 with more extravagant optimism than Edward E. Cooper. Late in July he itemized those benefits for the readers of his *Colored American:*

Our soldierly qualities have been proven. We have secured honorable stations in military life. . . . We are better represented upon

24. Des Moines *Iowa State Bystander,* September 30, 1898.
25. Baltimore *Ledger,* July 23, August 6, 1898.
26. Springfield *Illinois Record,* July 9, 1898; see also Indianapolis *World,* July 23, 1898; Coffeyville *American,* August 27, 1898; Indianapolis *Freeman,* August 27, 1898.

the official rolls than would have been probable in two decades of peace and still larger rewards are coming our way. The asperities of sectional and race hatred have been wonderfully softened. The Negro's confidence in himself has been inconceivably strengthened. The times are growing better. The sealed vaults of the public treasury have been burst open, and the hoarded wealth of the capitalists is finding its way into the arteries of trade. Money is diffused more widely among the plain people. Smoke is ascending in increased volume from the furnaces and the hum of commerce is awakening our dormant senses.[27]

Only the readers of the *Colored American* who, like its editor, equated the number of blacks on the military and civil rolls with the "progress of the race" were likely to agree with such rhapsodic prose. Others who read about the lynchings, new Jim Crow contrivances, and indignities suffered by black volunteers and regulars in the United States must have wondered whether racial prejudice had been so wonderfully softened.

In fact, few black Americans accepted Cooper's glowing assessment. The dominant tone in the Negro community remained one of skepticism. More typical than Cooper was Monroe Dorsey, who wondered how long the praise of the black soldiers would last and questioned whether it would have any practical effect. "But better a little praise than none," [28] Dorsey concluded. Others reminded the McKinley administration that as long as lynchers such as those who murdered Postmaster Baker went unpunished, all the official rhetoric about humanitarianism in Cuba would continue to smack of hypocrisy.[29] Early in July, 1898, John Mitchell listed in the *Planet* a dozen lynchings which had occurred in the South since the declaration of war. Contrary to the prediction that the war would dissipate "race prejudice and bring closer together the races," he argued, it had "had the opposite tendency for the number of lynchings has been steadily on the increase." [30]

Black spokesmen who doubted that the black man's role in the Cuban campaign would substantially improve his condition also pointed to the opposition which Negroes encountered in their

27. Washington *Colored American*, July 23, 1898.
28. *Parsons Weekly Blade*, July 23, 1898.
29. Cleveland *Gazette*, August 17, 1898.
30. *Richmond Planet*, July 3, 1898.

efforts to win admission to the volunteer army. Although few spoke in such strident terms as Bishop Henry M. Turner of Atlanta, many agreed that his assessment was essentially valid. Turner claimed that throughout the war the Negro soldier had served as "the butt of ridicule" for whites who magnified his every fault and snubbed him in matters of promotions and recognition. In the bishop's view, Negro soldiers had died "for nothing," fighting for a country where enough of his kinsmen had been "lynched to death to reach a mile high if laid one upon the other." [31] George L. Knox of Indianapolis might disagree with Turner's emigration schemes, but he confessed that the racial climate appeared to confirm the bishop's pessimism regarding the black man and the war. "The millennium that is to be has not dawned," Knox declared late in October, 1898, "and El Caney and Santiago may as well not have been." Paul Laurence Dunbar, whose poetry extolled the heroism of Negro soldiers, detected what he termed "a new attitude" produced by the war which was anything but favorable for black citizens. He described this attitude as one which said to Negroes: "You may fight for us but you may not vote for us. You may prove a strong bulwark when the bullets are flying but you must stand from the line when the ballots are in the air. You may be heroes in war but you must be cravens in peace." [32]

Such gloom was only reinforced by all the evidence of growing reconciliation between the North and South. Negroes read with alarm articles which explained how white soldiers from the North and South "forgot the past" as they sat around the canteen in a military camp in Florida or recounted the sentiments expressed by a New York volunteer stationed in South Carolina who served as an honor guard at the funeral of a Confederate veteran. More disturbing to Negroes, however, was the evidence that northern whites were becoming "southernized" in their racial attitudes. Nor did their fears appear to be altogether imaginary. Iowa sol-

31. *Voice of Missions*, VI (June 1, 1898), 2. Bishop Turner was in Africa at the time of the declaration of war between the United States and Spain, but upon his return to Atlanta late in May, 1898, he spoke out strongly against Negro participation in the conflict.

32. George L. Knox in Indianapolis *Freeman*, October 29, 1898; Paul Laurence Dunbar in Cleveland *Gazette*, December 17, 1898.

diers, for example, admitted that their experience in the South
had made them sympathetic with the white Southerner's approach
to the Negro Problem. In Augusta, Georgia, the men of the First
Maine were so free in expressing their hostility toward the black
immunes in their camp that "a small race war" ultimately resulted.[33] According to the Chattanooga *Daily Times,* northern
white soldiers at nearby Chickamauga Park had "caught the negrophobia which in some respects is worse than typhoid fever."
Some white Southerners rather smugly noted that those Yankees
who had come South singing "Uncle Tom and Little Eva" had
abandoned that tune after a few weeks of direct contact with
Negroes. "They are now singing 'Don't Like a Nigger Nohow,'"
a white Georgian declared with obvious satisfaction.[34]

Negroes admitted that unfortunately the Georgian's observation was all too valid. "The Negro might as well know it now as
later," a black editor in Norfolk lamented, "the closer the North
and South get together by this war, the harder he will have to fight
to maintain a footing." [35] Harry C. Smith of the Cleveland *Gazette*
fully agreed, and for several weeks he discussed the implications
of sectional reconciliation upon black people. His thesis was that
the dissipation of sectionalism would worsen the predicament of
the black man everywhere in the United States because it meant
that the North had acquiesced in southern racial attitudes. Increasingly, black Americans came to look upon the "road to reunion" as leading to "racial calamity." They believed that the reconciliation of the North and South marked the end of the last
major restraint—northern influence and opinion—upon the
growth of that species of Negrophobia which had hitherto flour-
ished primarily in the South.[36] Even the cautious Booker T. Washington, speaking at the Peace Jubilee in Chicago in October,

33. *Leslie's Weekly,* LXXXVI (August 4, 1898), 95; James E. Whipple, *The Story
of the Forty-Ninth* (Vinton, Iowa: n.p., 1903), p. 14; *Augusta Chronicle,* August 25,
1898, March 2, 1899. For a perceptive treatment of the North-South reconciliation,
see Richard E. Wood, "The South and Reunion, 1898," *The Historian,* XXI (May,
1969), 415–430.

34. Chattanooga *Times* quoted in *Augusta Chronicle,* August 30, 1898.

35. Norfolk *Recorder* quoted in Cleveland *Gazette,* August 13, 1898.

36. Cleveland *Gazette,* July 2, August 6, 13, 1898. See also *Richmond Planet,*
July 16, 1898; Indianapolis *Freeman,* August 6, 1898; Des Moines *Iowa State Bystander,* November 25, 1898.

1898, declared that even though the role of black citizens in the war had done much "to blot out sectional and racial lines," the "cancer" of race prejudice which continued to grow at the heart of the republic promised "one day [to] prove as dangerous as an attack from an army without or within." [37]

The performance of the black soldiers in the Cuban campaign may well have provided Negroes with a "much needed feeling of pride" in an era which otherwise contributed little to their esteem and confidence,[38] but those who anticipated that the black man's bravery would at least open the way for him to enter the officer corps of the regular army were greatly disappointed. Notwithstanding their praise of the black regiments, few white Americans were willing to grant the one concession most desired by Negro soldiers—the opportunity to become commissioned officers in their own regiments. Even those whites so generous in their praise of the role played by black troops in Cuba almost without exception credited their performance to the discipline and leadership provided by their white officers.[39] The persistence of the idea that Negroes made good soldiers only if commanded by white officers was a source of profound frustration for men who had gone to Cuba with high hopes of winning respect and honor for their race.

Black veterans of the Santiago campaign were quick to point out that they were without white "commissioned officers half of the time" and performed efficiently under the command of their own black noncommissioned officers. Such men, in their opinion, at least deserved to hold commissions in the regular army.[40] Throughout the United States Negroes took up the cause and urged President McKinley to see that black soldiers received fair play in the distribution of military honors. Numerous organiza-

37. Springfield *Illinois Record*, October 22, 1898; Booker T. Washington, "An Address at the Chicago Peace Jubilee," Washington Papers. See also Samuel R. Spencer, *Booker T. Washington and the Negro's Place in American Life* (Boston: Little, Brown, 1955), pp. 130–131; Booker T. Washington to the Editor, November 10, 1898, Birmingham *Age-Herald*, November 13, 1898.

38. Logan, *The Great Betrayal of the Negro*, p. 335.

39. "The Negro as a Soldier," *New York Tribune Illustrated Supplement*, August 24, 1898, p. 4; *Southern Churchman* quoted in Baltimore *Ledger*, August 6, 1898.

40. See the letters from John E. Lewis and Presley Holliday in Gatewood, *"Smoked Yankees,"* pp. 58–60, 62–65, 72–73, 76–81, 85–97.

tions as well as individuals petitioned the President to recognize Negro troops who had distinguished themselves before Santiago by removing the traditional barriers against them in the regular army. At its annual meeting late in 1898, the Mosaic Templars of America, a black fraternal order, demanded that the "black heroes of San Juan Hill" be rewarded with something other than the mob violence which had greeted them in the South. The Western Negro Press Association noted with "profound regret" that the president had promoted white West Point graduates "over the heads of Negro sergeants" who "had so long and so acceptably served" in the four black regiments.[41] When the McKinley administration protested that the regulations governing these regiments stipulated that all officers were to be white, Negroes responded by claiming that the military code should be changed to conform with the provisions of the Fourteenth Amendment. Because such changes seemed unlikely, a group of Negroes in Boston proposed that the federal government establish a separate all-black military academy so that black men might qualify for commissions in the regular army. The idea gained little support in the black press because most editors believed that such an institution would in no way guarantee the entrance of black men into the officer corps and would, in fact, only serve to close the door of West Point to colored youths.[42]

Although the agitation failed to win regular army commissions for the black heroes of the Cuban campaign, President McKinley did recognize some of these men by appointing them as lieutenants in the four immune regiments. However, few Negroes were satisfied with such recognition because commissions in the volunteer regiments were temporary; black regulars who held them would have to return to their own regular army regiments as noncommissioned officers as soon as the volunteer army was disbanded. The Savannah *Tribune* maintained that black regulars entitled to commissions ought to hold them "in the regiments

41. Little Rock *Arkansas Democrat*, December 6, 1898; Omaha *Afro-American Sentinel*, August 27, 1898; Baltimore *Ledger*, September 17, 1898.
42. Springfield *Illinois Record*, July 30, August 6, 13, 20, 1898; Washington *Colored American*, July 2, 1898; Cleveland *Gazette*, December 10, 1898. For Secretary Alger's ambiguous statement regarding commissions for Negroes, see *Army and Navy Journal*, November 12, 1898, p. 246.

they fought in." Chaplain George W. Prioleau of the Ninth Cavalry fully agreed: "Give us promotions as regulars for regulars and not as regulars for volunteers." Calvin Chase described the manner in which President McKinley chose to "honor" the black heroes of the war as "discrimination pure and simple." [43] Early in 1899, when all hope of black soldiers receiving commissions in the regular army had disappeared, a black Georgian concluded that "the Negro's valor has *intensified* the prejudice against him." [44]

Such assessments appeared to be verified by the racial violence which erupted in the months immediately following the Cuban campaign. White volunteers themselves often terrorized black citizens in the vicinity of their camps. Reports from Miami claimed that white soldiers "shot down Negroes like dogs" and caused many to flee the city for safety. At Camp Cuba Libre in Jacksonville the cry of "lynch him" was "heard often . . . issuing from the throats of certain U. S. volunteers" whenever a Negro was "involved in any contention with a white person." A black editor in Jacksonville warned white soldiers that Negroes in that city would not be so easily intimidated as those in Miami. "We would remind those 'defenders of the flag,' " he wrote, "that they are . . . in a city where the Negro has the courage and manhood to defend himself, and to send to the grave any man or set of men who attempt to lynch a Negro. . . ." [45] Although Negroes maintained that white volunteers preyed upon black civilians without fear of punishment, not all military authorities were indifferent to acts of racial violence committed by men under their command. In San Francisco several volunteers from Tennessee, Kansas, and Iowa received lengthy prison terms for wounding a Negro fisherman and wrecking his house. At Camp Alger, Virginia, General M. C. Butler, a South Carolinian whose past record scarcely placed him among the friends of black people, ordered the dis-

43. H. C. Smith to William McKinley, November 27, 1898, H. C. Corbin to H. C. Smith, December 5, 1898, #164178, Adjutant General's Records; Savannah *Tribune,* August 13, 1898; Washington *Colored American,* October 8, 1898; *Washington Bee,* August 13, 1898.
44. Savannah *Tribune,* March 19, 1899.
45. Jacksonville *Florida Evangelist* quoted in Cleveland *Gazette,* August 27, 1898; see also Willard B. Gatewood, Jr., "Negro Troops in Florida, 1898," *Florida Historical Quarterly,* XLIX (July, 1970), 12; Birmingham *Age-Herald,* July 14, 1898.

charge of the Third Virginia Regiment because of its attempt to lynch a Negro accused of attacking a white hospital steward.[46]

More alarming to black Americans than the acts of white volunteers were the eruptions of racial violence in Wilmington, North Carolina; Phoenix, South Carolina; and Pana, Illinois, late in 1898. Even Edward E. Cooper admitted that the "race war in the Carolinas" was sufficient to cause Cubans to reject "the American brand of civilization." [47] In a lengthy poem entitled "Santiago de Wilmington," F. B. Coffin, a Negro pharmacist in Little Rock, expressed the overwhelming sentiment of Negroes when he wrote: "On Santiago's bloody field/ where Spanish hosts were made to yield/ The Negro like a phalanx great/ Fought hard to save the ship of state/ And Wilmington with her disgrace/ Stares Santiago in the face/ And shows her heartless feelings clear/ For those who fought without a fear." [48] The outbreak of violence, and especially the "Wilmington Massacre," prompted Negroes again to remind President McKinley that any nation which could not protect the lives and property of its own citizens was scarcely in a position to promise protection and good government to peoples elsewhere. In a widely publicized lecture entitled "Cubans Protected but the American Negro Neglected," the Reverend Philip A. Hubert of Livingstone College developed a theme that gained considerable popularity; he thought it both ironic and tragic that a Republican administration which Negroes helped to bring to power should be so quick to respond to the call of oppressed Cubans and so indifferent to the troubles of oppressed black citizens at home.[49] Hubert and others suggested that a single battleship and a few troops dispatched by the president to Wilmington could have prevented the wholesale slaughter of black people which occurred there. But Negroes lamented that rather than utilizing all the resources

46. Indianapolis *Freeman,* August 20, 1898; Des Moines *Iowa State Bystander,* September 9, 1898; *Review Budget* (Lodi, Calif.) quoted in *Parsons Weekly Blade,* October 15, 1898; Richmond *Dispatch,* August 10, 11, 12, 14, 16, 17, 19, 1898.

47. Washington *Colored American,* November 12, 1892. For accounts of the Wilmington and Phoenix riots, see Helen Edmonds, *The Negro and Fusion Politics in North Carolina, 1894–1901* (Chapel Hill: University of North Carolina Press, 1951); Tom Wells Henderson, "The Phoenix Election Riot," *Phylon,* XXXI (Spring, 1970), 58–69.

48. F. B. Coffin, "Santiago de Wilmington," in Indianapolis *Freeman,* January 7, 1899.

49. Cleveland *Gazette,* December 3, 1898.

at his disposal to protect blacks in the South, President McKinley had chosen to make a goodwill tour of the region in December, 1898, to ingratiate himself with those responsible for the heinous crimes against their race. Nor did McKinley's visits to Tuskegee Institute and the state college for Negroes in Georgia (whose president, R. R. Wright, had been appointed a paymaster in the volunteers with the rank of major) compensate for the inaction of the federal government during the disturbances in the Carolinas. Negroes were no less critical of the president's State of the Union message, because in their opinion it demonstrated that the Republican administration was far more concerned with the welfare of Cubans than with protecting the civil rights of black Americans. According to John Mitchell, the message offered undeniable evidence that the party of Lincoln and emancipation had used the war to make its final peace with the white racists of the South.[50]

Earlier, in October, 1898, when the black veterans of the Cuban campaign left Montauk Point for camps elsewhere, they had an opportunity to learn for themselves whether their combat record had produced a revolution in white sentiment, as some claimed. Three regiments, the Twenty-fourth and Twenty-fifth Infantry and Ninth Cavalry, returned to stations in the Far West, while the Tenth Cavalry was assigned to Camp Forse, Huntsville, Alabama. Although whites in Salt Lake City extended a cordial welcome to the men of the Twenty-fourth upon their return to Fort Douglas,[51] other black soldiers found little evidence that their performance in Cuba had dissipated anti-Negro prejudice. Chaplain George W. Prioleau's description of the reception of the Ninth Cavalry in Kansas City tended to confirm predictions that all the praise of the black regulars by whites would be not only brief but also without tangible results. According to Prioleau, the Negro cavalrymen were refused service in restaurants, while the white soldiers of the First Cavalry who arrived in the city at the same

50. Washington *Colored American,* December 3, 24, 1898; *Richmond Planet,* December 17, 1898; Salt Lake City *Broad Ax,* November 26, December 24, 1898; *Savannah Tribune,* December 10, 1898; *Washington Bee,* December 24, 1898; *Parsons Weekly Blade,* November 12, December 17, 1898; Kansas City *American Citizen,* December 2, 1898; Topeka *Kansas State Ledger,* November 12, 1898.
51. Salt Lake City *Broad Ax,* October 8, 1898.

time were "invited to sit down . . . and eat free of cost." Such discrimination, the black chaplain concluded, could only be perpetrated by the most "hellish minds." [52]

But at least the ultimate destination of the Ninth Cavalry, a remote area of the Arizona Territory, promised to remove the men from contact with such overt manifestations of prejudice. The Tenth Cavalry, confronted with the prospect of a tour of duty in Alabama, envied the good fortune of the Ninth. The men of the Tenth much preferred to take their chances in the jungles of Cuba than be subjected to the insults and intimidation of whites in the South.[53] The experiences of the black cavalrymen in Alabama scarcely fell short of their expectations.

Repeated clashes occurred between black and white soldiers in the Huntsville camp, and a white civilian posted a standing reward "for every black 10th Cavalryman that was killed." The Negro troopers especially resented being disarmed while encamped in such hostile country; their resentment was all the more acute because white soldiers at Camp Forse were allowed to retain their arms. Such discrimination, the black troops argued, was inexcusable in view of the fact that they were seasoned veterans with a distinguished record for discipline and good behavior.[54] "The war department knows of what hatred there is against the colored troops in the south and what troubles they have," a member of the Tenth Cavalry wrote. "Why don't they send us to Cuba, or to the north, anywhere, or give us our side arms so that we might protect ourselves." [55] The black troopers enthusiastically welcomed the order early in 1899 transferring them to a post along the Rio Grande. By mid-May the regiment was back in Cuba as a part of the occupation army. In view of their recent experiences

52. Quoted in Cleveland *Gazette*, October 22, 1898.
53. Member of the Tenth Cavalry to the Editor, Springfield *Illinois Record*, October 8, 1898.
54. Birmingham *Age-Herald*, October 12, 13, 1898; Memphis *Commercial Appeal*, October 12, 1898; Cleveland *Gazette*, November 26, 1898; Springfield *Illinois Record*, November 5, 1898; Report of an Investigation of a Shooting Affray . . . Involving Members of the 10th Cavalry, October 10, 1898, Captain S. L. Woodward to the Adjutant General, October 26, 1898, Captain F. N. Dunning to the Adjutant General, November 3, 1898, #2046322, Adjutant General's Records.
55. Member of the Tenth Cavalry to the Editor, Springfield *Illinois Record*, December 3, 1898.

in Alabama, it is perhaps understandable that the men of the Tenth Cavalry looked upon their assignment in Cuba as the finest they ever had.[56]

By mid-August, 1898, it was obvious that Negro volunteers would have little opportunity to emulate the combat record of the regulars even if they went to Cuba. With few exceptions, however, they manifested a lively interest in being assigned to the island. Some Negroes argued that they were better equipped to serve in the occupation army for reasons other than their so-called immunity to heat and tropical diseases. Monroe Dorsey, a black editor in Kansas, declared: "The Negroes of America can better understand the condition of the Cubans and can better treat with them and make everlasting friends, while the white soldier, with his bundle of hatred for anything not of a white skin, haughty airs and bulldozing disposition, can make nothing but enemies out of the Cubans." [57] Dorsey and others who depicted the Negro volunteer soldier as an ideal "instrument of empire" calculated that such a role promised diverse rewards. It would not only allow the Negro soldier an opportunity to win respect for the American flag among the dark-skinned inhabitants of the Caribbean, but would also make him a "useful factor in the national make-up" whose influence could be exercised to relieve the burdens of black people in the United States.[58] Other black Americans who took a somewhat different approach argued that the Negro volunteer in Cuba would at least have "a chance to be . . . a man" and would have an opportunity to explore economic conditions there with a view toward becoming a permanent resident of the island upon being mustered out of military service.[59] For these reasons as well as others, most black volunteers indicated that they preferred duty in Cuba to being shuffled from camp to camp within the United States.

In August and September, 1898, three black volunteer regiments—the Eighth Illinois, Twenty-third Kansas, and Ninth Im-

56. Glass, *History of the Tenth Cavalry*, p. 39; *Army and Navy Journal*, January 13, 1900, p. 467.

57. *Parsons Weekly Blade*, August 27, 1898.

58. *Ibid.;* Des Moines *Iowa State Bystander*, July 1, 1898.

59. Coffeyville *American*, October 29, 1898; Des Moines *Iowa State Bystander*, September 25, 1898.

munes—were dispatched to the island as part of the occupation army. Colonel Marshall of the Eighth Illinois notified the War Department early in August that his men had voted "enthusiastically in favor of being sent to relieve the First Illinois at Santiago," a white unit decimated by yellow fever. Major General Shafter shortly afterward ordered a white immune regiment out of Santiago because of its disorderly conduct and requested that it be replaced by the black volunteers from Illinois. Shafter's request, backed up by the entreaties of Governor Tanner and other influential Republicans from Illinois, helped persuade the War Department to assign the regiment to Cuba.[60] Regardless of the motives of those who made the decision to utilize the Eighth Illinois for garrison duty, the choice of a black regiment from a politically doubtful state was an astute move from the standpoint of Republican strategy. Colonel Marshall was assured by an acquaintance who conferred with McKinley that he and his regiment stood "well at the White House." The president was reported to have said that "the happiest moment of his life" was when he received Governor Tanner's telegram informing him that the Eighth Illinois was ready for service in Cuba.[61]

On August 8, 1898, the Illinois troops boarded the train for New York. All along the route the regiment was greeted by enthusiastic crowds of black citizens who, like the soldiers themselves, were keenly aware of the symbolic significance of the occasion—a black regiment with a complete roster of black officers entrusted with a delicate mission in a foreign country. Despite the pride displayed by Negroes in the Eighth Illinois, the soldiers were never allowed to forget that they were something less than first-class citizens. In Baltimore several officers who attempted to secure a meal in a restaurant were thrown out because of their color. And when

60. *Chicago Tribune,* August 1, 6, 10, 12, 1898; *Biennial Report of Adjutant General of Illinois, 1897–1898,* pp. 38–39; Steward, *Colored Regulars,* pp. 285–286; H. C. Corbin to J. R. Tanner, August 5, 1898, J. R. Tanner to H. C. Corbin, August 6, 1898, in *Report of the Commission Appointed by the President to Investigate the Conduct of the War Department in the War with Spain,* Senate Document No. 221, 56 Cong., 1 sess., II, 1074, 1445; hereafter cited as *Conduct of the War with Spain* with appropriate volume number.

61. ? to John R. Marshall, October 17, 1898, Regimental Book Records of 8th Illinois Colored Infantry, Records of the Adjutant General's Office, Record Group 94, National Archives; hereafter cited as Eighth Illinois Regimental Records.

the regiment passed through Martinsburg, West Virginia, a white laborer in a local brewery was on hand to hurl verbal insults. As the train pulled out of the station, he loudly proclaimed that "all niggers ought to go to Cuba where they'd get killed." [62] Such evidence of anti-Negro sentiment scarcely bode well for the black volunteers who remained in the United States.

On August 11, 1898, the Eighth Illinois sailed from New York aboard the *Yale,* arriving in Cuba after an uneventful five-day voyage. Their first camp was on a site near San Juan Hill, where the sky was black with vultures feasting on the limbs of Spanish corpses which poked out of shallow graves. As soon as the Illinois soldiers had rid the countryside of this macabre sight and potential health hazard, they traveled by rail to the city of San Luis about eighteen miles from Santiago, and on August 18, 1898, installed themselves in the old Spanish barracks and arsenal there. Colonel Marshall served as commander of the post and as governor of the province of San Luis. A detachment of his men under Major Robert R. Jackson was sent to Palma Soriano, where their performance brought praise from the War Department.[63]

Two other regiments of black volunteers landed in Cuba shortly after the arrival of the Illinois troops and joined them at San Luis. One of these, the Twenty-third Kansas, left home in the midst of a heated political contest in which both Republicans and Populists claimed credit for the "honor" which the War Department had bestowed upon black Kansans. Although the Populist governor was responsible for organizing a Negro regiment with Negro officers, the Republicans maintained that its selection for duty in Cuba had actually been arranged by Republican congressman Charles Curtis. According to their version, the black volunteers would never have left their camp at Topeka if Curtis had not rushed to Washington and used his influence with Presi-

62. Goode, *"Eighth Illinois,"* pp. 108–112, 116–117; Springfield *Illinois Record,* August 13, 1898; *Pioneer Press* (Martinsburg, W. Va.), quoted in Cleveland *Gazette,* September 17, 1898.

63. Goode, *"Eighth Illinois,"* pp. 128–129, 149–150; John R. Marshall to John R. Tanner, August 28, 1898, in Springfield *Illinois Record,* September 3, 1898; Charles W. Hall, "The Eighth Illinois, U.S.V.," *Colored American Magazine,* I (June, 1900), 94–103. For an excellent treatment of the occupation of Cuba, see David F. Healy, *The United States in Cuba, 1898–1902: Generals, Politicians, and the Search for Policy* (Madison: University of Wisconsin Press, 1963).

dent McKinley.[64] But whether political pressure figured in the War Department's selection of either the Twenty-third Kansas or the Ninth Immunes (the other black unit sent to San Luis) cannot be ascertained with any degree of certainty. Indeed, several non-political considerations may have been decisive: not only did departmental officials believe that black soldiers were "especially suitable" for service in tropical climates, but General Shafter had also indicated that he favored their use for garrison duty. Furthermore, the pressing need for regiments to replace the weary veterans of the Santiago campaign undoubtedly helps explain why the department selected the Twenty-third Kansas and Ninth Immunes as well as the Eighth Illinois; all other black regiments were still in the process of being organized. Conceivably the Negro volunteers from North Carolina might have been assigned to Cuba if Governor Russell had not informed the Department that he desired to have Colonel James H. Young, the politically influential black commander of the Third North Carolina, readily accessible until the fall elections. Apparently he considered Young's presence essential for the Republicans in North Carolina to retain the black vote.[65]

At San Luis the soldiers of the three Negro regiments performed a variety of functions. They took charge of the Spanish prisoners of war interned there and supervised their shipment back to Spain. For several weeks Negro troops were kept on constant alert by reports claiming that 1,500 Spanish soldiers were hiding in nearby mountains and planning an attack.[66] The possibility of engaging in combat with Spaniards rekindled their hope of following in the steps of the black regulars. Private Simon Brown of the Twenty-third Kansas wrote home: "I am ready to die upon the battlefield defending our country, 'Grand America,' and the poor Cubans as well, because I am convinced that these people are of our Negro race, although they cannot speak the English language but they have the complexion of our race." Private Brown was undoubtedly

64. Topeka *Colored Citizen*, September 1, 8, 15, 29, October 6, November 4, 1898; Wichita *Tribune*, November 5, 1898; Coffeyville *American*, October 15, 1898. For a crude poll of black opinion regarding the political impact of Leedy's organization of a Negro regiment, see *Topeka Weekly Call*, July 28, 1898.
65. Raleigh *News and Observer*, August 7, 1898.
66. Goode, "*Eighth Illinois*," pp. 133–137.

disappointed that the rumored attack by the Spanish guerrillas never materialized, and he had no opportunity to prove himself "upon the battlefield." [67] The nearest thing to combat which the black soldiers witnessed was the pursuit of bands of Cuban banditti who for years had preyed upon the inhabitants in the eastern part of the island. They curbed the lawless activities of the bandits and even captured one of their most notorious leaders, Troncon. All the while the Negro soldiers assisted in the rehabilitation of Santiago province, including the construction of roads and bridges and the repairing of streets and plazas. Colonel Marshall was commended by his superiors for improving sanitation conditions and for restoring order by the use of competent policing methods. Under his supervision, according to one commentator, "business revived and the stagnation which had long hung like a fog over the little city [San Luis] disappeared." [68]

The black volunteers seem to have made a conscious effort to cultivate the good will of the Cubans. At Palma, Major Jackson sponsored an organization made up of black soldiers and Cuban civilians called the Mannana Club; it was designed to encourage friendly relations between the military forces and civilian population. Captain W. B. Roberts and several other officers of the Twenty-thrd Kansas made a pilgrimage to the home of Antonio Maceo, the fallen hero of the Cuban revolution, and spoke at length with his mother and sisters. Everywhere in the province the impoverished condition of the people elicited sympathy among the black troops. They were generous in their treatment of the women and children who visited the military camps in search of food. Cubans were welcomed at religious services and social functions sponsored by the three Negro regiments. About a dozen soldiers married Cuban senioritas; others became so enamored of the economic possibilities in the island that they vowed to remain there permanently, and a few either bought or acquired options on local real estate. Among these was Captain John L. Waller of the Twenty-third Kansas, formerly American consul in Madagascar whose real estate dealings there were largely responsible for the

67. Simon Brown to Citizens of Oswego, Kans., September 2, 1898, in *Parsons Weekly Blade*, October 22, 1898.
68. Fletcher, "Negro and the U.S. Army," pp. 256–258; Goode, *"Eighth Illinois,"* p. 218; Steward, *Colored Regulars,* p. 287.

celebrated incident in American diplomacy mentioned in the first chapter.[69]

Nor did soldiers fail to apprise their friends and relatives of the opportunities open to black men in Cuba. Numerous letters published in the black press provided abundant advice about the climate, soil, and growing season, also itemizing the trades and professions in which black Americans could seek their fortunes.[70] Even more important, according to some soldiers, was the absence of an institutionalized color line. Whatever racial segregation and discrimination they encountered in Cuba was usually of American origin. In a much-publicized letter Captain Roberts of the Twenty-third Kansas described how he thwarted the efforts of a white American who attempted to maintain a color barrier in the dining room of a Santiago hotel. Roberts told the proprietor that colored soldiers in Cuba had no intention of allowing "any discrimination on account of color." With the full backing of General Ezra P. Ewers, the black captain forced the management of the hotel, which ironically was named The American, to abandon for a time at least its policy of racial segregation.[71]

As might be expected, not all the black volunteers were favorably impressed by Cuba, nor did all Cubans welcome their presence. Some of the soldiers abhorred the hot climate and pointed to the sick lists of the three regiments as proof that Negroes were no more immune to tropical diseases than other Americans. Others described the Cuban people as dirty and indolent.[72] The Reverend C. T. Walker of Augusta, Georgia, known as the "black Spurgeon" who served as chaplain of the Ninth Immunes at San Luis, was consistently critical of the native population. For him, they were a treacherous lot who spent most of their time "lying

69. Goode, "Eighth Illinois," pp. 154–155, 190–191, 239; Gatewood, "Smoked Yankees," pp. 187–212; John R. Marshall to Adjutant General, January 24, 1899, Eighth Illinois Regimental Records. For informative letters regarding life in Cuba, see Sgt. John W. Botts, Co. H, 23rd Kansas, to J. Sterling Morton, no date, J. Sterling Morton Papers, Nebraska State Historical Society, Lincoln; Allen A. Wesley to Booker T. Washington, October 5, 1898, Washington Papers.

70. Coffeyville American, November 5, 1898; Parsons Weekly Blade, October 15, 1898; Savannah Tribune, August 15, 1898.

71. Letter from Captain W. B. Roberts, in Topeka Colored Citizen, November 11, 1898; see also Lynk, Black Troopers, pp. 120–124.

72. Gatewood, "Smoked Yankees," pp. 197–198; Topeka Colored Citizen, September 29, 1898; Dennis Matthews to Mrs. S. L. Gross, October 15, 1898, in Kansas City American Citizen, November 13, 1898.

around in the shade sleeping and dreaming how to cheat" Americans. Walker pronounced them totally incapable of self-government and urged the United States to abandon any thought of Cuban independence. His claim that Cubans "hated American soldiers, both white and black," may have been somewhat exaggerated,[73] but it was not totally without basis in fact. The Cuba Libre element of the population in particular made little effort to hide its contempt for the occupation army. This highly vocal element, anxious for immediate self-government, was probably responsible for the charges made against the Eighth Illinois shortly after its arrival in San Luis.[74] Reports to the War Department that the penchant of the Illinois troops for brawling and criminal assault made them feared and hated by Cubans finally prompted an official investigation. The result was a complete vindication of the black soldiers. Colonel Charles Starr, the white officer in charge of the investigation, pronounced the charges against them utterly groundless. In fact, the colonel was profoundly impressed by the conduct of the Illinois volunteers and by their desire to excel, because, as he noted, they realized "fully that colored troops commanded by colored officers are on trial." [75]

Racial considerations probably figured more significantly in the relations among the three regiments at San Luis than in any charges made by Cubans against the black soldiers. The men of the Eighth Illinois and Twenty-third Kansas considered themselves superior to the Ninth Immunes, whom they described as reckless and lacking in discipline—a charge stoutly denied by Colonel Charles J. Crane, the Mississippian who commanded the immune regiment. The fact that the immunes were under the command of white officers accounted in part for the condescending attitude of the troops from Illinois and Kansas. Although they felt that black men who enlisted in the immune regiments compro-

73. *Augusta Chronicle*, October 30, December 30, 1898, January 17, 1899; Silas X. Floyd, *Life of Charles T. Walker* (New York: Negro Universities Press, 1969), pp. 83–87.

74. *Chicago Tribune*, August 23, 1898; Springfield *Illinois Record*, August 27, 1898.

75. Order No. 21, Eighth Illinois Regimental Records; *Chicago Tribune*, August 23, 1898; *New York Daily Tribune*, August 23, 1898; Springfield *Illinois Record*, August 27, 1898; H. W. Lawton to H. C. Corbin, August 21, 1891, in *Conduct of the War with Spain*, II, 1113.

mised their self-respect and did so for reasons other than winning "honor for the race," they held the white officers of the Ninth primarily responsible for the "sorry condition" of the regiment. A member of the Eighth Illinois who claimed that the white officers "did not hold themselves in the self-esteem which their position and rank demanded" specifically noted their fondness for "imbibing in common with the men in the ranks" and their free use of profanity on the drill field. "In the southern white officers' eye," the Illinois soldier declared, "the man who did the most grinning . . . and could dance the best or make the most monkey shines was the best negro soldier." [76] Such an attitude on the part of the officers scarcely inspired the men with a sense of pride or made them feel that they were on trial. Pointing to the low morale and rapidly deteriorating health of the black immunes, H. C. C. Astwood, the resident missionary of the African Methodist Episcopal Church in Santiago, corroborated the claim made by Illinois and Kansas troops that the Ninth Regiment had "been rendered useless by inefficient and prejudicial white officers." [77] Although the officers of the regiment were quick to refute such charges, they made little effort to hide their contempt for the black officers of the Illinois and Kansas units, especially those who outranked them. Colonel Crane obviously did not relish having his regiment assigned to a remote station where the only other troops were blacks with black officers. He insisted that the men of his regiment were better disciplined than those of the Eighth Illinois and Twenty-third Kansas because the latter had only colored officers. But of more concern to him were the rumors which claimed that "Crane has lost his grip." The colonel came to the conclusion that his principal enemy was General Leonard Wood, the commander of the Department of Santiago who, in his opinion, was intent upon besmirching the reputation of his regiment.[78]

An incident involving the Ninth Immunes in mid-November, 1898, tended to confirm the idea that their discipline was not good. Ironically, though, the other two black regiments at San Luis also suffered the consequences of the immunes' misdeeds. On

76. Goode, "Eighth Illinois," pp. 157–159, 167–169, 173.

77. Ibid., p. 173.

78. Ibid., p. 171; J. C. Crane to the Adjutant General, November 2, 1898, #162002, Adjutant General's Records.

the evening of November 14, following a visit from the paymaster, the black immunes flocked to local saloons. When Cuban policemen attempted to arrest one of them for creating a disturbance, "many other soldiers congregated around interfering with the arrest." The situation became so menacing that the Cuban police lieutenant, José Ferrara, withdrew his men to a neighboring building to prevent a clash with the soldiers. But the soldiers, many of whom had been drinking, were bent upon revenge for what they considered the presumptuousness of the police in trying to arrest one of their comrades. Fully armed, they laid siege to the building into which the policemen had retreated. When order was finally restored, two soldiers and four Cubans (including Ferrara) were dead.[79]

General Leonard Wood immediately ordered a full investigation and posted a $1,000 reward for the names of the soldiers responsible for the affray. In his report to the War Department, Wood by no means confined his comments to the details of the San Luis affair but also discussed black volunteers in general. Although he believed that "the three colored regiments . . . have done, everything considered, very well," he nonetheless warned that "the massing together of three thousand negroes" was "liable at any time to be followed by outbreaks" such as the one at San Luis. He also questioned the wisdom of having so many Negro troops in Cuba, because the general claimed that "the Cuban negro cordially hates the American negro soldier." [80] Indeed, several editors of the Cuba Libre persuasion seized upon the San Luis incident to castigate all black troops as "cutthroats who ever since they came here have acted worse than the Spaniards ever did." [81] In view of the many protests concerning Negro soldiers which General Wood received from citizens in the vicinity of San Luis, he ordered all three black regiments to establish new camps several miles outside the city and promised to take "the most rigid measures to insure absolute quiet in the future." But the gen-

79. Leonard Wood to the Adjutant General, November 16, 1898, Leonard Wood to the Adjutant General, November 18, 1898, #162002, Adjutant General's Records; *Chicago Tribune*, November 16, 1898; Coston, *Spanish-American War Volunteer*, p. 17.

80. Leonard Wood to the Adjutant General, November 18, 1898, #162002, Adjutant General's Records.

81. *Chicago Tribune*, November 16, 1898; Early, "The Negro Soldier in the Spanish-American War," pp. 79–80.

eral's suggestion that two of the Negro regiments be assigned "to some other part of the island" failed to win the approval of the War Department.[82]

No other aspect of the black volunteers' service in Cuba received as much publicity as the San Luis affair. Editorials entitled "Negro Soldiers Proved Outlaws" appeared in white newspapers throughout the South.[83] Even the *Army and Navy Journal* cited the incident as an "example of the vicious violence" common among Negro troops.[84] The publicity of the San Luis affair had a profound effect upon the public judgment of the Negro as a volunteer soldier. The *Nashville American* concluded that "the negro has shown himself utterly unfit for the honorable calling of a soldier." [85] Those whites who had opposed the use of Negro volunteers to the San Luis affair as proof that Negroes were immune to discipline and self-control even if they were not immune to yellow fever. But none of these critics bothered to suggest that the black soldiers responsible for the disorder were from a regiment commanded by white officers; typically, the *Atlanta Constitution* claimed that "all the negro regiments were more or less mixed up in the affair." Others thought it significant that no ranking white officer was present in San Luis at the time of the disturbance because both Colonel Crane and General Ewers, the brigade commander, were "resting" in Santiago. "I don't know that my presence would have prevented it [the San Luis affair]," Colonel Crane later wrote, "but I believe so." [86]

The San Luis incident took a serious toll upon the morale of the Negro volunteers, especially those from Illinois and Kansas, who resented being blamed for offenses committed by the Ninth Immunes merely because they happened also to be black. The Eighth Illinois felt even more victimized when it was reported that General Wood had described its men as "the scums . . . of Chi-

82. Leonard Wood to the Adjutant General, November 18, 1898, #162002, Adjutant General's Records.

83. *Morning News* (Savannah), November 17, 1898; New Orleans *Daily Picayune*, November 16, 1898; *Atlanta Constitution*, November 16, 1898; Birmingham *Age-Herald*, November 17, 1898; Mobile *Daily Register*, November 17, 1898.

84. *Army and Navy Journal*, November 19, 1898, p. 283. The *Journal* pointed out that Colonel Marshall, the black commander of the Eighth Illinois, was the senior officer at San Luis at the time because both General E. P. Ewers and Colonel J. C. Crane were ill.

85. Quoted in Little Rock *Arkansas Democrat*, November 25, 1898.

86. *Atlanta Constitution*, November 16, 1898.

cago." Whatever the validity of the report, the Illinois troops believed that Wood "never had much love for the Eighth from the outset." [87] Frustrated by what they considered prejudice "in high places," the Negro volunteers increasingly expressed a desire to escape from "this accursed country" with its sweltering heat and interminable rains. The strict discipline imposed upon them following the San Luis affair and the monotonous life in the new camps only intensified their homesickness. Within the Illinois regiment the discontent came to focus upon Colonel Marshall, who was accused of "treating the boys like dogs." Even the colonel's light complexion figured in their grievances. One soldier described him as "too near white"; another referred to him as "the man with the white face and the black heart." [88] The sense of frustration and disillusionment among the black volunteers was best expressed perhaps by Corporal George J. Beard, who wrote a friend: "We came here to fight and not to clear up ground for these Cubans, but came to make them free and avenge our country's wrong . . . and now that we have assisted in accomplishing our aim we do not think it fair that we should stay here. . . ." [89]

The black volunteers responded enthusiastically to reports early in 1899 that they were to be transferred to the Philippines. At least there, so the argument ran, they would have an opportunity to share in the glory that came to troops who participated in combat. When such reports proved erroneous, the soldiers manifested profound disappointment and contemplated the prospect of prolonged service in Cuba with considerable misgiving. However, early in March, 1899, the War Department announced that they would be sent home, and within two months all three black regiments in Cuba were returned to the United States and mustered out. [90]

87. Goode, "Eighth Illinois," p. 171.
88. Gatewood, "Smoked Yankees," pp. 209–231. Earlier (August 13, 1898) the Washington Colored American had noted that a newspaper in Springfield, Illinois, had devoted "nearly half a column to convince its readers that Colonel John R. Marshall is a colored man." According to the Colored American "the few drops of Negro blood in his veins are so powerful that they overtop all the rest and establish his identity."
89. George J. Beard to the Editor, February 21, 1899, in Springfield Illinois Record, March 11, 1899.
90. Goode, "Eighth Illinois," pp. 272, 280–281; Chicago Tribune, March 8, 1899; Special Order No. 51, March 2, 1899, Eighth Illinois Regimental Records.

Six

Black Volunteers at Home

All these black boys can go to war that want to, but when
I go, rest assured there will be infinitely more than glory
in it for me. I am like you, no fighting for the U. S. for me
as long as the nightmare of Lake City remains undispelled.
>   —Ralph W. Tyler to George A. Myers,
>   May 11, 1898

Everything bad that the Colored soldiers do is heralded
over the country, but similar acts by the other ones are kept
quiet and the former are branded as being the worst in the
world.
Our Colored soldiers must be very careful in their actions.
They must keep in mind that they are on trial and more is
expected of them than any other class.
>   —*Savannah Tribune,* December 3, 1898

Whatever the grievances of those Negro soldiers who served in
Cuba, their experiences did not inspire as much bitterness and
disillusionment as those of the 7,000 black volunteers who never
left the United States. Wherever these men were stationed, their
presence aroused hostility and resentment among whites. The transfer of the volunteers to winter quarters in Georgia and other southern states scarcely improved the plight of the black soldier. A few
years later a colonel in the regular army candidly admitted before
a congressional investigating committee that there still existed "a
very strong prejudice throughout the old slave states against colored troops . . . quite a separate feeling from the ordinary race
prejudice." "Colored man in uniform represents authority," the
white colonel noted, "and this idea suggests superiority, which is
bitterly resented." [1] In the fall of 1898 the southern press continu-

1. Quoted in John M. Carroll, *The Black Military Experience in the American
West* (New York: Liveright, 1971), p. 525.

ally described black soldiers as so inclined to insolence, rowdyism, and criminality as to pose a serious menace to "peaceful race relations." White Southerners concluded that the soldier's uniform transformed the Negro "from a docile, tractable and peaceable individual into an offensive, insolent creature." The governor of Georgia even cited "the baneful influence" of the black volunteers encamped in his state as the cause for the upsurge in racial violence that occurred there—a charge which Negroes disputed in view of Georgia's extraordinary lynching record prior to the arrival of a single black soldier in the state.[2]

Black Americans concluded that Negro volunteers were targets of a campaign of vilification. The soldiers themselves, frustrated by what they called "yellow journalism," complained that they were maligned by those bent upon validating their own prophesies that blacks in uniform would be nothing more than "undisciplined thugs" with license to swagger and commit depredations. "I have newspaper clippings," a black volunteer stationed at Macon wrote, "showing that the very coming of Negro troops was heralded with unfounded contempt which poisoned the public mind before they arrived."[3] The black editor of the *Washington Bee* became so outraged by what he described as the *Washington Post*'s deliberate attempt to discredit Negro volunteers by publicizing only their misdeeds that he promised to call attention to "all the dastardly deeds of white soldiers which the *Post* carefully overlooks."[4] Often incidents involving Negro volunteers which were headlined as a riot or mutiny scarcely warranted such descriptions. Even Colonel Bullard, the white commander of Alabama's black regiment, claimed that journalists were given to exaggeration and misrepresentation in writing about Negro volunteers. In their hands, he declared, "a fist fight became 'a riot' and a plain drunk 'a mutiny.'" But Bullard also believed that Negro soldiers were inclined to "turn merited punishment into martyrdom."[5]

2. Memphis *Commercial Appeal*, November 18, 1898; *Washington Bee*, March 25, 1899; Savannah *Tribune*, April 1, 1899; Des Moines *Iowa State Bystander*, March 24, 1899.

3. Allen S. Peal to the Editor, March 15, 1899, in Cleveland *Gazette*, April 8, 1899.

4. *Washington Bee*, September 17, 1898.

5. Robert L. Bullard Diary, pp. 90–91; see also Oswald Garrison Villard, "The Negro in the Regular Army," *Atlantic Monthly*, XCI (June, 1903), 727.

No one claimed, of course, that black volunteers were always models of military decorum or any more immune to the temptations of saloons, brothels, and gambling houses than any other volunteers. When a white correspondent reported from Santiago that the Negro volunteers in Cuba were not as well disciplined as the black regulars stationed there earlier, Calvin Chase agreed but pointed out that volunteers in general, white and black, suffered in any comparison with regulars. Chase reminded his readers that the black volunteers had been sent to Cuba primarily to replace white immunes who had made themselves offensive to the natives; [6] black volunteers were, as one of them explained, "not angels but average mortals." Like other civilians hastily marshaled into the volunteer service, they had difficulty adjusting to the discipline and rigors of military life.[7] Impatient to get on the battlefield, they wearied of camp routine and complained about not being allowed to share in the glory of combat. The surrender of Spain which eliminated the possibility of such glory seriously affected the morale of some Negro volunteers, because the prospect of garrison duty in Cuba offered a poor substitute for men whose main concern was winning plaudits for the race upon the field of battle. Several soldiers of the Third North Carolina dispatched a letter to the secretary of war in which they declared that they "did not join the service for garrison duty" and therefore should be allowed to return home.[8] A member of Ohio's black battalion concluded that his unit might as well be mustered out because the war was over and "Roosevelt, Miles, and others (white, of course) have all there is to be gotten out of it." [9]

Whatever motives may have prompted individual Negroes to enter the volunteer army, few failed to realize that they were participating in an experiment with extraordinary obligations. The black editor of the Savannah *Tribune*, himself a veteran officer in the Georgia militia, advised Negro volunteers to "be very careful of their actions" because they were "on trial and more is expected of them than any other class." [10] White officers of black units, anx-

6. *Washington Bee,* September 10, 1898.

7. Allen S. Peal to the Editor, March 15, 1899, in Cleveland *Gazette,* April 8, 1899.

8. The letter is printed in *The Journal and Tribune* (Knoxville, Tenn.), October 5, 1898.

9. Winslow Hobson to the Editor, in Cleveland *Gazette,* October 15, 1898.

10. Savannah *Tribune,* December 3, 1898.

ious to protect the good name of their commands and to compile records that would enhance their own prospects for promotion in the army in the future, also reminded their men that they were "on trial," but the term assumed greater significance for Negro troops under the command of Negro officers. Such units were never allowed to forget their special responsibility to perform in a manner that would disprove the notion that Negroes made good soldiers only if commanded by white officers, while at the same time reflecting credit upon all black Americans. "If we fail," Colonel Marshall of the Eighth Illinois repeatedly told his men, "the whole race will have to shoulder the burden." [11] Determined to diminish rather than increase the black man's burden, Marshall and other black commanders consistently stressed the importance of perfection in drill, "gentlemanly conduct," and cleanliness. Not all black commanders were able to transform their units into showpieces of military discipline, but in view of the obstacles which they encountered their labors were remarkably successful. Of the black volunteer units the Ninth Ohio Battalion was undoubtedly the most outstanding. Both military and civilian observers agreed that it was one of the best-drilled commands in the volunteer army—a condition which owed much to the fact that it was commanded by men of ability and education who had served either in the state militia or in the regular army.[12] Even the Third North Carolina, whose officers were largely political appointees without previous military experience, achieved a degree of efficiency which the ridicule and bombast of the state's white press tended to obscure. Only years later did Josephus Daniels, the archenemy of Colonel Young and the regiment in 1898, admit that the black North Carolinians "made much better soldiers than anyone expected." [13]

But in the fall of 1898, as the black volunteers were undergoing training, even such faint praise from whites was rare. Whatever

11. Goode, "Eighth Illinois," p. 231.
12. The Commonwealth (Harrisburg, Pa.), quoted in the Cleveland Gazette, November 19, 1898; J. Madison Pierce to the Editor, ibid., August 27, 1898; Charles Young to Captain Colquehan, October 21, 1898, Regimental Book Records of the Ninth Ohio Colored Battalion, Records of the Adjutant General's Office, Record Group 94, National Archives.
13. Josephus Daniels, Editor in Politics (Chapel Hill: University of North Carolina Press, 1941), pp. 275–276.

commendation they received was usually reserved for those under the command of white officers and often referred more to these officers' ability to discipline Negroes than to the achievements of the men themselves. Colonel Bullard and the other white officers of the Third Alabama won public acclaim for the orderliness which characterized that regiment.[14] When the Sixth Virginia and Third North Carolina arrived at Camp Poland near Knoxville, Tennessee, the local white press was quick to indicate that it preferred the black Virginians under the white commander to the black North Carolinians under their black colonel. Lieutenant Colonel Croxton of the Sixth Virginia was described as an able military man responsible for the "gentlemanly and quiet behavior of the colored soldiers" under his command.[15] On occasion the white officers of black units allowed Negro volunteers from units commanded by black officers to be held responsible for offenses actually committed by their own men. Croxton, for example, protected the reputation of his command by permitting men from the Third North Carolina to be charged with disorderly conduct during visits to Knoxville when in fact soldiers from the Sixth Virginia were the culprits.[16] When white citizens of Chattanooga complained about the behavior of the Eighth Immunes on visits to that city from their camp at nearby Chickamauga Park, Colonel Huggins stoutly defended his men against charges of misconduct and suggested that the two black companies from Indiana attached to his regiment were responsible for any breaches in discipline. "I have done what I could to discipline these [Indiana] companies," Huggins reported to the adjutant general, "but they had been several months in service before they came under my command and having their own colored captains who were their neighbors at home and familiar with them, they are more self assertive and less respectful in their demeanor than the men of my regiment." [17]

14. Mobile *Daily Register,* July 22, 29, August 19, September 6, 1898.
15. Knoxville *Journal and Tribune,* September 15, 16, 17, 26, October 2, 1898.
16. James H. Young to the Assistant Adjutant General, October 2, 1898, James H. Young to Colonel Kuert, October 16, 1898, Richard Croxton to James H. Young, no date, Regimental Book Records of the Third North Carolina Colored Infantry, Records of the Adjutant General's Office, Record Group 94, National Archives.
17. E. L. Huggins to H. C. Corbin, November 11, 1898, #157536, Adjutant General's Records.

The mere presence of Negro soldiers in military camps was sufficient to arouse the hostility of some white volunteers, especially from the South, who soon learned that they could vent their prejudices with little fear of punishment. Whites' strenuous objections to being placed in the same brigades with blacks prompted a succession of organizational changes throughout the existence of the volunteer army. In September, 1898, when the Sixth Virginia was brigaded with the Twenty-first Michigan and the Fourth Tennessee, both white units, the Tennesseans "stacked arms and refused to drill claiming they preferred to quit rather than be brigaded with a negro regiment." Only when their officers promised to have the black Virginians transferred to another brigade did the Tennessee troops stop their protests.[18]

Among the reasons for the resignation of Colonel Charles F. Woodward of the Sixth Massachusetts was a conflict concerning the regiment's all-black company. General George A. Garretson of Ohio, the commanding officer of the brigade of which the Sixth Massachusetts was a part, objected to the presence of the colored company and wanted it attached to the Ninth Ohio Battalion. When Woodward resigned his commission, it was charged that he had done so rather than allow such a reorganization. There were other reasons for Woodward's resignation, but Negroes generally interpreted his action as that of "a noble patriot" who would not acquiesce in the racial prejudices of General Garretson.[19] Although Company L remained a part of the Sixth Massachusetts, the War Department did on occasion seek "to avoid any embarrassment" by acquiescing in the requests of high-ranking volunteer officers who objected to having Negro units in their brigades and divisions.[20]

Nor did the department discourage the segregation of Negro soldiers within military camps. The physical location of black vol-

18. Knoxville *Journal and Tribune,* September 29, 189-.
19. On Woodward's resignation and black reaction to it, see *Copies of Correspondence from the Adjutant General Relating to the Campaign in Cuba* (Washington: Government Printing Office, 1898), pp. 290–291; Edwards, *'98 Campaign of the 6th Massachusetts,* pp. 42, 115, 124; *Richmond Planet,* August 13, 1898; *Parsons Weekly Blade,* September 3, 1898; Springfield *Illinois Record,* August 27, 1898; Richard H. Titherington, *A History of the Spanish-American War of 1898* (New York: D. Appleton, 1900), p. 343.
20. S. B. M. Young to H. C. Corbin, October 10, 1898, #149769, Adjutant General's Records.

unteers in most camps reflected the same emphasis upon racial segregation that existed outside the army. The black volunteers from Virginia, as well as others under white commanders, were repeatedly warned "to keep away from the camp of the white soldiers and to avoid places in town habitated by white soldiers." [21]

One of the volunteer army's most troublesome problems in racial etiquette concerned the presence of Negro officers. Black men with military commissions posed a threat to many white Americans' conception of proper relations between the races. The *Washington Post* undoubtedly expressed a widespread sentiment when it declared: "This is a white man's country and the whites are not willing and cannot be compelled to accept the Negro on equal terms in any relation of life. White soldiers will not salute Negro officers neither will they associate with enlisted men of color." [22] Because such notions existed among high-ranking military personnel, segregation was practiced in everything from the officer's mess to toilet facilities. But no amount of segregation or complicated subterfuges toward that end could prevent contact between white enlisted men and black officers. In view of the almost daily occurrence of incidents in which white soldiers refused to show proper respect for Negro officers, the *Washington Post's* declaration appeared all too valid. A member of the Second Tennessee who consistently refused to salute black officers claimed to express "the universal sentiment of the Southern [white] people" when he remarked that "all coons look alike to me." [23] Colonel James H. Tillman, commander of a volunteer regiment from South Carolina and nephew of Senator Benjamin R. Tillman, threatened to court martial any of his men who dared to salute Negro officers. "We are South Carolinians and white men," Tillman declared, "and no earthly power can force our boys to lift their hats to one of these negro officers. If I hear of one of the South Carolina boys

21. General Order No. 21, September 17, 1898, Regimental Book Records of the Sixth Virginia Colored Infantry, Records of the Adjutant General's Office, Record Group 94, National Archives. A private in the First Cavalry, U.S.A., who was in Cuba with the Negro regulars recalled that "there was never any social mixing" between white and black soldiers, and that as for himself, he "was always a little bit afraid of them." See transcription of a taped interview with A. S. Allen, July, 1970, United States Army Military History Collection, Carlisle Barracks, Pa.

22. Quoted in Washington *Colored American,* August 20, 1898.

23. Memphis *Commercial Appeal,* November 18, 1898.

saluting a negro I will kick him out of the company. We have enlisted to fight for our country and not to practice social equality
with an inferior race whom our fathers held in bondage." [24] The
arrival of the Third North Carolina with its complete roster of
black officers at Camp Poland early in September, 1898, so in-
censed the white volunteers of the First Georgia that they fired
upon the black soldiers whenever they ventured near the woods
adjacent to the camp. So serious did the menace become that a
company of Ohio troops had to be called in to protect the Third
North Carolina even during drill practice.[25] Negro officers fully
understood that unless they had the support of the camp com-
mandant, their protests of such behavior by white soldiers were of
little avail.

One widely publicized incident which dramatized the prejudice
against Negro officers involved Major John R. Lynch, a paymaster
in the volunteers. Because Lynch was colored, the white troops of
the Second Texas Regiment refused to accept their pay from him,
at least until they were notified by the War Department that they
would either be paid by the Negro major or not at all. Throughout the United States, Negro citizens condemned the "virulent
prejudice" of the white Texans and applauded the action of federal authorities in forcing them to retreat from their "irrational
position." [26] For Edward Cooper, the incident provided two "in-
structive lessons" regarding the most effective means of combatting
anti-Negro discrimination. He noted that the readiness with which
the "haughty Texans took their money rather than risk the alternative" pointed up the "commercial spirit of the white American and the supreme importance he attaches to the dollar." The
incident confirmed that Afro-Americans would command the respect of whites only as they acquired wealth and economic power.
The second lesson of the Lynch episode, according to Cooper, was
that "the massive power of the government" could indeed be utilized in combatting overt expressions of discrimination and caste.[27]

24. *The Enquirer* (Columbus, Ga.), August 4, 1898; see also Indianapolis *Freeman*,
August 13, 1898.
25. James H. Young to Captain Babcock, September 18, 1898, Third North
Carolina Regimental Records; Knoxville *Journal and Tribune*, September 27, 1898;
Gatewood, "*Smoked Yankees*," pp. 125–126.
26. *Richmond Planet*, September 24, 1898; see also Mobile *Daily Register*, September 23, 1898; Kansas City *American Citizen*, September 30, 1898.
27. Washington *Colored American*, September 24, 1898.

Unlike Cooper, however, most Negro editors were content to emphasize that any behavior by black troops comparable to that of the white Texans would surely have been headlined as a mutiny and punished severely. Apparently the only punishment meted out to the Texans was to force them to receive their pay from a Negro officer.[28]

A black volunteer unit which did acquire a reputation for mutinous behavior was the Sixth Virginia. Relations between the white commander and the black officers had been strained from the beginning; black officers and men resented what they considered the disrespectful manner in which Colonel Croxton treated them. According to one black enlisted man, the white colonel was a "peevish, fretful and irascible" commander who subjected his Negro officers to "oaths and general 'cussing' . . . after every regimental parade" no matter how well the troops performed. For his part, Colonel Croxton complained that because the regiment contained so few men who could write well enough to handle the routine paper work, much of his time was devoted to reports and other details normally assigned to subordinate officers. More important, he came to the conclusion that more than half of the officers of the regiment's Second Battalion, including Major William H. Johnson, were so incompetent that they should be replaced by whites. After the Sixth Virginia arrived at Camp Poland, Croxton called upon the black officers of the Second Battalion to stand examination before a board of review appointed by the corps commander. Although the board which was scheduled to convene on October 3, 1898, contained a black lieutenant colonel from North Carolina, the Negro officers of the Second Battalion were convinced that the proposed examination was nothing more than a maneuver by Colonel Croxton to discredit them and to appoint white men to their posts. Rather than submit to what they believed would be certain humiliation, Major Johnson and eight other officers resigned.[29]

28. *Richmond Planet,* September 24, 1898; Mobile *Daily Register,* September 23, 1898; Kansas City *American Citizen,* September 30, 1898.

29. Knoxville *Journal and Tribune,* September 27, 28, October 1, 2, 1898; "Testimony of Lieut. Col. Richard C. Croxton," in *Conduct of the War with Spain,* IV, 939–943; Johnson, *Colored Volunteer Infantry in Virginia,* pp. 54–55, 67, 69; Gatewood, *"Smoked Yankees,"* pp. 146–147; Richard C. Croxton to Adjutant General, October 4, 31, 1898, Sixth Virginia Regimental Records; *Richmond Planet,* October 8, 15, 1898.

The enlisted men as well as the black officers of the First Battalion viewed this turn of events with great anxiety. A letter to the adjutant general signed by these officers reminded the War Department of the condition upon which the black troops had agreed to enter service and urged that replacements for the Negro officers who had resigned be selected from the ranks of the regiment. If men of color were not to be placed in command of the Second Battalion, the letter concluded, the entire regiment preferred to be mustered out immediately. Colonel Croxton described their appeal as absurd, and the division commander refused to forward it to the War Department because it was "so contrary to military practice and tradition." Over the loud protests of Negroes in Virginia who blamed the resignation of the black officers upon the racial prejudices of their white commander, Governor Tyler filled eight of the vacancies in the battalion with white officers from a volunteer regiment in Virginia then in the process of being mustered out. At Croxton's request, the governor appointed to the remaining vacancy a Negro soldier of the Twenty-fifth Infantry who was detailed as adjutant. If Croxton's request for a black adjutant was designed to mollify the men of the Second Battalion, it could scarcely have been less successful.[30]

On November 2, 1898, when the white officers first appeared and issued orders to the battalion, not a man responded. Pronouncing the incident a mutiny, Colonel Croxton relieved the men of their rifles and had two white regiments placed under arms to handle the situation. Division officers joined him in pleading with the black soldiers to "return to reason." But only when Major Joseph B. Johnson, the Negro commander of the First Battalion, spoke to the men was discipline restored. Some of the men later claimed that they resumed their routine activities only upon receiving a promise from Croxton that Negroes would replace the white officers. Although a white editor in Knoxville characterized the incident as merely "a little stir," it was considered far more serious by most other commentators and gained for the Sixth Virginia the

30. J. B. Johnson et al. to Richard C. Croxton, October 25, Richard C. Croxton to Adjutant General, October 25, 28, 1898, Sixth Virginia Regimental Records; Johnson, Negro Soldiers in the Spanish-American War, pp. 149–152; Richmond Planet, October 29, 1898; James H. Hayes to Russell A. Alger, October 24, 1898, #240766, Adjutant General's Records.

"Mutinous Sixth" label which it was never able to overcome.[31]

If the affair provided ammunition for whites opposed to the use of Negro volunteers, Negro citizens throughout the United States viewed it as a bold stand against racial discrimination. Typical of their response was that of the *People's Defender* of Jackson, Mississippi, which declared: "Thank God, the day is dawning when colored men know how to assert their manhood and resent insults tendered their dignity. The noble action of the immortal Sixth Virginia cannot be too highly commended." The Louisville *American Baptist* also applauded the black Virginians because their conduct offered "positive contradiction to the argument that the colored soldiers do not desire nor respect officers of their own race." [32] Even though the men of the Sixth Virginia regretted the bad name which their action acquired for the regiment, they too viewed it as a strike against prejudice and proudly referred to the mutiny as "that memorable day at Camp Poland." John Mitchell and other black defenders of the regiment in Virginia concentrated their ire upon Colonel Croxton, rather than on the governor who was actually responsible for the appointment of the white officers. In Mitchell's view Governor Hoge had "played fair with the soldiers" but had been duped by Croxton, who was blamed for "all the troubles of the regiment." [33]

An uneasy calm prevailed in the Sixth Virginia by November 10, 1898, when the regiment moved from Knoxville to Camp Haskell near Macon. Three other Negro regiments, the Third North Carolina and the Seventh and Tenth Immunes, joined the black Virginians at the Macon camp. Regardless of their regimental affiliation, the Negro volunteers viewed their new post with considerable anxiety,[34] because to them Georgia represented the very nadir of the black man's existence. White Georgians had already amply demonstrated their hostility for Negroes in uniform. In

31. *Richmond Planet*, November 5, 12, 19, December 10, 1898; Richard C. Croxton to Adjutant General, December 8, 1898, Sixth Virginia Regimental Records; see also Gatewood, "Virginia's Negro Regiment in the Spanish-American War," 204–205; John H. Allen (formerly of Sixth Virginia Infantry), Questionnaire, January 15, 1969, United States Army Military History Collection, Carlisle Barracks, Pa.

32. *People's Defender* and *American Baptist* quoted in Johnson, *Colored Volunteer Infantry in Virginia*, pp. 70–71.

33. *Richmond Planet*, November 19, 26, December 10, 1898.

34. Knoxville *Journal and Tribune*, October 9, 1898.

August, Private James Neely of the Twenty-fifth Infantry had been killed when he presumed to ask for a glass of soda water in a drugstore in Hampton, Georgia. And while the Tenth Immunes were stationed at Augusta, their white officers had cooperated with city officials in maintaining the color line on all public conveyances and in cafes and saloons. Only the hope of Cuba as the ultimate destination of the 4,000 Negro volunteers stationed at Camp Haskell helped to lessen their dread of camp life in Georgia.[35]

Although economic motives had prompted businessmen in Macon to campaign for the establishment of a military installation near their city, they had not bargained for a camp manned primarily by Negro soldiers. In fact, the concentration of so large a contingent of black troops at Camp Haskell caused fear and alarm among whites, who increasingly viewed themselves as a beleaguered people. From the beginning white citizens made it plain that they had no intention of treating the "black boys in blue" any differently from other Negroes. The white newspapers in Macon, as well as those in nearby Atlanta, spoke disparagingly of the black soldiers whose "riotous mood" and contempt for local racial mores were producing an "unhealthy" effect on the Negro population in the area. The fears of whites were continually nourished by rumors that the black troops at Camp Haskell planned to invade Macon and "take over the city." Such an atmosphere tended to harden the prejudices of whites and to strengthen their determination to keep all Negroes "in their place." Even white merchants, anxious to tap the lucrative trade provided by the free-spending soldiers, were careful to avoid giving the impression that they solicited their business.[36]

What the press interpreted as the "riotous mood" of the soldiers was actually their determination not to tolerate insults from whites. To acquiesce in the racial customs of Georgia was, in the opinion of most soldiers, to defeat the purpose for which they joined the volunteer army. Their hope of rising "to the full height of manhood" precluded their bowing to indignities and discrimination

35. *Augusta Chronicle,* July 16, 26, August 11, 20, 31, 1898; *Richmond Planet,* August 27, 1898.
36. *Atlanta Constitution,* November 18, 21, 23, 24, 30, December 1, 5, 1898; *Atlanta Journal,* November 16, 21, 1898; *The Telegraph* (Macon, Ga.), January 6, 7, 1899; Allen S. Peal to the Editor, March 15, 1899, in Cleveland *Gazette,* April 8, 1899.

without protest. Like the black regulars in Tampa earlier, the
Negro volunteers at Macon were in a relatively favorable position
to insist upon respect for their rights, because they were armed and
numerous enough to risk forceful action against those who attempted to enforce "the ancient, barbaric customs" of the South.
As a member of the Seventh Immunes noted, the white citizens of
Macon quickly "learned that the boys are prepared for unwanted
insults." Black civilians, too, were affected by the presence of the
Negro soldiers. They agreed that whites "treated them very good,
now that the soldiers are here," but feared what would happen
when the soldiers left. According to one elderly black resident, the
departure of the Negro troops would inaugurate an era of repression more severe than the Negro population had ever experienced
before.[37]

Nevertheless, as long as the Negro volunteers were stationed at
Camp Haskell, they continued to strike out against what they considered insults to the dignity of black people. On the day after the
arrival of the Sixth Virginia, someone pointed out to the men a
persimmon tree, known as the hanging tree, where several Negroes
had been lynched. The latest victim, Will Singleton, had been
hanged, shot up, and castrated; his testicles were placed on display in a jar of alcohol in a local white saloon. Outraged by the
existence of such a tree, the black soldiers from Virginia chopped
it down and split it into firewood. Moving on to a public park on
the outskirts of Macon, they found a sign which read: "No Dogs
and Niggers Allowed." The soldiers tore down the sign and beat
up the park-keeper when he tried to stop them. A few of the
Virginia troops, fully armed, went into the city and demanded
service in "white only" saloons and restaurants. Rounded up by
the provost guard, the soldiers were escorted back to camp, where
the entire Sixth Virginia Regiment was disarmed and placed under
arrest for twenty days. The arrest of the regiment, as well as the
presence of the white officers in the Second Battalion and the racial climate in the area, left the Sixth Virginia in a thoroughly
demoralized condition.[38]

    37. See the letters of C. W. Cordin in Gatewood, "Smoked Yankees," pp. 157–
173.
    38. Ibid.; Richmond Planet, November 26, 1898; Atlanta Constitution, Novem-
ber 21, 22, 23, 1898.

The experiences of the black volunteers who ventured outside Camp Haskell confirmed their view of Georgia as the "pest hole of the south." [39] They were appalled at the extent to which Negroes in the state were subjected to discrimination, insults, and personal abuse. Civilian policemen regularly used such terms as "coon" and "nigger" in addressing black soldiers, at least until they learned better. The black volunteers agreed that the judicial system in Georgia rested on the assumption that there was "no law here that a white man is bound to respect where our people are concerned." [40] Allen S. Peal, a black lieutenant in the Seventh Immunes, supported his claim that even in the courtroom Negroes were treated with disrespect by judicial officials; he cited the comment of the Macon city prosecutor during the trial of a black noncommissioned officer. "I am going to show a nigger soldier," the prosecutor began, "that he is the same as any other nigger." The black volunteers, especially those from the North, expressed utter disbelief in observing at first hand the horrors of the chain gang and were outraged to learn that Negro women as well as men were assigned to gangs engaged in road work. Only when the soldiers threatened to release the female prisoners were they kept out of sight in the county workhouse.[41]

No less surprising to the volunteers was the rigid segregation practiced by business establishments and on public transportation facilities. Cafes, saloons, and steam laundries refused service to Negro soldiers, even on a segregated basis. A white tailor who consented to accept their trade insisted that all business be transacted in the back of the shop. Only after the arrival of the black troops at Camp Haskell did the Consolidated Railway Company make any provisions for colored passengers on its trolleys. Trailers hitched to streetcars were "set aside for the use of colored people" when white passengers complained to the company about the pres-

39. "Ham" to the Editor, December 29, 1898, in *Richmond Planet,* January 7, 1899.

40. C. W. Cordin to H. C. Smith, January 28, 1898, in Gatewood, *"Smoked Yankees,"* p. 167. Because of the friction between Macon civil authorities and the soldiers, the white commander of the Seventh Immunes, Colonel E. A. Godwin, recommended that Camp Haskell be abandoned. See General James Wilson, Memorandum, March 8, 1899, #202298, Adjutant General's Records.

41. Allen S. Peal to the Editor, March 15, 1899, in Cleveland *Gazette,* April 8, 1899; *Richmond Planet,* December 3, 10, 24, 27, 1898.

ence of so many Negro soldiers. The soldiers' insistence upon riding in the streetcars rather than the trailers produced a series of disturbances which resulted in the death of at least three Negro volunteers. The streetcar conductor who shot and killed Private Elijah Turner of the Sixth Virginia because he refused to move out of a seat reserved for whites won a verdict of justifiable homicide and was freed. The trial, like others involving blacks and whites in Macon, convinced the Negro soldiers that the southern judicial system made a mockery of justice.[42]

While the Sixth Virginia was under arrest and therefore confined to its quarters, the local white press concentrated on what it called "the rebelling spirit" of other black units at Camp Haskell. For a time the Tenth Immunes, who were accused of creating rackets and resisting arrest by white policemen, served as the principal target; however, whites ultimately singled out the Third North Carolina, the only regiment in camp with a complete roster of Negro officers, as "the cause of all the trouble." [43] Fully aware of local sentiment, Colonel Young sought to insure that his men would not antagonize whites. For example, he implemented the advice of Major John A. Logan, Jr., a white officer whom he trusted, by severely restricting the number of soldiers allowed passes to visit Macon. But such efforts did little to combat the criticism of his regiment. In describing the Third North Carolina, the *Atlanta Journal* declared: "A tougher and more turbulent set of Negroes were probably never gotten together before." [44]

In view of such unfavorable comments regarding the regiment, a white resident of Raleigh, Charles F. Meserve, decided to investigate the state of affairs on his own and to report his findings to President McKinley. A Massachusetts native who since 1894 had served as president of Shaw University, a Negro institution in Raleigh, Meserve made an unannounced visit to Camp Haskell late in December, 1898. Following his inspection he reported to the President that sanitary conditions in the regiment were "well nigh

42. Allen S. Peal to the Editor, March 15, 1899, in Cleveland *Gazette,* April 8, 1899; *Atlanta Constitution,* November 30, December 1, 21, 23, 24, 29, 1898; *Richmond Planet,* December 24, 1893; Gatewood, *"Smoked Yankees,"* p. 153.
43. *Atlanta Constitution,* November 18, 1898; *Atlanta Journal,* November 22, 23, 1898, February 2, 1899.
44. James H. Young to John A. Logan, Jr., November 27, 1898, Third North Carolina Regimental Records; *Atlanta Journal,* February 2, 1899.

perfect" and that the spirit and discipline of the men "reflected great credit upon the Old North State." In his opinion, the excellent conditions prevailing in the Third North Carolina owed much to the qualities of leadership exhibited by Colonel Young. According to Meserve, Young practiced as a military commander the same principles of clean living that characterized his personal habits, meaning that he paid particular attention to the religious needs of his men and allowed no alcoholic beverages in the regimental canteen. In conferring with several white officers at Camp Haskell, Meserve learned that (contrary to newspaper reports) the North Carolina regiment did not have a higher rate of arrests than other regiments. Captain J. C. Gresham of the Seventh Cavalry, a native of Virginia and a West Point graduate, was especially generous in his praise of the regiment and insisted that "he had never met a more capable man than Colonel Young." [45]

Such testimonials in no way slowed the barrage of criticism directed at Negro volunteers; nor were the soldiers at Macon the only ones to acquire a reputation for having a rebelling spirit. Late in November, 1898, an incident involving Alabama's Negro regiment preempted the headlines in the southern press. Previously the Third Alabama had attracted little attention—in fact, it was generally described as a well disciplined, efficient organization, a condition credited to Colonel Bullard and his staff of white officers. Early in September the regiment was transferred from its swampy quarters in Mobile to Camp Shipp in the hill country near Anniston; there it first encountered the open hostility of whites. The white troops already at Camp Shipp were quick to express their displeasure at having Negroes enter their camp. White volunteers from Tennessee, Arkansas, and Kentucky were particularly unrestrained with their threats and insults, and white civilians did not take kindly to the presence of black troops. Unlike editors in Birmingham and Mobile who manifested a kind of paternalistic interest in Alabama's "Negro soldier experiment," the leading editor in Anniston treated them in a vein worthy of the name of his newspaper—*The Hot Blast*.[46]

45. Charles F. Meserve to William McKinley, December 24, 1898, #168007, Adjutant General's Records; see also Washington *Colored American*, February 25, 1899.
46. Bullard Diary, pp. 92–94; Birmingham *Age-Herald*, September 8, 9, 1898; Anniston *Hot Blast* quoted in Little Rock *Arkansas Democrat*, November 30, 1898.

Despite the tense atmosphere at Camp Shipp, the men of the Third Alabama continued to conduct themselves in a manner that provided little basis for criticism. Colonel Bullard retained their confidence because he took seriously their reports of abuse from whites and requested the War Department to protect them from harassment. He also publicly denied false allegations regarding his men and was prompt in passing along compliments paid the regiment by divisional and corps commanders. By mid-autumn, 1898, Bullard was convinced that the Third Alabama "was now a regiment that could be relied on, that followed and respected its officers, that bore abuse and insult with manly patience for discipline's sake." [47]

But the verbal and physical abuse suffered by the soldiers finally became intolerable. On November 24, 1898, they turned upon their tormentors in the white volunteer regiments. The "Battle of Anniston," as the affair was described in the press, left one black soldier dead, one white soldier seriously wounded, and several soldiers and civilians slightly wounded. Official reports presented conflicting versions of the specific causes, but the white officers of the Third Alabama claimed that the resort to violence by their men was prompted by accumulated grievances against the free-wheeling activities of white volunteers. The incident by no means destroyed Colonel Bullard's faith in the regiment; he still believed that the men were orderly and well disciplined and that they would perform efficiently as garrison troops in Cuba.[48]

Other white Alabamians disagreed. The disturbance at Anniston which occurred just as the press was filled with accounts of the San Luis affair, the "mutiny" of the Sixth Virginia, and various incidents involving the Third North Carolina caused many white citizens in Alabama to question whether the black volunteers should be retained in service. Editors who a few weeks earlier had bestowed praise upon Colonel Bullard's Negro soldiers now saw them only as black savages "with murder in their

47. Bullard Diary, pp. 94–95; Order No. 37, October 2, 1898, Order No. 46, November 10, 1898, Memorandum by Colonel Robert L. Bullard, December 14, 1898, Regimental Book Records of the Third Alabama Colored Infantry, Records of the Adjutant General's Office, Record Group 94, National Archives.
48. Robert L. Bullard to the Adjutant General, November 25, 1898, Third Alabama Regimental Records; *Atlanta Constitution,* November 25, 1898; *Chicago Tribune,* November 25, 1898; Mobile *Daily Register,* December 1, 1898.

hearts." Governor Johnston's rival in the Democratic party, Senator John T. Morgan, condemned what he referred to as a policy of defending the nation's honor "with members of the dependent race"—a theme which allowed him to strike at both a policy and an individual, Governor Johnston, the man responsible for the formation of the Third Alabama. "By putting guns in the hands of negroes as soldiers and making them peers of white men," the senator declared, "race conditions have been greatly aggravated." [49]

White Americans, especially Southerners, were inclined to agree with Morgan's assessment. The incidents involving black volunteers at Anniston, San Luis, and elsewhere stiffened the prejudice of whites against all black soldiers, volunteers and regulars. The degree to which Negro regulars were affected by the misconduct credited to Negro volunteers was pointed up late in November, 1898, when the War Department assigned a detachment of the Twenty-fifth Infantry to Fort Logan Roots near Little Rock. White citizens in the city protested as never before. Although these same citizens had requested troops to garrison the fort, the men of the Twenty-fifth "were not of the color desired." The *Arkansas Gazette* conceded that Negro soldiers possessed "a good record as fighters in the Cuban campaign," but maintained that experience with black volunteers had amply demonstrated that their presence at military posts in the South only intensified "racial prejudice resulting in . . . disorders." "We have enough race troubles of our own," the *Gazette* argued, "without being subjected to the annoyance of negro troops wearing the uniform of the United States soldiers." [50] The white press throughout the South rushed to the defense of the white Arkansans and claimed that if the War Department insisted upon receiving "the negro into the regular army ad infinitum," it should first make sure there were "enough army posts in the north to accommodate him." The Little Rock Board of Trade under its Jewish president led the campaign to have the order stationing black troops at Fort Roots rescinded. The Board organized protest meetings and enlisted the aid of the state's congressional delegation in pressing the

49. Birmingham *Age-Herald*, November 25, 26, 1898; Mobile *Daily Register*, November 25, 26, 1898.

50. Little Rock *Arkansas Gazette*, November 27, 28, 29, December 1, 1898; Little Rock *Arkansas Democrat*, November 28, 29, December 1, 1898.

matter at the War Department. Senator James K. Jones, a powerful figure in national Democratic circles, assured Adjutant General Corbin that Negro troops at Fort Roots would cause serious trouble because white Arkansans simply would not tolerate "negro insolence." Impressed by such arguments, Corbin rescinded his order and instead sent to Little Rock a detachment of the white Twelfth Cavalry.[51] The Negro soldiers undoubtedly were as relieved as the white Arkansans at the change in their assignment, because their wartime experience had taught them to dread assignments in the South.

The protests of Little Rock citizens dramatized the extent to which white opposition to black soldiers had solidified in the three months after the Cuban campaign. In August, when reports circulated to the effect that the black regiments from Alabama and North Carolina were scheduled for immediate muster out as a part of the War Department's plan to dismantle the volunteer army, influential individuals from those states had arranged to have them retained in service.[52] By early December, 1898, strong pressures from both civilian and military sources were being exerted to have all Negro volunteers mustered out. Prominent citizens in Alabama, assisted by Senator Morgan in Washington, urged the War Department to disband the state's black regiment even though Colonel Bullard and 456 enlisted men signed petitions requesting that they be allowed to remain in the volunteer army.[53] In the cases of the black volunteers from Virginia, Indiana, and North Carolina, the disbandment effort was largely the work of military authorities who concluded that these units no longer served a useful function, either because of the incompetence of their officers or because of their low morale. Contrary to the report on the Third North Carolina sent to President McKinley by Charles Meserve, for example, General J. C. Bates, the divisional commander, informed the War Department that most of its officers were incompetent, and that the general condition of the

51. Little Rock *Arkansas Gazette*, November 30, December 1, 1898.

52. Raleigh *News and Observer*, September 4, 1898; Mobile *Daily Register*, August 28, 1898; Bullard Diary, p. 92.

53. Bullard Diary, pp. 95–97; George P. Ide to William W. Grout, March 4, 1899, #210401, Adjutant General's Records; Fletcher, "The Negro and the United States Army," p. 252.

regiment made it unfit to be "entrusted with such delicate duties as our troops are likely to have in Cuba." Bates also recommended the immediate muster out of the Sixth Virginia because of its persistently low morale and record of misconduct.[54]

The only black volunteer outfit stationed in the South in the fall and winter of 1898 which escaped serious censure was the Ninth Ohio Battalion. Transferred from its post in Pennsylvania, the black battalion arrived at Camp Marion, South Carolina, in mid-November. The only other volunteers at this small camp were two white regiments from Pennsylvania and Connecticut. The strict discipline imposed by Major Charles Young, coupled with the relative isolation of Camp Marion, prevented any serious encounters between the black Ohioans and local whites. But the Ohio volunteers unanimously agreed that South Carolina was "the worst place we have struck yet." They were convinced that their chance for service in Cuba had been lost at Camp Meade because General W. M. Graham, who considered them his pet unit, requested that they remain as his headquarters guard when their brigade shipped out for the island. Most of them were all too willing to be mustered out in order to escape the rigorous discipline enforced by Major Young and the dreary existence of their "wretched camp" in "the southern backwoods."[55]

Unlike the black Ohioans, Negro troops from North Carolina had reason for wanting to remain in service. Conditions in their state (in the wake of the Democrats' successful white supremacy campaign and the Wilmington race riot) scarcely promised them a heroes' welcome. Late in December, when Colonel Young heard rumors that his regiment was to be mustered out, he immediately enlisted the support of Senator Jeter C. Pritchard and Congressman George H. White in an effort to have the muster-out order delayed until April, 1899. "If the President desires to muster us

54. J. C. Bates to the Adjutant General, November 22, 1898, #168007, Adjutant General's Records. Colonel Croxton of the Sixth Virginia confided to a friend: "I doubt if they send any more negro troops to Cuba anyhow. They have either to be kept practically as prisoners or else they raise thunder." See R. C. Croxton to Francis R. Lassiter, January 2, 1899, Francis R. Lassiter Papers, Duke University Library, Durham, N.C.

55. Wilson Ballard, "Outline History of the Ninth (Separate) Battalion, Ohio Volunteer Infantry," in Steward, *Colored Regulars*, p. 297; Special Order No. 3, November 9, 1898, Ninth Ohio Battalion Records; Cleveland *Gazette*, November 19, 1898; Columbia *State*, November 24, 1898; *Augusta Chronicle*, January 30, 1899.

out because our services are not needed that is one matter," Young telegraphed White, "but if it is because of charges intimated in the press, then we are entitled to and demand a hearing." [56] Young finally journeyed to Washington to plead the case of his regiment in person. In the meantime one of his captains, James E. Hamlin, himself a prominent black Republican, called upon Senator Mark Hanna to use his influence in postponing the muster out of the regiment. In a letter to Hanna he explained why the black North Carolinians desired to remain in military service until April:

> Every officer in the regiment from colonel down has some promi-
> nence in the state; they are men of character, filling positions of
> trust . . . and that naturally prejudices the democrats against us
> and I really believe that if we go to our respective homes just now
> during the sitting of the [Democratic] legislature, they would enact
> even worse laws than now anticipated. Our very presence on the
> streets of the different cities would simply inflame them against the
> entire race.[57]

Several days earlier Charles Meserve assured President McKinley that the colored citizens of North Carolina had reason to feel despondent "just now," and that the muster out of the black volunteers could only worsen their situation. Despite such entreaties, the War Department proceeded with its dismantling of the volunteer army and in January, 1899, the Third North Carolina was mustered out, along with other regiments, black and white.[58]

Until official orders for their muster out were received, almost all black volunteers continued to operate on the assumption that they would ultimately be sent to Cuba. Even the men of the Third North Carolina and Sixth Virginia were expecting assignments in the island as late as December. Despite the proliferation of rumors about duty in Cuba, there was little basis for believing that more black volunteers would be sent there, least of all the Virginia and North Carolina troops. In the previous month General James H. Wilson had secured War Department approval for re-

56. James H. Young to George White, January ?, 1899, #190118, Jeter C. Pritchard to H. C. Corbin, December 26, 1898, #168007, Adjutant General's Records.

57. James E. Hamlin to Mark Hanna, January 5, 1899, #190118, ibid.

58. Charles Meserve to William McKinley, December 24, 1898, #168007, Jeter C. Pritchard to H. C. Corbin, January 9, 1899, #182215, H. C. Corbin to George H. White, January 13, 1899, #190118, ibid.

moving all Negro volunteers from his division before it sailed for Cuba. The general believed not only that "as a class" the men of the Sixth Virginia and Third North Carolina were "entirely unfit for foreign service," but also that the people of Cuba deserved more consideration and respect than to have black volunteers placed in their midst.[59]

When muster-out orders arrived during January and February, 1899, the loudest protests came from the Eighth Immunes at Chickamauga Park, who claimed that "all along this regiment has been promised a time in Cuba." Describing the Eighth as "the best disciplined, best drilled, best behaved and healthiest black regiment in service," one soldier claimed that its muster out could only be viewed as "discrimination against all black troops." Ten Negro lieutenants of the regiment urged Senator Hanna to intercede in their behalf. In their opinion the "discharge of colored troops in the immune regiments because of colored officers [lieutenants]" could well mean "the muster out of republican power in nearly every northern state." [60]

Such efforts were in vain. During the first three months of 1899 all Negro volunteers, including the three regiments in Cuba, were paid and discharged from military service. Both before and after the soldiers at Camp Haskell and Chickamauga Park boarded trains for home, they took advantage of one last opportunity to retaliate against those whites whom they considered responsible for their troubles. Merchants from Macon brought wagons loaded with all kinds of merchandise to Camp Haskell in an effort to entice the soldiers to spend their muster-out pay. Much to the consternation of the merchants, the black soldiers refused to purchase a single item, but they did wreck several of the wagons. En route home the Third North Carolina and Eighth and Tenth Immunes were accused of terrorizing the countryside by shooting wildly from the trains.[61] In Atlanta the police boarded the train carrying

59. *Richmond Planet,* December 17, 1898; Indianapolis *World,* December 10, 17, 31, 1898; James Wilson to the Adjutant General, November 30, 1898, #168007, H. C. Corbin to J. H. Wilson, December 9, 1898, #168007, Adjutant General's Records.

60. Felix to Mark A. Hanna, Thomas Clarke *et al.* to M. A. Hanna, George Henderson to M. A. Hanna, February 3, 1899, #293324, Adjutant General's Records.

61. *Richmond Planet,* January 21, 1899; Macon *Telegraph,* January 26, 27, 1899; Lt. Col. Charles Withrow to Assistant Secretary of War, March 14, 1899, #202298, Adjutant General's Records.

the North Carolina troops, presumably to arrest the ringleader of the disturbance. While making their search, they engaged in "so much clubbing" that when the train pulled out of Atlanta for Raleigh it contained "many bloody heads." [62] Even more serious was the encounter between the Eighth Immunes and a mob of whites led by policemen at the railway station in Nashville. At a subsequent investigation, despite testimony by whites and blacks describing the affair as a "wanton assault" on the Negro soldiers, the federal attorney in charge concluded that "no offense against the Federal Statutes" had been committed. He believed that "the rough handling of the negroes" had been necessary to prevent "more serious trouble." [63]

The white officers of the Eighth Immunes and other Negro regiments vigorously protested what they described as unprovoked assaults upon their men. Because the soldiers were discharged from the volunteer army before leaving Macon and Chattanooga, the War Department claimed that it was powerless to protect them. Nevertheless, white officers who themselves were sometimes ostracized for holding commissions in black regiments made certain that the department was fully apprised of the "rough handling" of the Negro volunteers by whites as they traveled home. Colonel Charles Withrow of the Tenth Immunes described in detail the attack which a mob of militiamen, policemen, and citizens made upon the train carrying his regiment as it pulled out of the station in Griffin, Georgia. According to Colonel E. A. Godwin of the Seventh Immunes, the attack on his men following their discharge was merely the climax to a succession of incidents growing out of "the friction between civil authorities and enlisted men" which had existed ever since his arrival at Macon the previous fall. Because of this friction, Godwin recommended that Camp Haskell be closed at once and that all troops under orders to report to the post be assigned elsewhere. No white officer was more openly critical of the treatment of black soldiers at the Macon camp than Captain Amos Brandt of the Seventh Immunes. Upon his return

62. Macon *Telegraph*, February 1, 2, 3, 1899; *Atlanta Constitution*, February 1, 2, 3, 4, 1899.
63. The voluminous papers relating to the investigation of the Nashville incident are found in the Adjutant General's Records under file #209169. For the report by the federal attorney in charge of the investigation, see A. M. Tillman to John W. Griggs, August 7, 1899, #209169, Adjutant General's Records.

home to Des Moines, he declared in a public address that his regiment "was treated shamefully" throughout its stay at Camp Haskell. Black soldiers were insulted, cursed, and tried "before an unjust bar." "Georgia is as black as hell," Brandt concluded, "and Macon a trifle worse." [64]

Because of the "rough handling" accorded other black volunteers en route home, the black citizens of Louisiana feared for the safety of the Ninth Immunes who were mustered out in Pennsylvania upon their return from Cuba. In a petition to the War Department these citizens requested that the regiment be transported to New Orleans by water rather than by rail. "Our husbands, fathers, brothers and sons are loyal to the flag," their petition concluded, "and we desire to have them to live to fight and die for their country in its hour of peril from its foes, but we solemnly protest against having their lives spared only that they may become a target and be killed by their own countrymen." [65] Although the Ninth Immunes returned to Louisiana by rail, they escaped any of the unfortunate experiences of other black soldiers.

Except for those units from Illinois, Ohio, and Indiana, the return of black volunteers to their homes was accompanied by little of the fanfare that greeted white soldiers. The Twenty-third Kansas was virtually ignored by the new Republican administration in Topeka. The arrival of the Eighth Illinois, though marked by parades and banquets, was marred by a rising tide of protest among black citizens over Governor Tanner's treatment of Negro miners during strikes at Pana and Virden.[66] In North Carolina and Virginia the Democratic legislatures recognized the black volunteers only by their negative actions—both states eliminated Negroes from the militia.[67] The same legislature in North Carolina, bent upon consigning the black colonel of the Third North Carolina Regiment to oblivion, passed a resolution directing that the

64. Lt. Col. Charles Withrow to Assistant Secretary of War, March 14, 1899, General James Wilson, Memorandum, March 8, 1899, #202298, *ibid.* For Brandt's speech, see Des Moines *Iowa State Bystander,* March 3, 1899.
65. Paul Bruce *et al.* to the Secretary of War, May ?, 1899, #234974, Adjutant General's Records.
66. *Chicago Tribune,* March 19, 1899; Springfield *Illinois Record,* March 25, April 1, 1899.
67. *Annual Report of the Adjutant General of North Carolina, 1899,* p. 75; Johnson, *Colored Volunteer Infantry of Virginia,* p. 96.

name of James H. Young be removed from the cornerstone of the new school for the deaf, dumb, and blind—the institution which Young had promoted as a legislator and as a member of its board of trustees.[68] This gesture aptly symbolized the fate of Negroes not only in North Carolina and the South, but also in the rest of the nation.

68. *Union Republican* (Winston, N.C.), January 12, 19, 1899.

Seven

Kinsmen of Cuba?

The color line is being fastly drawn here [Cuba] and the Cubans abused as Negroes.

—H. C. C. Astwood, August, 1898

By the autumn of 1898, the vision of empire had clearly captivated a sizable segment of the American public. During the ten months between the outbreak of hostilities and the ratification of the peace treaty early in 1899, the old themes of mission and destiny assumed a new relevance as the idea of "an imperialism of righteousness" won widespread public acceptance. Convinced that "the march of human events rules and overrules human action," [1] President William McKinley maintained that the nation could not escape the responsibilities imposed upon it by the fortunes of war and a wise deity. On July 7, 1898, while Shafter's army stood before Santiago and Dewey's fleet dominated Manila Bay, the President signed the congressional resolution by which Hawaii was annexed to the United States.[2] The implications of this precedent for acquiring overseas territories became clear with the defeat of the Spanish forces in Cuba. The preliminary peace protocol, signed on August 12, 1898, not only stipulated that Spain relinquish all sovereignty over Cuba, but also provided for the cession of Puerto Rico and Guam to the United States and for American possession of Manila pending the final disposition of the Philippine Islands at the subsequent peace conference. In the final

---

1. H. Wayne Morgan, *America's Road to Empire: The War with Spain and Overseas Expansion* (New York: John Wiley and Sons, 1965), p. 91; Foster R. Dulles, *America's Rise to World Power, 1898–1954* (New York: Harper and Row, 1963), pp. 48–50.

2. See Thomas A. Bailey, "The United States and Hawaii during the Spanish-American War," *American Historical Review*, XXXVI (April, 1931), 552–560.

treaty, signed in December, 1898, Spain reluctantly parted with the Philippines, technically as a war indemnity, for twenty million dollars. On February 6, 1899, the Senate approved the treaty by a margin of one vote.[3]

Like other Americans, black citizens followed these developments with keen interest. The imperialistic direction of national policy continued to prompt a wide variety of reactions in the black community, ranging from enthusiastic approval to bitter condemnation. Although the war in Cuba and the efforts of black men to gain equitable treatment in the volunteer army dominated their concerns in the summer of 1898, the annexation of Hawaii and the Philippine Question by no means escaped their attention. And whether they supported or opposed the acquisition of the Hawaiian Islands, they recognized it as an act of far-reaching significance. The anti-imperialist editor John Mitchell inveighed against annexation in an editorial entitled "The Rape of the Islands." For him, "the jingle and the possession of dollars" had made American leaders "impervious to reason" and blind to the nation's traditional principles.[4] Other opponents of Hawaiian annexation, emphasizing the racial affinity between themselves and the dark-skinned islanders, suggested that the Hawaiians would soon be subjected to the same treatment as Negroes in Louisiana and Mississippi. "Before the black natives of the Hawaiian Islands will have been subjects of America twelve months," Monroe Dorsey predicted, "many of them will wish the infernal regions to open and receive them rather than bear the torments, persecutions and abuses." [5]

Those Negroes who favored the annexation of Hawaii usually spoke in terms of its benefits to black Americans. Some argued that the black man more than any other should encourage the acquisition of such tropical islands because there he could have "a brighter outlook . . . climatically, industrially and socially." [6] As usual, the most eloquent spokesman for the expansionist view-

3. Morgan, *America's Road to Empire*, pp. 80–81, 98–99, 109–110.

4. *Richmond Planet*, August 27, 1898; see also Springfield *Illinois Record*, June 25, 1898; Indianapolis *Freeman*, July 9, 1898.

5. *Denver Statesman* quoted in Topeka *Colored Citizen*, July 14, 1898; *Parsons Weekly Blade*, December 10, 1898.

6. Coffeyville *American*, October 29, 1898; see also *The Radical* (St. Joseph, Mo.), quoted in the Milwaukee *Wisconsin Weekly Advocate*, October 14, 1898.

point was Edward E. Cooper of the *Colored American,* whose opinions often echoed the official rhetoric of the McKinley administration. Cooper greeted the annexation of Hawaii with unabashed enthusiasm. "Hawaii is ours," he exclaimed. "The wolf cry of imperialism cannot keep us in swaddling clothes forever. Expansion is the natural order of things in nations as well as individuals. Hawaii is the best subject to start with upon a new and broader policy." Cooper maintained that America's superior ideas of government imposed upon the nation a responsibility to see that these ideas "should obtain upon every inch of soil that we can get within our grasp." Even though " 'imperialism' may have an imposing sound," he assured his readers, there was not "a thing in it that will work harm to the colored American." Indeed, the planting of the American flag in Hawaii, Puerto Rico, and other islands promised only a brighter future for black people in the United States.[7]

In defending the positive contributions of expansionism to the welfare of Negro citizens, Cooper cited the changes in the nature of American government which such a policy would inevitably produce. He argued that control of the "turbulent and revolutionary inhabitants" of the territories that would come under the jurisdiction of the United States would necessitate a strengthening of the federal government. The centralization of power in Washington would, in turn, eliminate "the absurdities surrounding our idea of state sovereignty" which heretofore had been used to obstruct effective action by the federal government in preventing "lynchings, confiscation of property, unlawful restriction of suffrage and arbitrary conviction for alleged crimes." With the destruction of state rights and the pernicious influence exerted by the political "oligarchies of the South," Cooper envisioned the coming of a full measure of justice for black Americans under the aegis of a powerful federal government. In his opinion, such a prospect was sufficient reason for Negro citizens to give their full support to McKinley and his policy of imperialism.[8]

Few black Americans shared Cooper's enthusiasm for the Republicans' "new and broader policy." Even those most critical of

7. Washington *Colored American,* July 16, 30, 1898.
8. *Ibid.,* September 3, 1898.

the motives which prompted Senator Benjamin Tillman [9] and other Southern Democrats to oppose such a policy were seldom free of misgivings about the implications of an imperialistic program. Their anxiety bred a succession of ambivalent and contradictory responses. An extreme example was provided by J. L. Thompson, a black Republican editor in Des Moines, who in one breath opposed the acquisition of any territory which did not border on the United States or which had to be conquered or purchased and in another proclaimed: "We should not seek expansion . . . yet when . . . it becomes necessary to acquire territory for the progress of humanity and for the welfare of the nation . . . we should do so." Fred L. Jeltz of the *Kansas State Ledger* in Topeka feared that once "this territorial aggrandizement" began, it would be "pushed to the limit." Convinced that efforts to redirect national policy would be futile, Jeltz resigned himself "to the fact that America has outgrown the Monroe Doctrine and started in the competitive colonial scheme." [10] Underlying many of the reservations expressed by black editors was their persistent belief that "charity begins at home," coupled with the anticipated effects of expansion upon both Negro Americans and the dark-skinned natives of the lands likely to come under American jurisdiction. John H. Deveaux of the *Savannah Tribune* admitted that the more he pondered the expansionist policy, the more misgivings he had about it. Since only those white Americans interested in amassing wealth quickly would take up residence in Hawaii, Cuba, Puerto Rico, and the Philippines, the natives of these islands would be subjected to "severer tests of servitude than ever." But more important would be the impact of their behavior regarding the rights of colonial colored peoples upon race relations in the United States. Deveaux was certain that their example would inspire Anglo-Saxons at home to accelerate their oppression of Negro citizens. [11]

In the closing months of 1898, as the peace negotiators in Paris

9. Senator Tillman declared: "I am opposed to the annexation of anything. . . . We have enough negro troubles of our own without annexing more from Cuba." See Columbia *State*, August 9, 1898.

10. Des Moines *Iowa State Bystander*, September 23, 1898; Topeka *Kansas State Ledger*, July 23, 1898.

11. Savannah *Tribune*, July 9, 1898.

struggled to work out a final settlement, Negro Americans manifested a greater interest in the fate of Cuba than in the final disposition of the Philippines. They were particularly disturbed by
friction between the American military commanders and the Cuban insurgent leaders which flared into the open following the
surrender of Santiago.[12] American soldiers made little effort to
hide their contempt for their Cuban allies, claiming that they
would neither fight nor work. One white officer, in referring to
the insurgents, said he would not "give one Virginia nigger for a
score of them." [13] Some white soldiers expressed both dismay and
regret that so many of the rebel forces in Cuba were Negroes.
James K. Vardaman of Mississippi, a captain in a volunteer outfit
stationed on the island, wrote home from Santiago: "Here the
nigger is one of the few 'large pebbles on the beach.' He leads
the choir, commands the armies, is prominent in business circles,
and in many other ways 'cuts quite a figure.' I cannot say just
how long he will hold this prominence—not longer, I dare say,
than the Americans get hold of the offices." [14] Black Americans
came to believe that Vardaman's forecast was all too plausible, especially in view of the public assertions of General Shafter and
others that Cubans were "no more fit for self-government than
gun-powder is for hell." Their anxiety about the future of Cuba
became even more acute as a result of the growing clamor within
the United States for the annexation of the island.[15] Black citizens
in a dozen cities in the North and midwest staged mass meetings
to protest any U.S. effort to renege on its promise to help Cuba
establish itself as an independent republic. Negro Americans overwhelmingly endorsed the idea of an independent Cuban government in which blacks would be as prominent as they had been in
the war of liberation. A black republic in Cuba would not only
add luster to the reputation of the sons of Africa, the argument
ran, but would also provide a convenient refuge for black citizens

    12. For a description of the friction between the American military authorities
and the Cubans, see Healy, *United States in Cuba*, pp. 33–38; *Richmond Planet*,
July 23, 30, August 20, 1898; "General Garcia and Cuban Conduct," *Literary Digest*,
XVII (July 30, 1898), 121–123.
    13. *Washington Bee*, July 30, 1898.
    14. Letter in *The Commonwealth* (Greenwood, Miss.), April 14, 1899.
    15. Healy, *United States in Cuba*, p. 36; Walter Millis, *Martial Spirit*, pp. 361–
364.

in the United States who wished to escape the oppressive racial climate in the South.[16]

In the fall of 1898 Negro Americans feared that all their hopes regarding a Cuba Libre were in jeopardy. In their view race was the basic cause of the friction between the American military forces and the "dark-hued rebels." "The whole trouble in Cuba between Shafter and [Calixto] Garcia," Monroe Dorsey observed, "is the American stumbling block, the Negro. There are just a few more black soldiers in the Cuban ranks than Shafter cares to deal with and recognize as men." According to Calvin Chase of the *Washington Bee,* it was race prejudice, "pure and simple," which prompted white Americans to treat the vanquished Spaniards with more consideration and respect than their own comrades in arms.[17] The Kansas City *American Citizen* also condemned the War Department for drawing the color line against the armies of Garcia and Gomez, claiming that the "fear of Negro dominancy in Cuba" was the force behind a movement to circumvent the Teller Amendment and annex the island. Even Edward E. Cooper warned the McKinley administration against any attempt to violate its moral and legal obligations regarding Cuban independence.[18] Unlike Cooper, who had faith in McKinley's ability to withstand pressures to deny Cuba the full fruits of its long struggle for freedom, John Mitchell believed that the future of the "dark-skinned inhabitants of the island" promised little relief from their miserable existence. He predicted that whether Cuba became an independent republic or an American colony, wealthy Spanish residents and white Americans would exercise control over it in a way that would discriminate against Afro-Cubans. The disagreements between Garcia and Shafter, he claimed, merely confirmed his earlier prophecy that men of color in Cuba would be worse off under American rule than they had been under the Spanish monarchy.[19]

Despite the gloomy outlook of Mitchell and a few other black

16. *Richmond Planet,* December 17, 1898; see also Springfield *Illinois Record,* January 14, 1899; Indianapolis *Recorder,* January 14, 1899.
17. *Parsons Weekly Blade,* August 20, 1898; *Washington Bee,* July 30, 1898.
18. Kansas City *American Citizen,* September 23, 1898; Washington *Colored American,* August 6, September 17, 1898.
19. *Richmond Planet,* August 20, 1898.

observers, Negro Americans in general continued to express admiration for the courageous stand of their Cuban kinsmen against Spanish oppression. Calvin Chase was convinced that Afro-Cubans would greet American race prejudice with the same kind of manly resistance that had characterized their opposition to Spanish tyranny. Like other black Americans, he maintained that the War Department operated on the erroneous assumption that Negroes in Cuba were no different from those in the United States when in fact there was "a great deal of difference." In Chase's view the Afro-Cuban was "brave, bold and intelligent," while the Afro-American was "intelligent but submissive"—a condition he credited to the "so-called race leaders," especially Booker T. Washington. He suggested that Washington should depart at once for Cuba, as he could be "spared with ease" by black Americans, and possibly Afro-Cubans could teach him how to become bold enough to voice the highest aspirations of his people.[20]

Edward E. Cooper, always anxious to justify the policy of expansionism in terms of its benefits to Negro Americans, constructed an elaborate rationale based on the differences between blacks in Cuba and the United States. The "interjection of the Cuban and Puerto Rican problems" in the life of the nation would produce "an altered basis of calculation" concerning Negro Americans. In explaining how such problems would affect black citizens, he wrote:

> A new system of government is a probability and millions of black people will be deeply interested. Comparisons between the Cuban Negro and the American Negro will be instituted. The relative treatment will be watched and the effect noted. The Cuban Negro has not been trained to submission and obedience of his American brother and will imbibe our idea of civilization very slowly if the idea means degradation and segregation. The resistance our foster brethren are sure to make to all forms of tyranny may stir the latent manhood of the people here and lead to a revolt against a system of oppression that has been long but impatiently endured.[21]

20. *Washington Bee*, August 27, 1898. For a white man's analysis of Afro-Cubans, see Robert L. Bullard, "The Cuban Negro," *North American Review*, CLXXXIV (March 15, 1907), 623–630.
21. Washington *Colored American*, September 3, 1898.

Cooper, then, took the view that the future of Negro Americans was inextricably linked to the future of the colored people in Cuba in a way that was certain to operate to the advantage of the former. On one hand, any attempt to perpetuate a racist regime in Cuba would encounter resistance from Afro-Cubans whose example would inspire emulation by Afro-Americans. On the other hand, the establishment of a socio-political order in Cuba based on justice rather than color without alterations in the Jim Crow society at home was no less likely to prompt revolt by black Americans to win "as generous treatment and as full degree of protection as that accorded the inhabitants of Cuba and Puerto Rico." Despite his professed faith in McKinley's promise to give blacks and mulattoes in Cuba an equal chance, Cooper nonetheless warned whites that the outcome of the race problem in the United States depended in large measure upon the kind of civil and political code they established in Cuba.[22]

Whether black Americans accepted or rejected Cooper's rationale, they were likely to agree with his contention that Afro-Cubans were a proud, defiant people unwilling to tolerate any form of tyranny. In fact, the idea of Cuba as a black man's paradise retained its popularity among Negro Americans, perhaps understandably in view of the increasing incidence of racial violence and legalized discrimination in the United States. Even so virulent a negrophobe as James K. Vardaman admitted that blacks in Cuba enjoyed greater opportunities than colored Americans. ". . . if I was a nigger," Vardaman wrote from Santiago, "I would most assuredly move to Cuba. Here he has civil rights galore and no man dares say him nay."[23] John W. Cromwell, a prominent black attorney and writer, depicted Cuba as a country in which blacks and whites lived "on terms of perfect equality" and suggested that the island "could teach America one lesson, that of fraternity of races." Booker T. Washington, while conceding that the Cubans had "certain elements of weakness," nonetheless agreed that they had "surpassed the United States in solving the race problem in that they have no race problem."[24] Accord-

22. *Ibid.*, August 27, September 3, 1898.
23. Quoted in Greenwood *Commonwealth*, April 14, 1899.
24. Washington *Colored American*, November 2, 1898; *Nashville American*, April 16, 1899; see also Bullard, "The Cuban Negro," 626.

ing to a black editor in Des Moines, Cuba not only offered the black American an opportunity "to be a man," but also provided him "an equal chance as a planter or in some business pursuit." Furthermore, blacks in the United States generally espoused the notion that they were better adapted to tropical climates than white men and therefore could "bring out the rich soil of Cuba with better results." [25]

Since the Negro was a material factor in the population of Cuba, black Americans argued that they should be assigned an important role in the reconstruction of the island. In addition to the military function which they hoped Negro troops would perform in Cuba, black citizens desired to make their presence known there in civilian capacities, either as civil servants attached to the American military government or in the fields of religion and education. Although their agitation for the appointment of black men to positions in the military government produced negligible results,[26] Negro churches in the United States did succeed in establishing missions among their colored cousins there. In the summer of 1898 the African Methodist Episcopal Church took the initiative in this missionary effort by dispatching H. C. C. Astwood to Santiago as its representative. A clergyman, editor, and former consul to the Dominican Republic who spoke fluent Spanish, Astwood traveled to Cuba in August, 1898, with the Eighth Illinois Volunteers and claimed to have established the first Protestant church in Santiago "and possibly on the island." He was later joined by black missionaries representing the National Baptist Convention and the African Methodist Episcopal Zion Church. The latter denomination also sent representatives to Puerto Rico.[27]

While religious organizations were engaged in missionary activities, black American educators proposed various schemes for educating Afro-Cubans. Booker T. Washington suggested that the American government bring Afro-Cuban students to the United States for industrial education at Tuskegee Institute. Washington's idea was that the Tuskegee curriculum would provide the

25. Des Moines *Iowa State Bystander,* September 23, 1898.
26. Washington *Colored American,* July 30, November 2, 1898, April 6, 1901.
27. Washington *Colored American,* July 30, 1898; Baltimore *Ledger,* August 13, September 17, October 1, 1898; Indianapolis *Freeman,* September 17, 1898; Goode, "*Eighth Illinois,*" p. 145; Springfield *Illinois Record,* August 20, 1898.

students with the skills needed to aid in the material reconstruction of their homeland. Kelly Miller of Howard University supplemented Washington's proposal with the recommendation that those Cuban students interested in "the non-industrial aspects of education" be allowed to enter Howard. Washington's plan triggered a debate between those with widely different views regarding the appropriate type of education for Negroes, but the idea of educating black Cubans in the United States, whether under an industrial or classical curriculum, engendered little enthusiasm. Both the *Colored American* and the *Washington Post,* for example, preferred that the government send to Cuba "a selection of Negro graduates to do the instructing there." One reason the *Post* objected to proposals for bringing Afro-Cubans to the United States for study was its belief that Cuban Negroes, "having only been trained for fighting," would have an undesirable effect upon their American cousins.[28]

Despite such opposition, promising Cubans were brought to the United States for study in various educational institutions. The Cuban Educational Association of the United States, organized by General Joseph Wheeler, Nicholas Murray Butler, and other prominent men, provided much of the impetus for the movement. The avowed aim of the association was to inculcate bright young Cubans with American ideals so that they, as the future leaders of their nation, would become "beacon lights to create a stable pacific government in the Antilles." But even before the organization of the Cuban Educational Association, Booker T. Washington was busy recruiting students among the Cuban refugees in Florida. Ultimately he arranged with American officials in Cuba and Puerto Rico to have students from those islands attend Tuskegee Institute at government expense. The experience was not an altogether happy one for either Washington or his school. Cultural and language differences posed certain obvious problems; but more important, the islanders displayed "a very ugly spirit" and reacted so violently to the strict regimen at Tuskegee that the institution had to construct a guardhouse. Their pen-

28. Washington *Colored American,* August 27, 1898; Booker T. Washington, "Industrial Education for Cuban Negroes," *Christian Register,* LVIII (August 18, 1898), 924–925; *Washington Post* quoted in Columbia *State,* August 25, 1898.

chant for rebellion occasionally inspired restlessness and discontent among other Tuskegee students. Ironically, whatever success Washington had in reeducating the Cubans and Puerto Ricans under his tutelage was in academic rather than industrial work. If the *Washington Post* was aware of Tuskegee's troubles with the dark-skinned "colonials," it undoubtedly felt justified in opposing schemes for bringing colored islanders to the United States for education.[29]

In view of the prevailing image of Cuba as a black man's paradise and the deteriorating racial climate in the United States, Negro Americans manifested far greater interest in the question of emigration to the island than in any proposals for educating Cuban students in American institutions. Ever since the outbreak of the Spanish-American War there had been frequent references to the opportunities awaiting black citizens in Cuba, Hawaii, and other islands; however, according to one black observer, it was the wave of negrophobia in 1898–99 which started afresh the agitation for Negro emigration. Whatever the cause of the agitation, by 1899 the question of emigration had become the subject of lively debate between those blacks who considered the idea pure balderdash and those who favored large-scale emigration to Cuba or Puerto Rico as the most feasible means of escaping the atmosphere in the United States. Although black spokesmen displayed a wide diversity of views regarding the question, an overwhelming majority opposed any scheme which envisioned a mass exodus sponsored by the federal government—in short, any scheme which smacked of expulsion or deportation. At its organizational meeting in mid-September, 1898, the Afro-American Council took note of the interest in emigration and recognized that special facilities existed in Cuba for the "rapid development and substantial success of plans and purposes prosecuted by colored Americans." The council recommended that black citizens make "an intelligent

29. Gilbert K. Harroun, "The Cuban Educational Association of the United States," *Review of Reviews*, XX (September, 1899), 334–335; *New York Times*, December 8, 1898, June 12, 1899; W. J. Barnett to Booker T. Washington, September 23, 1898, Thomas J. Calloway to Booker T. Washington, October 9, 1898, Thomas Austin to Booker T. Washington, November 8, 1898, Washington Papers; Harlan, *Booker T. Washington*, pp. 283–284; Foner, *Spanish-Cuban-American War*, II, 463–464.

survey of the field" and act promptly "in taking front place with other Americans who shall seek fortune in that new territory." [30] But the well-known black clergyman John E. White of Georgia declared as wholly unworkable all solutions to the Negro Problem which involved "the deportation of the Negro race in any sizeable quantities." The Negro, he argued, was an American with every right to live in the United States and destined to remain in the country of his birth. Another prominent black Georgian, C. T. Walker, formerly a chaplain in the volunteer army stationed in Cuba, also opposed mass migration and recommended that Negroes follow the example of whites by emigrating "where we please and when we please." [31]

For a time the possibility of Negro Americans settling in Cuba had the endorsement of certain whites. The *Savannah Morning News*, for instance, claimed that the South "could spare a good many [Negroes] without feeling their loss seriously." The leading white daily in Columbia, South Carolina, whose editor Narsico Gonzales was a Cuban emigré, noted that a free Cuba would be a beginning toward fulfilling the "creole dream of empire" in the Caribbean and suggested that one of the unexpected dividends of the war with Spain might well be the solution of the race problem in the United States, since Cuba would be opened up as a "field of emigration" for black Americans.[32] The *Army and Navy Journal* agreed that Cuba was "the ideal home of the negro." It also predicted that the liberation of the island would aid "in the settlement of the so-called negro problem" by attracting black citizens from the United States who would serve as agents to Americanize Afro-Cubans. The paper encouraged black Americans to

30. Tokepa *Colored Citizen*, May 5, 1898; Springfield *Illinois Record*, May 21, 1898; Savannah *Tribune*, August 27, 1898; Washington *Colored American*, November 26, 1898; Indianapolis *Recorder*, May 7, 1899. On the action of the Afro-American Council, see Alexander Walters, *My Life and Work* (New York: Fleming Revell, 1917), p. 109.

31. Baltimore *Ledger*, December 31, 1898, June 17, 1899. The Indianapolis *Recorder* (May 7, 1899) maintained: "We cannot escape the white man's prejudices by emigrating to these new territories. As long as that prejudice is prevalent at home it will be felt abroad."

32. Savannah *Morning News*, November 15, December 17, 1898; Columbia *State*, May 28, August 25, 1898; *Leslie's Weekly* quoted in Indianapolis *Recorder*, February 18, 1899.

prepare for immediate emigration in order to take advantage of the existing demand for labor there. The editor of the *Journal* wrote:

> From the congested centers of the negro population in Louisiana, Mississippi, South Carolina and other states, we may safely assume that swarms of colored men will flock to Cuba, greatly to their own advantage and no less to that of the regions they are leaving. These negroes may not be the pick of the race, but if well treated they will make useful field hands. They are familiar with American ways and methods. They will speak English, at least the negro version of it, and the ideas and responsibilities of American citizenship which a third of a century has taught them, though still crude and imperfect, will be a decided advance upon those now current among the Cuban workmen of their race.[33]

Such sentiment had little in common with Negroes' views on the question of emigration.

Black Americans who espoused the cause of emigration invariably did so for reasons other than going to Cuba to become "useful field hands." They did not wish to leave familiar surroundings for a strange land merely for the sake of substituting one depressed condition for another; rather, they intended to escape "the daily grind and chafe and insult" to which they were subjected in the United States. In short, they desired to "breathe free air" and seek economic advancement in a country which, in their opinion, granted to blacks every privilege "enjoyed by people of any other color." [34] During their brief tour of duty in Cuba, Negro American soldiers contributed significantly to the utopian image of the island by their glowing accounts of the economic opportunities there. A typical account was provided by W. C. Warmsley, a black physician and army surgeon who urged his friends in the United States to emigrate to Cuba: "The businessman (colored) of Santiago say they would like to have one million colored men of education from the States." He insisted that black American physicians and teachers of English could easily amass fortunes on the island. Conceding that white Cubans were "prejudiced against the jet

33. *Army and Navy Journal*, June 11, 1898, p. 809.

34. John S. Durham, "Confessions of a Man Who Did," *Southern Workman*, XXVIII (May, 1899), 168–172; Des Moines *Iowa State Bystander*, September 23, 1898.

blacks," Warmsley argued that "their prejudice, unlike the American article, is not so bitter." [35]

Despite such reports, most black spokesmen remained skeptical of any mass exodus of Negro Americans to Cuba and insisted that only those who possessed capital or particular skills should consider taking up residence there. John S. Durham, a well-known Negro lawyer in Philadelphia and a former minister to Haiti, whose advice was sought by numerous blacks "considering taking their chances in Cuba," encouraged emigration for those who "have capital for investment or are without family and want adventure." [36] The ideal type to "grasp the expansion spirit and open the gates that lead to higher possibilities" was T. McCants Stewart, a black New York attorney who announced his intention to move his family to Hawaii.[37] But most Negro leaders repeatedly warned poor, unskilled black men that their plight in Cuba would be worse than that in the United States because they would be unable to compete successfully with native labor. Durham and Edward E. Cooper both favored selective emigration; nevertheless, they reminded black Americans that "the higher duty consists of manfully facing home conditions" and in striving to achieve "industrial independence" in the land of their birth. In 1906, however, Durham himself moved to Cuba to become manager of a sugar plantation in the province of Camagüey.[38]

To an extraordinary degree the agitation for large-scale black emigration to Cuba centered in Kansas. As one observer noted, the same people who had been part of the 1879 exodus of Negroes from the South to Kansas were now the most ardent advocates of emigration to Cuba. He concluded that they had "found the land

35. W. C. Warmsley to G. W. Jackson, May 19, 1899, reprinted in Gatewood, "Smoked Yankees," pp. 231–232.

36. Durham, "Confessions of a Man Who Did," pp. 68–70.

37. Washington Colored American, November 26, 1898. Thomas McCants Stewart, born in Charleston, S.C., in 1852 and educated at Howard University, the University of South Carolina, and Princeton Theological Seminary, moved to Liberia in 1883; however, after two years he returned to the United States and became a lawyer and influential black Democrat in New York. After residing for a time in Honolulu, he returned to Liberia in 1906 and became a justice on the Supreme Court of that country.

38. Durham, "Confessions of a Man Who Did," pp. 68–72; Washington Colored American, August 13, November 26, 1898; Indianapolis Freeman, March 24, 1906, November 9, 1907.

of John Brown inhospitable." [39] Although black Kansans were not subjected to as much legalized discrimination as Negroes in some other states, their condition scarcely warranted robust optimism. Whatever the reasons for the prominence of the emigration issue in Kansas, it received a thorough airing among black citizens in the state.[40] The Negro press (especially the Topeka *Colored Citizen* and the Coffeyville *American*) championed the idea, claiming that emigration to Cuba was the only opportunity for the black man to escape the assaults upon his dignity and manhood. Both subscribed to the view that "the treatment of the colored man among the Latin races everywhere has ever been more humane and equitable . . . than among the Anglo-Saxon or Teutonic races." As early as mid-June, 1898, the *Colored Citizen* reported that young black men in Kansas, impressed by the business opportunities open to them in Cuba, were busy studying the Spanish language so as to be prepared to embark for the island as soon as the war was over. By the following autumn the *American* was predicting that over half the members of Kansas's black regiment stationed at San Luis would not return to the United States but would remain in Cuba to take advantage of their opportunities in a society where color was not a stamp of inferiority.[41] Its prediction proved wholly inaccurate, but at least one officer of the regiment (Captain John L. Waller, who earlier in the decade had attracted national attention because of his controversial activities in Madagascar) remained in Cuba and encouraged other black Americans to join him.

In fact, Waller became one of the most eloquent spokesmen for the cause of emigration. Convinced that lynching and other forms of racial violence would ultimately annihilate Negroes if they remained in the United States, he urged them to come to Cuba, where they would "prosper and enjoy the ballot." He emphasized that the land was fertile and could be leased or purchased cheaply. To succeed in Cuba, emigrants ought to possess "nerve, determination, an independent spirit, $300 or $400, and a good team [of

39. Savannah *Morning News*, November 15, 1898.

40. See Marie Deacon, "Kansas as the 'Promised Land': The View of the Black Press, 1890–1900" (M.A. thesis, University of Arkansas, 1972).

41. Topeka *Colored Citizen*, May 26, June 16, 1898; Coffeyville *American*, November 5, 1898.

horses]." Emigrants should "burn their bridges behind them" in the United States and "come to stay." Waller assured black Americans that their presence on the island would be welcomed by the natives despite "the efforts of some white men high in station to discourage it." He thought "the kindly treatment accorded the distressed Cubans" by the black soldiers during their tour of duty had established "a friendship between the American colored people and the Cubans" that would "always make the former welcome." Since Waller believed that the emigration of two or three million black Americans would promote the material advancement of Cuba and contribute to the solution of the race problem in the United States, he urged Congress to appropriate $20,000,000 to help Negroes emigrate to Puerto Rico and the Philippines as well as Cuba. According to his calculation, such an appropriation would be "paid back into the treasury of the United States in the way of revenue and duties on exports in less than five years." With considerable fanfare, in mid-1899 Waller announced the organization of the Afro-American Cuban Emigration Society to promote his scheme. The society was scheduled to begin operations by the end of the year. Despite an impassioned plea for prominent black men in every state to support the project, the reaction of such men was considerably less than enthusiastic.[42]

Black editors were inclined to compare Waller's proposal with Bishop Turner's dreams of an African empire presided over by Negro Americans. As spokesmen for the black middle class, the editors usually thought that Waller, no less than Turner, was "talking through his hat." [43] But if they had been forced to make a choice, they probably would have agreed with George L. Knox of the Indianapolis *Freeman* in maintaining that Cuba was far preferable to Africa. Not only were the soil and climate of Cuba conducive to the prosperity of black men, according to Knox, but its people were also "kindly disposed toward Negroes" and undisturbed by "the question of amalgamation." Furthermore, emigration to Cuba was less expensive than the long journey to Africa

42. For a lengthy letter from Waller, see Indianapolis *Recorder*, July 8, 1899; see also Kansas City *American Citizen*, November 24, 1899, September 7, 1900; Gatewood, "Kansas Negroes and the Spanish-American War," 312.

43. *Atlanta Appeal* quoted in *Richmond Planet*, January 14, 1899; Indianapolis *Recorder*, July 8, 1899; Indianapolis *Freeman*, July 8, 1899.

which promised only "a dreary, backward existence." Despite his preference for Cuba, Knox refused to endorse Waller's or any other plan for mass emigration.[44]

The most grandiose emigration scheme originating in Kansas was one proposed by W. L. Grant, an influential Baptist minister in Topeka who had long manifested an interest in what he called "our 200,000 kinsmen in Cuba." Convinced that Negroes could never receive justice in the United States, he petitioned Congressman Charles Curtis and Senator L. C. Baker, both of Kansas, to sponsor a bill appropriating $100,000,000 for the purpose of settling 2,000,000 black Americans in Cuba, Puerto Rico, Hawaii, and Africa. The inclusion of Africa was obviously an attempt to broaden support for his project, especially among the adherents of Bishop Turner's back-to-Africa movement. Despite the endorsement of the executive board of the Negro Baptist Convention in Kansas, the scheme won little support in Congress or from middle-class blacks. T. Thomas Fortune accused Grant of pursuing a dream which was as futile as it was impractical. The solution to the race problem in the United States, according to Fortune, lay not in dumping black citizens abroad but in the formula suggested by Booker T. Washington. The failure of Grant's proposal was perhaps predictable in view of the fate of similar requests for federal assistance made earlier by Turner.[45]

Less amibitious than the projects of either Waller or Grant was the plan by John T. Vaney, another black Topeka clergyman who early in November, 1898, announced his intention to establish a colony of Negro Americans near Santiago. Vaney claimed that the time appeared propitious for fulfilling his long-cherished hope of establishing such a colony. Like others, he believed that the climate and soil of Cuba held great promise for the material success of black Americans and that the island would provide respite from the social ostracism which they suffered in the United States. There is, however, no evidence to indicate that Vaney ever arrived in Cuba with the twenty or thirty families who were to form the nucleus of his colony; he probably abandoned the project

44. Indianapolis *Freeman,* July 8, 1899.
45. Topeka *Kansas State Ledger,* December 12, 1898; *Parsons Weekly Blade,* December 24, 1898; Savannah *Morning News,* December 17, 1898; Springfield *Illinois Record,* March 18, 1899.

in view of the hostile response which its announcement elicited among Cubans, both black and white.[46]

Although black Americans often referred to the differences between themselves and Afro-Cubans, they were scarcely prepared for the Cuban reaction to their various emigration schemes. Some Cubans predicted "a race war should many negroes come from the United States." A well-known Santiago editor, in explaining the differences between men of color in the United States and Cuba, left no doubt that the Afro-Cuban considered himself superior to the "yankee negro": "It is simply that Cubans are a superior race who have the right to protect themselves from contamination." Perplexed by reports that "Cuban negroes are even more bitter than whites in denouncing the [emigration] movement," [47] black Americans refused to accept the explanation of whites who credited such animosity to the presence of Negro volunteers in Cuba on the grounds that their behavior alienated all Cubans regardless of color. At first Negro spokesmen either classified reports of Afro-Cuban hostility toward their American kinsmen as false, or held white Americans responsible for fomenting prejudice against them in order to eliminate any competition in the exploitation of the island.[48]

Whatever the validity of the latter charge, it was an undeniable fact that Cubans responded unfavorably to the prospect of a sizable influx of black Americans. Perhaps the most plausible explanation of this hostility was offered by Major John R. Lynch, the black Mississippian appointed army paymaster by President McKinley. During his three-year tour of duty in Cuba, Lynch found that nationality rather than race was the preeminent concern of colored people there and that they looked out "for what they believed to be the interest of Cuba and the Cubans." Therefore, "they had no sympathetic feeling for the colored American on account of race, for they have no race issue there such as we have in the States." Lynch declared: "As against the colored

46. *New York Daily Tribune,* November 13, 1898; *New York Evening Post* quoted in Columbia *State,* November 29, 1898; Savannah *Morning News,* November 15, 1898; Washington *Colored American,* December 3, 1898.

47. Savannah *Tribune,* November 26, 1898; Mobile *Daily Register,* November 19, 1898; Indianapolis *Recorder,* August 12, 1899.

48. Topeka *Kansas State Ledger,* January 12, 1899; Indianapolis *Recorder,* July 8, 1899.

American and the white Cuban, the colored Cuban was for the white Cuban. As against the colored Cuban and the white American, the white Cuban was for the colored Cuban. With the Cubans, white and black, it was not a question of race or color, but of country." [49]

Lyman Beecher Bluitt, a member of the Eighth Illinois Volunteers who remained in Santiago after the muster out of his regiment, fully corroborated Lynch's observations. After residing on the island for two years, Bluitt concluded that any Afro-American sympathy for or racial identity with colored Cubans was "greatly misplaced and proven by contact with them to be neither desired nor appreciated." The "clannishness of the Cubans" amounted to "a hostility toward Americans" which was "in no wise modified toward the American Negro." A failure to appreciate that nationalism counted for more than racial considerations with all Cubans, black as well as white, meant that those black Americans who settled in Cuba were without exception "disappointed in their expectations and eager for an opportunity to return to the United States." [50]

In spite of such discouraging reports, individual Negroes continued to emigrate to Cuba; apparently some prospered sufficiently to remain there permanently. As late as mid-1901, a black missionary in Santiago was still issuing appeals for black citizens to take advantage of the cheap land available in Cuba. David Massey, a paving contractor who had settled there, described the island as a virtual El Dorado for black businessmen. Another Negro American reported from Santiago late in 1899 that no matter how bad things were for his race in Cuba, they were infinitely better than conditions in the South.[51] All the while advertisements in the black press claimed that the "Gem of the Antilles" offered "the best opportunities upon this hemisphere" for Negro Americans who possessed "not less than $400" and a willingness to work. One

49. Lynch, *Reminiscences of an Active Life,* pp. 440–441, 448.

50. Lyman Beecher Bluitt in Washington *Colored American,* February 24, 1900. For a similar observation made early in 1899 by C. W. Cordin, a black Ohioan and former member of the Seventh Immune Regiment who traveled extensively in Cuba after being mustered out, see Cleveland *Gazette,* April 1, 1899. On the difficulties of R. M. R. Nelson, a Negro American civilian employed in the Quartermaster Department in Cuba, see Indianapolis *Freeman,* October 7, 1899.

51. Washington *Colored American,* May 5, 1900, August 24, 1901.

advertisement proclaimed: "Sugar offers an opportunity to make $5000 per annum for eight years after two years of hard labor." Those who desired to better their condition by going to Cuba were invited to send thirty cents to John E. Bruce or Edward E. Cooper for full details.[52] It is perhaps impossible to ascertain how many black Americans responded to such publicity by moving to Cuba, but clearly there was no migration of the dimensions envisioned by Waller and Grant. In fact, by the time Waller's Afro-American Cuban Emigration Society was scheduled to begin operations late in 1899, whatever enthusiasm black Americans had manifested for the scheme had cooled considerably.

Several factors were responsible for the decline of interest in Cuban emigration. The possession of "not less than $400" as a prerequisite for success largely eliminated lower-class blacks, the segment of the Negro population most likely to embrace the emigration idea. No less important was the conservative approach of middle-class blacks. Opposed to any mass exodus, they recognized that the type of individual likely to succeed in Cuba was precisely the one which the black community in the United States could least afford to lose; likewise, as the Indianapolis *Recorder* observed, "the colored men who would be the most desirable emigrant" were those most unlikely to emigrate.[53] Although middle-class Negro citizens had fewer reasons for wanting to leave the United States, their lack of enthusiasm for emigration to Cuba was also prompted by a belief that race prejudice had accompanied the establishment of the American military regime in Cuba and that blacks would have little more opportunity for achieving "the full height of manhood" than in the United States. Finally, by mid-1899 the interest of black citizens and other Americans had been diverted from Cuba to the Philippines, where a new war had erupted. In time the attention of emigrationists shifted from the Caribbean to the Pacific.

Even though few black Americans emigrated to the Caribbean and even fewer remained there permanently, they continued to manifest interest in the affairs of the islands under American

---

52. *Ibid.*, July 29, 1899, February 17, 1900; see also William S. Sweetser, "Opportunities for Stock-Raising in Cuba and Puerto Rico," *Southern Workman*, XXIX (July, 1900), 407–413.

53. Indianapolis *Recorder*, July 8, 1899.

control. Black citizens believed that the United States was "trying to read Porto Rico out of the benefits of the constitution" [54] and became increasingly suspicious of American motives concerning Cuba. Many expressed concern that the McKinley administration would disregard the Teller Resolution and ultimately annex the island. The Cleveland *Gazette* condemned "the delay upon the part of our government in securing to the people of that isle the great boon they contended for so many years, and at so great a sacrifice of life, money and property." Others suggested that the experience of black Americans, with all their unfulfilled promises from the American government, was to be repeated in Cuba.[55] H. C. C. Astwood reported from Santiago that as soon as white Americans "found out . . . the majority of Cubans are Negroes," they no longer desired "to have Cuban independence." [56] A black editor in Kansas predicted that those who were "foolish enough to believe that the United States interfered in Cuba" because of "Spanish inhumanity to the Cubans" would ultimately realize that the motive was actually "greed of gain." The Indianapolis *Recorder* regretted that the veteran Cuban patriots were "still blind to the handwriting on the wall." [57] In a similar vein Chris J. Perry, a prominent Philadelphia Negro, expressed fear that Cuba would learn too late that its scourge was not to be scorpions but something far more deadly—Americans who would thwart the goal of Cuban independence "by alleging a desire to teach her people self-government." According to Perry, the performance of the United States regarding the island only proved that "the Anglo-Saxon begins with you by an appeal to heaven to witness his innocence and honesty and ends by 'stealing your spoons.' " For black anti-imperialists like John Mitchell, the Platt Amendment in 1901 was nothing more than a contrivance to thwart the Cubans' aspirations for a sovereign republic.[58]

54. Indianapolis *Freeman*, March 10, 1899.
55. Cleveland *Gazette*, March 10, 1899; *Parsons Weekly Blade*, January 21, 1899; Salt Lake City *Broad Ax*, January 14, 1899; Washington *Colored American*, January 21, 1899.
56. Quoted in *Voice of Missions*, VI (October 1, 1898), 2.
57. *Parsons Weekly Blade*, January 21, 1899; Indianapolis *Recorder*, March 4, 1899.
58. Salt Lake City *Broad Ax*, January 14, 1899; *Richmond Planet*, June 8, 1901; Indianapolis *Freeman*, April 20, 1901.

The aspect of the American military regime in Cuba upon which black Americans lavished most of their attention concerned its racial policies. The prevailing view was that the military authorities had introduced prejudice into a society where racial relations had previously been harmonious, a view shared by the *New York Evening Post* and a few other white anti-imperialist journals. In the fall of 1899 the black press in the United States reported that the colored people of Cuba "were clamoring for recognition." "It seems," George L. Knox observed, "that it is about the same fight that had been on in the United States in the last score of years, only the colored Cubans are more aggressive." [59] T. Thomas Fortune held white Americans responsible for the unrest among Afro-Cubans, claiming that the black men of the island resented the discriminatory practices of the military regime. "There was not race distinction, as we know it," Fortune concluded, "before the Americans carried it there." [60] As early as August, 1898, H. C. C. Astwood, the black missionary in Santiago, reported: "The color line is being fastly drawn here and the Cubans abused as Negroes." A year later a report that a Cuban had been lynched near Havana prompted John Mitchell to conclude that American occupation of the island had been "followed by American atrocities." The *Kansas City Star*, a leading white daily in the midwest, agreed that the establishment of "the American color line in Cuba" would place "most influential men and families in the island . . . under 'the ban of blood.' " [61]

During the next two years other black Americans in Cuba confirmed Astwood's views, indicating that the color line had be-

59. See Healy, *United States in Cuba*, p. 61; Indianapolis *Recorder*, February 18, 1899; *Washington Bee*, March 4, 1899; Indianapolis *Freeman*, September 9, 1899.

60. *New York Age* quoted in Kansas City *American Citizen*, May 14, 1900; see also John E. Bruce ("Bruce Grit") in Washington *Colored American*, April 29, 1899. An incident cited by Negro Americans as evidence that the color line had been introduced in Cuba concerned Washington's Cafe, a restaurant in Havana owned by three white Americans and operated for whites only. The refusal of the proprietors to serve a mulatto general in the Cuban insurgent army because of his color attracted much attention among blacks in the United States. For a discussion of this celebrated incident, see *Parsons Weekly Blade*, March 11, 1899; Baltimore *Ledger*, November 25, 1899; Lynk, *Black Troopers*, p. 124.

61. *Voice of Missions*, VI (October 1, 1898), 2; *Richmond Planet*, October 7, 1899; *Kansas City Star* quoted in Coffeyville *American*, March 11, 1899. See also a letter from J. E. Greenlease, steward at the headquarters of the American commander in Havana, to J. H. Downes, in Washington *Colored American*, December 16, 1899.

come increasingly rigid under the administration of General Leonard Wood, the American military governor of the island. Early in 1901 a Negro American living in Santiago reported:

> Already the damnable serpent of American race hatred is palpably insinuating . . . [itself] into all insular affairs. . . . There would be today a wide field for colored stenographers, typewriters, civil engineers and horsemen if it were not for this hydra-headed monster . . . but I regret to say there is not one. The departments employing men of the above professions are controlled by two or three Negro-hating southern democrats of very low birth and breeding who will permit no one except the Cuban and a few Spaniards to hold positions higher than that of stableman. . . .[62]

Nor did General Wood himself escape censure. Black Americans condemned his order barring colored Cubans from the artillery organization and held him responsible for suffrage regulations during the municipal elections of 1900 which they described as worthy of the most prejudiced politicians in Mississippi and Louisiana.[63] However, the Cleveland editor and politician Harry Smith reminded those so critical of Wood that the ultimate responsibility for drawing the color line in Cuba lay with the general's superior, President McKinley, who was manifesting the same disregard for the rights of black Cubans that characterized his attitude toward the disfranchisement of black Americans.[64] The Kansas City *American Citizen* announced in mid-1900 that colored Cubans were "sick of the color line" imposed by American military authorities, citing as evidence their demand that such descriptive words as black, brown, and colored be eliminated from all official documents.[65]

Although Negroes in the United States applauded Cuban resistance to racial discrimination, their attitude toward Cuba had undergone a substantial change by the autumn of 1901. References to the island as "the black man's paradise" had virtually dis-

62. Quoted in Washington *Colored American,* March 30, 1901. See also a statement by R. W. Kimball, who had recently returned from Cuba, in *New York Daily Tribune,* March 2, 1903.

63. *Washington Bee,* January 13, 1900; Topeka *Colored Citizen,* June 29, 1900; Cleveland *Gazette,* August 31, September 7, 1901; *New York Daily Tribune,* August 26, 1901.

64. Cleveland *Gazette,* August 31, 1901.

65. Kansas City *American Citizen,* May 25, 1900.

appeared. That the concept of a Cuba Libre retained little of its original symbolic meaning for black Americans was evident in their unenthusiastic response to the official establishment of the Cuban Republic in 1902. For them the new republic, modeled after the United States, had incorporated the bad as well as the good features of the American system; in the words of T. Thomas Fortune, it promised to make "our priceless principles" the "priceless curse" of dark-skinned Cubans.[66] The failure of the colored party to occupy a position of power in the Cuban Republic was interpreted as evidence that the racial legacy of the American military regime was indeed to be perpetuated upon the island. Clearly those who had anticipated the emergence of another black republic in the Caribbean had grossly miscalculated.[67]

But even more important in explaining the disillusionment which came to characterize the attitude of colored Americans toward the Cuban enterprise was their failure to benefit from it. Their preeminent concern had always focused upon the oppressed condition of black people in the United States—a condition which they had hoped to alleviate by participating in a war to free Cuba. Ever since the outbreak of the Cuban revolution, Negroes in the United States had identified the cause of a Cuba Libre with the cause of justice for colored peoples, themselves as well as Afro-Cubans. But rather than arresting the deterioration of their status at home, their display of patriotism and sacrifices on the battlefield appeared to have intensified prejudice against them. Edward A. Johnson, an alderman and prominent black educator in Raleigh, stated categorically in 1899 that "the mob spirit is growing—prejudice is more intense." He insisted that it was no longer confined to the white rabble; rather, "now it has taken hold of those of education and standing." [68] Between the end of the war

66. *New York Age* quoted *ibid.*, May 4, 1900. See also Indianapolis *Freeman*, May 24, 1902; Washington *Colored American*, May 24, 1902.

67. Cleveland *Gazette*, July 5, 1902. In 1906, when the Cuban government placed restrictions upon Chinese and West Indian Negro immigrants, a black American editor remarked: "If there was ever a people that should sympathize with the oppressed Negro, it should be the Cuban, for only eight years ago the Negro shed his blood to help free that people from the dreadful tyranny of Spain. The painful thorn has been pulled out of the lion's paw and that same paw has wielded an awful slap at one of its main liberators. Cuba, too, is to be a white man's country." See "Cuban Immigration," *Alexander's Magazine* II (August 15, 1906), 14.

68. Johnson, *Negro Soldiers in the Spanish-American War*, p. 220.

and the official transfer of sovereignty to the Cuban Republic in 1902 three states (North Carolina, Virginia, and Alabama) disfranchised their black citizens. Certainly the rich harvest envisioned by black imperialists such as Edward E. Cooper had failed to materialize. In addition, the opposition with which Afro-Cubans greeted emigration schemes impressed upon all Negro Americans, whether or not they favored emigration, the validity of Lyman Bluitt's observation that their kinsmen in Cuba neither appreciated nor desired their sympathy.

The growing disillusionment within the black community resulted in the revival of the theme which actually never disappeared in all the discussion of Cuba: namely, the idea that charity begins at home. It reemerged dramatically in 1902 when Congress began discussing the Cuban tariff reciprocity. Although a lower tariff on Cuban sugar might benefit the colored people of the island, black Americans were concerned with their own interest and therefore opposed any reciprocity arrangement which would be detrimental to the sugar plantations of Louisiana—"an industry carried on by the brawn and muscle of Negro labor." In view of all the assistance which Americans had given Cuba, according to a black editor in New Orleans, it was high time that the people of the island made some sacrifices themselves.[69] Although black opponents of Cuban reciprocity railed against the sugar trust as the prime beneficiary of such a treaty, their concern was clearly the welfare of blacks in Louisiana. George L. Knox of the Indianapolis *Freeman* claimed that in Louisiana, where legal disfranchisement had already been enacted, the economic blow that would be dealt by Cuban reciprocity would render the black people of the state utterly helpless.[70] Like other black Americans who were convinced that welfare of black citizens took precedence over that of the island, by 1902 Knox had substantially altered his views of Cuba, suggesting that the "Cubans' future would be safer and more glorious by being a part of our commonwealth of states rather than

69. *National Advocate* (New Orleans) quoted in Indianapolis *Freeman*, March 15, 1902; Washington *Colored American*, December 13, 1902; see also Rubin Weston, *Racism in U.S. Imperialism: The Influence of Racial Assumptions on American Foreign Policy, 1893–1946* (Columbia: University of South Carolina Press, 1972), pp. 162–170.
70. Indianapolis *Freeman*, March 1, 22, 29, 1902.

an uncertain, unstable republic." [71] Even though few Negroes went that far in abandoning the cause of Cuba Libre, the metamorphosis which occurred in Knox's thought was not actually so different from that which other black Americans had experienced.

71. *Ibid.*, May 11, 1902; Washington *Colored American*, December 13, 1902.

Eight

A Swell of Anti-Imperialism

It is a sorry, though true, fact that wherever this government controls, injustice to the dark race prevails. The people of Cuba, Porto Rico, Hawaii and Manila know it as well as do the wronged Indian and outraged black man in the United States.

—Lewis H. Douglass, December, 1899

By the time President William McKinley submitted the Treaty of Paris to the Senate on January 4, 1899, the policy of overseas expansion had become the target of severe criticism by a relatively small though highly articulate group of white citizens. The acquisition of the Philippine Islands, provided by the treaty, served as a focus for their opposition. Individuals of diverse political affiliations and socioeconomic backgrounds—wealthy businessmen, mugwumpish editors and intellectuals, labor leaders, politicians, race-baiting Southerners, and humanitarians—spoke out against McKinley's expansionist program. An organized anti-imperialist movement launched in Boston in June, 1898, spawned a succession of anti-imperialist leagues which waged vigorous propaganda campaigns against the ratification of the treaty.[1]

Even before the signing of the document on December 10, 1898, several resolutions which sought either to restrict the acquisition of territory or to limit retention of the Philippines by the United States had set off a fierce verbal battle in the Senate. One of these, introduced by Senator George C. Vest of Missouri, maintained that "under the Constitution . . . no power is given to the Federal Government to acquire territory to be held and governed permanently as colonies." Like the Vest resolution, anti-expansionist

1. Fred H. Harrington, "The Anti-Imperialist Movement in the United States, 1898–1900," *Mississippi Valley Historical Review,* XXII (September, 1935), 211–230.

measures by Senators Augustus O. Bacon of Georgia and Stephen Donaleson McEnery of Louisiana also went down to defeat. Nor was the eloquence of Senator George Hoar, a Massachusetts Republican, sufficient to block Senate ratification of the treaty. But the triumph of the expansionists involved more than the skill of administration spokesmen and the use of presidential patronage at critical junctures in the deliberations of the treaty.[2] Events in Manila also operated to their advantage.

For several years prior to the arrival of Admiral George Dewey in Manila Bay in April, 1898, a group of Filipinos had been in rebellion against Spanish rule. At first the rebels hailed the Americans as their deliverers from Spanish tyranny, but they gradually came to understand that the American promise of a free Cuba did not imply a free Philippine republic. On orders from President McKinley and the War Department, American military forces in the Philippines avoided any actions which might intimate recognition of rebel authority or Philippine independence. On January 5, 1899, the rebel leader Emilio Aguinaldo proclaimed himself head of the Philippine Republic and indicated his determination to resist his new American masters as vigorously as he had the Spaniards. A month later, on the night of February 4, 1899, the growing tension between Aguinaldo's forces and American troops erupted in open fighting which signalled the beginning of a protracted and bloody guerrilla war. The timing of the clash—two days before the final Senate vote on the Treaty of Paris—was important; the unfavorable reaction which it provoked in the United States against the Filipinos strengthened the hands of those senators bent upon ratifying the treaty and thereby bringing the archipelago under American jurisdiction.[3]

The issues raised by the treaty and by the outbreak of the so-called Filipino Insurrection were matters of concern to most Americans, but it is difficult to imagine that any other segment of the population devoted more attention to the implications of the ex-

2. Morgan, *America's Road to Empire*, pp. 105–109; Lala Carr Steelman, "Senator Augustus O. Bacon, Champion of Philippine Independence," in Joseph F. Steelman, ed., *Essays in Southern History* (Greenville, N.C.: Department of History, East Carolina College, 1965), pp. 92–97.

3. Garel A. Grunder and William E. Livezey, *The Philippines and the United States* (Norman: University of Oklahoma Press, 1951), pp. 52–55.

pansionist policy than Negro citizens. Beginning early in 1899 the discussion of expansionism reached a new level of intensity within the black community. The topic occupied a prominent if not preeminent place in the columns of black journals and produced numerous pronouncements and resolutions by gatherings of Negro citizens. The black press placed so much emphasis upon the nation's "imperialistic programme" that some Negroes feared that other questions "of more vital interest to the race" were being neglected. "Why don't our Negro weeklies give us more editorials on race matters and let the Philippines and other international questions be discussed in the dailies. . . ?" [4] a Negro journalist asked early in 1900. For most black Americans, however, the acquisition of the Philippines was indeed a race matter, one with important ramifications for themselves as well as for the colored inhabitants of the islands.

In many respects their approach to the Filipinos' struggle was similar to that which they took toward the Cuban rebellion. As was the case in their view of Cubans, color was of crucial importance in determining attitudes toward the Filipinos. Even though their claims of racial kinship with the dark-skinned natives of the Philippines could scarcely be taken literally, black citizens in the United States did identify racially with the Filipinos, whom they called "our kinsmen" and "our colored cousins." No less important was the sympathy which they displayed toward the Filipinos' strivings for freedom, often interpreting the insurrection in the Philippines as but one phase of the larger struggle of all colored people to escape Anglo-Saxon oppression. Fully aware of the similarity between the predicament of the black man in America and the brown man in the Philippines, black Americans could never quite rid themselves of doubts and misgivings about a policy which called upon them to take up arms against a people with whom they had racial and ideological ties. Their doubts and misgivings gave rise to a highly vocal opposition to "McKinley imperialism."

Whether he favored or opposed expansionism, the white American was also likely to interpret the issue in racial terms; however, his approach bore little resemblance to that of the black citizen.

4. *Afro-American Advance* (St. Paul), February 10, 1900.

Even though racial considerations may not have been a dominant factor in the initial imperialist impulse, racial ideas came to occupy a prominent place in attitudes of whites toward overseas expansion. After America's bid for world power was already well underway, a racialist rationale emerged to serve the new imperialism. Contributing to the popularity and plausibility of such a rationale was the fact that it fitted so well the paternalist or accommodationist approach of whites toward their black countrymen.[5] Studies of white anti-imperialists indicate that with few exceptions they, like their adversaries, "thought of peoples in the categories of racism" and subscribed to the notion of racial inequality.[6] Because black Americans recognized that racism pervaded the thoughts of whites, imperialists and anti-imperialists alike, they could never become wholly reconciled to the arguments postulated by either.

The reaction of blacks to Rudyard Kipling's poem, "The White Man's Burden," first published in the United States in February, 1899, indicated the degree to which they took exception to the imperialist rationale. Kipling described the "white man's burden" in terms of the Anglo-Saxon's duty to serve the needs of the "new-caught, sullen peoples, half-devil and half-child" who inhabited the lands coming under the influence of Western civilization. Governor Theodore Roosevelt of New York classified Kipling's verse as "poor poetry but good sense from the expansionist standpoint." His friend, Senator Henry Cabot Lodge, disagreed only to the extent that he thought it better poetry than Roosevelt did. Although the phrase "white man's burden" acquired a more benevolent, humanitarian meaning in the hands of white apologists for American expansionism than Kipling's poem contained,[7] black citizens were quick to denounce the whole concept as "sham and hypocrisy."

5. Frederickson, *Black Image in the White Mind*, pp. 305–309.

6. Robert L. Beisner, *Twelve against Empire: The Anti-Imperialists, 1898–1900* (New York: McGraw Hill, 1968), pp. 232–233; Christopher Lasch, "The Anti-Imperialists, the Philippines and the Inequality of Man," *Journal of Southern History*, XXIV (August, 1958), 319–331; Richard E. Welch, "Motives and Policy Objectives of the Anti-Imperialists, 1898," *Mid-America*, LI (April, 1969), 119–129; Philip W. Kennedy, "Race and American Expansion in Cuba and Puerto Rico, 1895–1905," *Journal of Black Studies*, I (March, 1971), 306–316.

7. Dulles, *America's Rise to World Power*, p. 48n; Grunder and Livezey, *Philippines and the United States*, p. 49; Frederickson, *Black Image in the White Mind*, p. 308.

Black reaction was so violent that George L. Knox observed in March, 1899, that "the air is filled with replies to the 'white man's burden.' " [8]

Dozens of poems entitled "The Black Man's Burden" appeared in the months immediately following the publication of Kipling's work. The basic theme of most of these poems was contained in a piece by H. T. Johnson, a well-known black clergyman and editor of the influential *Christian Recorder:*

> Pile on the Black Man's Burden.
>   'Tis nearest at your door;
> Why heed long bleeding Cuba,
>   or dark Hawaii's shore?
> Hail ye your fearless armies,
>   Which menace feeble folks
> Who fight with clubs and arrows
>   and brook your rifle's smoke.
>
> Pile on the Black Man's Burden
>   His wail with laughter drown
> You've sealed the Red Man's problem,
>   And will take up the Brown,
> In vain ye seek to end it,
>   With bullets, blood or death
> Better by far defend it
>   With honor's holy breath.[9]

The title of Johnson's poem proved a popular and durable motif, the subject not only of verse but also of essays, editorials, orations, debates, and sermons. Late in 1899 J. H. Magee of Chicago organized the Black Man's Burden Association for the purpose of dramatizing the plight of Negroes in the United States and of depicting the treatment of the brown people in the Philippines as an extension of the government's domestic policy toward its own black citizens.[10]

The idea of the "white man's burden" became the target of especially severe criticism by Negro editors, including some who had previously been friendly to expansion. According to the Indianap-

8. Indianapolis *Freeman,* March 11, 1899.
9. *Voice of Missions,* VII (April, 1899), 1.
10. Washington *Colored American,* January 27, February 10, 1900.

olis *Recorder,* for example, events in the Philippines indicated that white Americans were disposing of their "burden" in the islands in the same manner which had "proven so effective with the North American Indians." In a similar vein, Calvin Chase of the *Washington Bee* argued that the race prejudice of white Americans precluded the success of their efforts to Christianize and civilize nonwhites. The real burden, he concluded, belonged not to the white man but to the colored man whose advancement was always "encumbered by the prejudice and opposition" of Anglo-Saxons.[11] Other Negro Americans viewed the "outburst of Anglo-Saxonism" as pernicious and "full of mischief" for all colored peoples, both at home and in the distant islands under American control. A black correspondent in the Savannah *Tribune* defined the "white man's burden" merely as "an imperialistic cry" to justify the desire of white men to "oppress weaker races and rob them of the rights and liberties God has given them."[12]

Some editors, echoing the old theme "charity begins at home," suggested that if white Americans had a duty or responsibility toward their colored brothers, it existed not in the Pacific but in the United States among black citizens who still awaited the fulfillment of promises of justice and liberty. John Mitchell of the *Richmond Planet,* as ardently opposed to expansion as ever, characterized all the talk of "white man's burden" as a rhetorical subterfuge for the conquest and murder of the feeble, dark-skinned people in the Philippines. High-sounding phrases could not obscure the fact that the United States was committing acts in the islands which could not be "defended either in moral or international law." Mitchell argued that the most promising field for missionary service was in the South among whites, rather than among the liberty-loving Filipinos. "With the government acquiescing in the oppression and butchery of a dark race in this country and the enslaving and slaughtering of a dark race in the Philippines," he concluded, "we think it time to call all missionaries home and have them work on our own people."[13] Although Edward E. Cooper of the *Colored American* rarely agreed with the editor of the *Planet*

11. Indianapolis *Recorder,* March 4, 1899; *Washington Bee,* March 11, 1899.
12. Savannah *Tribune,* March 18, 1899.
13. *Richmond Planet,* February 18, March 4, 1899.

on questions related to expansion, his response to the white man's burden concept was remarkably similar to Mitchell's. Dismissing the notion as "a lot of sickly sentimentality," Cooper maintained that "it is the black man's burden that cries out to heaven." "The white man has few burdens that are not self-imposed," he concluded, "while the black man has few that are not imposed upon him by the tyranny of unavoidable conditions." [14]

From the moment when Admiral George Dewey sailed into Manila Bay in 1898, black Americans had followed events in the Philippines with considerable interest. Although the war in Cuba and issues related to the island's postwar development dominated their concerns until early 1899, their references to the Philippines usually revealed little support for American annexation of the islands and widespread sympathy for the cause represented by Aguinaldo.[15] Even those who supported an expansionist policy favored either a temporary protectorate or the acquisition of a single coaling station. But virtually every black American endorsed the idea of ultimate autonomy for the Filipinos.[16]

Shortly after Dewey's arrival in Manila Bay, a few Negro editors began to talk of the Philippines as an excellent field for Negro colonization. Proposals for emigration to the islands came to be linked with similar schemes for settling black Americans in Cuba; for a time they prompted heated debate.[17] In the meantime, blacks also began to notice the "growing feeling of ill-will between American troops and the insurgents." Aguinaldo quickly assumed the status of a hero among black citizens who by mid-1898 began to refer to him as "kinsman" and to applaud his "spunk." The image of the Filipino leader was not only that of a bold colored leader, but also of one manfully holding his own against the whites who were oppressing colored people in the United States.[18]

14. Washington *Colored American*, March 4, 1899.

15. See Baltimore *Ledger*, April 30, 1898; Omaha *Afro-American Sentinel*, May 7, 1898; Topeka *Colored Citizen*, May 5, 1898; Milwaukee *Wisconsin Weekly Advocate*, May 11, 21, 1898; Coffeyville *American*, May 28, July 23, 1898; Des Moines *Iowa State Bystander*, September 23, 1898; Washington *Colored American*, July 30, November 12, 1898.

16. Indianapolis *Freeman*, September 17, 1898.

17. Topeka *Colored Citizen*, May 5, 12, 1898; Milwaukee *Wisconsin Weekly Advocate*, May 21, 1898; Coffeyville *American*, May 28, 1898; Springfield *Illinois Record*, May 21, 1898.

18. *Richmond Planet*, July 23, 30, August 20, 1898; *Parsons Weekly Blade*, August 23, 1898.

Clearly, when Booker T. Washington opposed annexation of the islands, he approached the issue within a racial context: "My opinion is that the Philippine Islands should be given an opportunity to govern themselves. They will make mistakes but will learn from their errors. Until our nation has settled the Negro and Indian problems I do not believe that we have a right to assume more social problems." [19] Washington's friend and loyal supporter George L. Knox of Indianapolis also viewed the Philippine question in terms of race, but his argument against American annexation was more characteristic of Benjamin Tillman than of a black anti-imperialist like John Mitchell. In mid-1898 Knox declared that the Philippines were undesirable for acquisition because the "natives, half-breeds and Spaniards" would "be always restless and discontented no matter how modern or enlightened" they became. The Filipinos could never be assimilated into the American system and therefore should be given "a wide berth." [20] Knox's attitude is all the more noteworthy in view of the fact that by early 1899 he had become an ardent champion of McKinley's Philippine policy. Other prominent Negroes revised their views regarding the Philippines, especially after it became clear that the president's policy did not include autonomy for the inhabitants of the islands, but few wound up on the same side as Knox.

Black spokesmen who had assumed that the United States would seek nothing more than a single coaling station in the Philippines were profoundly disturbed by the decision late in 1898 to acquire the entire archipelago. Their initial response to what many considered a new and unexpected direction in American policy was characterized by indecisiveness and vacillation. In contemplating the future of the islands under American rule, black editors changed positions so often and dramatically that one well-informed observer concluded in January, 1899, that the Negro press was very much "at sea on the subject of expansion." [21] Behind their editorial contentions lay a dilemma that Negro Americans never completely resolved throughout the Philippine Insurrection, a dilemma born of the conflict between their obligations as American citizens and their ideological and racial identity with the insur-

19. Indianapolis *Freeman*, September 24, 1898. For Washington's opposition to the annexation of Hawaii, see *Boston Transcript*, August 26, 1898.
20. Indianapolis *Freeman*, July 30, 1898.
21. Washington *Colored American*, January 28, 1899.

rectionists. Aware of the tendency in some quarters to equate criticism of expansion with disloyalty and treason, they were reluctant to take a position that would cast doubt upon their patriotism. At the same time, however, black citizens were deeply concerned "about the treatment of . . . the dark-skinned races" [22] in the Philippines and recognized that for them to endorse American rule in the islands in order to prove their own patriotism was to place themselves in the difficult position of opposing for a colored people in the Pacific the same freedom and liberty which they sought at home. The outbreak of hostilities between the colored followers of Aguinaldo and the Anglo-Saxon forces of the United States early in 1899 tended to diminish the indecisiveness of Negroes regarding America's role in the Philippines and to harden their opposition to McKinley's policy. "The anti-expansion sentiment, as evidenced in all our public gatherings, is growing among Negroes," Edward E. Cooper reported in February, 1899.[23] But lest such sentiment be interpreted as evidence of the black man's lack of Americanism, Negroes usually accompanied their criticisms of expansion with ringing professions of patriotism, insisting that their sense of civic responsibility compelled them to speak out whenever their government departed from national traditions and ideals.

The ideological difficulties posed by the Philippine question for Negro Americans were graphically demonstrated by the tortuous editorial course pursued by Calvin Chase of the *Washington Bee.* Convinced that the primary mission of the United States in the archipelago was to free its inhabitants from Spanish rule and to assist them in establishing a republican government, Chase criticized President McKinley for making the disposition of the Philippines a subject of negotiation. "The government . . . should never have asked Spain for these islands," he declared in November, 1898. "We should have . . . taken possession [of them]." He dismissed as wholly specious the argument of Southern Democrats who questioned "the wisdom of accepting the Philippines without the consent of the governed" and maintained that in view of the plight of black people in the South, the white Southerner was "the

22. *American Baptist* quoted in Coffeyville *American,* February 11, 1899.
23. Washington *Colored American,* February 4, 1899.

last person who should talk about the consent of the governed."
Chase suspected that racism, rather than any commitment to republican principles, was responsible for the anti-expansionist
rhetoric of Southern Democrats. It was, he concluded, "the same
old fear of 'nigger domination' albeit . . . 8000 miles away." [24]

Although Chase castigated white Southerners for their hypocritical position on the Philippines, he also became increasingly suspicious of the motives of the McKinley administration. Abandoning
hope that the President would utilize American jurisdiction over
the archipelago to promote the liberty and welfare of its people,
Chase began to refer to expansion as a fraud by which a colored
race in the Orient was to be placed "under the yoke of American
prejudice." Describing himself as a patriot who subscribed to the
principles of the Declaration of Independence and desired to keep
the "flag pure and unstained," he protested McKinley's course in
the Philippines on the grounds that it would work "disastrously
both to the Filipinos and ourselves." The crusade for humanity
which had begun in the spring of 1898 to rescue Cuba from
Spanish tyranny had degenerated into a war of greed and oppression within less than a year. Although Chase admitted that the
Filipinos may have embarked upon a hopeless struggle, he applauded their "spirit of heroism . . . in the interest of independence" and doubted whether any black American could in good
conscience endorse the use of military force to thwart their aspirations. As for himself, Chase recognized the natural bond of sympathy between colored people in the United States and "a similar
race in the orient," since both were engaged in a struggle "for
constitutional liberty." Finally, the Washington editor seriously
questioned whether the United States should presume to "establish and maintain government for others" until it learned to "protect the lives and property of its own citizens," especially those of
color who lived in the South.[25]

The themes expressed by Chase were echoed by other black
spokesmen as they manifested increasing hostility to President Mc-
Kinley's policy. In fact, the anti-expansion theme became so prevalent that it appeared to verify Chase's contention that "a majority

24. *Washington Bee,* November 12, December 10, 17, 1898.
25. *Ibid.,* February 4, 11, March 11, 1899.

of the negroes in this country are opposed to expansion." [26] Booker T. Washington doubted that the American government could do "for the millions of dark-skinned races to be found in Cuba, Porto Rico, Hawaii and the Philippine Islands that which it has not been able to do for nearly 10,000,000 negroes and Indians" at home.[27] Ida Wells Barnett included the anti-expansion theme in her crusade against lynching, asserting that the McKinley administration should protect black citizens from lynch mobs before assuming the white man's burden in the Philippines.[28] John Mitchell took pride in the "brilliant fight for liberty" being waged by the colored people of the Philippines and held the McKinley administration responsible for the slaughter of helpless Filipinos by American troops. Citing Senator Hoar, the Richmond editor claimed that the decline of the United States would "date from the time we annex the Philippine Islands and with gun and sword force its unwilling people into abject submission." [29]

No less severe in their indictment of the administration's Philippine policy were Monroe Dorsey of the *Parsons Blade,* Harry Smith of the Cleveland *Gazette,* and Julius Taylor of the Salt Lake City *Broad Ax,* who likened Aguinaldo's love of liberty to that of Patrick Henry and claimed that American troops in the islands were guilty of more cruelty and robbery than the Spaniards had ever committed.[30] For the well-known Negro columnist John E. Bruce, American involvement in the Philippines was nothing if not an unjust war of conquest waged by Anglo-Saxons against a people whom they considered inferior. In his opinion the Filipinos had "an American Weyler on their hands" in the person of General Elwell Otis, the American commander.[31] Even the Indianapolis *Recorder,* "on sober second thought," concluded that the Filipinos were wise in refusing "to come under the sheltering wing of a country which has repeatedly demonstrated its inability to protect

26. *Ibid.,* February 4, 1899.
27. Quoted in Healy, *U.S. Expansionism,* pp. 240–241.
28. Cleveland *Gazette,* January 7, 1899.
29. *Richmond Planet,* February 11, April 1, 1899.
30. *Parsons Weekly Blade,* January 4, 21, 1899; Cleveland *Gazette,* January 7, 1899; Salt Lake City *Broad Ax,* January 28, February 5, 11, March 11, 1899; see also Gibbs, *Shadow and Light,* pp. 284–287.
31. John E. Bruce wrote under the pen name Bruce Grit. See Washington *Colored American,* March 18, April 8, 1899.

the lives and property of its own citizens a stone's throw from the seat of government." When P. B. S. Pinchback and James Lewis spoke out in defense of American acquisition of the Philippines, a black editor in their hometown of New Orleans characterized them as mere "negro political pap seekers" who "ought to be read out of good society" for daring to sell out their kinsmen in the Pacific in an effort to win some patronage crumbs from the White House. Even the Savannah *Tribune,* usually so reluctant to criticize a Republican administration, took exception to President McKinley's course in the Philippines and urged him to adopt a conciliatory policy which would "allow the natives to feel that it is the purpose of the government to protect them and ultimately give them an independent government." [32]

The course of events in the Philippines early in 1899 seriously eroded the ranks of black imperialists. Those Negroes who favored the acquisition of the islands and supported military action against Aguinaldo were usually motivated more by personal political considerations than by any commitment to the establishment of American rule over the Filipinos. In fact, the most persistently vocal exponents of imperialism within the black community were those who had been appointed to office by McKinley or who expected to be. Even though they echoed the official views of the administration and attempted to describe overseas expansion in terms of its benefits to colored citizens, their rhetoric was usually defensive in tone and often lacking in conviction.[33] The plight of black people in the United States made the discussions of duty and destiny by Negro expansionists appear all the more awkward.

Black editors who supported the president's Philippine policy generally eschewed a racial interpretation of the war in the islands and looked upon American involvement as an unavoidable, ugly situation forced upon the nation. The Des Moines *Iowa State Bystander* and the Milwaukee *Wisconsin Weekly Advocate* characterized Auguinaldo as an ingrate and traitor who subordinated the welfare of his deluded followers to his own personal ambitions.

32. Indianapolis *Recorder,* January 28, 1899; New Orleans *Southern Republican* quoted in *Washington Bee,* January 28, 1899; Savannah *Tribune,* February 25, 1899.

33. See George B. Cortelyou to Judson W. Lyons, August 19, 1899, Judson W. Lyons to Albert W. Washington, August 21, 1899, McKinley Papers.

"It is hoped,' 'the *Bystander* declared in mid-February, 1899, "that these brief engagements will be a good lesson to the natives and they will kindly submit to American rule." [34]

By early 1899 the most enthusiastic black editorial advocate of the Philippine policy was George L. Knox of the Indianapolis *Freeman,* who believed that the United States should "prosecute the war until it reaches the ends mapped out." Otherwise he believed that "the political integrity of the nation" would be seriously compromised. In replying to those black Americans who argued in favor of immediate independence for the Filipinos, Knox declared: "The bushman of today cannot be the legislator of tomorrow." The duty of the United States, he maintained, was to provide these "bushmen" with experience in "the best form of government possible under the circumstances" so as to insure the future tranquility of the islands.[35]

Convinced that patriotism compelled support for the president's policy, Knox castigated black spokesmen who applauded Aguinaldo and reminded them that "it was a poor bird that befouls its own nest." Nor did he believe that the black man's troubles at home provided a legitimate excuse for desiring the failure of American arms abroad. Outraged by all the praise of Aguinaldo's courage which appeared in the Negro press, Knox maintained that he had "nothing more against the heroism of Aguinaldo" than "against the heroism of General Lee and Stonewall Jackson," both of whom battled for independence and lost. Like the Confederates, Aguinaldo was a rebel against legally established authority, and he too would lose.[36]

Knox was most severe in his criticism of those black Americans who supported Aguinaldo on racial grounds. He conceded that there might be legitimate reasons for opposing American actions against the Filipino rebels, but race was not one of them. "To oppose the government in the Philippine war on the issue of color," he warned, "is suicidal." The sooner Negro Americans got rid of the bad habit of identifying and sympathizing with every foreigner of color, the better off they would be. Rejecting the notion that

34. Des Moines *Iowa State Bystander*, February 17, 1899; Milwaukee *Wisconsin Weekly Advocate*, May 11, 1899.
35. Indianapolis *Freeman*, February 4, March 11, 1899.
36. *Ibid.*, April 8, 22, 29, 1899.

racial sympathy for the brown people of the Philippines took precedence over loyalty to the government of the United States, the *Freeman* editor proclaimed that he was one black citizen who was "not going to erect racial walls by fighting the white Spaniard and play the Achilles when it comes to the black Philippinos." [37]

Black supporters of the administration's Philippine policy staged loyalist meetings in several northern and midwestern cities. In one such meeting in Chicago, Theophile T. Allain, formerly a state senator in Louisiana who had been appointed a documents clerk in the House of Representatives, presented a rousing speech justifying American presence in the islands. He expressed great resentment that someone had compared Aguinaldo to Toussaint L'Ouverture; in his opinion, there was not the slightest resemblance between the courageous Haitian leader and "that half-breed Mongolian Chinese" who posed as a leader of the Filipinos.[38] In Washington black federal officeholders utilized their influence and considerable forensic skills in public gatherings of Negroes to combat the growing anti-expansionist sentiment. For example, John P. Green, a former state senator in Ohio whom McKinley appointed chief of the U.S. Stamp Agency in 1897, was an eloquent defender of the administration's policy in the Philippines. Not only would American rule bring "physical, intellectual, and moral regeneration" to the Filipinos, according to Green, but it would also open avenues of "usefulness, honor and wealth" for the black American. "I expect to live," he declared, "to see the day [when] great generals, merchant princes, bankers, railway magnates and others belonging to our race will be in evidence in our new possessions." [39]

Of the loyalist meetings held by black Republicans, none received more publicity than a gathering in Indianapolis late in the spring of 1899. Sponsored by the Anacostia Colored Republican Club, the meeting heard speeches by Indiana's most influential black Republicans, including George L. Knox, James H. Lott, Dr. S. A. Furniss, and Gurley Brewer. In the opening address Brewer set the tone by declaring:

37. *Ibid.,* May 6, July 15, 1899.

38. Washington *Colored American*, May 13, 1899.

39. For Green's address see *The World* (Seattle), January 4, 1899; see also John P. Green, *Fact Stranger Than Fiction: Seventy-five Years of a Busy Life* (Cleveland: Riehl Printing, 1920), pp. 266–271.

. . . the natives in these far-away islands in the Pacific are now being offered the same boon that was offered the American negro in 1861—the opportunity to become subjects of a great and good government. This is the greatest blessing that could possibly fall upon the people of the Philippines. . . . The Filipinos are fighting against their saviors because they do not understand what a future this country has to offer them. The future that Lincoln offered the negro is being fulfilled.

The proceedings concluded with the adoption of a resolution expressing "confidence in the United States government and belief in the high honor and just action of the army and navy in the Philippine Islands." [40] The hostility with which the black press throughout the country reacted to the Indianapolis gathering provided some indication of the extent to which imperialism had become unpopular among Negro Americans. Even a local black newspaper characterized the proceedings as "the subservient and lickspittle action" of a "little coterie of so-called negro leaders" which only reflected discredit upon the whole race.[41]

Although black expansionists had a strong editorial spokesman in George L. Knox, their cause suffered a serious blow early in 1899 with the temporary defection of Edward E. Cooper of the Washington *Colored American*. Cooper had enthusiastically endorsed McKinley's Philippine policy as long as he interpreted it to mean a temporary protectorate over the islands. But the use of troops to crush the Filipino insurrection profoundly disturbed him, not only because it appeared to indicate permanent occupation, but also because it placed the McKinley administration in the position of thwarting the aspirations of a "freedom-loving" colored people. "Lovers of free government may not wholly agree with . . . the practices of Aguinaldo and his followers," Cooper wrote, "but they cannot fail to admire the principles for which the little band so gamely contends." [42]

Like other Negro Americans, the editor of the *Colored American* argued that the ratification of the Treaty of Paris did not preclude the establishment of a Philippine Republic protected and

40. Indianapolis *Freeman*, June 3, 1899; Salt Lake City *Broad Ax*, June 6, 1899; Gurley Brewer to James A. Mount, May 18, 1899, Mount Correspondence.

41. Indianapolis *World*, June 3, 1899.

42. Washington *Colored American*, February 11, 1899.

guided by the United States. Such a course, in his view, would at least spare the nation the frightful consequences certain to result from a perversion of its republican principles. Early in February, 1899, Cooper wrote:

> Since they [Philippines] came to us as a military necessity, and stand for no fixed national policy—rather the abandonment of republicanism—why not place the Philippines upon the same footing with Cuba. . . . An American protectorate will bring to us all the advantages of trade, spread a healthful influence over the islands and preserve in tact the heritage of our fathers, with none of the evils attending the annexation of an indigestable and unsympathetic population.[43]

Nor did Cooper fail to note the similarity between the predicaments of the Filipinos and black Americans: both were colored peoples struggling for freedom and recognition against Anglo-Saxon domination. He described the war in the Philippines as "a costly, unnecessary and illogical conflict" which could be terminated quickly if Americans would treat Aguinaldo "as we would have had George III treat us something more than a hundred years ago." But the Philippine war was contrary to American principles, and its continuation was also certain to cost the Republican party the support of black voters.

Throughout the first eight months of 1899 the *Colored American* repeatedly warned party leaders that no amount of rhetoric about Christianizing and civilizing Filipinos would convince Negro citizens that the war was anything more than a "gigantic scheme of land-grabbing and dollar making" at the expense of a dark-skinned people who "had no rights the Anglo-Saxon is bound to respect." According to Cooper, the hypocrisy of the American role in the Philippines was only heightened by the fact that as a nation which claimed to be intent upon bestowing Christian civilization upon the islands, the United States continued to tolerate barbaric and un-Christian treatment of its own colored citizens.[44] "We have acquired," he observed, "the doubtful habit . . . of rushing around among our neighbors and condemning them be-

43. *Ibid.*
44. *Ibid.*, January 21, 28, February 11, March 11, 25, April 15, May 27, July 15, 29, 1899.

cause of the untidy conditions of their premises, sweetly unmindful of the fact that dirt is an inch thick upon our own floor." In fact, Cooper believed that any comparison between the "enlightened civilization" of the United States which tolerated mob violence against its own citizens and "the customs of barbarians" in the Philippines would "not appear to our advantage." [45]

For so loyal a Republican as the editor of the *Colored American*, a war which pitted white Americans against the darker Filipinos was obviously a source of much agony. But to preclude any doubts about his loyalty to party and country, Cooper consistently voiced criticism of the Philippine policy as a prophetic patriot anxious to keep both faithful to their ideals. "The best patriot," he explained early in March, 1899, "is he who holds up his finger of warning when his country seems about to depart from its safe moorings of humanity." [46] Despite such explanations, Cooper was never able to reconcile satisfactorily his sympathy for the Filipinos with his conviction that black Americans would be accorded full rights only to the degree that they assumed their duties as citizens—even if such duties meant participating in a movement to thwart the independence and freedom of a colored people in far-off Asia. The result was a succession of editorials in the *Colored American* which revealed the contradictory and ambivalent attitudes of its editor in regard to the Philippine war. The only theme pursued with consistency was his commitment to an early termination of the fighting. Convinced that the United States could arbitrate its differences "with the liberty-loving islanders without loss of dignity," Cooper continued to argue, at least until the fall of 1899, that "a Philippine Republic under an American protectorate would settle the whole controversy . . . in accord with our pretensions of Christian duty and fair play." [47]

In a sense, the rising tide of opposition to American involvement in the Philippines so evident in the black community early in 1899 represented a culmination of grievances and thwarted aspirations. Those who had anticipated that the war with Spain would yield handsome dividends for black patriots in Cuba and the United States felt that men of color in both countries had been

45. *Ibid.*, April 15, 1899.
46. *Ibid.*, March 11, 1899.
47. *Ibid.*, April 1, 1899.

consistently shortchanged. Increasingly skeptical about the fate of their "colored cousins" in Cuba, black Americans believed that the war had actually worsened their own plight because it had "drawn the Anglo-Saxons together." The fear, first expressed in the summer of 1898, to the effect that black people would "be ground to dust between the upper and nether millstone of national cohesion" appeared to have been realized.[48] Commenting on the reunion of the North and South produced by the war, a black Georgian noted that one effect was the subjection of the Negro to a "deeper humiliation and degradation." "His former friends are silent and indifferent," the Georgian declared. "His enemies have grown bolder and more defiant. It looks as though annihilation is what is desired, and the Christian public fold their arms and say, 'Let him die' he is not Anglo-Saxon." [49]

As evidence that the war had removed the last restraints against negrophobia, blacks cited the outbreak of mob violence in the months immediately following the end of the fighting in Cuba. They emphasized that black men in the uniform of the U.S. Army were no more immune to racial repression than other Negroes. Early in December, 1898, the Baltimore *Afro-American* expressed a widespread sentiment when it observed: "Just as the black heroes had covered themselves with glory on the battlefields of Cuba, this old time spirit of half dead slavery days returns to make trouble with the colored people in the Southland." [50] John Mitchell claimed that lynchings increased dramatically in the wake of the armistice with Spain. Regardless of the accuracy of his statistics, certainly racial violence appeared to assume a more brutal and inhuman character.[51]

Beginning with the "massacre" in Wilmington, North Carolina, and the mine wars in Illinois in the fall of 1898, reports of racial incidents appeared in the press almost daily for the next two years, culminating in the bloody race riots in New Orleans, Akron, and New York in the summer of 1900. At the Afro-American Council meeting in December, 1898, there was considerable sentiment for issuing an appeal to foreign powers "to lend their influence toward

48. Indianapolis *Freeman,* July 23, 1898; see also *Richmond Planet,* January 21, 1899.
49. Savannah *Tribune,* March 18, 1899.
50. Baltimore *Afro-American* quoted in *Richmond Planet,* December 3, 1898.
51. *Richmond Planet,* July 3, August 20, 1898, July 29, 1899.

bringing about harmony between the negro and white races in this country." A gathering of prominent Negroes at Oberlin College a few months later actually passed a resolution imploring foreign governments to protect black Americans from lynchers.[52] One Negro editor noted that black citizens, having contributed their "brawn and sinew to this Government to help overthrow the bonds of oppression and tyranny of Spain from her colonies," were now calling upon other nations to do for them what they had done for the suffering Cubans. John Mitchell claimed that the condition of Negroes in the South had become so bad that their survival seemed to depend upon a foreign power taking up the cause of humanity in their behalf.[53]

Two particularly gruesome lynching incidents in Georgia early in 1899 prompted great alarm and indignation among black Americans and strengthened their opposition to the Philippine policy of the McKinley administration. One of these was the slaughter of a half-dozen defenseless black citizens in Palmetto, Georgia, on March 15, 1899, by a large mob of whites. As if the act itself was not cause enough for an outpouring of indignation, Governor Allen D. Candler of Georgia placed the blame for the Palmetto crime upon the pernicious influence of black volunteers recently encamped in his state. The governor maintained that their presence had disturbed "the peaceful race relations" existing in Georgia and produced tensions which were responsible for violent acts against blacks.[54] In April, 1899, a black man named Sam Hose who was accused of several crimes including rape was caught and burned at the stake in Newnan, Georgia, in the presence of a mob of over 2,000 persons. His body was mutilated by souvenir hunters; one of his fingers was placed in an envelope and given to his son as a reminder that he should "make himself scarce." In the meantime Elijah Strickland, a black minister who had dared to defend Hose, was hanged.[55] Such outrages strengthened the conviction of

52. Coffeyville *American*, January 28, 1899; Cleveland *Gazette*, June 3, 1899.
53. *Richmond Planet*, July 29, 1899.
54. Brawley, *Social History of the American Negro*, pp. 313–314; *Washington Bee*, May 25, 1899; *Richmond Planet*, April 1, 1899; Savannah *Tribune*, March 18, April 1, 1899.
55. *Richmond Planet*, April 29, 1899; Indianapolis *Freeman*, May, 6, 1899; Indianapolis *Recorder*, May 7, 1899. On the Hose lynching, see also Brawley, *Social History of the American Negro*, p. 314.

black Americans that any government which could not or would not protect its own citizens from atrocities was in no position to become the standard-bearer of enlightenment among other people. An early expression of this attitude was a speech by William H. Lewis, a black member of the Cambridge City Council, before a mass meeting of Negroes in the Boston area shortly after the lynching of Sam Hose. "What a spectacle America is exhibiting today," Lewis declared. "Columbia stands offering liberty to the Cubans with one hand, cramming liberty down the throats of the Filipinos with the other, but with both feet planted upon the neck of the negro." If Georgia was any indication of Anglo-Saxon civilization, blacks argued, the Filipino would do well to continue his fight for full freedom and independence.[56]

The deteriorating racial situation in the United States figured significantly in the growth of anti-expansionist sentiment among black Americans. They believed that a nation which oppressed and degraded its own colored citizens was unlikely to pursue a different course among colored peoples in colonial possessions. Earlier predictions that America's crusade in Cuba would involve a Jim Crow war and result in a Jim Crow empire appeared by early 1899 to have been remarkably accurate. Negroes were well aware that white troops referred to Aguinaldo and his followers as "niggers" and the war in the Philippines as "the nigger fighting business."[57] Some, in fact, claimed that Aguinaldo opposed American control of his country precisely because he feared that Filipinos would be accorded the same treatment as Negroes in the United States. That they were not dealing in idle speculation became apparent a few months later when Aguinaldo invoked the name of Sam Hose and other lynching victims in his propaganda efforts aimed at the black American soldiers sent to the Philippines.[58]

In an address before the Afro-American Council in the summer

56. Des Moines *Iowa State Bystander*, April 28, 1899. *Washington Bee* (June 24, 1899) proposed sending Negro American representatives to all European capitals, where they would publicly expose the plight of black citizens in the United States with a view toward marshaling international opinion against "lynch law."

57. Cleveland *Gazette*, May 6, 1899; Salt Lake City *Broad Ax*, June 6, 1899; Indianapolis *World*, June 17, 1899.

58. *Washington Bee*, February 11, March 11, 1899; Cleveland *Gazette*, May 6, June 24, 1899; Salt Lake City *Broad Ax*, April 8, 1899; see also John M. Gates, "An Experiment in Benevolent Pacification: The U.S. Army in the Philippines, 1898–1902" (Ph.D dissertation, Duke University, 1967), pp. 45–46.

of 1899, Bishop Alexander Walters of the A.M.E. Zion Church summarized the position of most black citizens toward the Philippine crisis. Although the bishop had no objections to commercial expansion, he opposed the imperialistic course undertaken by McKinley. Walters declared:

> I do not think that America is prepared to carry on expansion at this time, especially if it be among the dark races of the earth. The white man of America is impregnated with color-phobia. He has been taught for centuries that the black man, no matter where he dwells, has no rights which the white man is bound to respect, hence he is not prepared to grant dark skinned people the most favorable opportunities for development. No matter how intelligent or cultured a man might be, if his skin is dark, his rights should be ignored. Had the Filipinos been white and fought as bravely as they have, the war would have been ended and their independence granted a long time ago.[59]

Against the background of the Palmetto crime, the Hose lynching, and numerous similar incidents, black citizens had little difficulty in interpreting American action in the Philippines as an attempt to foist upon the islands a civilization that had very little to commend it to any people of color. As one Negro editor noted, the conflict being waged by the United States against the Filipinos was contrary to national ideals and traditions, and it was all the more insidious because it was "a race war." [60]

Although black citizens feared for the future of the Filipinos lest they too become the victims of racism, another factor which helps explain their hostility to McKinley's Philippine policy concerned their own military experience during and after the Spanish-American War. Most black Americans agreed that Negro regulars had not received rewards commensurate with their heroic performance on the Cuban battlefields and that black volunteers had been subjected to abuses which no white man would have tolerated. Even in the uniform of a United States soldier, the editor Harry Smith insisted, the Negro was "made the cur dog of the nation," charged with all kinds of "crimes and murderous affrays," but seldom complimented for his bravery and display of discipline under try-

59. Milwaukee *Wisconsin Weekly Advocate,* August 17, 1899.
60. Indianapolis *World,* June 17, August 12, 19, 1899.

ing circumstances. The Chicago *Conservator* declared in April, 1899, that the black heroes of San Juan Hill had gotten their "passing mention," then become "lost in that sublime Americanism which forgets all that the Negro does but his crimes." [61] Those who pressed the claims of Negro regulars and sought greater opportunities for black men under the army reorganization bill of 1899 met with little success. In February, 1899, Congressman George White, Judson Lyons, Henry P. Cheatham, and Bishop B. W. Arnett waged a vigorous campaign in an attempt to obtain colored officers for colored regiments, admission of blacks to artillery units, and the "establishment of a more liberal policy in recognition, treatment and promotion of colored soldiers." [62] Their failure to win concessions for Negroes under the new army bill dissipated any remaining hopes that black veterans of the Cuban campaign would be rewarded with commissions in the regular army. With the muster out of the last black volunteers early in the spring of 1899, no Negro held a commission in the military service except Lieutenant Charles Young and several chaplains. In North Carolina, Georgia, Virginia, and other states movements to reduce or disband colored militia units were already underway.[63]

An additional blow to the Negro American's pride in his role in the war with Spain came from an unexpected source—Theodore Roosevelt, the hero of San Juan Hill who had been elected governor of New York in 1898. Colonel Roosevelt had on several occasions praised the performance of black regulars in Cuba, and Negroes generally considered him a friend of the race. Then, in an article on the Rough Riders which appeared in *Scribner's Magazine* in April, 1899, he included references to Negro soldiers which outraged black citizens. While Roosevelt commended the black soldiers, especially the cavalry, for their gallantry in Cuba, he emphasized that all Negro soldiers were "peculiarly dependent upon their white officers." He believed that blacks were more likely to break under strain than whites, citing as evidence the behavior of some black infantrymen during the heat of the battle at San Juan

61. Cleveland *Gazette*, April 1, 1899; Chicago *Conservator* quoted in Kansas City *American Citizen*, April 21, 1899.

62. Washington *Colored American*, February 11, 25, March 18, 1899.

63. *Ibid.*, March 18, 1899; Savannah *Tribune*, March 18, 1899; Baltimore *Ledger*, April 22, 1899.

Hill. According to Roosevelt, the infantrymen "began to get a little uneasy and to drift to the rear." "This I could not allow, as it was depleting my line," he wrote, "so I jumped up . . . drew my revolver, halted the retreating [black] soldiers." [64]

For black Americans, nothing Roosevelt had said or would say in the presidential campaign of 1900 could compensate for this slur, which was retained unchanged when his article was incorporated into his book *The Rough Riders*.[65] Because of the widely held view that black soldiers had saved Roosevelt and his Rough Riders from annihilation and had displayed remarkable qualities of leadership under fire in the absence of their white officers, the reaction of Negroes to his statement was both immediate and vociferous. Presley Holliday and other black veterans of the Santiago campaign, as well as Robert J. Fleming, a white lieutenant of the Tenth Cavalry, challenged the accuracy of Roosevelt's suggestion that black soldiers had been guilty of any cowardice. Holliday claimed that indeed Roosevelt had threatened to shoot some black soldiers whom he thought were retreating, but that he had apologized to them upon being informed that they had been ordered to the rear to bring up rations and entrenching tools. Holliday thought Roosevelt "was sufficiently conscious of his error not to make a so ungrateful statement about us at a time when the nation is about to forget our past service." [66]

The reaction of the black press was far less generous. In the *Richmond Planet* John Mitchell printed compilations of eyewitness testimony by both black and white soldiers disputing Roosevelt's assertions, noting that even though the *Scribner's* article referred to numerous heroic individuals by name, it failed to include the name of a single black soldier. Mitchell speculated that had Roosevelt's article been published prior to the gubernatorial campaign in New York, the opposition of black voters would have been sufficient to insure his defeat. As far as the Richmond

64. Theodore Roosevelt, "Rough Riders," *Scribner's Magazine*, XXV (April, 1899), 436.
65. See Theodore Roosevelt, *The Rough Riders* (New York: Charles Scribner's Sons, 1899), pp. 144–145.
66. Presley Holliday to the Editor, April 22, 1899, in *New York Age*, May 11, 1899; see also Theodore Roosevelt to Robert J. Fleming, May 21, 1900, in Elting Morison, ed., *Letters of Theodore Roosevelt*, 8 vols. (Cambridge: Harvard University Press, 1954–56), II, 1304–6.

editor was concerned, his "favorable impression of the Governor" had been totally "dissipated." In commenting on the possibility that Roosevelt might eventually become the Republican presidential candidate, Mitchell remarked that "his elevation to the presidency would tend to increase rather than alleviate the ills from which we [Negroes] suffer." [67]

Monroe Dorsey, Edward E. Cooper, and a host of other black editors [68] joined Mitchell in condemning Roosevelt, but their criticisms paled beside those of Harry Smith of the Cleveland *Gazette*. Referring to the New York governor as a "man of foreign blood," Smith denounced his reference to the cowardice of Negro soldiers as "a malicious slander" upon men who had saved his life. According to the *Gazette*, the *Scribner's* article confirmed blacks' suspicions that Roosevelt was intent upon magnifying his own deeds and the performance of his Rough Riders at the expense of the Negro regulars who "actually carried the day in Cuba." A "man so small as to withhold credit from his saviors," Smith confidently predicted, would "never wear the presidential robes." [69]

Roosevelt's article, appearing just as Negroes began to discuss seriously whether black troops ought to serve in the Philippines, only compounded the difficulty of those who attempted to revive notions of a rich harvest awaiting black men willing to assume their civic duty by shouldering the "white man's burden" in the islands. By the spring of 1899 most black Americans were skeptical of any suggestion that rallying to the flag in the Philippines would advance the progress of the race. Their experience during the Cuban war had impressed upon them the peculiar harvest reaped by the black patriot; his reward was not the receipt of military commissions or even minimal recognition of his manhood, but lynchings by Georgia mobs and insults to his dignity by the nation's most conspicuous military hero. Within such a context it could hardly be expected that rumors about black soldiers being sent to the Philippines would meet with an enthusiastic reception. In fact, George L. Knox appeared to be the only prominent black editor

67. *Richmond Planet,* April 22, 1899.
68. *Parsons Weekly Blade,* April 29, 1899; Washington *Colored American,* May 6, 1899; T. Thomas Fortune to Booker T. Washington, April 6, 1899, Washington Papers.
69. Cleveland *Gazette,* April 22, 23, May 6, 27, June 10, 1899.

to favor the use of colored troops in the islands. Knox pleaded with Negroes to understand that any enemy of the United States was "a common enemy and the color of his face has nothing to do with it." [70]

But for most black Americans the color of the Filipino was important. Julius Taylor claimed that, precisely because the Filipinos were colored, "no Negro possessing any race pride can enter heartily into the prosecution of the war." [71] Edward E. Cooper joined the veteran black anti-expansionist George Dudley of the Kansas City *American Citizen* in the earnest hope that no black troops would be assigned to duty in the Philippines. Dudley was unalterably "opposed to pitting negro against negro," and to dispatch black troops to the islands would be just that. "God forbid," he exclaimed, "the sending of a single negro soldier from this country to kill his own kith and kin fighting for the cause they believe to be right." [72]

Few Negroes took seriously reports that the War Department had decided to send Negro regulars to the Philippines because "the majority of the natives there are Negroes, and our colored troops could do much to allay bitter feelings toward Americans, and thus pave the way for assimilation." The only reason for sending Negroes to the islands, the Indianapolis *Recorder* argued, was the failure of white troops to subdue the Filipinos and the need for black soldiers to bring about the victory that had eluded them.[73] Others who agreed with the *Recorder* pointed out that the War Department's view of Negroes as "things" to be "killed as a means of saving the white man" hardly constituted a source of encouragement for black soldiers. Aware that men in the regular army had to perform whatever duties they were assigned, John Mitchell nevertheless warned black regulars against anticipating any rewards for service in the Philippines other than disease and death. They would receive "no promotions, no honor, only humiliating insinuations and ribald jest at the hands of an

70. Indianapolis *Freeman*, July 1, 1899.
71. Salt Lake City *Broad Ax*, May 16, 1899.
72. Washington *Colored American*, April 29, 1899; Kansas City *American Citizen*, April 28, 1899.
73. Indianapolis *Recorder*, April 29, 1899.

ungrateful nation." [74] The Omaha *Progress* was of the opinion that any black soldier who met death while fighting in the Philippines would do so without "feeling that he was fighting in a righteous cause." Rather, he would "go to meet his Maker feeling that he was an accessory to a great land-grabbing scheme" that would enslave people his own color. [75]

Reports concerning the use of black soldiers in the Philippines which gained wide circulation within the black community in April, 1899, were not unfounded. As early as February the War Department had suggested that the Twenty-fourth Regiment was available for service in the islands, but General Otis did not consider the transfer of the black infantrymen to Manila "wise . . . at present." [76] At approximately the same time, black volunteers from Illinois and Alabama who were about to be mustered out requested that their regiments be retained for service in the Philippines. Although the black volunteer units were disbanded on schedule, the idea of using Negro volunteers to put down the Filipino Insurrection was viewed with favor by General Nelson A. Miles, the commanding general of the army. Late in April, 1899, Miles proposed the organization of a corps of 10,000 Negro volunteers "specially for service in the Philippines." "In order that the most positive discipline will be enforced and thorough equipment supplied," the general wrote, "I earnestly recommend that these troops be placed under commanding officers of the highest experience and highest ability and who have already made records for themselves by their ability to organize, discipline and command in the field troops, companies, regiments and brigades. . . ." Although Miles did not explicitly state that colored troops should be commanded by white officers, such an arrangement was apparently his intention. The secretary of war rejected his proposal on the grounds that the military situation in the Philippines at the time did not require additional troops. [77]

74. *Richmond Planet,* June 17, 1899.
75. *Omaha Progress* quoted in Salt Lake City *Broad Ax,* April 15, 1899.
76. Elwell Otis to the Adjutant General, February 28, 1899, in *Correspondence Relating to the War with Spain,* II, 918.
77. Nelson A. Miles to the Secretary of War, April 26, 1899, #242070, Adjutant General's Records; see also Fletcher, "Negro Soldier and the United States Army," pp. 287–288.

Contrary to rumors circulating in the United States that Aguinaldo was on the verge of surrender, American military authorities in the Philippines recognized late in the spring of 1899 that the war would be neither easy nor brief. Furthermore, the tour of duty of the white volunteer regiments dispatched to Manila the previous year had expired. In view of the situation General Otis in June, 1899, requested the War Department to transfer regulars to replace the departing volunteers. Among those regular army units which arrived in the Philippines in July and August were parts of the Twenty-fourth and Twenty-fifth Infantry. After a brief period of training in camps near Manila, the Negro infantrymen moved into the interior of Luzon in pursuit of the elusive Filipino forces. Within a year Negro troopers of the Ninth and Tenth Cavalry joined the infantrymen in the struggle against the Filipino insurrectionists.[78]

The departure of the black regulars for the Philippines was attended by few of the patriotic orations and festive activities which marked their embarkation for Cuba a year earlier. Most black newspapers expressed regret that Negro soldiers had been sent to distant islands to fight "for God only knows what." Harry Smith of the Cleveland *Gazette* saw something sinister in the decision to send black troops to the Philippines at the height of "the rainy and sickly season." Like other black spokesmen, Smith believed that Negroes had again been called upon to do the dirty work of whites and to suffer the loss of life.[79] The distinguished A.M.E. clergyman H. T. Johnson succinctly summarized the views of most black spokesmen who commented on the decision of the government to use Negro troops in the fight against the Filipinos:

> It would be difficult, however, for the Negro to deprive others of the things so dear to himself, even if he were spurred on by the hope of future rewards; and the assurance of future good treatment. He knows that the people of the Philippines are struggling for freedom, that they are in their own land; that they are foreign

78. William T. Sexton, *Soldiers in the Sun: An Adventure in Imperialism* (Harrisburg, Pa.: Military Publishing Co., 1939), pp. 176, 242; *Manila Times*, July 24, 31, 1899, December 27, 1900, May 15, 1901.

79. Cleveland *Gazette*, June 10, 24, 1899; see also Savannah *Tribune*, July 22, 1899; Des Moines *Iowa State Bystander*, July 7, 1899; Indianapolis *Recorder*, July 23, 1899; *Richmond Planet*, June 17, August 19, 1899; *Washington Bee*, August 12, 1899.

members of his own racial household; that he will get no thanks for being killed himself, or for killing others; that he is only needed because his white comrade cannot stand the fearful odds which daily tasks his ranks.[80]

Notwithstanding such reservations, Johnson, like other black Americans, praised "the pluck and patriotism" of the Negro regulars assigned to the Philippines and expressed confidence that they would, as usual, perform with valor. Although John Deveaux of the Savannah *Tribune* had doubts about the whole Philippine enterprise, he took pride in the fact that colored men could "be relied on to fight for the old flag of freedom in any clime or against any enemy." [81]

Expressing a view which appeared often in the comments of those who took note of the decision to use black troops in the islands, Julius Taylor maintained that if black men were to be forced to participate in "this unholy war," they should at least be allowed to go under officers of their own color.[82] The persistent clamor for black commissioned officers was not altogether barren of results: Charles Young ultimately went to the Philippines with a regular army regiment and was promoted to captain in 1901; more significant, perhaps, in the same year Benjamin O. Davis became the first Negro to receive a commission by examination.[83] But the most immediate effect of the agitation was the commissioning of black men as lieutenants and captains in two volunteer regiments of Negroes recruited especially for service in the Philippines.

The opposition of black Americans to the Philippine war appears to have intensified with the departure of the Negro regulars for the islands. Political, civic, fraternal, and religious organizations in the black community passed resolutions condemning "McKinley imperialism" and the president's disregard for the rights of

80. Quoted in Marks, ed., *Black Press Views American Imperialism,* p. 133.
81. *Ibid.;* Savannah *Tribune,* July 22, 1899.
82. Chicago *Broad Ax,* July 15, 1899; see also Cleveland *Gazette,* July 15, 1899. The *Daily American Citizen* (Kansas City) on August 1, 1898, proposed that Negro newspapers pool their resources and send a correspondent to the Philippines to cover the activities of black soldiers since past experience had indicated that their valor would otherwise be ignored. The proposal, like a similar one during the Cuban War, was not implemented.
83. For Young's career, see Abraham Chew, *A Biography of Colonel Charles Young* (Washington: R. L. Pendleton, 1923); on Davis, see Washington *Colored American,* July 13, 1901.

Negro citizens at home, issues which Negro Americans interpreted as closely interrelated. One observer stated that "the sentiment against President McKinley's policy in the Philippine islands is practically unanimous . . . so far as the citizens of color are concerned." [84] Such a claim appeared to be substantiated by the resolutions adopted by gatherings of black citizens and by the editorial position of most black newspapers. "Intelligent Afro-Americans" were overwhelmingly opposed to the Philippine policy, according to Harry Smith, "because they feel that the American people generally, and the present administration particularly, lack the breadth of mind that would enable them to govern properly colored people abroad when those here at home are so sadly neglected, ignored, mistreated and lynched in defiance of law, order and civilization." [85]

The treaty signed with the Sultan of Sulu by General John C. Bates on August 20, 1899,[86] which sanctioned slavery in the Sultan's Philippine domain, prompted anxiety among even the most loyal black Republicans. So staunch a friend of McKinley's Philippine policy as George L. Knox was clearly shaken by the news of the so-called Bates treaty; he asserted that Negroes of the United States would insist that no relations be effected with the Sulu ruler until slavery had been abolished in his domains. The Indiana Conference of the African Methodist Episcopal Church officially called upon Congress to disavow the Bates treaty and to banish "forever slavery in the Philippines." [87] The treaty confirmed most black anti-imperialists' worst fears regarding the implications of the president's course in the Philippines.

By the late summer of 1899 criticism of the Republican administration had assumed strong political overtones. Edward E. Cooper repeatedly warned that a continuation of the Philippine war would "spell disaster for the party in power." In August, T. Thomas Fortune publicly called for McKinley's defeat in the next presidential election. Among the arguments which Fortune mar-

84. *Richmond Planet,* July 22, 1899.
85. Cleveland *Gazette,* July 15, 1899.
86. On the Sulu Treaty see Grunder and Livezey, *Philippines and the United States,* pp. 139–140.
87. Indianapolis *Freeman,* September 9, 1899; see also *The Southern Republican* (New Orleans), September 9, 1899.

shaled in support of his position were the failure of Negro soldiers to receive anything approaching equitable treatment during the Spanish-American War and the president's refusal to appoint Negroes to the various commissions to determine the government for Cuba and the Philippines, in spite of the fact that these areas were inhabited by colored people. John Mitchell, in assessing the Republican prospects for 1900, claimed that neither McKinley nor Roosevelt promised much hope because they were both imperialists who were little concerned with the rights of colored people. A black editor in Norfolk suggested, however, that "with Messrs. Mc-Kinley and Roosevelt on the ticket, the Negro can get his full revenge in one fell swoop." [88]

The most vocal opposition to "McKinley imperialism" among black citizens in 1899 probably emanated from those in Massachusetts, the home of the anti-imperialist movement. Early in the year at a gathering in Boston to commemorate the 129th anniversary of the death of Crispus Attucks, Negro speakers vigorously protested the Philippine war on the grounds that Aguinaldo was "fighting for just what our forefathers sought thirty-five years ago." Throughout the spring and summer prominent figures in Boston's black community, including Archibald H. Grimké; the Reverend W. H. Scott, minister to a suburban Baptist congregation; and Clifford H. Plummer, an attorney who was secretary of the National Colored Protective League, continued to criticize the president's Philippine policy, which they usually considered in connecton with his position regarding outrages against black citizens in the South. In mid-July plans were made for the addition of a colored auxiliary to the New England Anti-Imperialist League—an arrangement which allowed black and white anti-imperialists in Massachusetts to cooperate within a segregated organizational structure.[89]

Plummer described the creation of the auxiliary as the beginning of "an uprising of the colored race" to bring about "the downfall of McKinley, imperialism and the Republican Party."

88. Washington *Colored American*, February 4, May 27, July 29, August 19, 1899. For Fortune's indictment of McKinley, see *Washington Bee*, August 5, 1899; *Richmond Planet*, September 30, 1899; Norfolk *Recorder* quoted in Cleveland *Gazette*, July 29, 1899.

89. Daniel B. Schirmer, *Republic or Empire: American Resistance to the Philippine War* (Cambridge: Schenkman Publishing, 1972), pp. 138, 172–173.

The activities of Boston's black citizens in the fall of 1899 indicated that Plummer was not engaging in idle boasts. At a mass meeting on October 3 sponsored by the National Colored Protective League and chaired by Grimké, the "colored people of Massachusetts" addressed an open letter to President McKinley. One of the most stinging indictments of the president's expansionist policy, the document condemned McKinley for his racist policies both at home and abroad. It pointed out that while he had used federal power "for the liberation of alien islanders and the subjugation of others," he always claimed to be powerless to protect colored Americans at home. Instead he courted the favor of those white Southerners who humiliated and oppressed their black neighbors. "We felt," the letter declared, "that the President of the United States, in order to win the support of the South to his policy of 'criminal aggression' on the Far East, was ready and willing to shut his eyes, ears, and lips to the 'criminal aggression' of that section against the Constitution and the laws of the land. . . ." [90]

While black Bostonians in general envisioned "a revolt at the ballot box," Plummer claimed that their supporters included some who were not opposed to armed resistance and "who, were it possible, would offer their strength to aid the Filipinos in their struggle for independence." In discussing the sentiment toward an "armed uprising," he revealed that during the Spanish-American War some black citizens had wanted to strike a blow against their white American oppressors by aiding the Spaniards.

> During the war with Spain a proportion of the more enthusiastic of the colored people of New England and some of the Middle and Southwestern States were ready to make an armed revolt against the United States and to espouse the cause of Spain. The feeling still exists to a large degree, and . . . were it possible to render the fighting Filipinos armed assistance, it would be done. It was, in fact, only the cooler minds and trained intelligence of certain of the race that successfully prevented the more open expression of feeling and the actual offer of services. It was the purpose of some of the people to raise troops as quietly as possible, to get out of the country in detachments, and to join the forces of Spain.[91]

90. Herbert Aptheker, ed., *Documentary History of the Negro People in the United States* (New York: Citadel Press, 1951), 787–791, 824.
91. *Ibid.*, p. 824.

While validity of Plummer's assertion cannot be corroborated by other direct testimony, the prospect of an uprising by Negroes during the war had troubled some white Southerners. It is possible too that the repeated warnings in 1898 against unpatriotic acts and utterances issued by the more conservative elements in the Negro community may have been prompted by rumors of a movement to aid Spain.

Regardless of its factual validity, the notion of a revolt by Negroes during the Spanish-American War figured prominently in a novel published in 1899 by Sutton E. Griggs, a black Baptist minister in Nashville. Griggs's *Imperium in Imperio*, described by one authority as "the first political novel by an American Negro," focused on the activities of a national Negro organization and two of its members, Bernard Belgrave and Belton Piedmont. The Imperium in Imperio was a secret, militant league established "to unite all Negroes in a body" with a view toward freeing them from the oppression of a white racist government. As president of the league, Belgrave proposed that black Americans engage in an open revolt for the purpose of seizing control of Louisiana and Texas. The revolt which was to take place during the Spanish-American War would be carried out with the aid of an unidentified foreign power. Once the revolution succeeded, according to Belgrave's plan, Louisiana was to be ceded to the foreign ally in return for its assistance, and Texas was to become an independent black nation. Piedmont, who perhaps represented one of the cooler heads, opposed Belgrave's resort to armed revolt and chose death by execution rather than take part in such a treasonous plan. Griggs's novel was virtually unknown to white Americans, but it probably circulated more widely among blacks than the fiction of Charles W. Chesnutt, Paul Laurence Dunbar, and other more prominent Negro literary figures.[92]

Although the name of Frederick Douglass was often invoked by those interested in keeping Negroes loyal to the Republican

92. Sutton E. Griggs, *Imperium in Imperio: A Study of the Negro Problem* (Cincinnati: Editor Publishing, 1899); Hugh M. Gloster, *Negro Voices in American Fiction* (Chapel Hill: University of North Carolina Press, 1948), pp. 56–58; Marks, *Black Press Views American Imperialism*, p. xxin; John W. Cromwell, "Review of *Imperium in Imperio,*" Washington *Colored American*, April 9, 1899; Robert E. Fleming, "Sutton E. Griggs: Militant Black Novelist," *Phylon*, XXXIV (March, 1973), 73–77.

party, even members of the Douglass family expressed grave misgivings about the party's imperialist program. Douglass's son-in-law Nathan Sprague resigned from the Republican state committee in Maryland in protest against McKinley's policy of imposing upon the colored Filipinos "a warped civilization" which allowed its own citizens of color to be "lynched and burned at the stake." Lewis H. Douglass, the son of the revered black leader, was no less critical of President McKinley, claiming that his administration lacked "the courage to deal with American citizens without regard to race or color." "It is a sorry, though true, fact," Douglass declared, "that wherever this government controls, injustice to dark races prevails." Therefore the president's grandiose promises of liberty and justice to the Filipinos constituted "hypocrisy of the most sickening kind." References to the Filipinos as "niggers" confirmed Douglass's suspicions that McKinley imperialism meant "the extension of race hate and cruelty, barbarous lynchings and gross injustice" to the brown people of the Orient.[93]

Black Democrats were even less restrained in their criticism of McKinley's Philippine policy and obviously hoped to capitalize upon its unpopularity in persuading Negro voters to abandon the Republican party. Two leading black Democratic journals, the Indianapolis *World* and Julius Taylor's *Broad Ax,* concentrated their editorial fire upon Republican imperialism for months and repeatedly referred to the military conflict in the Philippines as "a race war." Both newspapers (and especially the *Broad Ax* after its transfer from Salt Lake City to Chicago in mid-1899) endorsed the position of the Anti-Imperialist League and equated the Democratic party and William Jennings Bryan with the cause of liberty for "the dark skinned Filipinos." Black Democratic politicians, unusually active in the state campaigns in the fall of 1899, invariably interpreted the plight of Negroes in the United States and the war in the Philippines as evidence of the Republicans' oppression of colored races. Among the new organizations launched by Negro Democrats in 1899, the one with the most imposing title was the National Negro Anti-Expansion, Anti-Imperialist, Anti-Trust and Anti-Lynching League. Its founder was William T.

93. *Washington Bee,* November 4, 1899; Lewis H. Douglass in Kansas City *American Citizen,* November 17, 1899.

Scott of Cairo, Illinois, a native of Ohio and a veteran of the Civil War who had amassed considerable wealth as a saloonkeeper and dabbler in real estate. Scott abandoned the Republican party in 1880 and functioned as an independent until four years later, when he switched his allegiance to the party of Grover Cleveland. In the fall of 1899 his newly created League, with branches in Illinois, Ohio, and Kentucky, actively campaigned for Democratic candidates in those states and promised to take an even larger role in the forthcoming presidential campaign.[94]

The political implications of the anti-expansionist clamor among black citizens placed loyal Negro Republicans on the defensive. Despite their eloquence in behalf of McKinley's Philippine policy and their efforts to convey the impression that black opposition to the administration was limited to a handful of discontented editors, they actually feared that Negroes would abandon the Republican party in sizable numbers. Reverdy Ransom, a well-known black clergyman in Chicago, informed John P. Green that all prominent colored citizens whom he knew were opposed to the president because of his failure to reward the black soldiers of the Cuban campaign and his timidity regarding racial atrocities in the South.[95] In conveying Ransom's letter to McKinley, Green also informed the president: "I might add that so far as my information goes, the war in the Philippines is *exceedingly* unpopular amongst all colored people, without regard to conditions." Green pleaded with the president to arrange for him to secure a railroad pass so that he could contact black leaders in various sections of the country in an effort to quiet their discontent with the administration's policies.[96]

Late in July, 1899, when the departure of the black regulars for the Philippines quickened opposition to these policies, Green, Judson Lyons, Henry P. Cheatham, and other prominent Negro officeholders in Washington hastened to the White House to assure McKinley of the loyalty of black citizens to his administra-

94. See Chicago *Broad Ax* and Indianapolis *World*, January 14–December 30, 1899; W. T. Scott to James Russel, in Chicago *Broad Ax*, September 30, 1899. For a lengthy biographical sketch of Scott, see Indianapolis *Freeman*, October 19, 1899; on the Negro voter in the campaigns of 1899 in Ohio, Kentucky, and Maryland, see Washington *Colored American*, October 14, 28, 1899.
95. Reverdy C. Ransom to John P. Green, June 27, 1899, McKinley Papers.
96. John P. Green to William McKinley, June 29, 1899, *ibid.*

tion and the Republican party.[97] A similar gesture at the outbreak of the Spanish-American War had prompted a hostile reaction from a relatively small segment of the black press; in 1899 the response was overwhelmingly negative. Harry Smith summarized the editorial reaction when he characterized "Messrs. Lyons, Cheatham and Co." as a group of "self constituted and white man made" black leaders "whose eagerness to toady to the administration seems to exceed their loyalty to the race." [98]

President McKinley himself was troubled by the mounting dissatisfaction among black voters. He was especially anxious about the anti-administration position of the *New York Age* and its editor, T. Thomas Fortune. In the fall of 1899 Democrats in the president's home state of Ohio urged Fortune to deliver speeches in behalf of their gubernatorial candidate. They specifically requested that he emphasize the anti-expansionist theme. At McKinley's request, R. R. Wright and Booker T. Washington used their influence to persuade the New York editor to decline the invitation and to remain loyal to the Republican party.[99]

In a conference with Bishop Abram Grant of the A.M.E. Church, the president indicated that he was perplexed by the attitude of Negroes in view of the fact that he had appointed more black men to federal office "than any other president." Bishop Grant told him that the issue was not his appointment policy, but his failure to speak out boldly against the wanton persecution of Negroes in the South. All the while others, like Green, impressed upon him the toll which his treatment of Negro soldiers and his Philippine policy were taking among his black constituency.[100] Even if the president had been inclined to make one, a strong statement on the Georgia lynchings probably would have been inappropriate at such a late date. But it was not too late to attempt to overcome the hostility arising from what colored citizens considered the government's shabby treatment of black soldiers who served during the Spanish-American War. Register of the Trea-

97. Cleveland *Gazette*, July 22, 1899.
98. *Ibid.*, July 29, August 12, 1899.
99. Booker T. Washington to R. R. Wright, October 20, 1899, T. Thomas Fortune to Charles W. Dick, October 23, 1899, R. R. Wright to William McKinley, October 24, 1899, McKinley Papers.
100. Cleveland *Gazette*, July 29, 1899; see also "Atkinson, McKinley, Expansion and the Negro," *A.M.E. Church Review*, V (October, 1899), 275–276.

sury Judson Lyons in particular urged McKinley to take some step to mollify blacks on this issue. At Lyons's prodding the president joined General Miles in recommending that black volunteers be recruited for service in the Philippines. While Miles believed that Negroes were "better adapted for this work than their white brethren," McKinley's recommendation seems to have been motivated by more political considerations. If the move was designed to allay the discontent among blacks, it was obvious that they would accept as satisfactory nothing less than black regiments with all black officers. McKinley may well have had such an arrangement in mind, but the War Department obviously did not.[101]

Early in July the black press reported that the War Department would not call up black volunteers for service in the Philippines because its experience with such soldiers in the Spanish-American War had been unsatisfactory. Although War Department officials may have opposed a repetition of what they considered an unhappy experiment, there were perhaps other reasons for their reluctance to accept black volunteers under "their own officers." [102] The crucial question which confronted them, according to Calvin Chase, was "Will Darkey Fight Darkey?" [103] An official in the department was quoted as saying: "I doubt whether half-disciplined Negroes, under the command of Negro officers, if brought face to face with their colored Filipino cousins, could be made to fire upon them or fight them. If the Negro understands the Filipinos are fighting for liberty and independence, ten chances to one they would take sides with them." [104] No such doubt existed about the Negro regulars, presumably because they were better trained and under the command of white officers.

Ultimately, however, pressure from the White House resulted in a decision to form two regiments of Negro volunteers, the Forty-eighth and Forty-ninth Infantry, for use in the Philippines. The regiments were to be recruited directly by the War Depart-

101. Cleveland *Gazette*, August 19, 1899. Lyons was apparently the individual most persistent in urging McKinley to recommend black volunteers for service in the Philippines; see *Washington Bee*, September 30, 1899.

102. Kansas City *Daily American Citizen*, July 2, 1899.

103. *Washington Bee*, September 9, 1899.

104. *Dispatch* (Richmond, Va.) quoted *ibid*. See also *Parsons Weekly Blade*, July 1, 1899; A. R. Abbott, "Negro Soldiers for the Philippines," *Anglo-American Magazine*, II (November, 1899), 453–457.

ment without regard to state boundaries, and Negroes were to be allowed to hold commissions below the rank of major. The decision regarding commissions obviously represented a compromise between the demands of Lyons, the black official most intimately involved in the negotiations regarding the formation of the regiments, and the opposition of the War Department to black volunteer officers. Those Negroes commissioned as lieutenants and captains in the new regiments were either regulars who had distinguished themselves in Cuba or volunteers from the state and immune regiments who had indicated an aptitude for company positions. The twenty-five regulars who received commissions were granted leaves from their own regiments for the duration of the volunteers' tour of duty. At the expiration of that leave they were to return to their own regular army units at their former rank. Of the other company officers, fifteen had formerly served with the immunes and twenty-nine had been officers in state units. Early in September, 1899, orders were issued for the organization of the Forty-eighth to take place at Fort Thomas, Kentucky, and the Forty-ninth at Jefferson Barracks, Missouri.[105]

Most black spokesmen, whether they supported or opposed the president's Philippine policy, viewed the formation of these two regiments as an effort to eradicate "Negro discontent with McKinley" before the presidential election year. The president himself took credit for the regiments. In conferring with a delegation of Negro lawyers at the White House, he revealed that strong pressure had been exerted upon him to prevent the appointment of any Negro officers, but that he had held out for an arrangement that would allow the competent black soldier "to make a record for himself." In the fall of 1899 McKinley paid increasing homage to the valor of Negro soldiers and appealed to the pride and patriotism of black voters.[106] If his object was to allay the criticism of his administration emanating from the black community, his efforts were not altogether in vain.

105. *Washington Bee*, September 2, 16, 1899; Washington *Colored American*, September 23, 1899; Richard Johnson, "My Life in the U. S. Army, 1899–1922," (typescript, U.S. Army Military History Collection, Carlisle Barracks, Pa.), pp. 17–19; Colonel William Beck to the Adjutant General, October 30, 1899, Regimental Records, Forty-ninth United States Volunteer Infantry, Record Group 94, National Archives.
106. *Washington Bee*, September 16, October 14, 1899.

After a visit to the White House in mid-September, 1899, Calvin Chase announced that while he had hoped the black volunteer regiments would have complete rosters of black officers, he was certain that the president's action would "put an end to so much dissatisfaction among Negro Republicans." Chase discovered quite suddenly that McKinley was "on the right track" in the Philippines and began to argue that expansion meant constant association with darker races abroad, which in turn would "liberalize racial attitudes at home." The editorial reversal of the Indianapolis *Recorder* was no less dramatic. By December, 1899, the paper viewed Aguinaldo not as a hero but as a "sham leader" willing to destroy his "poor, ignorant" followers for self-gain. The editors of the *Washington Bee* and the Indianapolis *Recorder,* like other traditionally black Republicans, had perhaps come to appreciate George L. Knox's warning that opposition to the McKinley administration would either place them in strange company or leave them without a political home in the presidential election of 1900. As for Calvin Chase, he believed that the Democratic and Republican parties were "two great political evils" and urged blacks to take the lesser evil and remain loyal to the party of Lincoln.[107]

The organization of the two volunteer regiments with partial rosters of black officers was the signal for Edward E. Cooper to renew his courtship with the McKinley administration and rejoin the ranks of the imperialists. Unlike Chase, Cooper provided an elaborate (if somewhat awkward) rationale for the change in the editorial stance of his *Colored American,* which had always been uncomfortable in its role as a critic of McKinley's Philippine policy. Shortly after the announcement of the decision regarding the Forty-eighth and Forty-ninth Infantry, the *Colored American* declared:

> The administration has realized the failure to utilize the valor and experience of Negro soldiers in the Philippines was an unjust discrimination and mistake. By this change of policy and evident desire to recognize the gallant black boys who fought at San Juan and served so faithfully in the United States camps last year,

107. *Ibid.,* September 30, October 7, 1899; Indianapolis *Recorder,* November 19, December 2, 1899.

President McKinley has raised himself high in the esteem of the
Afro-American. . . . He has furnished his party adherents with a
fine lot of campaign rhetoric.[108]

However, Cooper neither criticized black Americans for allowing
their racial sympathies to rest with the dark-skinned Filipino nor
denied that Aguinaldo was a man of character and ability; rather,
he argued that the higher duty of the black citizen was to his
country and that the Filipino chieftain, for all his admirable qualities, was bound to lose. Borrowing an argument from the white
expansionists, he declared that the Filipinos would benefit from
contact with the civilization of a superior race. For the United
States to abandon the helpless natives of the islands would be an
evasion of responsibility forced upon the nation by the fortunes
of war. Cooper still desired a speedy end to the "cruel and expensive war" in the Philippines which would result in establishing
"the purest system of self-government" for the natives. Both objectives could best be promoted by uniting in support of President
McKinley, whose "righteous judgment" could always be relied
upon to find a way out of the imbroglio that would be "honorable alike to all concerned." [109]

Unlike Cooper, George L. Knox of the Indianapolis *Freeman*
did not have to reverse himself in order to applaud the president
for creating two regiments of black volunteers for service in the
Philippines. In fact, Knox had long urged black citizens to "go
slow" in opposing McKinley's Philippine policy lest they find
themselves in league with the "party of Tillman" in the next election. By the summer of 1899 he was calling upon the president to
organize black volunteer units for duty in the Philippines, and
when the decision to send Negro regulars to the islands was announced, he encouraged black men to do their duty. Knox assured
them that the conflict in the Philippines was not a race war, but
a war to sustain the nation's legitimate authority: "It is quite time
for Negroes to quit claiming kindred with every black face from
Hannibal down," he declared. "Hannibal was no Negro, neither
is Aguinaldo." Patriotism, Knox repeated, required all Ameri-

108. Washington *Colored American*, September 16, 1899.
109. *Ibid.*, October 7, 21, 28, November 4, 11, 1899.

cans, black and white, to uphold the flag and "share in the glories or defeats of the country's wars." [110]

Few black Americans were prepared to accept Knox's advice or to see in the creation of the two regiments of black volunteers any reason for relaxing their opposition to the war in the Philippines. They felt that the president's concession was "too little and too late." [111] Many, like Harry Smith, considered the color line drawn against black officers in the two regiments as an insult to Negro citizens. Outraged by the administration's attempt to woo black voters by a policy that kept "competent Afro-Americans from serving in the highest military ranks," Julius Taylor's Chicago *Broad Ax* declared: "We would rather be called traitors . . . than permit ourselves to shoulder a musket for the purpose of deliberately murdering Filipinos who are fighting for liberty and independence." [112] The *Richmond Planet* and Omaha *Progress* continued to oppose what they termed McKinley's "cruel and imperialist war," chiding men such as Chase and Cooper for selling their editorial souls for two regiments in which Negroes were not allowed to hold a rank higher than captain. Even the Democratic governor of Virginia had been more generous during the Spanish-American War, they pointed out. The *Progress* expressed the hope that the regiments would never be organized and, if organized, never be sent to the Philippines.[113]

Other outspoken opponents of the Philippine war either directly or indirectly discouraged black men from enlisting in the regiments. Ralph W. Tyler, a prominent Negro Republican in Ohio, claimed that no Afro-American with "a spark of manhood or race pride" would join one of the president's "colored regiments, to go to the Philippines, there to fight their own color, who like we in America are fighting for liberty." [114] Despite his declining health, the senior bishop of the A.M.E. Church, Henry M.

110. Indianapolis *Freeman*, March 11, July 1, September 30, October 17, 1899.

111. Washington *Colored American*, September 16, 1899.

112. Cleveland *Gazette*, September 9, 1899; Chicago *Broad Ax*, September 23, 1899.

113. *Richmond Planet*, September 9, 30, October 14, 21, 1899; Omaha *Progress* quoted in Indianapolis *Freeman*, September 30, 1899, and in *Washington Bee*, September 30, 1899.

114. Quoted in Washington *Colored American*, September 16, 1899.

Turner, was still strong enough to issue a broadside against any black American who dared take up arms against the dark-skinned natives of the Philippines. Such a black man was either a fool or a villain; Turner's "sincere prayer" was that any black citizen who responded to the president's call for volunteers should "get ball stung." [115] In a similar vein the Democratic editor of the Indianapolis *World* argued that any Negro who volunteered for service in the Philippines did "not himself deserve freedom." [116]

Throughout the early fall of 1899, as the two black volunteer regiments were being organized, opponents of the Philippine war continued to castigate those who had so little race pride as to enlist in such outfits. Anti-expansionist newspapers printed numerous letters from black regulars in the Philippines, who described the discrimination practiced by military authorities against them as well as the other "niggers" there, the Filipinos.[117] They also noted incidents in which colored officers of the new volunteer regiments were subjected to insults and the usual taunts from white soldiers, such as "all coons look alike to me." [118] The *Richmond Planet* urged more Negroes to follow the example of Benjamin Graves, formerly an officer in the Sixth Virginia who refused a commission as captain in one of the regiments being recruited for service in the Philippines. Graves, the *Planet* maintained, preferred a teaching position in the public schools to a commission in an army of conquest. Although the salary of a captain was double that of a public school teacher, Graves desired a position that would allow him to contribute to the uplift of colored people rather than to their annihilation.[119] Although the response of black men to the president's call for volunteers indicated that the protests of the anti-expansionists had not been without effect, the Forty-eighth and Forty-ninth Regiments were finally organized and readied to take up the "white man's burden" in the Philippines. In January, 1900, the black volunteers began to arrive in Ma-

115. Quoted in Cleveland *Gazette,* November 25, 1899.
116. Indianapolis *World,* October 28, 1899.
117. See *Richmond Planet,* September–December, 1899, for numerous letters from black regulars in the Philippines.
118. *Ibid.,* October 7, 1899; Cleveland *Gazette,* January 27, 1900.
119. *Richmond Planet,* September 30, 1899.

nila.[120] During the next ten months the expansionism debate passed through its most acrimonious phase among black citizens at home.

In 1899 the misgivings of black Americans regarding the policy of the McKinley administration hardened into forthright opposition as a result of the Philippine crisis. Only a few Negroes, notably McKinley's black appointees, consistently supported the administration's policy in the islands. Anti-imperialism became the prevailing sentiment within the black community; increase in this sentiment coincided with the upsurge in anti-imperialist opinion among white Americans. But the motives behind each movement differed along racial lines. To be sure, Negroes applauded the utterances of such white anti-imperialists as Senator Hoar, Thomas Wentworth Higginson, and others inclined to draw a parallel between the lynching of black people in the United States and the extermination of brown people in the Philippines. Only rarely, however, did white opponents of McKinley's policy, including the mugwumpish Anti-Imperialist League, recognize the existence of black anti-imperialist sentiment.

120. William P. Duvall to the Adjutant General, January 24, 1900, #312490, Adjutant General's Records.

Nine

Black Americans and the Paramount Issue in 1900

The whole trend of imperial aggression is antagonistic to the feebler races. It is a revival of racial arrogance. It has ever been the boast of the proud and haughty race or nation that God has given them the heathen for their inheritance and the uttermost parts of the earth for their possession. . . . Will the Negro stultify himself and become part of the movement which must end in his own humiliation?
—Kelly Miller, October, 1900

At the opening of the twentieth century a sense of crisis pervaded the black community in the United States. In fact, James M. Trotter of Boston maintained, "There never has been such a crisis in the history of the American negro as there is today." The proliferation of personal liberty leagues and protective associations suggested the gravity of the situation. Increasingly Negro citizens recognized that racial prejudice was no longer confined to Dixie. In August, 1900, a prominent black woman in Minnesota remarked that there was "an epidemic of Negrophobia all over the country." In a report to the North Ohio Conference of the African Methodist Episcopal Church, the Reverend Charles Bundy of Cleveland took cognizance of the anxiety and uncertainty which existed throughout the black community as a result of the swell of anti-Negro sentiment. "We find to our sorrow," Bundy's report noted, "that prejudice is increasing to an alarming degree." [1] The view that the "close and harmonious alliance" forged between the North and South by the war with Spain had placed upon Negroes "a larger measure of eternal vigilance" found sup-

1. *The Boston Globe*, August 17, 1900; St. Paul *Afro-American Advance*, August 25, 1900; *Colored American Magazine*, II (November, 1900), 50.

port in America's postwar imperialist activities. If black Americans detected a relationship between the upsurge of racism at home and the nation's war against "the little brown brothers" in the Philippines, they also recognized that colorphobia, rather than being a problem peculiar to the United States, existed among whites throughout much of the Western world. Late in 1899 a writer in the *A.M.E. Church Review* observed that the colonial thrust of Western nations against the "darker races in Africa and Asia" had initiated "a startling world movement . . . which is no less than the stirring of the spirit of civilization and prowess among the dark-skinned races." [2]

The impact of Western imperialism upon such races was a principal concern of the black Americans who attended the first Pan-African Conference which met late in July, 1900, in London. Bishop Alexander Walters and W. E. B. Du Bois were among the eleven delegates from the United States who participated in the deliberations at Westminster Hall concerning the "present condition and outlook of the darker races of mankind." Bishop Walters was elected president of the body, and Du Bois, one of its vice-presidents, was also head of the committee charged with drafting an Address to the Nations of the World. Du Bois's committee wrote a document which stated that "the problem of the Twentieth Century is the color line" and which appealed to the Western powers to repudiate racism in their dealings with the nonwhite peoples of their colonial empires. Taking cognizance of the plight of black Americans, the memorial urged that they be guaranteed "the right of the franchise" and "security of person and property," calling upon all Americans to keep alive "the spirit of Garrison, Phillips and Douglass." [3]

By the time the American delegates to the Pan-African Conference returned home, however, such a spirit seemed to be virtually

2. *New York Age*, January 4, 1900; *A.M.E. Church Review*, October 1899, quoted in Marks, ed., *Black Press Views American Imperialism*, p. 154.

3. Walters, *My Life and Work*, pp. 253–264; Elliott M. Rudwick, *W. E. B. Du Bois: Propagandist of Negro Protest* (New York: Atheneum, 1968), pp. 208–209; *The Times* (London), July 24, 25, 26, 1900; Richard B. Moore, "DuBois and Pan Africa," in Okon Edet Uya, ed., *Black Brotherhood: Afro-Americans and Africa* (Lexington, Mass.: D. C. Heath, 1971), pp. 156–158; George Shepperson, "Notes on Negro American Influence on the Emergence of African Nationalism," *ibid.*, pp. 221–222; Indianapolis *World*, August 18, 1900.

extinguished. Late in August Bishop Walters told the Afro-American Council that black citizens in the United States were in the midst of one of their most critical periods. The crude rhetoric of negrophobes, the enactment of discriminatory legislation, and the eruption of diverse forms of racial violence testified to the accuracy of the bishop's observation. White audiences throughout the United States applauded Senator Benjamin R. Tillman's racist lectures on the Negro Problem, while legislators in various states of the South were busily engaged in seeking constitutional and legal devices to solve it. In 1900 North Carolina disfranchised its black electorate, and Virginia joined the growing list of states with statutes segregating the races on public transportation facilities. Movements for racially separate schools in Kansas and Illinois lent credence to the view that Jim Crowism was a national rather than a sectional phenomenon.[4]

In the first year of the twentieth century, nothing created more anxiety among black Americans than the outbreak of violence which threatened their personal security. Large race riots erupted in New Orleans, New York, and Akron in the summer of 1900, while brutal lynchings continued to occur with alarming frequency. Although the South still dominated the pages of this bloody record, at least a half-dozen blacks were lynched in 1900 in Indiana, Kansas, Colorado, and Nebraska.[5] The threats to the life and liberty of the black man which appeared to assume particularly menacing proportions between 1898 and 1900 caused some Negro spokesmen to long for a "new allotment of Joshua E. Giddings, Lovejoys and Charles Sumners . . . to [take up] the cause of the down-trodden Afro-American in his humiliated condition. . . ."[6] Those who looked to President McKinley to assume such a role were consistently disappointed. Neither the Wilmington "massacre" of 1898 nor the racial outrages in Georgia in 1899 prompted him to take a strong stand against lynching, and

4. Washington *Colored American,* September 8. 1900; William A. Mabry, *The Negro in North Carolina Politics since Reconstruction* (Durham: Duke University Press, 1940), pp. 57–72; *The Reformer* (Richmond), January 27, 1900; *The National Pilot* (Petersburg, Va.), February 1, 1900.

5. Seth M. Schiener, *Negro Mecca: A History of the Negro in New York City, 1865–1920* (New York: New York University Press, 1965), pp. 121–127; Brawley, *Social History of the American Negro,* pp. 315–317; Cleveland *Gazette,* September 1, 1900; Aptheker, *Documentary History of the Negro People,* pp. 800–803.

6. Cleveland *Gazette,* March 18, 1899; Washington *Colored American,* February 10, 1900.

Congress allowed the anti-lynching bill introduced by Representative George H. White to remain buried in committee.[7]

In his third annual message to Congress on December 5, 1899,
the president did devote several paragraphs to lynching, but his
remarks were concerned solely with the hanging of "five unfor-
tunates of Italian origin" in Tallulah, Louisiana, an incident
which had brought forth strong protests from the Italian government. Although McKinley's message also promised justice to Filipinos and Cubans, it included no comparable commitment to
black Americans; in fact, it omitted any reference to the so-called
Negro Question. Only by the most liberal interpretation of the
president's remarks on the Tallulah lynchings could Negro parti-
sans of the Republican administration make them applicable to
black citizens.[8] Even Edward E. Cooper, who described the message as "a refreshing draught" which would "do much to silence
one very strong ground for complaint on the part of our people,"
admitted that he would have been much more encouraged if
McKinley had spoken as "directly on the lynching of Negroes as
of Italians."[9] Other black spokesmen, in a state of near despair
over the number and brutality of crimes committed against their
race, found little in the address to inspire optimism.[10] They were
only too well aware that it was the lynching of Italians, rather
than Negroes, which had elicited a response from the White
House. Though they expressed doubts about the sincerity of Mc-
Kinley's promises to the Cubans and Filipinos, they were nonetheless resentful that he ignored the crisis which confronted black
citizens at home. While the beleaguered Filipinos had the sympathy of much of the black community, many Negroes continued
to be disturbed by the ordering of the nation's priorities which
allowed the welfare of "alien peoples" to take precedence over
that of its own black minority.

The presidential campaign of 1900 witnessed a climax to the
public debate over imperialism, and the Negro Americans' concern about national priorities figured significantly in their choice

7. *Wide-Awake* (Birmingham), January 24, 1900; Maurine Christopher, *America's
Black Congressmen* (New York: Thomas Y. Crowell, 1971), pp. 165–166.

8. Fred Israel, *The State of the Union Messages of the Presidents, 1790–1966*,
3 vols. (New York: Chelsea House–Robert Hector, 1966), II, 1937–38.

9. Washington *Colored American*, December 9, 1899.

10. See Cleveland *Gazette*, December 9, 1899; Chicago *Broad Ax*, December 9,
1899.

of candidates. Whether the black voter remained loyal to the Republican party or shifted his support to the Democratic party depended largely upon what he perceived to be the route offering the best prospects for alleviation of racial prejudice. Ideally, of course, the promise of racial justice would embrace the colored people of the overseas possessions as well as those at home, but among other factors complicating the political decisions of Negro American voters was the absence of a single party which held out the hope of such justice both for them and for their cousins overseas. The choice that confronted them was between one party which offered little to black Americans and much to the Filipinos and another party which, though committed to thwarting Aguinaldo's fight for independence, at least possessed a tradition of being the black citizens' friend.

In the presidential contest of 1900 the Democrats and Republicans adopted opposing positions regarding imperialism. The Democratic party and its presidential nominee, William Jennings Bryan, pronounced imperialism the paramount issue of the campaign and tried for a time to make the election a popular referendum on the issue.[11] The anti-imperialist platform of Bryan's party condemned as un-American the course pursued in the Philippines by the McKinley administration. The Republicans countered with a vigorous defense of expansionism and promised only to grant the Filipinos "the largest measure of self-government consistent with their welfare and our duties." [12] They renominated McKinley and chose Governor Theodore Roosevelt of New York as his vice-presidential running mate.

By 1900 the twenty-year process of excluding black voters from the national political structure seemed to be almost complete. Disillusioned with the Republicans because they had abandoned the cause of the black man's civil rights, some black Americans who advocated political independence took up residence in the Democratic camp. Such a shift in allegiance often proved to be

11. On Bryan and the Democratic campaign of 1900, see Paolo Coletta, *William Jennings Bryan: Political Evangelist, 1860–1908* (Lincoln: University of Nebraska Press, 1964), pp. 259–263.

12. *Official Proceedings of the Twelfth Republican National Convention Held in the City of Philadelphia, June 19, 20, 21, 1900* (Philadelphia: Press of Dunlap Printing, 1900), p. 108; see also Philip W. Kennedy, "Racial Overtones of Imperialism as a Campaign Issue, 1900," *Mid-America*, XLVIII (July, 1966), 196–205.

only temporary, because Negroes rarely felt comfortable for long in a party dominated by race-baiting white Southerners.[13] Although black Democratic organizations existed in certain areas such as New York, where Richard Croker's Tammany Hall machine sponsored the United Colored Democracy,[14] most Negroes preferred to remain within the Republican party no matter how far it had retreated from its original ideals. But their presence in Republican ranks did not imply uncritical acceptance of party performance. As one historian has noted, Negro voters remained "loyal but critical of the Republican Party" in the closing years of the nineteenth century.[15]

In the presidential campaign of 1900 even this precarious loyalty appeared to be in jeopardy, not only because the party of emancipation continued to ignore its black constituency, but also because its imperialist stance was considered inimical to the interests of colored people in the overseas possessions. As Charles Winslow Hall noted, by 1900 the Republican party had so completely "turned its back upon its heritage" that party leaders "practically declared that every dark-skinned race is unfitted to exercise self-government."[16] For Negroes who viewed the political situation in such a vein, it mattered not that the Republican platform of 1900 condemned the disfranchisement of black voters in the South or that Senator Henry Cabot Lodge reaffirmed the party's commitment "to the rights of man." Similar pronouncements had been made before with little practical effect. Indeed, Lodge's justification of imperialism on the grounds that "the liberator may be trusted to watch over the liberated" offered scant reassurance to disenchanted black Republicans.[17] Many dismissed it as sheer cant.

13. For the tendency of Negroes to display political independence, see Lewis, "Political Mind of the Negro," 189–202.

14. On the origins of the United Colored Democracy in 1898, see Scheiner, *Negro Mecca*, pp. 193–194.

15. See August Meier, "The Negro and the Democratic Party, 1875–1915," *Phylon*, XVII (2nd Quarter, 1956), 182–191.

16. Charles Winslow Hall, "The Old or the New Faith, Which?" *Colored American Magazine*, I (August, 1900), 173.

17. For Lodge's remarks, see *Official Proceedings of the Twelfth Republican National Convention*, p. 87. A delegation from the Afro American Council which attended the convention and urged the party's platform committee to take a forthright stand against lynching was disappointed that the platform was no more explicit on the subject; see Washington *Colored American*, June 30, 1900.

During the opening months of the campaign year, the anti-imperialist sentiment among Negro Americans showed few signs of relaxing despite the reversals made by Calvin Chase, Edward E. Cooper, and several other well-known black editors. In fact, developments in the spring of 1900 tended to strengthen rather than weaken their opposition to the president's expansion policy. Few Negro citizens were happy over the drift of affairs in either Cuba or Puerto Rico. They resented what they called General Leonard Wood's introduction of "southern race prejudice" into Cuba and feared that Afro-Cubans would be relegated to a status of permanent inferiority in the new Cuban republic. Even black Americans who had no intention of bolting the Republican party understood why Cubans of all colors "were in sympathy with Mr. Bryan and the Democratic Party." Although Cooper's *Colored American* refused "to get excited" early in 1900 when Congress passed a Puerto Rican tariff bill and a law establishing a civil government on the island, other Negroes interpreted these measures as explicit denials of McKinley's claim that "our priceless principles undergo no change under a tropical sun." [18]

The outbreak of the Boxer Rebellion in China in June, 1900, and the subsequent participation of the United States in an international military expedition to crush it also served to magnify the doubts of black Americans who had reservations about the policy of imperialism. John Mitchell was certain that the use of American troops in China would work "to the benefit of the Democratic leaders, who have declared that Imperialism is the paramount issue in the campaign." That it might enhance their anti-imperialist overtures to black voters appeared to be a distinct possibility.[19] Even the more avid supporters of McKinley's policies within the Negro community could muster little enthusiasm for sending military forces to Peking. For example, although Edward E. Cooper commended Secretary of State John Hay's note on the Chinese crisis and encouraged black men to enlist for military service in case the United States became involved in a full-fledged war with China, he did "not blame the Chinese for resenting the

18. Lynch, *Reminiscences of an Active Life,* pp. 447–448, Washington *Colored American,* April 8, 1900; Indianapolis *Recorder,* June 9, 1900; *The Negro World* (St. Paul), April 28, 1900; *The New Age* (Portland, Ore.), April 7, 28, 1900; Indianapolis *World,* March 24, 1900.
19. *Richmond Planet,* July 21, 1900.

interference of foreigners" and seriously questioned the wisdom of sending Christian missionaries among them. Other pro-McKinley spokesmen agreed with Cooper that in spite of the fact that local evils made it difficult for black men to become enthusiastic about participating in a war with China, it was their duty as citizens to come to the defense of the beleaguered American missionaries and diplomats in Peking. But their support of intervention was almost invariably predicated upon the condition that the United States "should have no part in such a land grabbing scheme as will result from the dismemberment of China." [20]

Outspoken Negro anti-imperialists, Democrats as well as independents and some Republicans, loudly protested American involvement in the Chinese crisis and pointed to McKinley's tendency to disregard the nation's nonentanglement tradition as evidence of the dangers inherent in his imperialist course. A report that the president intended to send the Ninth Cavalry to rescue white Americans in Peking and to uphold Secretary Hay's Open Door policy prompted blistering retorts from the more militant Negro critics of McKinley expansionism. Some demanded that the government concern itself with maintaining the "open door" for Negroes in the United States by combatting "the work of American Boxers" such as the Red Shirts, White Cappers, and other vigilante groups rather than interfering in the affairs of China. John E. Bruce claimed that the atrocities committed by whites against black citizens in New Orleans during the riot in that city surpassed anything done by the Boxers.[21] "This is not our war," Bishop Henry M. Turner thundered, "and the black man who puts a gun upon his shoulder to go and fight China should find the bottom of the ocean before he gets there." The bishop was certain that only "the low, ignorant and scullion class" of black citizens would be taken in by the arguments that they had a duty to perform in China.[22] Prominent colored citizens in Chicago petitioned the president to revoke orders directing black

20. Washington *Colored American*, July 28, August 4, 25, 1900; Milwaukee *Wisconsin Weekly Advocate*, July 26, 1900; Indianapolis *Recorder*, June 23, 1900; Topeka *Kansas State Ledger*, October 4, 1900.

21. *Richmond Planet*, July 21, 1900; Cleveland *Gazette*, August 13, 1900; John E. Bruce in Washington *Colored American*, July 7, August 4, 1900; F. J. Loudin to John P. Green, August ?, 1900, Green Papers.

22. Henry M. Turner to the Editor of the *New York Age*, July 27, 1900, in Cleveland *Gazette*, August 18, 1900.

cavalrymen to Peking and urged him to dispatch them to the South, where black people were in dire need of protection.[23] Late in August, 1900, the international military force subdued the Boxers, and the Ninth Cavalry was among those American units en route to China which were diverted to the Philippines [24]—a destination that did little to quiet the noisy anti-imperialists in the Negro community.

In fact, the war in the Philippines was of far greater significance in shaping the black citizens' attitude toward overseas expansion in 1900 than affairs in Cuba, Puerto Rico, or China. By the time the presidential campaign was underway in the United States, communications from black soldiers stationed in the islands filled the columns of black newspapers. While these letters covered a wide variety of topics, the racial aspects of the war were important concerns of most correspondents. They identified racially with the Filipinos, whom one soldier described as "the best mulatto people I have seen," and viewed themselves as part of an experiment which "pitted Greek against Greek." Few of the black correspondents in the Philippines failed to comprehend the irony and contradiction inherent in their position as enemies of a colored people striving for freedom in distant Asiatic islands; nor were they oblivious to the contempt with which white Americans regarded Filipinos. In a letter to the Cleveland *Gazette* Patrick Mason of the Twenty-fourth Infantry described the Filipinos as "a patient, burden-bearing people" whom white soldiers referred to as "niggers" and treated as creatures without any rights whatsoever. Another Negro soldier admitted that the Filipinos had a just grievance because, as he described it, the "Americans, as soon as they saw that the native troops were desirous of sharing in the glories as well as the hardships of the hard-won battles . . . began to apply home treatment for colored peoples." In his letters to the *Richmond Planet* Sergeant John W. Galloway corroborated charges that white soldiers abused Filipinos and explained the cordial relations existing between Negro troops and natives of the islands in terms of their "affinity of complexion." The sergeant predicted

23. Cleveland *Gazette*, September 8, 1900.
24. Colonel T. B. Dugan, "History of the Ninth U. S. Cavalry, 1866–1906," #1374702, Adjutant General's Records. (Pages are unnumbered and the contents arranged by years.)

that the status of the Filipino under American rule was destined to be "that of the Negro in the South." [25]

The letters from black soldiers in the Philippines tended to confirm the view that the military struggle there was "a race war." George L. Knox might continue to insist that "imperialism and race issues have no connection," but a substantial segment of the black population saw the two phenomena as intimately related. In explaining the unpopularity of McKinley expansionism in the black community, Archibald Grimké maintained that "the absolute supineness of the executive" on the subject of lynching made Negroes "shudder for other peoples who may come under the yoke." [26] And a black editor in Helena, Arkansas, insisted that Negro Americans who took up arms against the dark-skinned Filipinos did so knowing that they were fighting to bestow upon the islands "color-phobia, jim crow cars, disfranchisement . . . and everything that prejudice can do to blight the manhood of darker races." [27] J. C. Reid, a well-known black citizen in Minnesota, claimed that the first-hand reports from the Philippines by Negro soldiers ought to serve as "a warning lesson to Afro-American expansionists." Reid referred not only to the treatment accorded Filipinos by white Americans, but also to the color line established in the Philippines against the Negro soldiers themselves. Segregated barbershops and restaurants in Manila appeared to proliferate in the wake of the American occupation of the islands.[28] The army was also accused of engaging in a variety of discriminatory practices. One story which aroused strong reaction in the black community concerned attempts to segregate the black and white officers of the Forty-ninth Volunteers during mess on board ship en route to the Philippines. "And thus," Monroe Dorsey of Kansas commented, "we send the government's representatives to subdue and civilize a dark race, who carry their American prejudice to color to a country where it never existed." [29]

Throughout the first six months of 1900 the anti-imperialist

25. For these letters, see Gatewood, "Smoked Yankees," pp. 248, 251–253, 257.
26. Cleveland Gazette, October 31, 1900.
27. The Reporter (Helena, Ark.), February 1, 1900.
28. St. Paul Afro-American Advance, December 2, 1899.
29. Washington Colored American, January 20, 1900; Monroe Dorsey in Parsons Weekly Blade, January 26, 1900.

theme continued to figure prominently in the editorial columns of the black press. H. C. C. Astwood, having relinquished his missionary post in Cuba and resumed his editorial duties in Philadelphia, gave eloquent expression to a prevalent sentiment among Negro Americans when he wrote:

> The slaughter in the Philippines is one of the most unrighteous acts ever perpetrated by any government even during the Middle Ages. The doings of Weyler in Cuba pale in significance by those of the nation who, with hypocritical humanity, made haste to stop the blood feud, to secure independence, happiness and contentment to the natives. Spain stands aghast at America's cruelty upon her once colonists, rescued from under such a hypocritical guise, without the power of protesting or aiding those who are being so mercilessly chastised by a government of liberty and justice. American manliness and the spirit of the fathers are trampled under the feet of the imperialists, and those who pretend to have the spirit of independence and human liberty in their breast are called traitors if they raise their voices against this diabolical outrage.[30]

Although other editors such as Harry C. Smith of Cleveland and John Mitchell of Richmond accused the Republican administration of hypocrisy, duplicity, and unconstitutional actions in pursuit of its expansionist policy, they were not willing to join Astwood in calling upon Negro voters to assist in defeating "the dynasty of imperialism at the polls in November next." [31]

Their refusal to embrace William Jennings Bryan and the Democratic party pointed up the dilemma which confronted many black Americans in 1900. "I don't think," Kelly Miller declared, "there is a single colored man, out of office and out of the insane asylum, who favors the so-called expansion policy." But the notion that Negroes would shift their allegiance to the Democratic party was altogether "another question"; Miller did not believe that they were "yet ready for a departure so radical." [32] Few were willing to place their faith in a party so thoroughly tinged with "Tillmanism" and the colorphobia manifested by many white Southern Democrats. "Mr. Bryan is all right in wanting to give the

30. *The Defender* (Philadelphia), January 27, 1900.
31. Cleveland *Gazette*, June 30, 1900; *Richmond Planet*, February 10, July 17, 1900.
32. Quoted in Cleveland *Gazette*, October 31, 1900.

so-called Negroes in the Philippines their independence," John
Mitchell argued, "but his party is all wrong concerning the rights
of Negroes in this country." The position of black anti-imperialists
was similar to that of Senator Hoar and other white Republicans
who opposed President McKinley's policy in the Philippines. In
spite of Bryan's anti-imperialist rhetoric, they could not bring
themselves to support the Democratic ticket. For those black men
who essentially agreed with Mitchell, there was not sufficient reason to depart from Frederick Douglass's advice: "the Republican
party is the ship—all else is the sea." [33] They belonged to that
sizable group of black Americans who gave only perfunctory support to the Republican ticket in 1900.

A few black citizens who were unwilling to choose between
the lesser of two evils proposed placing a national Afro-American
ticket in the field. As early as 1898 there had been agitation for a
Negro party, but the first steps toward that end seem to have
been taken by a group of Negroes in Philadelphia, including
Thomas Wallace Swan, an editor of *Howard's American Magazine,*
whom Ida Wells Barnett later described as a "shrewd soldier of
fortune." Among the most prominent blacks to endorse the idea
were Bishop Alexander Walters and H. C. C. Astwood. At this
juncture Walters believed that such a party offered Negroes in
the northern states the only effective means for exercising an
influence in the political arena commensurate with their voting
strength. In a letter accompanying a proposed platform of principles for an Afro-American party which was circulated among
"representative" black citizens in all sections of the country,
Swan admitted that the movement was "revolutionary in character" but maintained that Negroes had no alternative since both
Democrats and Republicans had betrayed popular government.[34]
"We recognize in the spirit of Imperialism, inaugurated and fos-

33. *Richmond Planet,* May 26, 1900. On the party choices of leading white anti-
imperialists, see Beisner, *Twelve against Empire,* pp. 120–130.

34. The launching of a Negro party had been the subject of discussion at least
since the fall of 1898, and efforts were made by a group in Chicago in the following
year to organize a Negro Protective party. See Caesar A. A. Taylor to John P.
Green, October 14, 1898, Green Papers; Washington *Colored American,* October 15,
1898, May 5, 1899, June 23, 1900; Marks, ed., *Black Press Views American Imperialism,* pp. 173, 209–211; Indianapolis *Freeman,* June 16, 1900; Kansas City
American Citizen, June 15, 1900; Wells, *Crusade for Justice,* p. 360; Indianapolis
World, June 16, 1900.

tered by the administration of President McKinley," he wrote, "the same violation of Human Rights, which is being practiced by the Democratic party in the recently reconstructed States, to wit, the wholesale disfranchisement of the Negro." In response to Swan's circular a conference chaired by Bishop Levi J. Coffin of the A.M.E. Church met in Philadelphia on June 6, 1900, to discuss the possibility of organizing a third party. The group issued a call for a national convention, but so negative was the reaction among black leaders that the idea was abandoned. The experience of the supporters of an all-Negro party was similar to that of white anti-imperialists who attempted at about the same time to launch a third party.[35]

Despite the coolness of Negroes toward the proposed Afro-American party and their reluctance to forsake Republicanism, some Negroes—perhaps more than at any time since 1888—did shift their allegiance to the national Democratic ticket. They received encouragement from veteran advocates of black political independence such as George T. Downing of Newport, Rhode Island, who claimed that every time McKinley toured the South and consented "to wear the Confederate button, an emblem of contempt for the black man," he aided and abetted those who oppressed Negroes in that region.[36] Frank Putnam of Chicago, an enthusiastic champion of McKinley's cause in 1896, announced his intention to work for Bryan's election. Putnam did not feel that as a working man he could continue to support a party as thoroughly committed to plutocracy and imperialism as he believed the Republican party had become by 1900.[37] Albert M. Thomas, a Yale-educated Negro lawyer prominent in local Republican circles in New York, also came out in support of Bryan, whose election he believed would be "in the interest of the country and incidentally for my race." Among his primary objections to McKinley was the policy of imperialism. Specifically, Thomas

35. Swan quoted in Marks, ed., *Black Press Views American Imperialism*, p. 209; Kansas City *American Citizen*, June 15, 1900; Schirmer, *Republic or Empire*, pp. 199–203.

36. George T. Downing to the Editor, May 8, 1900, in *New York Daily Tribune*, May 14, 1900.

37. Frank Putnam, "The Negro's Part in National Problems," *Colored American Magazine*, I (June, 1900), 69–79.

opposed the "hopeless war in the Philippines," the "dilatory tactics toward Cuba" and its independence, and the discriminatory tariff against Puerto Rico.[38] From Cuba, John L. Waller, the enthusiastic emigrationist, announced his decision to abandon his life-long commitment to the Republican party in order to support a presidential candidate who favored immediate independence for Cuba and the Philippines. "I am one of those," he declared, "who believes that ours is too great a people and government to longer harass and shoot to death a small nation of colored people who have so long contended for . . . liberty." But Waller had another reason for being disillusioned with the McKinley administration; he complained loudly that Negroes had failed to receive any appointments under the military regime in Cuba—a complaint which may well have revealed a significant source of his grievance against the Republicans.[39]

Among those Negroes who threatened to defect from the Republican ranks in 1900, few attracted more publicity than several well-known clergymen. Three bishops of the A.M.E. Church, Abram Grant, Benjamin Arnett, and W. B. Derrick, were reported to have cast their lot with Bryan; Bishop Alexander Walters of the A.M.E. Zion Church first counseled Negroes to divide their vote in the election, then toyed with the idea of a national Negro party, and finally wound up endorsing the Republican ticket.[40] In mid-May, 1900, the Colonial Baptist Association of New England, consisting of thirty Negro congregations in Connecticut and Massachusetts, arraigned President McKinley for the plight of both black Southerners and colored Filipinos. In what was interpreted as an unwarranted "fling at McKinley," the association singled out Grover Cleveland for special commendation as a president "who did his duty." [41] The Reverend W. H. Scott, militantly anti-imperialist minister of St. John's Baptist Church in Woburn, Massachusetts, drew up a bill of particulars against McKinley which emphasized his role in provoking "a war of extermination

38. Cleveland *Gazette,* August 4, 1900.
39. For Waller's letter, see Topeka *Colored Citizen,* September 14, 1900.
40. Meier, "The Negro and the Democratic Party," 182. On Bishop Arnett, see *Colored American Magazine,* 1 (October, 1900), 330.
41. Indianapolis *Freeman,* May 26, 1900; Chicago *Broad Ax,* June 9, 1900.

in the Philippines" and his display of prejudice against those Negro soldiers who "helped to save the honor of the nation in the Spanish-American War." [42]

Of those Negro churchmen who decided to support the candidacy of Bryan in 1900, none was more devastatingly critical of McKinley and the Republicans than Bishop Henry M. Turner. "For sixteen years I have been cooling toward the Republican party," the bishop declared.[43] In fact, on at least one previous occasion he had forsaken the party of Lincoln to vote for Cleveland. Returning to the Republican fold in 1896, he quickly became disillusioned with McKinley, especially with his policy of imperialism. Bishop Turner claimed that under such a policy the United States had not only defied its own constitutional principles by taxing the inhabitants of Puerto Rico without allowing them representation, but it had also violated the basic rules of humanity by recognizing the existence of slavery in parts of the Philippines. The bishop solemnly protested what he described as America's "unholy war of conquest" in the archipelago against a "feeble band of sable patriots . . . maintaining a heroic but pitifully unequal struggle for their God-given rights and . . . liberties." The fact that black soldiers were in the Philippines aiding in the execution of McKinley's "diabolical will" only served to augment his disgust. Despite his indictment of the Republican administration, Turner suffered few illusions about the Democrats. He explained that his decision to support Bryan was prompted not by any misconception that the Democrats were any better on racial questions than the Republicans, but by the notion that any change was better than blind loyalty to a party which took the black vote for granted.[44]

At the annual session of the Afro-American Council which convened in Indianapolis late in August, 1900, political partisanship was much in evidence. A reference by one speaker to "Negro Democrats" prompted Colonel James Lewis of New Orleans to question whether any such political creatures existed; the remark

42. *Voice of Missions*, VIII (November 1, 1900), 2. On Scott's anti-imperialist activities, see Schirmer, *Republic or Empire*, pp. 85, 214–215.

43. Quoted in Meier, "The Negro and the Democratic Party," 182.

44. Bishop Turner in *Voice of Missions*, VIII (October 1, 1900), 3. See also *Washington Bee*, September 15, 1900; *Richmond Planet*, September 15, 1900.

brought J. Milton Turner of St. Louis, a well-known supporter of Bryan, to his feet. Undoubtedly aware that the leadership of the council was dominated by men and women who were unwilling to abandon the Republican party regardless of their disenchantment with McKinley, Turner insisted that no partisan political rhetoric should creep into the convention and forthrightly opposed any attempt to have the organization issue a statement of political preference. Such a view coincided with those of T. Thomas Fortune and other pro-McKinley officials of the council who had been worried lest an effort be made to censure the McKinley administration for its disregard of Negro rights.[45]

Campaign officials of both the Democratic and Republican parties manifested a keen interest in the proceedings at Indianapolis. H. C. C. Astwood claimed that he was approached with a proposition to obtain from the Afro-American Council an official endorsement of Bryan. He rejected the idea because he believed it to be a plot to embarrass the president engineered by the political organization of Senator Matthew Quay, which was not on good terms with the McKinley administration.[46] Although Republican campaign officials would undoubtedly have welcomed the council's approval of the McKinley-Roosevelt ticket, their immediate concern was with heading off a motion of censure. Prior to the convention Republican party chairman Mark Hanna informed President McKinley that he had arranged to "have four or five good men there to look after the delegates from the East" and suggested that John P. Green and Ferdinand Barnett, a key black Republican in Chicago, be instructed "to see that the Western delegates are looked after." [47] Green was not satisfied merely to

45. Cleveland *Gazette*, September 8, 1900; Washington *Colored American*, September 1, 1900; St. Paul *Afro-American Advance*, September 1, 1900; Emma Lou Thornbrough, *T. Thomas Fortune: Militant Journalist* (Chicago: University of Chicago Press, 1972), p. 204.
46. H. C. C. Astwood to William McKinley, July 25, 1900, McKinley Papers. On the activities of Quay's organization, see the *New York Daily Tribune*, August 22, 24, 1900.
47. Marcus A. Hanna to William McKinley, August 16, 1900, McKinley Papers; F. L. Barnett to John P. Green, August 9, 1900, Green Papers; H. P. Cheatham to George A. Myers, August 20, 1900, Harry S. New to George A. Myers, August 22, 1900, F. L. Barnett to Charles Dick, August 22, 1900 (copy), F. L. Barnett to George A. Myers, August 22, 1900, George A. Myers to Charles Dick, August 23, 1900, Barney McKay, August 23, 1900, Jere Brown to George A. Myers, August 27, 1900, Myers Papers.

stop an anti-administration resolution; he proceeded to call on the Council to go on record endorsing President McKinley. Bishop Walters ruled him out of order, but he continued "to beshower the convention with pro-administration platitudes." Finally, Walters deputized Colonel Lewis to eject Green from the hall, which he did "with neatness and dispatch." Although the Address to the People ultimately issued by council condemned the suffrage restrictions placed upon black voters in the South, it contained no reference to McKinley's record with regard to Negro rights and omitted taking a stand in favor of either Bryan or McKinley.[48]

In 1900 William Jennings Bryan and his aides assiduously courted Negro voters and attempted to convince them that the Democratic party would be more attentive to their plight than the Republicans had been. According to one observer, the enthusiasm of white Southern Democrats for Bryan cooled considerably during the closing weeks of the campaign when it became apparent that he was seeking the support of Negroes in the North. *The Nation* claimed that Bryan told black voters that "Filipinos are colored people like themselves, that the Republican Party is trying to deprive them of their liberties, that the only hope for such people is with the Democrats, and that the Republicans have not given the Negroes as many offices as they are entitled to. . . ." Although Bryan's appeal may not have been as explicit as the *Nation* asserted, those made by his followers in the black community were.[49]

Bryan did not ignore the Negro vote. He remained in close touch with diverse black organizations, including the Afro-American Protective League, whose president W. P. McAlister predicted that "free thinking Negroes" would support the Democratic ticket. The United Colored Democracy of Greater New York under Edward E. Lee, which launched a local proselytizing campaign in Bryan's behalf, devoted especial attention to the imperialist policy of the Republicans and "their oppression of colored Filipinos." [50]

48. St. Paul *Afro-American Advance,* September 1, 1900; Cleveland *Gazette,* September 8, 1900; Thornbrough, *T. Thomas Fortune,* p. 204; Indianapolis *World,* September 1, 1900.

49. *The Nation,* LXXI (November 1, 1900), 337.

50. Louis W. Koenig, *Bryan: A Political Biography of William Jennings Bryan* (New York: G. P. Putnam's Sons, 1971), pp. 334–335. On Bryan's views of race and

Frederick L. McGhee, a well-known attorney and Catholic layman in St. Paul who was the most influential black Democrat in Minnesota, pursued a similar theme in speeches and articles during the campaign. He insisted that the acquiescence of the McKinley administration in the "fiendish slaughter" of helpless Filipinos by "the proud Anglo-Saxon" was wholly consistent with the Republican party's disregard "for the life, liberty, freedom and rights of the American Negro." McGhee held that the "murder and assassination" being committed by Americans in the Philippines "under the guise of war" was responsible for "the spirit of mob rule, the prevalence of lynch law in all parts of our country." [51] Such views naturally found expression in the public statements issued by the Negro National Democratic League, since McGhee was chairman of its committee on address.

The sixth biennial session of the league which convened in Kansas City in July, 1900, was one of the largest gatherings of black Democrats ever assembled. Among those who figured prominently in its deliberations were George F. Taylor of Oskaloosa, Iowa, who succeeded Edward E. Lee of New York as league president in 1900; Colonel W. T. Scott of Illinois, founder of the National Negro Anti-Expansion, Anti-Imperial and Anti-Trust League; and four well-known editors, Julius Taylor of the Chicago *Broad Ax,* Alexander E. Manning of the Indianapolis *World,* James A. Ross of the Buffalo *Globe and Freeman,* and James H. W. Howard of *Howard's American Magazine.*[52] The leaders of the league "worked out with Bryan the details of ambitious plans to increase the numbers of Negroes voting Democratic."[53] The league's Address to the Public reviewed McKinley's record and found "little if anything to commend it to the Negro voter." The league condemned the president and his party for their support of the gold standard, their coddling of trusts, and their discrimination against black soldiers during the Spanish-American War.

black citizens, see Willard H. Smith, "William Jennings Bryan and Racism," *Journal of Negro History,* LIV (April, 1969), 127–147. In July, 1900, a key Republican in Indiana reported that the Democrats were at work to win over "our colored people"; see W. T. Durbin to William McKinley, July 25, 1900, McKinley Papers.

51. McGhee quoted in Marks, ed., *Black Press Views American Imperialism,* xi–xii; see also St. Paul *Afro-American Advance,* March 31, 1900.

52. Chicago *Broad Ax,* July 7, 21, 1900.

53. Koenig, *Bryan,* p. 335.

In view of such a record, Negroes were urged to support the party of "that great commoner of the plain people—William Jennings Bryan." The most severe indictment leveled against McKinley by the black Democrats concerned his policy of imperialism. Their Address to the Public declared:

> We hold that the policy known as imperialism is hostile to liberty and leans toward the destruction of government by the people themselves. We insist that the subjugation of any people is "criminal aggression" and is a pronounced departure from the first principles taught and declared by Washington, Lincoln, Jefferson and all the great statesmen. . . . Whether the people who will be affected by such a policy be or consider themselves Negroes, nor yet because the majority of them are black, is of but little moment. They are by nature entitled to liberty and freedom. We being an oppressed people . . . should be the "loudest in our protestations against the oppression of others."

The black Democrats maintained that if Negro citizens were willing to support the Republican party in its suppression of liberty "in our so-called possessions," then they had little justification in complaining "of the same thing being done in any part of our own land." Their Address to the Public concluded with the warning that a nation "could not oppress a people without the borders of the country without sooner or later introducing such oppression within its [own] borders." [54]

Throughout the campaign similar themes appeared in black newspapers that favored Bryan. Such traditionally Democratic journals as the Indianapolis *World* and Chicago *Broad Ax* had the editorial support of the Cleveland *Gazette*, Richmond *Reformer*, Martinsburg, West Virginia, *Pioneer Press*, and other Negro weeklies which did not officially endorse the Democratic ticket. All were inclined to agree with the sentiment expressed in a bit of verse which appeared in the *Broad Ax:* "One who steals a ham is a thief/ One who steals a fortune is a financier/ One who assists in stealing the Philippines is a patriot." [55] *The Negro World,* the editorial mouthpiece of black Democrats in Minnesota, combined the themes of anti-trust and anti-imperialism and

54. For the League's Address to the Public, see Chicago *Broad Ax,* July 21, 1900.
55. *Ibid.,* October 27, 1900.

attempted to refute the idea that McKinley's administration had ushered in an era of general prosperity by charging that only the rich were prosperous. The *World's* editor, Joseph Houser, took the position that because Bryan was the candidate of the common people and made equal rights the cardinal principle of his platform, Negroes, of all Americans, should give him their support.[56]

In June, 1900, James Beck, the commander of Kansas's black regiment during the Spanish-American War, assumed the editorial reins of the Topeka *Colored Citizen;* he immediately announced that the paper would henceforth "be for Bryan." A prominent figure in the fusionist convention of the Democrats and Populists in Kansas in 1900, Beck criticized the McKinley administration for its refusal to grant Cuba immediate independence and for "killing Philippine negroes in an endeavor to deprive them of their liberty." But the focus of his attack was on the "slave policy of McKinley in the Sulu Islands." Week after week, the *Colored Citizen* expounded on the implications of an expansion policy which "spread the protecting folds of Old Glory over human slavery, polygamy and paganism." [57] Other black supporters of Bryan who took up the issue of the Sulu Treaty asked Negro citizens whether they as former slaves themselves could in good conscience support a man who approved of slavery.

To an extraordinary degree the hostility of Negroes toward the Republican ticket in 1900 was directed at the vice-presidential candidate, Theodore Roosevelt. Not only those who supported Bryan but also independents and some loyal Republicans were critical of Roosevelt because of his unfavorable comments on the behavior of Negro troops in Cuba which had appeared in *Scribner's Magazine* the previous year. At the Republican National Convention Roosevelt's candidacy prompted more concern and discussion among Negro delegates than any other issue.[58] In much of the black community the image of the Republican vice-presidential candidate was that of a racist ingrate who had called into

56. St. Paul *Negro World,* March 24, May 19, June 2, 1900.

57. Topeka *Colored Citizen,* June 15, 29, July 20, 27, August 3, 10, 17, 24, 31, September 21; October 26, November 2, 1900. See also Indianapolis *World,* September 22, 1900.

58. Cleveland *Gazette,* June 23, 1900. Negro Republicans served as either delegates or alternates in the delegations from Alabama, Arkansas, Illinois, Indiana, Louisiana, Mississippi, North Carolina, Ohio, South Carolina, and the District of Columbia.

question the bravery and gallantry of the Negro soldiers who had saved his life. George W. Ford, a black Republican in Topeka, wrote Roosevelt that his remarks about black soldiers were "hurting us with the colored voters." When Edward E. Cooper pleaded for a retraction of the offensive paragraphs in the *Scribner's* article, Roosevelt replied: "I never repudiate anything I have written. . . ."[59] Black Republicans, as far as possible, ignored Roosevelt's slur on Negro troops. But when compelled to deal with the issue, they explained it as either an "honest error" which had nothing to do with the color of the soldiers or as a molehill transformed by Democratic demagogues into a mountain. For George L. Knox, it was merely "a little incident that was more pleasantry than otherwise." Other black Republican publicists preferred to emphasize Roosevelt's fair treatment of Negroes while he was governor of New York, noting particularly his stand against segregated schools.[60]

But neither black Democrats nor independent Republicans such as Harry C. Smith of Cleveland would allow Roosevelt's slur to be cast aside so lightly. Smith believed that only a full retraction of his statement about Negro soldiers would make Roosevelt acceptable to black voters. Black Democrats ridiculed T. Thomas Fortune, Calvin Chase, John E. Bruce, and others who, after a year of condemning the Colonel, swallowed all their past criticisms in order to urge Negroes to vote for "their reviler and slanderer." According to some, such shifts had nothing to do with any ideological change but could be explained only by the fact that these journalists had been placed on the payroll of the Republican party's publicity bureau.[61] Lest any black voter forget what Roosevelt had actually said about the Negro regulars in Cuba, Julius Taylor reprinted the pertinent paragraphs from his controversial article in the *Broad Ax* week after week. Other black

59. George W. Ford to Theodore Roosevelt, June 30, 1900, Theodore Roosevelt to George W. Ford, July 9, 1900, Theodore Roosevelt to E. E. Cooper, July 20, 1900, Theodore Roosevelt Papers, Manuscript Division, Library of Congress. See also J. Madison Vance to George A. Myers, July 3, 1900, Myers Papers.

60. Portland *New Age*, October 20, 1900; Indianapolis *Freeman*, October 27, 1900; Washington *Colored American*, October 6, 1900; F. J. Loudin to John P. Green, August ?, 1900, Green Papers; Barney McKay to George A. Myers, August 17, 1900, Henry W. Arnett to George A. Myers, September 13, 1900, Myers Papers.

61. Cleveland *Gazette*, July 7, 28, August 4, 18, October 27, 1900; Indianapolis *World*, July 7, 21, 1900.

Democrats depicted the New York governor as a negrophobe unfit to occupy any position in the federal government. Bishop Turner dismissed him as "a flash light hero and tin soldier whose pen is mightier than his sword." The mere mention of Roosevelt's name brought forth loud protests and hisses at several gatherings of Negroes during the late summer of 1900.[62]

Such overt expressions of hostility from the black community prompted Roosevelt to elaborate on his comments about Negro soldiers. Late in May he wrote a letter to Robert J. Fleming, a white lieutenant who had been present at San Juan Hill and who had challenged his assertion that the black regulars had displayed any signs of cowardice. Conceding that "colored regular troops usually fight excellently," Roosevelt nonetheless reiterated his claim that some of them had panicked under pressure, which he attributed "to the superstition and fear of the darkey, natural in those but one generation removed from slavery and but a few generations removed from the wildest savagery." Roosevelt maintained that "the only way to work out our political salvation" was to "treat each man on his merits as a man," a policy which he followed in regard to blacks no less than whites. "I strive my best," he wrote, "to secure to the colored men an exact equality with their white neighbors." As evidence of his lack of prejudice he noted that his own children "sat in the same school with colored children" and that he had invited colored men to "eat at my table and sleep in my house." But Roosevelt told Lieutenant Fleming that he had no intention of flattering Negroes, soldiers or civilians, by saying what he knew to be untrue. "Such flattery," he concluded, "would only be wrong and not in their real interest." [63]

Despite his efforts to "look dispassionately at the exact facts," the political significance that his comments on black soldiers assumed in the summer and fall of 1900 caused Roosevelt to modify the position he had taken in the letter to Lieutenant Fleming. The governor first began to include complimentary references to the black veterans of the Spanish-American War in his campaign

62. Chicago *Broad Ax*, October 20, 27, 1900; Topeka *Colored Citizen*, August 3, 24, October 5, 1900; *Parsons Weekly Blade*, May 18, 1900; Indianapolis *World*, July 7, 21, August 11, September 15, October 20, 1900.
63. Theodore Roosevelt to Robert J. Fleming, May 21, 1900, in Morison, ed., *Letters of Theodore Roosevelt*, II, 1304–6.

speeches; then early in October he discussed the controversial *Scribner's* article in a lengthy interview with a Chicago newspaper reporter. The interview made no reference to any panic by black soldiers but emphasized that the order of a white captain was responsible for the movement of several colored regulars to the rear. In his revised version of the incident Roosevelt stated:

> I had an order to hold a certain position and was supported by the Tenth Cavalry (colored). The position was uncertain and we needed every man available to make the stand. Two or three of the colored soldiers started to the rear in search of water as ordered by their captain. I rebuked the captain for lessening our force, and commanded the men to remain. The statement I made after that, as near as I can remember, was "I have orders to hold this hill and intend to do it. I will shoot any man that gives up this position." This is the whole story in a nutshell. . . .

Then, disregarding his earlier warning about the dangers of flattery, Roosevelt heaped praise upon the gallantry of Negro troops in Cuba and claimed that victory at San Juan belonged to them "as much if not more than any other soldiers there." He condemned the Democrats for attempting to make political capital out of the incident and felt that his position with the colored people was "too well-known for these political tricksters" to profit from their distortions of it.[64]

Although black Republican spokesmen pronounced Roosevelt's explanation altogether satisfactory, many Negroes remained skeptical of his sincerity and wondered why he had waited until a national political campaign to revise his opinion of black soldiers. Even in speeches which were obviously designed to atone for the slur against Negro troops, Harry C. Smith detected a patronizing attitude which was no less distasteful than his accusations against "the brave boys of the colored regiments." Exasperated by Roosevelt's welter of contradictory statements, Smith concluded that Roosevelt was "disposed to manipulate the race question in a way so as to magnify the name and greatness of himself, or to ingratiate himself into the good feeling of that class that might oppose his promotion." [65]

64. For Roosevelt's interview of October 7, 1900, which appeared in the *Chicago Daily News*, see Indianapolis *Freeman*, October 13, 1900.
65. Cleveland *Gazette*, September 1, October 27, 1900.

But as the campaign progressed, attention seemed to shift from Roosevelt's "position with the colored people" to the relationship of Bryan and the Democratic party to black citizens. In a speech at Newburgh, New York, late in October, Roosevelt himself called upon Bryan to reconcile his demand for Filipino self-government with the treatment of black Americans by the Democratic state governments in the South. He suggested that as long as the Democrats disfranchised "our fellowmen of duskier hue" in North Carolina and other southern states, their loud expressions of sympathy for the "little brown brothers" of the Philippines would have the unmistakable ring of hypocrisy.[66]

The most difficult problem confronting Bryan in his effort to win support of Negroes was the important position of white Southerners within his party. While Senator James K. Jones of Arkansas, the Democratic national chairman, did not engage in the kind of race-baiting that characterized the behavior of some of his southern colleagues, he was scarcely the broad-minded "friend of the race" described by Julius Taylor in the columns of the *Broad Ax*. Nor was Joseph Houser any more convincing in his efforts to deal with the disfranchisement of blacks by Democratic politicians in the South. The readers of his *Negro World* probably found little solace in his claim that "many intelligent colored men" in North Carolina had approved the literacy test recently enacted in that state. Like Houser and other black supporters of Bryan, George E. Taylor of the Negro Democratic League ignored the fact that the party's platform remained silent on the issue of civil rights and attempted instead to distinguish between the national Democratic party and its racist southern wing. On matters affecting the rights of black people, he argued, Bryan bore little resemblance to the party's negrophobes in the South. Taylor placed the responsibility for the disfranchisement of black voters in the South upon the McKinley administration and the Republican Congress because of their refusal to take appropriate federal action. According to him, the correction of such "local evils" rested "with the party in power and not with the party out of power." Taylor clearly implied that the election of

66. Quoted in the *New York Times*, October 23, 1900. See also Howard K. Beale, *Theodore Roosevelt and the Rise of America to World Power* (New York: Collier Books, 1968), p. 77.

Bryan would bring an end to the despotic tendencies spawned by imperialism and would inaugurate an era of justice for colored peoples in the Philippines as well as in the South.[67]

But the most serious embarrassment to Bryan and his Negro supporters was Senator Benjamin R. Tillman of South Carolina, whose racist outbursts during the campaign undoubtedly frightened off prospective black voters and confirmed the idea that all paths leading Negroes out of the Republican party led them "away from our friends and directly to our enemies." In answer to the persistent charge that no self-respecting black man could vote for a party represented by Tillman, black Democrats suggested that Republicans omit all references to the South Carolina senator until they had purged "the Tillmans" from their own party. James Beck noted that the same white Republicans from the North who attempted to besmirch the Democratic party by their discourses on the evils of Tillmanism fell "over each other to do him [Senator Tillman] honor" whenever he delivered a lecture on the race question in their hometowns.[68] However valid such an observation may have been, it probably did little to discount the liability posed by the conspicuous presence of Tillman and other southern racists in the Democratic party.

Early in October three elderly anti-imperialists from Boston who had formerly been active in the abolitionist movement commented on the problem raised by the racism of Southern Democrats. Their "Address to the Colored People of the United States" was intended as an appeal for Negroes to support Bryan. In this document Thomas Wentworth Higginson, William Lloyd Garrison, Jr., and George S. Boutwell focused upon the "war of races" in the Philippines and counseled Negro voters to "cut adrift from every organization which wars on darker races." Such organizations included "the imperialistic Republican party" which was no longer the "liberty loving party" that had emancipated the slaves. Since the new Republican party had made freedom "a matter of complexion," it offered little hope for the colored race in the United States. The address also maintained that there had been

67. Chicago *Broad Ax*, June 16, 1900; St. Paul *Negro World*, March 31, 1900; George E. Taylor in the Indianapolis *World*, August 4, 1900.

68. Koenig, *Bryan*, pp. 334–335; Topeka *Colored Citizen*, August 17, 31, September 21, 1900.

"far more outrages on the American Negro during the term of McKinley than two terms of Cleveland." In an obvious attempt to overcome black voters' objections to Bryan's white supporters in the South, the document explained: ". . . the Southern Democrats are at least doing the colored race this service; that they as a rule oppose the national policy of imperialism. This may seem an inconsistency but it is really very simple. The very fact of their unwillingness to give equal rights to the American Negro makes them unwilling to undertake the government of ten millions more belonging to the colored race. This much, at least, experience has taught them. Thus, at any rate, they are on your side." [69] Negro Democrats seized upon the address by three white men whose loyalty to black people had "never been questioned" and urged all black voters to "read it and ponder over its contents." Although a few Negroes loyal to the Republican party admitted that no black American could "pass lightly by the appeal" of Garrison, Higginson, and Boutwell,[70] it is doubtful that their statement did much to dissipate black citizens' misgivings about Bryan.

But other appeals by white anti-imperialists did strike a responsive chord among Negroes in Massachusetts, especially those in the Boston area. Through the combined efforts of black and white opponents of the Philippine war, anti-imperialism emerged as a dominant issue in the campaign there. A pamphlet written by Kelly Miller of Howard University and issued by the New England Anti-Imperialist League emphasized the relationship between the war and the deteriorating condition of Negro Americans, sounding the basic theme of the anti-McKinley forces in the Bay State. The Reverend W. H. Scott traveled for the League during the campaign, maintaining a steady fire of criticism against Roosevelt for his slur upon the gallantry of black soldiers in Cuba and condemning the racist implications of McKinley's policy of imperialism. Early in October, 1900, Scott, Clifford H. Plummer, and other black anti-imperialists in Boston convened a mass meeting of Negro citizens in Faneuil Hall; it passed a resolution call-

69. For the "Address to the Colored People of the United States," see Chicago *Broad Ax*, October 27, 1900, and St. Paul *Afro-American Advance*, November 3, 1900.

70. St. Paul *Afro-American Advance*, November 3, 1900; see also Topeka *Colored Citizen*, October 19, 1900.

ing upon black voters to use their ballots to defeat the Republican ticket. Shortly afterward Archibald H. Grimké and five other prominent black Bostonians issued an appeal for Negroes either to vote for Bryan or at least to abstain from voting for McKinley. Grimké maintained that McKinley, Roosevelt, and their cohorts in the Republican party had adequately demonstrated that they were imbued with a belief "in the divine right of the Anglo-Saxon to govern the republic and subjugate darker races." [71]

The hostility which Boston Negroes manifested toward McKinley's policies both at home and abroad also expressed itself against Booker T. Washington and his formula for racial progress. Although Washington had earlier indicated that he favored independence for Cuba and the Philippines, he was not one to embrace the anti-imperialist cause or to relate the Philippine war to racial problems at home. In fact, Washington so thoroughly subscribed "to the 'White Man's Burden' of leadership and authority" that he appeared to forget that he was a Negro and himself took up the burden before the presidential campaign was over by arranging to assist in the development of cotton culture in Germany's African colonies. In 1900 he remained loyal to McKinley and helped keep his friend T. Thomas Fortune faithful to the party of Lincoln.[72] As far as the Reverend Scott and other militant black Bostonians were concerned, the so-called Tuskegee Idea was objectionable for the same reason as McKinley's "Southern policy" and imperialistic program: both represented acquiescence to racism. Scott and his group protested vigorously against the meeting of Washington's National Negro Business League scheduled to convene in Boston late in August. Although their protest was supported by George S. Boutwell, president of the New England Anti-Imperialist League, Washington's organization met on schedule and presented through the press an image of complete harmony and unanimity. Washington allowed no references to the recent outbreaks of racial violence and boasted that black businessmen had come to Boston "for a definite purpose with which

71. Schirmer, *Republic or Empire*, pp. 213–215.
72. Louis R. Harlan, "Booker T. Washington and the White Man's Burden," *American Historical Review*, LXXI (January, 1966), 441–467; see also *Colored American Magazine*, II (November, 1900), 49–50.

politics had no connection." Despite the well-orchestrated proceedings of the convention, there was at least one unexpected occurrence with political overtones: the most enthusiastic demonstration by delegates was in response to remarks by J. W. Pullen,
a black veteran of San Juan Hill who praised the performance of
Negro troops in Cuba and "condemned Roosevelt for maligning
the race" in his account of the Santiago campaign.[73]

During the closing week of the presidential campaign a lengthy
letter in the black Democratic press constituted a final, eloquent
appeal for Negroes to vote for William Jennings Bryan. Written
by Sutton E. Griggs, the Nashville minister and novelist, the document was a ringing indictment of the Republicans' policy of imperialism—a policy described as responsible for enslaving "the
colored peoples of the Philippines and for worsening the plight
of black citizens in the United States." Convinced that the principal burden of Negro Americans was the "ponderous chain of
gratitude" that shackled them to the Republican party, Griggs
called upon black voters to break free of the chain and exert their
political independence. He emphasized the changed condition of
party politics and explained that in 1900 Negroes confronted the
choice between "a former friend gone wrong and a former foe
treading gloriously the path of rectitude." The Republican party
under McKinley, having "drifted into idolatry" and worship of
the golden calf, was bent upon depriving the Filipinos of independence and justice in order to exploit the wealth of their homeland; in contrast, the Democratic party under Bryan offered them
"that same political freedom for which Patrick Henry pleaded."
"If the Negro aids the Republican party in the political murder
of the Filipino," Griggs declared, "we will not have long to wait
before there is a political hanging in America with the Negro as
the victim." The "dinner pail may be full," as the Republicans
claimed, but "the man with a heart will not stop to eat dinner if
the giver thereof is engaged in robbing the helpless." Griggs envisioned Negro support for Bryan as the means for restoring har-

73. Schirmer, *Republic or Empire*, p. 216; Louis R. Harlan, *Booker T. Washington: The Making of a Black Leader, 1856–1901* (New York: Oxford University
Press, 1972), p. 268; Washington *Colored American*, September 1, 1900.

monious relations between the races in America: "Let the freedom of the Filipino be the bridge across the chasm, on which
bridge we meet to clasp glad hands and renew the bonds of
friendship of former days." [74]

Despite the tendency of black anti-imperialists to exaggerate
the dimensions of the exodus of Negro voters from Republican
ranks, the threat appeared menacing enough to arouse concern
among the Republican campaign managers. In an effort to bolster the party's appeal among black voters, they took pains to cultivate those Negro journalists who had been most critical of the
McKinley administration. Both President McKinley and Governor Roosevelt were anxious about T. Thomas Fortune and interceded to have him assigned a role in the campaign. In a letter to
party chairman Mark Hanna early in July, Roosevelt described
Fortune as "an able and rather discontented black man." The
president agreed and suggested that "it would be most useful to
get him at once." Ultimately, Fortune, John E. Bruce (Bruce
Grit), and other "discontented" black journalists were employed
by the party's Afro-American Literary Bureau. The temperamen-
tal Fortune, who was hopeful that his services would be rewarded
later by a federal appointment, seems to have followed the advice
of his friend Booker T. Washington and avoided any disruptive
antics for the remainder of the campaign. In the case of Bruce,
no black journalist equaled the abruptness with which he abandoned the anti-imperialist cause for one extolling the wisdom of
McKinley's Philippine policy.[75]

Those Negroes who called themselves loyalists to the party of
Lincoln and Douglass (especially Judson Lyons, John P. Green,
and Henry P. Cheatham, the three highest ranking black appointees in the McKinley administration) were active throughout the
campaign. They stumped Illinois, Maryland, New York, and other
states where the Negro vote was supposed to hold the balance of
political power. Such loyalists clearly recognized that a major
source of discontent among black citizens was related to the racial

74. Sutton E. Griggs to the Editor, Indianapolis *World*, November 3, 1900.
75. *Boston Globe*, September 5, 1900; Theodore Roosevelt to Mark Hanna, July 7,
1900, Mark Hanna to Theodore Roosevelt, July 11, 1900, Roosevelt Papers; Thornbrough, *T. Thomas Fortune*, pp. 205–207; Cleveland *Gazette*, September 29, October
20, 27, 1900.

implications of the Philippine War. They had to combat the idea that the policy of imperialism toward the Filipinos was but another manifestation of the same sentiment which allowed black people to be lynched in the South.[76]

J. C. Reid, a staunchly Republican editor in Minnesota, insisted that the "apathy among the rank and file of negro voters of this vicinity" could be "traced to their opposition to the war in the Philippines, which they have been told by some demagogues was due to the fact that the Filipino is a dark race, whom Americans think designed by nature to be vassals of the superior white race." According to Reid, anti-imperialist pamphlets had been "distributed with a lavish hand in the homes of colored citizens, most of whom have read them and can reproduce the arguments contained therein." To combat the idea that the United States was engaged in a racist mission in the Philippines, he suggested that an appeal be made to the black man's patriotism: "Explain to him that the presence of American troops in the Philippines was for the purpose of preserving order, originally, until the rebellion by the Tagals made it necessary to bring them in to subjection to American authority, and then appeal to his patriotism and loyalty." For a time such a formula, which Reid described as "simple and effective," became popular with black Republican editors; they argued that Negro Americans could ill afford to oppose the administration during a major national crisis.[77]

Other black editorial spokesmen relied heavily upon the arguments of Senator Albert Beveridge in constructing a rationale for imperialism. George L. Knox declared that the issue in the Philippines was not humanity or race but the prestige and international reputation of the United States. For Americans to shirk their responsibility in the islands "would be simply a confession of weakness" which no patriotic citizen, black or white, was willing to allow. The editor of a black weekly in Seattle, who fully agreed with Knox, claimed that "our duty in the Philippines" necessitated forcing the surrender of "those devils" led by Aguinaldo, because they had turned upon the American friends and rejected the promise of good government and internal tranquility.

76. Cleveland *Gazette,* September 22, 1900; *Washington Bee,* October 20, 1900.
77. St. Paul *Afro-American Advance,* July 28, 1900.

"All this Philippine sympathy in the United States," he concluded, "was nothing more nor less than Bryan-Demo-Pop political clap-trap for campaign purposes." [78]

In fact, some Negro Republicans refused to consider imperialism a question which concerned black voters at all. Instead, they focused attention on domestic issues, notably what was described as McKinley prosperity. Black Republican journals such as the *Washington Bee* and the Des Moines *Iowa State Bystander* characterized imperialism as a false issue raised by Bryan to divert attention from the silver plank in his platform—a heresy that would destroy the economic progress achieved under McKinley.[79] For the St. Paul *Afro-American Advance,* the reelection would not only mean the continuation of economic stability and "plenty of work" for blacks, but would also insure that steps would be taken to reduce the congressional representation of those southern states which had disfranchised their black citizens.[80]

Following his rather sudden change of heart about American involvement in the Philippines, Calvin Chase, delegate to the Republican national convention for the District of Columbia, began to equate anti-imperialists with "anti-good-governmentists" and urged black Americans not to be seduced by the "well-dressed platitudes and barren sentimentality" by which the Democrats were attempting to bolster their declining fortunes. Negro defenders of the McKinley administration characterized the arguments against imperialism as "tommyrot," also charging that critics of American action in the Philippines were guilty of aiding and abetting enemies of the republic. In fact, Chase claimed that the only thing sustaining Aguinaldo's resistance was the hope of Bryan's election. The tendency to question the loyalty and patriotism of those who opposed McKinley's policy in the islands and to label as a "turncoat"—a racial Judas—anyone who declared in favor of Bryan became more pronounced as the campaign progressed.[81]

78. George L. Knox in the Indianapolis *Freeman,* January 27, 1900; *Republican* (Seattle), January 19, 1900.

79. *Washington Bee,* August 25, September 1, 1900; Des Moines *Iowa State Bystander,* August 31, September 14, 1900.

80. St. Paul *Afro-American Advance,* August 4, 1900. See also Des Moines *Iowa State Bystander,* August 10, September 14, 1900.

81. *Washington Bee,* January 27, August 25, September 1, 22, October 20, 27, 1900; Des Moines *Iowa State Bystander,* October 19, 1900; Portland *New Age,*

As much as any black Republican, Edward E. Cooper of the *Colored American* attempted to make imperialism ideologically palatable to black citizens. Cooper never ruled out the possibility that the United States would ultimately grant autonomy to the Filipinos. The most immediate concern of the United States, he argued, was to establish its sovereignty over the archipelago, "after which the question of permanent retention can be disposed of as a separate proposition." Cooper was also careful to distinguish between expansion and imperialism: the former brought commercial advantages to the United States and the fruits of civilization to the natives of "our overseas islands;" the latter was "suggestive of tyranny, wars of conquest, thirst for lands . . . robbery of the natives." The presence of American troops in the Philippines was the result not of imperialism but of "logical expansion," which promised to bring about "the establishment of better conditions on the islands." He interpreted the appointment of such "a whole-souled, liberal-minded gentleman" as William Howard Taft to the position of civil governor in Manila as evidence of President McKinley's intention to treat the natives generously.[82]

In championing McKinley's candidacy Cooper and other black Republicans attempted to exonerate the president of any responsibility for the deteriorating status of Negro citizens. They emphasized that under his administration 26,000 black men, earning collectively more than seven million dollars, had been employed by the federal government. They also pointed out that the disfranchisement of Negroes in the South was the work of Democrats at the state level, which meant that the president was powerless to intervene. In his campaign speeches and statements John P. Green reminded black voters that despite the criticism of McKinley's inaction regarding the murder of Postmaster Baker in Lake City, South Carolina, the president had actually made maximum use of his power and had brought the culprits to trial. In Green's view, nothing more could be expected of him. Perhaps even more effective than these efforts in dissipating the hostility of blacks to-

September 22, 1900; *New York Daily Tribune*, November 3, 1900. When Alex Manley, editor of the Washington *Daily Recorder*, showed an inclination to support Bryan, he was mercilessly ridiculed by black Republican stalwarts and reminded that it was white racist Democrats who drove him out of Wilmington, N.C., during the riot in 1898. See Indianapolis *Freeman*, October 6, 1900.

82. Washington *Colored American*, February 10, March 24, April 21, 1900.

ward McKinley were reports which circulated widely throughout the campaign to the effect that his "silence upon the lynchings and outrages in the South" had resulted from the "bad advice" of Henry P. Cheatham, Judson Lyons, and Bishop B. W. Arnett. "As soon as this was generally known," George A. Myers of Cleveland wrote, "all opposition from that source disappeared. . . ." Although Myers may have exaggerated, it does appear that such reports, by diverting responsibility for the administration's "Southern policy" from the White House to three black men, made it easier for Negroes to support McKinley's bid for reelection.[83]

Unlike the black Democrats who condemned the president for discriminating against Negro troops, their opponents in the Republican party maintained that he had given black citizens an opportunity to demonstrate their patriotism by allowing them to serve in the volunteer army. The Savannah *Tribune* dismissed as absurd the talk about the president being responsible for the prejudice toward black men once they were in the army, and it placed more importance on the fact that McKinley was the first president to allow the mustering in of regiments "composed of Negroes and officered by men of their own race from colonel down to corporal." Like other stalwart black Republicans, the editor of the *Tribune* called upon Negro voters to demonstrate their gratitude for this signal honor by unanimously supporting the president's reelection. To honor both McKinley and the black soldiers who had "saved the Rough Riders from annihilation" in Cuba, Negro Republicans in Indiana formed clubs known as the Rescue Riders, whose members would presumably tilt the political contest in favor of the Republicans and thereby save the party in that state from a Democratic ambush.[84]

Perhaps the most effective argument used by black Republicans

83. Green, *Fact Stranger Than Fiction*, pp. 268–269; Washington *Colored American*, September 29, October 13, 1900; *Congressional Record*, 56 Cong., 1 sess., Appendix, pp. 442–444; Indianapolis *Freeman*, October 13, 1900; George A. Myers to William McKinley, November 15, 1900 (copy), Green Papers; John P. Green to George A. Myers, August 15, 1900, Judson Lyons to George A. Myers, August 25, 1900, Cyrus F. Adams to George A. Myers, October 30, 1900, Myers Papers.

84. Savannah *Tribune*, September 22, 1900; Topeka *Kansas State Ledger*, September 5, 1900; Washington *Colored American*, May 26, 1900; Kansas City *American Citizen*, September 28, 1900; Indianapolis *Recorder*, July 21, 1900; *Parsons Weekly Blade*, October 12, 26, 1900.

in their efforts to prevent Negro voters from shifting their support
to Bryan was their claim that the Democratic party was the party
of "mobocracy," disfranchisement, and racial oppression. Bishop
George W. Clinton of the A.M.E. Zion Church maintained that
even though Bryan himself might "be well inclined toward the
negro," black voters should "not lose sight of the fact that no man
is greater than his party." [85] Negro Republicans argued that Bryan's highly vocal sympathy for the brown people of the Philippines and his silence on the plight of black citizens in the South
constituted "a spectacle of hypocrisy which all history may search
in vain to equal." Lest black voters succumb to Bryan's anti-
imperialist rhetoric, Negro Republicans never allowed them to forget that the Democratic party was synonymous with "Tillmanism"
and the most virulent form of racism. They also predicted that
the election of Bryan would put into positions of national importance a "horde of negro haters" who had succeeded at the state
level in stripping black people of virtually all constitutional
rights. Bryan's party, they claimed, had not only been the champion of statutory discrimination against Negroes in North Carolina and Virginia earlier in 1900 but had also been largely re
sponsible for the "disgraceful riot" in New York during the
summer, since the real instigators had been white policemen who
owed their allegiance to Tammany Hall.[86] Voicing a theme persistently pursued by black Republican publicists, Edward E.
Cooper declared that Senator Tillman and other veteran white
racists of the South were anti-imperialists for precisely the same
reasons they were anti-Negro—they despised all colored people.[87]
Unlike Higginson, Garrison, and Boutwell, needless to say, Cooper
did not believe that such colorphobia could be interpreted to
mean that white Southerners were on the side of black Americans.

During the final weeks of the presidential campaign black Republicans closed ranks and exerted every effort to win endorse-

85. Quoted in the *New York Daily Tribune,* November 3, 1900.
86. *Washington Bee,* September 1, 22, October 20, 27, 1900; Indianapolis
Recorder, August 11, October 13, 27, 1900; Des Moines *Iowa State Bystander,* June
2, September 14, 28, November 2, 1900; Indianapolis *Freeman,* September 22, 1900;
Washington *Colored American,* September 29, 1900; Cyrus Fields Adams to John P.
Green, November 5, 1900, Green Papers.
87. Washington *Colored American,* October 13, 1900.

ment for the McKinley-Roosevelt ticket from individuals and organizations that had hitherto remained uncommitted. Although the Afro-American Council officially omitted any such endorsement at its annual session in August, fifty-two of its most prominent members including Bishop Walters, John P. Green, Judson Lyons, and William A. Pledger signed a petition signifying their unqualified support of the "foreign and domestic policy of the national Republican administration." Over 80 percent of the members of the Afro-American Press Association, an organization that represented about one-fifth of the nation's black newspapers, committed themselves to a similar position.[88] It is difficult, however, to ascertain with any precision the degree to which the Negro press ultimately came out in favor of the Republican ticket; estimates by contemporary observers ranged from 20 percent to almost 98 percent.[89] Certainly the most important Negro journals such as the *New York Age,* the Indianapolis *Freeman,* the Washington *Colored American,* and the *Washington Bee* remained faithful to the Republican party.

The numerically superior pro-McKinley journals also aimed their editorial fire at the weakest point in Bryan's armor. They depicted the Democratic candidate as a cheap demagogue attempting to garner support in the black community by emphasizing an issue that was not of vital concern to black people; George L. Knox, for example, maintained that "the high-flown notion of Imperialism" was largely irrelevant to the needs of the American black man.[90] Late in July, Calvin Chase's *Washington Bee* sounded a theme which became increasingly popular with Negro Republicans; it described the Democrat party as the "unequivocal advocate of imperialism," because it had no regard for law, reason, and human rights insofar as black citizens were concerned. Chase and other black editors argued that Bryan's own definition of

88. Indianapolis *Recorder,* September 1, 8, 1900; Judson Lyons to George **B.** Cortelyou, August 25, 1900, McKinley Papers; Marks, ed., *Black Press Views American Imperialism,* p. 172.

89. Indianapolis *Recorder,* November 10, 1900; Washington *Colored American,* August 25, 1900.

90. Indianapolis *Freeman,* October 6, 1900. See also Washington *Colored American,* March 24, 1900; *Washington Bee,* August 25, 1900; Des Moines *Iowa State Bystander,* July 20, 1900.

imperialism as "government without the consent of the governed" was a perfect description of the way Democrats ruled in the South. What could be more hypocritical, they asked, than Democrats who practiced imperialism at home being agitated by McKinley's imperialistic program in the Philippines? [91]

A majority of those disenchanted with the McKinley administration because of its imperialist policy and failure to take a forthright stand against racial outrages in the South ultimately followed Calvin Chase's advice and decided that "of the two great political evils" they would "take the lesser"—the Republican party. Even H. C. C. Astwood, who early in 1900 had called upon Negroes to assist in the defeat of the "dynasty of imperialism" in Washington, made his peace with the McKinley administration. In a letter to the President late in July, he described himself as "one of your admirers and supporters" and praised McKinley's foreign policy as being "so eminently proper and wise." [92] When the election was less than two weeks away, Harry C. Smith came out in support of McKinley's reelection, despite the fact that he had maintained a consistently critical view of the Republican administration. In editorials which amounted to a political confession, he explained why Negroes had no alternative in 1900 except to vote Republican: unlike the Democratic party, which had never displayed any concern for citizens of color, the Republican party at least had a rich heritage of abolitionism and emancipation, and Negroes could hope that in the future the party would revive its commitment to the ideals of Sumner and Lovejoy. [93] John Mitchell, another veteran anti-imperialist who took a similar view, summed up the attitude of many blacks when he declared: "Mr. Bryan holds out no star of hope for the Negro in this country but promises everything to the brown brothers in the Philippines." Reflecting on the reasons why Bryan failed to win greater black support, a prominent Negro in Topeka noted shortly after the election that "hugging Aguinaldo and

91. *Washington Bee,* July 28, August 18, 1900. See also Indianapolis *Recorder,* August 25, 1900; Washington *Colored American,* September 29, 1900.
92. H. C. C. Astwood to William McKinley, July 25, 1900, McKinley Papers.
93. Cleveland *Gazette,* October 20, 27, November 3, 1900.

preventing an honest ballot and a fair count in the Confederate
states was more than the colored brother could stand. . . ." [94]

John R. Lynch was essentially accurate when he claimed that
"fully ninety percent of the colored voters" remained loyal to the
Republican party.[95] Even in New York City, where Bryan gained
a majority, the efforts of black Democrats appear to have produced
disappointing results. The United Colored Democracy, having
entered the presidential campaign with high hopes of capturing
a larger share of the black vote, saw its prospects evaporate with
the outbreak of race riots late in the summer. Negro residents of
the city believed that police brutality had sparked the riots, and
they tended to agree with William Henry Brooks, a prominent
black clergyman, who placed the responsibility at Tammany's
door. Once the city's Democratic organization had been identified
with police outrages and racial violence, it was unlikely that many
Negroes, regardless of their grievances against the Republicans,
would be impressed by the appeals of the United Colored Democracy, itself a segregated unit within the Tammany machine.[96] Although Negro voters probably helped to make Boston "the banner Bryan city in the country" in 1900, even there the black
community was divided.[97]

Black Americans in 1900 kept the faith, but their enthusiasm
for the Republican party's platform and candidates was at a low
ebb. A substantial number responded favorably to the appeals of
Bryan, despite a reluctance to support a candidate whose party
was identified so directly with the oppression of black people in
the South. For some, the time had arrived to escape enslavement
to a political organization that consistently ignored them once
elections were over. Few black supporters of Bryan expected a
Democratic victory to usher in a racial millennium; rather, they
believed that the Democratic party could not "treat the Negro any
worse than he is being treated by the Republicans," and that a

94. John Mitchell in the *Richmond Planet*, September 15, 1900; Topeka *Kansas State Ledger*, November 27, 1900.
95. Lynch, *Autobiography*, p. 447.
96. John E. Bruce in the Indianapolis *Freeman*, September 8, 1900; Gilbert Osofsky, *Harlem: The Making of a Ghetto, Negro New York, 1890–1930* (New York: Harper and Row, 1966), p. 161; Scheiner, *Negro Mecca*, p. 125; *New York Daily Tribune*, November 8, 1900.
97. Schirmer, *Republic or Empire*, pp. 215, 220.

display of political independence might cause the Republicans to return to the original ideals of their party as far as the civil rights of black people were concerned. For many black voters, however, such a rationale had little appeal; the campaign of 1900 seemed to offer them little choice. Writing from England shortly after the election, F. J. Loudin, the director of Fisk University's Jubilee Singers, expressed the sense of bewilderment which gripped Negro Americans. "Well, I see McKinley is in again as the least of two evils," he wrote. "I am not sorry but I would not have voted for him, though I am not a Democrat and scarcely think I would have voted for Bryan. . . . I shall expect to see more Negroes disfranchised and lynching increased. . . ." [98]

Although the outcome of the election was disheartening to the black supporters of Bryan, few were as pessimistic as Alexander E. Manning, a veteran Negro Democrat in Indiana. For him the voting statistics had ominous implications for the political future of Negroes. He claimed that the increase in Republican strength among northern whites and the "attitude of the Republican leaders" during the campaign signaled "the passing of the Negro out of politics." The party of Lincoln no longer depended upon black voters in pivotal states; in the future the party would be even more crass in ignoring them, if they continued to remain so solidly loyal to it. According to Manning, the black man's only hope for exercising any leverage in politics was to free himself from what Sutton Griggs called "the ponderous chain of gratitude" that bound him to the Republican party.[99]

Following the Republican victory in 1900, Negro protests against the policy of imperialism declined dramatically. Most black spokesmen seemed to acquiesce in American's status as a colonial power on the grounds that it was "a fact of national life." A few did not, such as the Negro editor in Savannah who continued to lambast the president's expansionist course on the grounds that the Filipinos were "distant kindred" of black Americans and the "common destiny" of the two colored peoples was more important than "a nonprotecting flag at home." Wearied by what he considered such futile sermonizing, Calvin Chase re-

98. F. J. Loudin to John P. Green, November 23, 1900, Green Papers.
99. Indianapolis *World,* November 10, 1900.

sponded: "Well, suppose you don't endorse it [imperialism]? Neither do you endorse the policy of being disfranchised in Georgia but what are you going to do about it?" [100] Chase's question aptly pointed up the hopelessness of the black citizenry in the United States, especially in the South, at the turn of the century.

100. *Washington Bee,* December 22, 1900.

Ten

The Philippines: Black Soldiers and the White Man's Burden

Would to God it lay in my power to rectify the committed error and compensate the Filipino for the wrong done!
> —Sergeant John W. Galloway (Twenty-fourth Infantry) to Thomas Consunji, February 5, 1900

. . . all enemies of the U.S. Government look alike to us hence we go along with the killing [in the Philippines].
> —Captain W. H. Jackson (Forty-ninth Infantry), August, 1900

In the fall of 1900, as the public debate over imperialism reached a climax in the United States, the war in the Philippines entered a new and more ominous phase. Not even the heavy-handed censorship imposed on military news from the islands could obscure the fact that the program of pacification was no closer to realization than it had been a year earlier. In the wake of the successful American offensive late in 1899, a speedy end to the insurrection was anticipated by officials in Manila, including General Elwell Otis and his successor as military commander, General Arthur MacArthur, and Judge William Howard Taft, the head of the civil commission. So certain were they that the Philippine people had been won over that late in June, 1900, General MacArthur issued a proclamation offering amnesty to all Filipinos who would renounce insurrection and take an oath of allegiance to the United States within ninety days. The response indicated the extent to which American officials had miscalculated. The vast majority of the islanders did not avail themselves of the offer, and at the end of the ninety-day period "everyone seemed to be satisfied to let the proclamation expire without renewal." [1]

What Americans had interpreted as the disintegration of Aguinaldo's insurgent movement was really only a shift in strategy— a change from conventional to guerrilla warfare. Instead of large regular formations, the Filipino insurgents reorganized their forces into small, highly mobile units which avoided pitched battles and engaged in ambush, sniping, and sabotage. These units, dispersed over a large geographical area and rarely in communication with Aguinaldo's headquarters, constituted an elusive, almost invisible enemy. Aguinaldo himself was constantly on the move in the mountains of northern Luzon, where disease and terrain took their toll on the American army which pursued him. The insurgents' objective was to exhaust the Americans and make their occupation of the islands so costly that they would withdraw rather than suffer the losses necessary to establish their authority.[2]

In an attempt to win greater support among his own countrymen, Aguinaldo utilized various techniques ranging from patriotic appeals to terror. Insurgent propagandists devoted much attention to the outbursts of racial violence in the United States, as well as to the activities of anti-imperialists. Detecting a ray of hope in the forthcoming American presidential election of 1900, Aguinaldo stepped up insurgent military operations in the belief that any appearance of inactivity would be interpreted as evidence of American success and therefore would contribute to the triumph of McKinley and the imperialists. Assured that William Jennings Bryan had a good chance of victory and that his election would mean their independence, Filipinos were encouraged to stiffen their resistance to the pacification program. Despite the long-term risks involved in predicting Bryan's election, the insurgents at least gained time in which to perfect their new strategy and to

1. Gates, "Experiment in Benevolent Pacification," pp. 151–158; Grunder and Livezey, *Philippines and the United States,* pp. 65–66.

2. Gates, "Experiment in Benevolent Pacification," pp. 198–200. Especially useful on military activities in the Philippines between 1899 and 1902 are John R. M. Taylor, "The Philippine Insurrection against the United States—A Compilation of Documents with Notes and Introduction," 5 vols. (Unpublished MS, microfilm, National Archives); James A. LeRoy, *The Americans in the Philippines,* 2 vols. (Boston: Houghton Mifflin, 1914); Sexton, *Soldiers in the Sun; Annual Reports of the Department of War, 1899–1902.*

strengthen their base of popular support. General MacArthur testified to the effectiveness of Aguinaldo's approach when he declared that insurgents disbanded whenever they were closely pressed and sought safety in the nearest village, "a manuever quickly accomplished by reason of the assistance of the people." [3]

Black regulars were among the American troops whose service in the Philippines spanned the shift in insurgent strategy from conventional to guerrilla warfare. Arriving in Manila in July and August, 1899, Negro soldiers of the Twenty-fourth and Twenty-fifth Infantry immediately took stations around the city from Calacoon to Balic Balic road. By mid-1900 the number of black regulars in the Philippines had increased to 2,100 men. In January and February, 1900, the Forty-eighth and Forty-ninth Infantry, the two Negro volunteer regiments recruited specifically for service in the islands, disembarked at Manila and remained in the field in Luzon until their enlistment terms expired a year and a half later. Eight troops of the Ninth Cavalry, originally destined for China to help put down the Boxer Rebellion, arrived in mid-September, 1900. The Ninth first saw action in southern Luzon in the vicinity of Nueva Caceres and Legaspi, and later participated in operations in Samar and Panay. By December, 1900, when the total strength of American forces stood at 70,000 men and officers, there were over 6,000 black regulars and volunteers stationed at dozens of small outposts scattered from northern Luzon to Samar. Not until mid-1901, at about the time the two black volunteer regiments returned to the United States, did any unit of the Tenth Cavalry arrive in the islands. In May the regiment's famous Second Squadron took station in Samar, where it immediately encountered "many Samaritans but not any good ones." [4]

In the weeks immediately after their landing in Manila in 1899 the Twenty-fourth and Twenty-fifth Infantry joined other troops stationed on the perimeter of the city. Detachments of the black

3. Gates, "Experiment in Benevolent Pacification," pp. 131–134, 210–211, 218.

4. "Record of Events," Regimental Returns of the Regular Army, Twenty-fourth and Twenty-fifth Infantry, July–September, 1899; "Record of Events," Regimental Returns of the Regular Army, Ninth and Tenth Cavalry, September, 1900, May–June, 1901, Record Group 94, National Archives; Elwell Otis to the Adjutant General, February 6, 1900, in *Correspondence Relating to the War with Spain*, II, 1142; Glass, *History of the Tenth Cavalry*, p. 39.

regiments guarded the city's water pumping station on the Mariquina River and helped protect the strategically important railroad linking Manila with Dagupan, a city 150 miles to the north. Other Negro infantrymen performed scouting and patrol duties in the area beyond the American lines.[5] For those who had participated in the Santiago campaign, it was soon apparent that the war in the Philippines was vastly different from the one waged against the Spaniards in Cuba. Although the tropical heat and torrential rains of the Philippines were reminiscent of Cuba, the enemy employed tactics which bore little resemblance to those of the Spaniards before Santiago. The type of warfare involved in subduing the Filipino insurgents promised to produce few heroes and little glory.

During their first weeks in the Philippines the black soldiers became intimately acquainted both with the hazards of a tropical climate and with the deadly tactics of the insurgents. On August 21, 1899, eleven men of the Twenty-fourth Infantry who had started on a reconnaissance mission toward San Mateo drowned when their boat capsized in the Mariquina River, a swift stream swollen by several days of heavy rain.[6] Early in September a party of the Twenty-fourth, on a scouting expedition in the mountains north of Manila, discovered in a valley "a body of Filipinos, drilling on extended order, such as used only in fighting." But upon descending to the site, the soldiers found only "peaceful citizens planting rice"—an occurrence that was to be repeated many times as they pursued their elusive enemy. A month later, on October 9, 1899, the Twenty-fifth had a similar experience when stationed around Calacoon and the battle-scarred church at La Loma. The black soldiers on picket duty near the church noticed a file of men dressed as Chinese coolies coming out of the nearby woods and assumed that they were the Chinese laborers who had been employed to furnish bamboo for constructing a road. Much to their surprise, however, the "queer looking men" were insurgents attired in Chinese garb who "threw out their skirmish line" and

5. "Record of Events," Regimental Returns, 24th and 25th Infantry, July–August, 1899; see also Muller, *Twenty-fourth Infantry;* Nankivell, *Twenty-fifth Regiment,* p. 88.

6. "Record of Events," Regimental Returns, 24th Infantry, August, 1899; *Richmond Planet,* August 26, 1899.

opened fire. The pickets, aided by reinforcements from a regimental outpost, "worked like demons" for more than an hour to hold their position. Ten men of the Twenty-fourth lay dead by the time the insurgents vanished into the woods. The day after the engagement, three companies of the regiment marched ten miles into the interior in search of the band of insurgents "but could see nothing of them." [7]

Throughout the early fall of 1899 the black regulars were "constantly on the jump," engaging the enemy in a succession of small skirmishes at such places as San Mateo, Mexico, Santa Ana, and San Nino.[8] The soldiers sensed that a major offensive was in the offing. Late in September a sergeant in the Twenty-fifth wrote a friend: "Everything is hustle and bustle; great preparations are being made, and everything indicates a hard campaign in the near future." [9] With the approach of the dry season, General Otis launched such a campaign in northern Luzon, a pincer movement designed to drive the insurgent forces, including Aguinaldo, into a *cul de sac*. Both Negro regiments were assembled at San Fernando on the Manila-Dagupan Railroad in preparation for the northern offensive. The farther the American army moved away from Manila, the more acute became its supply problem. At one point during the so-called northern expedition the food supply of the Twenty-fifth Infantry became so short that the men resorted to shooting monkeys for meat.[10] But neither the shortage of food nor the "grueling work up and down the steep and slippery trails" dampened the spirits of the black soldiers. Colonel Frederick Funston accompanied a battalion of the Twenty-fourth Infantry in a search for insurgents in the rugged country around San Jose; it was his first opportunity to observe colored troops in action. He was profoundly impressed by their performance, and

7. R. B. Lemus to the Editor, September 22, 1899, in Gatewood, *"Smoked Yankees,"* pp. 246–247; C. W. Cordin to the Editor, Cleveland *Gazette,* October 15, 1899, *ibid.,* pp. 249–250.

8. Nankivell, *Twenty-fifth Regiment,* pp. 88–89; Muller, *Twenty-fourth Infantry;* Captain Marcus D. Cronin, *Historical Sketch of the Twenty-fifth Infantry, United States Army* (Fort Bliss, Texas: n.p. 1907).

9. M. W. Sadler to Indianapolis *Freeman,* n.d., in Gatewood, *"Smoked Yankees,"* p. 247.

10. Fletcher, "Negro Soldier and the United States Army," pp. 274–275; Sexton, *Soldiers in the Sun,* pp. 174, 200.

especially by the "everlasting good nature" of the men as they waded through knee-deep mud and scaled towering mountains.[11]

Among the numerous engagements in which black regulars participated during the northern offensive, few attracted as much attention as the battle at O'Donnell. The Twenty-fifth, with headquarters at Bamban, learned that a large force of insurgents was encamped fifteen miles away at O'Donnell. Led by a Filipino guide, a detachment of 400 black soldiers under the command of Captain H. A. Leonhauser left Bamban on the night of November 17, 1899, headed for O'Donnell on a roundabout route through the foothills of the Zambales Mountains. Arriving at their destination just before sunrise, the troops staged a surprise attack on the insurgent stronghold.[12] Once inside O'Donnell, the colored soldiers "showed a grim and great earnestness in their work of gathering in prisoners, rifles and bolos." One eyewitness reported: "Strong black arms caught fleeing insurgents upon the streets and hauled them from under beds and beneath houses. Native women screamed in alarm and on their knees offered money and food to the American troops." [13] But the soldiers apparently refrained from acts of unnecessary brutality. In fact, a young white officer was deeply impressed by the "humanity and forebearance of the colored men of the 25th Infantry" in their taking of O'Donnell. "There might have been a hundred of these pitiful Filipino warriors killed," he wrote, "but the men apparently couldn't bring themselves to shoot them." Instead, the soldiers were satisfied to capture over 100 insurgents and a large supply of weapons, food, and ammunition.[14]

Despite complaints by some members of the Twenty-fifth that white Americans had paid little attention to their successful raid on O'Donnell, the affair did attract a good deal of favorable pub-

11. Frederick Funston, *Memories of Two Wars: Cuban and Philippine Experiences* (New York: Scribner's, 1914), p. 343.

12. On the battle at O'Donnell, see *Annual Reports of the Department of War for the Fiscal Year Ending June 30, 1900* ["Report of the Lieutenant General Commanding the Army"], 56 Cong., 2 sess., House Doc. 2, Pt. VI, 351–356; Cronin, *Twenty-fifth Infantry;* letters of black soldiers in Gatewood, *"Smoked Yankees,"* pp. 258, 265.

13. Nankivell, *Twenty-fifth Regiment*, p. 104.

14. Samuel P. Lyons, "The 25th at O'Donnell," in Samuel Powell Lyons Papers, United States Army Military History Collection, Carlisle Barracks, Pa.

licity. An Associated Press story spoke in glowing terms of the black soldiers' behavior. Even more complimentary were the official reports filed by the white officers in charge of the attack. Captain Leonhauser praised their performance in the highest terms, and Colonel Andrew S. Burt, the regimental commander, informed his superiors that the black soldiers deserved "credit for their untiring energy on the night march over unknown and difficult country, for the spirited manner in which they entered the town and for their orderly conduct afterward." Colonel Burt specifically called attention to the conspicuous bravery displayed by Sergeant James K. Lightfoot of Company K, Twenty-fifth Infantry, and recommended him for a Medal of Honor.[15]

If the Twenty-fifth won plaudits for its capture of O'Donnell, the Twenty-fourth added new luster to its reputation by participating in an extraordinary march of over 300 miles through northern Luzon into areas where no American troops had previously been. On November 18, 1899, a battalion of the Twenty-fourth and a company of native scouts under the command of Captain Joseph B. Batchelor, Jr., departed from Cabanatuan. After joining the army of General Henry W. Lawton five days later at Tayug, Batchelor received instructions (described as vague and "indefinite") to take his force through the mountainous country to Bayombong, the town in which Aguinaldo intended to establish the next insurgent capital. The object of the expedition was "to intercept and shut off Aguinaldo from crossing into the Cagayan Valley," a fertile tobacco-growing region. On November 24 Batchelor's force of Negro infantrymen and native scouts, weighted down with supplies of rice and salt, began the ninety-mile trek to Bayombong over a route appropriately called the "infernal trail."

Five days later, after encountering several bands of insurgents, the soldiers arrived at their destination only to find that it had already been occupied by a troop of American cavalrymen and that Aguinaldo planned to enter the Cagayan Valley to the north. Taking advantage of his vague instructions, Batchelor decided to lead his men across the mountains to the Cagayan River and to

15. P. C. Pogue to the Editor, Cleveland *Gazette*, November 24, 1899, in Gatewood, *"Smoked Yankees,"* p. 258; Nankivell, *Twenty-fifth Regiment*, pp. 104–105; *Annual Reports of the Department of War, 1900* ["Report of the Lieutenant General . . ."], Pt. V, 356.

follow the stream to its mouth at Aparri, a town on the coast of northern Luzon. Such free-wheeling, unsupplied expeditions were anathema to General Otis, who immediately dispatched a courier with orders to overtake and arrest Batchelor for refusing to abide by Lawton's instructions. When the courier was not heard from, Otis ordered gunboats to enter the Cagayan River at Aparri and move southward in an effort to assist the black battalion.

In the meantime Batchelor and his men, cut off from contact with other American forces and in dire need of food and clothing, continued their push toward the Cagayan River. Dispersing a rebel force at Fuerte San Luis on December 3, they entered the valley a few days later and began to move through mud and water along the Cagayan River toward Aparri. As they pushed northward the Negro soldiers captured insurgent installations, planted the American flag in towns and villages where it had not previously appeared, and secured the release of several hundred Spanish prisoners. On December 14 the flag was hoisted over Tuguegarao, the provincial capital of Cayagan, where Batchelor was met by the naval officers who had steamed the sixty miles up the Cagayan River from Aparri to bring relief. Except for a company left to garrison Tuguegarao, Batchelor and his men went by boat first to Aparri, then to Manila. Although General Otis reportedly abused Batchelor "like a pickpocket" for his liberal interpretation of Lawton's orders, the daring expedition of the Negro soldiers under his command became one of the most celebrated feats of the Philippine War.[16]

While the battalion of the Twenty-fourth pushed toward Aparri, other black troops engaged in a series of significant battles with the insurgents in another part of Luzon. Marching across the mountains toward the South China Sea, units of the Twenty-fifth Infantry captured the important towns of Iba and Botolan. Those who took part in the fighting at Iba during the first week of January, 1900, won special commendation for their efficiency and coolness. In the same week two companies of the Twenty-fifth under the command of Captain Leonhauser attacked an insurgent

16. On the Batchelor expedition, see Sexton, *Soldiers in the Sun*, pp. 215–219; "Record of Events," Regimental Returns, 24th Infantry, November–December, 1899; Elwell Otis to the Adjutant General, December 7, 1899, *Correspondence*, II, 1115.

fortress at the base of Mount Arayat, known as Camansi, which was described as "a veritable Gibraltar . . . a sort of second Lookout Mountain." The black troops ultimately took possession of the fortress, but not before the insurgents murdered five American soldiers whom they had captured earlier. In commenting on the Camansi engagement, General MacArthur declared that the Negro infantrymen were "worthy of all commendation." [17]

Despite the victories won by the American army during its offensive in northern Luzon, the pacification of the Philippines was far from complete. In fact, the campaign had resulted neither in the capture of Aguinaldo nor in the destruction of his army. By early 1900 resistance to American rule was almost wholly in the form of guerrilla warfare. Few engagements thereafter deserved to be called battles. But the hit-and-run tactics of Aguinaldo's widely dispersed forces and the marauding bands of robbers (ladrones) proved to be no less deadly to American troops who were constantly on patrol and scouting duty. Black volunteers of the Forty-eighth and Forty-ninth Infantry arrived in the Philippines early in 1900 anxious to confront the insurgents in conventional warfare; they were disappointed to discover that most of their efforts were devoted to "looking for rebel forces which are no where to be found." [18] A Negro lieutenant probably expressed the sentiments of his comrades when on January 31, 1900, he wrote home: "While there is no enemy in sight, yet we are always on the lookout and we have slept in our shoes ever since we landed. The war may be over or it may have just commenced. No one can tell what these devils will do next." [19]

In 1900 Negro soldiers ranged far and wide over Luzon in pursuit of Aguinaldo and his scattered army. John Hill of the Twenty-fourth Infantry recalled that his regiment "mostly walked from

17. "Record of Events," Regimental Returns, 25th Infantry, January, 1900; Cronin, *Twenty-fifth Infantry*; C. W. Cordin to the Editor, January 7, 1900, in Cleveland *Gazette*, March 17, 1900; Michael H. Robinson, Jr., to the Editor, Washington *Colored American*, March 24, 1900; *Annual Reports of the Department of War, 1900* ["Report of the Lieutenant General . . ."], Pt. VI, 360–361. The fortress at the foot of Mount Arayat was referred to either as Comanche or Camansi in official documents.
18. F. H. Crumbley to the Editor, February 7, 1900, in Gatewood, "Smoked Yankees," p. 269.
19. J. H. Thomas to A. C. Richardson, January 31, 1900, in Indianapolis *Recorder*, March 17, 1900.

place to place," occasionally accompanied by supply carts drawn by water buffalo. A veteran of the Twenty-fifth described the regiment's activities in 1900 as "one of unremitting field service and hard work, all of it guerrilla warfare." [20] In addition to participating in many skirmishes, the black troops built and maintained telegraph lines, constantly performed patrol and scouting duties, provided protection for work crews constructing roads, escorted supply trains, and "located and destroyed insurgent ordnance and other supplies." [21] Richard Johnson, a black enlisted man in the Forty-eighth Volunteers, maintained that the activities of his regiment consisted primarily of "hiking over mountains in the broiling sun and drenching rain; slushing through rice paddies and wading rivers with a few days respite at garrison duty." [22]

In order to prevent the insurgents from reestablishing themselves in areas already "pacified," American military authorities stationed small detachments of troops in the larger towns of each province. By April, 1900, for example, eight companies of the Twenty-fifth Infantry garrisoned ten towns scattered along the South China Sea coast from Subig to Santa Cruz, a distance of ninety miles.[23] Although duty in these small outposts offered welcome relief from "the hike," it left much to be desired. In a classic understatement one black soldier wrote: "Our recreation was meager." Lounging around village shops watching the girls and drinking beno, a potent alcoholic beverage, helped some of the soldiers overcome their boredom. On occasion these small posts suffered shortages in food and medicine, especially when insurgents prevented such supplies from "being forwarded from one town to another." The scarcity of medicines meant that the soldiers

20. John Hill, Questionnaire, December 14, 1968, in United States Army Military History Collection, Carlisle Barracks, Pa.; Cronin, *Twenty-fifth Infantry;* see also a letter from Private Edward Brown of the Twenty-fourth Infantry in the Indianapolis *Recorder,* June 9, 1900.
21. *Manila Times,* June 29, 1902; "Record of Events," Regimental Returns, 24th and 25th Infantry, January–December, 1900.
22. Johnson, "My Life in the U. S. Army, 1899–1922," p. 37; see also Osceola E. Jones to Booker T. Washington, November 4, 1900, Washington Papers.
23. T. H. Wiseman to Indianapolis *Freeman,* April 13, 1900, in Gatewood, *"Smoked Yankees,"* p. 276.

had little relief from the fevers and bowel troubles which so frequently plagued them.[24]

With the approach of the presidential election in the United States, Aguinaldo's army stepped up its resistance to American pacification. Throughout Luzon the insurgents launched attacks against American troops who garrisoned the small towns, ambushed scouting and escorting parties, and destroyed telegraph lines. Late in July, 1900, the Filipino insurgents struck a small detachment of the Twenty-fifth at Cabangan; among the casualties was James K. Lightfoot, the Negro sergeant who had earlier been commended for his bravery in the battle at O'Donnell. On October 10, 1900, eighteen men from the Twenty-fourth, en route from San Jose to repair a break in the telegraph line eight miles away, "were ambushed by 500 Insurgents who opened fire on the detachment at a distance of 50 feet." Only six of the black soldiers survived the attack.[25] All the while, the Negro volunteers were boasting of their brilliant work in the field, where disease and climate seemed to pose as much of a threat as insurgents' bullets. Frank R. Steward, a Negro captain of the Forty-ninth Infantry, explained in a letter to a friend how his men had routed the rebels after "a considerable scrap . . . in and around Las Pinas and Zapote." The captain claimed that "the Insurrectoes had increased their activity" in an attempt to hasten the defeat of McKinley. They assumed that with Bryan's election "was to come their 'Indepencia.' [sic]" But for a Republican as dedicated as Steward, the cause of Bryan was as hopeless as that of Aguinaldo.[26]

Following McKinley's election triumph, there was a gradual decrease in insurgent activity. This is not to say that resistance disappeared; for several months after the election black infantrymen,

24. J. H. Thomas to A. C. Richardson, January 31, 1900, in Indianapolis *Recorder*, March 17, 1900; Johnson, "My Life in the U.S. Army," p. 37.

25. Nankivell, *Twenty-fifth Regiment*, p. 92; Muller, *Twenty-fourth Infantry;* "Record of Events," Regimental Returns, 24th Infantry, October, 1900.

26. Frank R. Steward to Thomas H. R. Clark, January 22, 1901, in Gatewood, *"Smoked Yankees,"* pp. 294–296. For information on the diverse activities of the Negro volunteers, see Regimental Records, 48th and 49th Infantry, Adjutant General's Records; *Army and Navy Journal,* January 19, 1901, p. 504, July 6, 1901, p. 1097; "The Negro as Soldier and Officer," *The Nation,* LXXIII (August 1, 1901), 85–86; Fletcher, "Negro Soldier and the United States Army," pp. 287–294.

regulars as well as volunteers, were only too well aware of the rebels' presence. Reconnoitering parties were often fired upon by insurgent snipers or attacked by bands equipped with the bolo, a type of knife which was employed with deadly precision. Late in November, 1900, several troops of the Ninth Cavalry engaged in hard fighting in the interior of Albay Province around the insurgent capital of Jovellar. Their action finally cleared the province of "organized bands of insurgents." [27] Even so, sporadic attack by disorganized, free-wheeling guerrilla forces in Albay and elsewhere continued to pose a threat to the American pacification effort.

McKinley's victory in November was the signal for General MacArthur to inaugurate a new policy designed to insure the establishment of permanent control over the islands. This policy represented a shift from "benevolent pacification" to a more stringent approach, promising punishment for natives who continued to resist American authority and stressing the importance of isolating insurgents from their bases of supply in the villages. It also emphasized the need to protect villagers from intimidation and terror at the hands of insurgents.[28] For the black soldiers, including the Tenth Cavalry which arrived in May, 1901, the new military policy meant not only garrison duty in towns and villages scattered over hundreds of miles across the archipelago, but also an endless succession of expeditions through rice paddies and dense forests and over treacherous mountains and swollen streams. Writing in mid-March, 1901, a black infantryman noted that pitched battles were "few and far between." [29] An officer of the Ninth Cavalry described the pursuit of insurgents and ladrones by his men as "persistently and continually running the quarry to his lair [only] to find, in the majority of the cases, that he had

27. "Record of Events," Regimental Returns, 9th Cavalry, November, 1900; T. B. Dugan, "History of the Ninth Cavalry, 1866–1906," #1374702, Adjutant General's Records.
28. On the shift in American military policy, see Gates, "Experiment in Benevolent Pacification," pp. 261–271.
29. "Record of Events," Regimental Returns, 10th Cavalry, May–August, 1901; R. B. Lemus to the *Planet*, March 17, 1901, in *Richmond Planet*, April 17, 1901; MacArthur to the Adjutant General, May 15, 1901, *Correspondence*, II, 1278; Robert Patterson to C. Patterson, January 21, 1901, in Kansas City *American Citizen*, March 8, 1901.

escaped to some other hiding place." [30] However, such expeditions often resulted in the capture of sizable quantities of insurgent arms and food supplies.

The most notable event in the Philippine War during 1901 was the capture of Aguinaldo. Early in January a black soldier "picked up a suspicious looking native" who turned out to be an insurgent courier with documents which revealed the whereabouts of the Filipino leader's hideout in the Benguet Mountains of north-eastern Luzon. On the basis of these documents, Colonel Frederick Funston devised a plan—"a masterpiece of deceptive strategem"—which resulted in the capture of Aguinaldo on March 23, 1901. Funston was rewarded by being made a brigadier general in the regular army. While under arrest in Manila, Aguinaldo issued a proclamation calling upon his followers to accept American authority over the islands. Within a few weeks several of the most notable insurgent military leaders, including Manuel Tinio, Mascardo Alexandrino, and Urbano Lucuna, laid down their arms.[31] When General Arsi surrendered his force to the commander of Company K of the Twenty-fifth Infantry at Castillejos, a black enlisted man of that company wrote home: "The fact that they surrendered to the company they fought so often shows they appreciated their foes and speaks well of Company K, 25th Infantry." Like many others, the black soldiers believed that the capture of Aguinaldo meant "the practical winding up of the insurrection." [32] By mid-1901 such a view seemed to be substantiated by the reduction of American troop strength and the transfer of authority over the islands from the army to the civil commission under governor William Howard Taft.

While American authorities in Manila busied themselves with the establishment of civil governments in the provinces pacified by the army, the scene of combat shifted to Batangas and Samar. In these areas the insurgent generals Miguel Malvar and Vincente

30. Dugan, "History of the Ninth Cavalry." For a graphic description of life among black soldiers in the Philippines, see Rienzi B. Lemus, "The Enlisted Man in Action, Or the Colored American Soldier in the Philippines," *Colored American Magazine*, V (May, 1902), 46–54.

31. Johnson, "My Life in the U.S. Army," pp. 44–45; Sexton, *Soldiers in the Sun*, pp. 260–264; Gates, "Experiment in Benevolent Pacification," pp. 304–305; *Manila Times*, March 28, 1901.

32. R. B. Lemus to the *Planet*, April 23, 1901, in *Richmond Planet*, June 8, 1901.

Lukban continued their resistance to American rule.[33] Few black troops took part in the campaigns waged in these provinces: the two Negro volunteer regiments returned to the United States in mid-1901, and the Twenty-fourth and Twenty-fifth Infantry, as well as most of the Ninth Cavalry, were busy in Luzon garrisoning numerous outposts. From May until August several detachments of the Ninth Cavalry and the Second Squadron of the Tenth Cavalry did serve in the wild, sparsely settled areas of Samar. According to one observer, they "had a terrible time up in the interior" of that island. Undoubtedly the best-known black soldiers in Samar were Sergeant Major Horace Bivins of the Tenth Cavalry and Charles Young of the Ninth Cavalry, who had rejoined the regular army after serving as commander of Ohio's black volunteer battalion during the Spanish-American War. Promoted to captain early in 1901, Young commanded a company of dismounted cavalry in Samar which for almost three months went on daily scouting and reconnoitering expeditions into the country along the Gandara River. By September, 1901, the Negro cavalrymen, including Captain Young and his outfit, had left Samar and taken stations in Panay and southern Luzon.[34]

From early 1901 until their departure from the Philippines more than a year later, the black troops who garrisoned numerous outposts on the islands did more than perform the usual scouting, patrol, and guard duties and other activities involved in keeping the peace. They also assisted in laying "the foundations of civil government" and generally fuctioned as agents of the Americanization process. Their civil duties included the supervision of elections, the organization of educational and legal systems, and the maintenance of public health facilities.[35] Lieutenant David J. Gilmer of the Forty-ninth Infantry, a former member of the Third North Carolina Volunteers, not only was popular with enlisted

33. Gates, "Experiment in Benevolent Pacification," Ch. 9.

34. "Record of Events," Regimental Returns, 9th Cavalry, May–August, 1901; Glass, History of the Tenth Cavalry, p. 40; "Record of Events," Regimental Returns, 10th Cavalry, May–September, 1901; Crane, Colonel of Infantry, pp. 383–384; Annual Reports of the Department of War for the Fiscal Year Ending June 30, 1902 ["Report of the Lieutenant General Commanding the Army"], 57 Cong., 2 sess., House Doc. 2, Pt. IX, 464–465, 596, 597, 598, 601.

35. Manila Times, June 29, 1902; A. S. Burt to the Adjutant General, June 6, 1901, in Nankivell, Twenty-fifth Regiment, pp. 107–108; Muller, Twenty-fourth Infantry.

men but also won the affection of the people of Linao as commander of the post there. Gilmer later secured a commission in
the Philippine Scouts, an army of natives organized and officered
by Americans.[36] Captain Frank R. Steward, also of the Forty-ninth,
who was a graduate of the Harvard Law School, served as provost
judge in San Pablo; there he organized and presided over the first
American-type court.[37] His father, Chaplain Theophilus Steward
of the Twenty-fifth Infantry, supervised a series of schools taught
by soldiers in the towns and villages north of Manila under the
protection of his regiment. According to one observer, the chaplain's command of the Spanish language and capacity for hard
work enabled him to achieve excellent results and to instill in
Filipinos an appreciation for American values.[38] Black soldiers
often displayed considerable pride in their nonmilitary activities,
which they described as significant contributions to the improvement of life among the natives. An enlisted man in the Twenty-
fifth Infantry boasted in 1902 that "the colored American soldier
has taught the Filipino thrift, economy and above all the customs
of polite society." [39]

The performance of Negro troops in the Philippines, volunteers
as well as regulars, won praise from diverse quarters. Black officers of the volunteer units such as Edward L. Baker, Frank R.
Steward, and David J. Gilmer amply demonstrated their qualifi-
cations to hold military commissions. The battles at O'Donnell,
Camansi, Botolan, and other places again testified to the fighting
prowess of the enlisted men of the Negro regiments. The *Manila
Times* claimed that the black soldiers "created a distinctly favorable impression" during their tour of duty in the islands, in
spite of disparagement by those "who do not believe in enlisting
colored men." The *Times* also insisted that "in smartness of dress
and general military appearance they have easily stood first among

36. See especially Gilmer's "Address to the People of Linao," in Washington
Colored American, January 19, 1901.

37. Frank R. Steward to Thomas H. R. Clark, January 22, 1901, in Gatewood,
"Smoked Yankees," pp. 295–296.

38. R. B. Lemus to the Editor, January 15, 1902, *ibid.,* pp. 309–310; see also
Theophilus Steward, "Two Years in Luzon," *Colored American Magazine,* IV (November, 1901), 4–10.

39. R. B. Lemus to the Editor, January 15, 1902, in Gatewood, *"Smoked Yankees,"*
p. 310.

the regiments that have done garrison duty in Manila." [40] Official military reports filed with the War Department frequently referred to the coolness and efficiency displayed by Negro troops in combat. Several regulars were recommended by their white commanding officers for Medals of Honor and Certificates of Merit. At the conclusion of a tour of the islands the inspector general declared that the Twenty-fifth Infantry was "the best regiment I have seen in the Philippines"—a view heartily endorsed by Colonel Andrew S. Burt, the regiment's commander. [41] Promotion to brigadier general in April, 1902, ended Burt's connection with the Twenty-fifth; before leaving for his new assignment he delivered a farewell address to the men which revealed his high regard for their services in the Philippines.

> That you are as gallant as the best, remember El Caney, O'Donnell, Iba, Arayat and numbers of lesser fights in Zambales. Zambales! One province in Luzon that was absolutely cleaned up of ladrones and insurrectos, this by your untiring efforts, night and day, marching and fighting in and out of the rainy season. Oh! that was a grand piece of good soldiering! and don't you forget, my comrades, that I will tell the story on all public and private occasions.

In Burt's opinion black enlisted men were no less entitled to praise for their "record of good behavior in these Islands"—a record which proved that their race was "as law abiding as any in the world." [42]

Other observers, military as well as civilian, echoed Burt's sentiments. The Manila police chief commended the black soldiers of the Twenty-fourth Infantry for their exemplary conduct, asserting that no regiment stationed near the city had given the police so little trouble. [43] Of course, such compliments were not intended to suggest that every Negro soldier was a paragon of military virtue. One black soldier noted that the men of his company "ranged . . .

40. *Manila Times,* June 29, 1902.

41. Nankivell, *Twenty-fifth Regiment,* pp. 106, 108–110; 112; Muller, *Twenty-fourth Infantry; Manila Times,* January 17, 1900.

42. Nankivell, *Twenty-fifth Regiment,* pp. 112–113; see also Savannah *Tribune,* June 14, 1902.

43. *Manila Times,* June 29, 1902.

from pious gentlemen to habitual rowdy belligerents," [44] a description which undoubtedly could have been applied generally to Negro troops. No less than whites, blacks suffered from the boredom endemic to existence in remote outposts. Their diversions sometimes included activities considerably less wholesome than fishing, swimming, playing baseball, or participating in choral groups. Gambling and overindulgence in various alcoholic concoctions constituted the chief diversions of some soldiers, and drinking gamblers had a tendency to spawn fights. Black soldiers on leave in Manila sometimes became involved in disturbances in the tenderloin districts, especially in houses of prostitution which attempted to establish a color line.[45]

For many soldiers, black and white, female companionship offered the best respite from a monotonous existence. It was common practice for a Negro soldier to acquire a "squaw." Richard Johnson of the Forty-eighth Infantry claimed that the "first to acquire a 'querida' or lover (kept woman) was our captain and this set the pattern for all the men." [46] Perhaps, as Archibald Cary Coolidge later wrote, "their pursuits of the native women provoked much anger among the [Filipino] men." But whether such activity gave "rise to fresh insurrection in districts which had been pacified," as Coolidge claimed, is open to question.[47] Some black soldiers, especially those who planned to remain permanently in the Philippines at the termination of their military service, married Filipino women and settled in various parts of Luzon. For most soldiers, however, these relationships ended when they sailed for the United States in 1902. An enlisted man of the Twenty-fifth observed that in view of the number of deluded women who crowded

44. Johnson, "My Life in the U.S. Army," p. 49; see also William H. Cox, Jr., to John Mitchell, Jr., September 3, 1900, in Gatewood, "Smoked Yankees," p. 283.
45. Manila Times, August 26, September 2, 26, October 6, 1899, June 21, 22, 1902.
46. Johnson, "My Life in the U.S. Army," pp. 32, 60; see also George Rhodes, Questionnaire, January 13, 1969, and Walter Ervin, Questionnaire, January 23, 1969, in United States Army Military History Collection, Carlisle Barracks, Pa. For interesting observations on Filipino women by black soldiers, see D. J. Gilmer to E. E. Cooper, ?, 1900, in Washington Colored American, December 1, 1900; George E. Payne to Mrs. Isaac Drake, February 16, 1901, in Kansas City American Citizen, May 24, 1901.
47. Archibald Cary Coolidge, The United States as a World Power (New York: Macmillan, 1908), pp. 73–74.

the pier as soldiers shipped out for home, it was altogether appropriate for the band to play "The Girl I Left Behind." [48]

Whatever the consequences of their relations with native women, black soldiers generally appear to have treated Filipinos with respect and compassion. Throughout the war, and especially after the army adopted a harsher policy toward insurgents, reports of atrocities circulated widely in the United States. Few prompted as much indignation as those regarding the use of the so-called water cure as "a persuader . . . to induce bad hombres to talk." [49] Some Americans maintained that troops in the Philippines engaged in brutalities which surpassed anything committed by "Butcher" Weyler in Cuba. In May, 1900, black newspapers in the United States published a letter from a Negro soldier who expressed horror at the looting, stealing, desecration of churches, and daily indignities against Filipinos committed by his white comrades.[50] Even some high-ranking military officers protested against the severity of the war. The charges of unwarranted brutality achieved even greater credence late in 1901 when General Jacob Smith, in retaliation against the insurgents for their massacre of a contingent of American troops in Samar, ordered his army to turn the island into "a howling wilderness" and to kill every human being over the age of ten.[51]

Although one writer asserted in 1904 that "the brutal conduct" of black soldiers "in the interior seriously jeopardized the hope of a peaceful solution" to the Philippine insurrection, the weight of testimony in regard to their treatment of natives contradicts this observation.[52] Oswald Garrison Villard maintained that "neither the officers nor the men of any colored regiment" figured in "the charges and counter-charges arising out of the use of the water tor-

48. Steward, "Two Years in Luzon," 4–10; Manila Times, July 15, 1902; R. B. Lemus to the Planet, April 17, 1902, in Gatewood, "Smoked Yankees," p. 315.

49. Samuel P. Lyons to Mrs. Samuel P. Lyons, May 13, 1901, Lyons Papers; see also LeRoy, Americans in the Philippines, II, 225–228.

50. Milwaukee Wisconsin Weekly Advocate, May 17, 1900. See also Washington Bee, May 10, 1902.

51. Sexton, Soldiers in the Sun, pp. 273–275; Schirmer, Republic or Empire, pp. 237–240; Gates, "Experiment in Benevolent Pacification," pp. 331–334; Stuart C. Miller, "Our Mylai of 1900: Americans in the Philippine Insurrection," Transaction, VII (September, 1970), 17–29.

52. John Foreman, "The Americans in the Philippines," Contemporary Review, LXXXVI (September, 1904), 395.

ture, except one man who at the time of his offense was not with his regiment." [53] There were, of course, other exceptions of which Villard was undoubtedly ignorant. For example, Lieutenant Samuel Lyons of the Twenty-fifth confided in a letter to his wife that he and his men had on occasion administered the water cure to recalcitrant insurgents.[54] Nevertheless, it does appear that the black regiments used this particular form of torture far less frequently than some of the white outfits.

The Ninth Cavalry developed its own method for extracting information from captured insurgents. In describing it one authority wrote: "A native . . . was taken into a semi-dark room and securely bound. Then a huge black, dressed only in a loin cloth and carrying a cavalry sabre, entered and danced around the victim making threatening gesticulations with the sabre. To an ignorant Filipino he undoubtedly looked like a devil incarnate." [55] The method proved amazingly successful as a persuader; whatever its psychological consequences, it was obviously preferable to the physical torture inflicted by the water cure.

By the time the black troops departed from the Philippines, it was generally agreed that their relationships with natives were more cordial than those of white soldiers. When the Negro soldiers first arrived in the islands, Filipinos viewed them with awe and fear as an "American species of bete noir." A typical reaction was: "These are not Americans; they are Negritoes." But their fear quickly turned into friendliness and their awe into admiration. Filipinos came to accept black Amercans as "very much like ourselves only larger" and gave them the affectionate appellation, "Negritos Americanos." [56] Negro soldiers generally reciprocated the good will of peaceful natives and treated them with consideration and respect. In letters home they often referred to the contempt which white soldiers displayed toward all Filipinos and insisted that such an attitude underlay much of the natives' hostility to American rule.[57] Military authorities, quick to recognize

53. Villard, "The Negro and the Regular Army," 726.
54. Samuel P. Lyons to Mrs. Samuel P. Lyons, May 13, 1901, Lyons Papers.
55. Sexton, *Soldiers in the Sun*, p. 242.
56. *Manila Times*, June 29, 1902; see also George Rhodes, Questionnaire.
57. For samples of such letters, see Gatewood, *"Smoked Yankees,"* pp. 252–254, 257, 279–290.

the rapport between black soldiers and natives, generally agreed that in towns and districts "garrisoned by colored troops the natives seem to harbor little or no enmity toward the soldiers and the soldiers themselves seem contented with their lot and are not perpetually pining for home." [58] In 1902 Colonel Burt could "not recall of the many places where the 25th Infantry has been stationed on these Islands that the inhabitants were not genuinely sorry when they have been ordered to leave their towns." General Robert P. Hughes fully agreed, noting that black soldiers "mixed with the natives at once" and "whenever they came together, they became great friends." Hughes recalled that when he withdrew "a darkey company" from Santa Rita, the residents wept and begged him to allow the black soldiers to remain.[59]

Not all white Americans in the Philippines were so favorably disposed toward black soldiers and their friendly relations with Filipinos. "While the white soldiers, unfortunately, got on badly with the natives," the correspondent Stephen Bonsal reported, "the black soldiers got on much too well." Some white officers came to suspect that Negro troops had more sympathy for the Filipinos' aspirations for independence than for American policy regarding the islands. Others complained that the racial identity which black soldiers established with the natives had resulted in a color line that discriminated against whites.[60] Governor Taft apparently shared some of these concerns. He felt that black troops "got along fairly well with the natives . . . too well with the native women"; the result was "a good deal of demoralization in the towns where they have been stationed." Taft was credited with engineering the withdrawal of Negro troops from the islands in 1902 "out of their regular turn." [61]

Whatever the reaction of white soldiers to the rapport between their black comrades and the Filipinos, their overt expressions of

58. *Hearings before the Committee on the Philippines of the United States Senate*, Senate Doc. 331, 57 Cong., 1 sess., Pt. 1, p. 647.

59. Burt quoted in Nankivell, *Twenty-fifth Regiment*, pp. 112–113; Hughes quoted in *Hearings before the Committee on the Philippines*, Pt. 1, p. 647. See also Captain Thomas C. Carson's testimony, *ibid.*, Pt. 3, p. 2543.

60. Stephen Bonsal, "The Negro Soldier in War and Peace," *North American Review*, CLXXXVI (June, 1907), 325.

61. *Ibid.*, p. 326; Philip W. Kennedy, "The Concept of Racial Superiority and United States Imperialism, 1890–1910" (Ph.D. dissertation, St. Louis University, 1962), p. 96.

racial prejudice toward both only strengthened that relationship. Writing about American forces in the Philippines early in 1900, Frederick Palmer maintained that color was a crucial factor and that if a man was nonwhite, "we include him in a general class called 'nigger,' a class beneath our notice, to which, so far as our white soldier is concerned, all Filipinos belonged." [62] Another correspondent, Albert Gardiner Robinson, reported from Manila that "the spirit of our men is far too much one of contempt for the dark-skinned people of the tropics." [63] White soldiers "almost without exception" referred to the natives as "niggers," and, as Major Cornelius Gardner of the Thirtieth Infantry observed, "the natives are beginning to understand what the word 'nigger' means." In 1899 both the *Manila Times* and the *Army and Navy Journal* became so concerned about the mischief done by the widespread use of the term in referring to black soldiers and Filipinos that they called upon Americans to banish it from their vocabulary.[64] For quite a different reason white Southerners in the islands also objected to calling Filipinos "niggers"—a term which they reserved for Negro Americans, soldiers as well as civilians. James H. Blount of Georgia, an officer in the Twenty-ninth Infantry who remained in the Philippines as a civil judge, claimed that Southerners "instinctively resented any suggestion comparing Filipinos and negroes," because such comparison implied that their social intercourse with natives was "equivalent to eating, drinking, dancing and chumming with negroes"—things which no self-respecting white man would do.[65]

Black soldiers were keenly aware of the racial attitudes of their white comrades toward all colored people, themselves as well as Filipinos. The men of the Twenty-fifth Infantry had scarcely

62. Frederick Palmer, "The White Man and the Brown Man in the Philippines," *Scribner's Magazine*, XXVII (January, 1900), 81; see also James A. LeRoy, "Race Prejudice in the Philippines," *Atlantic Monthly*, XC (July, 1902), 100–112.

63. Albert Gardiner Robinson, "The Outlook in the Philippines," *The Independent*, LII (February 8, 1900), 349. Jacob Schurman, formerly head of the Philippine Commission, admitted that the Filipino's "color and stature make it impossible for the Anglo-Saxon to treat him with respect." *Ibid.*, LIV (May 8, 1902), 1104–7.

64. Gardner quoted in *Hearings before the Committee on the Philippines*, Pt. 2, p. 884; *Manila Times*, November 17, 1899; *Army and Navy Journal*, August 26, 1899, p. 1240.

65. James H. Blount, *The American Occupation of the Philippines, 1898–1912* (New York: Putnam, 1912), pp. 364–365.

landed in the islands in 1899 when, as they marched into Manila, a white spectator yelled: "What are you coons doing here?" [66] The sentiment implicit in the question found expression in the establishment of "white only" restaurants, hotels, barber shops, and even brothels, and in tunes such as "I Don't Like a Nigger Nohow" sung by white soldiers. In mid-1900 a Negro regular observed that "already there is nowhere in Manila you can hardly [sic] get accommodated and you are welcomed nowhere." The color line being drawn against the black soldier in the Philippines was, in his opinion, "enough to make a colored man hate the flag of the United States." [67] Patrick Mason of the Twenty-fourth Infantry wrote home not long before he was killed in combat: "The first thing in the morning is the 'Nigger' and the last thing at night is the 'Nigger.'" Such talk, according to Mason, was prompted by the assumption of white soldiers that no one except Caucasians had "any rights or privileges." [68] Late in 1899 a black infantryman on duty near San Isidro wrote: "The whites have begun to establish their diabolical race hatred in all its home rancor . . . even endeavoring to propagate the phobia among the Spaniards and Filipinos so as to be sure of the foundation of their supremacy when the civil rule . . . is established." [69] White officers often expressed admiration for the light-hearted, cheerful mood with which black soldiers undertook even the most difficult assignments, but few indicated an awareness of their deep resentment of the insults and discrimination to which they were regularly subjected.

A major source of black soldiers' grievances was the racial prejudice displayed by some of their white officers. While in the Philippines, the officer personnel of the four Negro regiments of the regular army changed frequently; [70] according to black enlisted men and noncommissioned officers, the replacements too often in-

66. Mary Curtis, *The Black Soldiers, or the Colored Boys of the United States Army* (Washington: Murray Brothers, 1915), p. 41.
67. "Colored Regular" to Paul Dana, July 16, 1900, #342217, Adjutant General's Records.
68. Patrick Mason to the Editor, Cleveland *Gazette*, November 19, 1899, in Gatewood, *"Smoked Yankees,"* p. 257.
69. John W. Galloway to the Editor, November 16, 1899, *ibid.*, p. 252; see also Washington *Colored American*, January 11, 1902.
70. Samuel P. Lyons to Mrs. Samuel P. Lyons, September 13, 1899, December 4, 1900, Lyons Papers.

cluded whites who, protected by their rank, gave full vent to their animosities against people of color. Though always generous in their praise of white officers whom they considered fair-minded, black soldiers complained bitterly about their treatment at the hands of those with a prejudice against Negroes. Specifically, they charged such officers with cursing and abusing enlisted men and with subjecting them to inhuman treatment for even minor infractions of military regulations. In a few instances the grievances found their way to the War Department; but as a member of the Twenty-fifth who filed a complaint correctly predicted, "an abnegation will confront this statement as has been the case heretofore. . . ." [71]

The color prejudice manifested by white Americans in the Philippines substantially affected the black soldiers' view of the Filipino. The soldiers early classified the natives as colored people and looked upon themselves as part of an experiment pitting "Greek against Greek." [72] Although some white Americans claimed that Filipinos deeply resented the presence of black troops because they regarded themselves "as belonging to a race superior to the African," [73] such a view was contradicted by the testimony of black soldiers who almost without exception noted how the affinity of complexion between themselves and the natives provided the basis for mutual respect and good will. After a series of interviews with well-educated Filipinos, a black infantryman reported that although natives had been told of the "brutal natures" of black Americans and had at first feared for the safety of their senoritas, personal experience had demonstrated that Negro soldiers were "much more kindly and manly in dealing with us" than whites.[74]

71. "Colored Regular" to Paul Dana, July 16, 1900, H. C. Corbin to Paul Dana, September 7, 1900, #342217, Frederick Schaffen to the Secretary of War, October 16, 1900, #350548, Adjutant General's Records. See also letters in *Army and Navy Journal:* July 7, 1900, p. 1068, December 1, 1900, p. 328, October 12, 1901, p. 141.
72. M. W. Saddler to the Editor, no date, in Indianapolis *Freeman*, November 18, 1899.
73. Coolidge, *United States as a World Power*, p. 74n; Savannah *Tribune*, July 22, 1899. See also Theodore Friend, *Between Two Empires: The Ordeal of the Philippines* (New Haven: Yale University Press, 1965), p. 35.
74. John W. Galloway to the Editor, November 16, 1899, in Gatewood, "*Smoked Yankees*," pp. 251–255. See also W. H. Jackson, "From Our Friends in the Far East," *Colored American Magazine*, I (August, 1900), 149; F. H. Wheaton, "A Feast with the Filipinos," *ibid.*, III (June, 1901), 154–155.

Black soldiers might refer to Filipino insurgents as "gugus," a term used by white Americans usually to identify hostile natives, but they obviously did not join white soldiers in applying the more general term "nigger" to all Filipinos.[75] Nor did they "kick and cuff" natives at will. According to one Filipino, the black soldier differed from his white comrade in one principal respect: he did not "connect race hatred with duty." [76] Eugene R. Whitted of the Twenty-fifth Infantry agreed that the Negro soldier's lack of racial animosity toward colored people gave him an advantage over whites in dealing with the Filipinos. "Our men met treatment with like treatment," he declared, "and when they were in the field they were soldiers and when in town gentlemen." [77] Despite breaches in the gentleman's code, Negro troops appear, as one Negro regular put it, to have gotten "along well with everybody but American [white] people." [78]

Although color was important in determining the attitude of black soldiers toward Filipinos, it was not the only consideration. Some soldiers early detected a similarity between the predicament of the black man in the United States and the brown man in the Philippines: both were subjects of oppression. For such soldiers the struggle of colored Filipinos against their white oppressors had obvious ideological as well as racial implications. In view of the plight of colored citizens in the United States, it was not surprising that some black soldiers expressed doubts as to whether Filipinos under American rule would "be justly dealt by." [79] Private William R. Fulbright of the Twenty-fifth described the war against the Filipinos as "a gigantic scheme of robbery and oppression." [80] Writing from a military station on Luzon on Christmas Eve, 1900, a Tuskegee alumnus confided to Booker T. Washington that "these

75. Frank R. Steward to Thomas H. R. Clark, January 22, 1901, in Gatewood, "Smoked Yankees," p. 295; Samuel Waller, Questionnaire, January 11, 1969, in United States Army Military History Collection, Carlisle Barracks, Pa.

76. John W. Galloway to the Editor, November 16, 1899, in Gatewood, "Smoked Yankees," p. 253.

77. Whitted quoted in The Searchlight (Wichita), December 27, 1902.

78. "Colored Regular" to Paul Dana, July 16, 1900, #342217, Adjutant General's Records.

79. For letters of black soldiers expressing this view, see Gatewood, "Smoked Yankees," pp. 253, 257, 268; Richmond Planet, February 3, 1900.

80. William R. Fulbright to the Editor, June 10, 1901, in Gatewood, "Smoked Yankees," p. 305.

people are right and *we* are wrong and terribly wrong." The black soldier assured Washington that he would not reenlist because no man "who has any humanity about him at all" would desire "to fight against such a cause as this." Another Negro infantryman who believed that the Filipinos had "a just grievance" maintained that the insurrection would never "have occurred if the army of occupation . . . [had] treated them as people." But the occupation forces, he declared, attempted to apply to the Filipinos the "home treatment for colored people" which they would not tolerate.[81]

Few black soldiers were so forthright in expressing doubts about the wisdom and correctness of the American position in the Philippines. More typical was a statement by Sergeant M. W. Saddler: "Whether it is right to reduce these people to submission is not a question for the soldier to decide." Like others, Saddler preferred to emphasize the resolve with which Negro troops in the Philippines performed their duty in order to "add another star to the already brilliant crown of the Afro-American soldier." [82] Captain W. H. Jackson of the Forty-ninth acknowledged that the soldiers of his regiment identified racially with the natives, but he insisted that, as members of the American army, black men took the position that "all enemies of the U. S. government look alike to us, hence we go along with the killing." [83]

Despite such explanations, the correspondence of Negro soldiers revealed that they were continually plagued by misgivings about their role in the Philippines. For black regular William Simms of Muncie, Indiana, such misgivings were forcefully driven home by a Filipino boy who asked him: "Why does the American Negro come from America to fight us when we are much a friend to him and have not done anything to him [?] He is all the same as me and me all the same as you. Why don't you fight those people in America who burn Negroes, that make a beast of you. . . ?" [84] For

81. Robert L. Campbell to Booker T. Washington, December 24, 1900, Washington Papers; unsigned letter in Milwaukee *Wisconsin Weekly Advocate*, May 17, 1900.

82. M. W. Saddler to the Editor, no date, in Indianapolis *Freeman*, November 18, 1899.

83. Jackson, "From Our Friends in the Far East," 149.

84. Quoted in Indianapolis *Freeman*, May 11, 1901.

introspective and thoughtful soldiers like Simms, their racial and ideological sympathy for a colored people struggling to achieve freedom seemed always to be at war with their notions of duty as American citizens and their hope that the fulfillment of that duty would somehow ameliorate the plight of their people at home. As Sergeant John W. Galloway indicated, "the black men here are so much between the 'Devil and the deep sea' on the Philippine Question." [85] But even those without such qualms who believed that the soldier's oath knew "neither race, color nor nation" were troubled by the increasing hostility of black Americans at home toward the war in the Philippines. Negro soldiers, according to one infantryman, were "rather discouraged over the fact that the sacrifice of life and health has to be made for a cause so unpopular among our people." [86]

Anti-imperialists in the United States were quick to detect the irony involved in the use of black troops to suppress the Filipino insurrection. A succession of poets, novelists, humorists, and journalists attacked the racist notions implicit in the doctrine of the white man's burden and pointed up the disparities between the rhetoric and realities of "benevolent assimiliation." George Ade and Finley Peter Dunne called attention to the incongruities in the nation's use of black troops to shoulder the "white man's burden" in the Philippines where they, as representatives of an unassimilated segment of the American population, were supposed to bring about the "benevolent assimilation" of the Filipino. According to Dunne's Mr. Dooley, the government's policy in the Philippines was to "Take up th' white man's burden an' hand it to th' coons." Having succeeded to the presidency in September, 1901, upon McKinley's assassination, Theodore Roosevelt admitted that Dunne's "delicious phrase about 'take up the white man's burden and put it on the coons' exactly hit off the weak spot" in his ex-

85. J. W. Galloway to the Editor, no date, in *Richmond Planet*, September 30, 1899. Galloway was later accused of sympathizing with the insurgents and discharged from the army without honor; for the voluminous records regarding his case, see the correspondence in #17043, #198322, and #356799, Adjutant General's Records.

86. Michael H. Robinson, Jr., to the Editor, no date, in Washington *Colored American*, March 24, 1900.

pansionist theory. But Roosevelt assured Dunne that he was not willing "to give up the theory yet." [87]

No less aware of the "weak spot" were the Filipino insurgents, who were also thoroughly familiar with the plight of Negroes in the United States and of the widespread anti-imperialist sentiment within the black community. Cognizant of the ambivalent attitude of the black troops who found themselves combatting an independence movement by another people of color, insurgent propagandists directed special appeals "To the Colored American Soldier." [88] Here is one such proclamation signed by Aguinaldo and addressed to the Twenty-fourth Infantry during its operations in 1899 in the vicinity of Mabalacat:

> It is without honor that you are spilling your costly blood. Your masters have thrown you into the most iniquitous fight with double purpose—to make you the instrument of their ambition and also your hard work will soon make the extinction of your race. Your friends, the Filipinos, give you this good warning. You must consider your situation and your history, and take charge that the blood . . . of Sam Hose proclaims vengeance.[89]

Such appeals were sources of embarrassment for the vast majority of black soldiers who protested that they were "just as loyal to the old flag as white Americans." [90] Nevertheless, the insurgents' propaganda was not altogether barren of results, and a few black soldiers actually joined the rebel ranks.

Although probably no more than a dozen men deserted to the insurgent cause, their acts appeared all the more dramatic because the desertion rate among the Negro regiments had traditionally been extremely low. What usually occasioned comment was not the number but the motivation of the Negro deserters. According to Stephen Bonsal, desertions from Negro regiments in the Philippines "were invariably of a different character" than those from white regiments. The white soldier "deserted because he was

87. Gianakos, "Spanish-American War and Double Paradox," 42–43.

88. Jackson, "From Our Friends in the Far East," 149.

89. Quoted in Rienzi B. Lemus to the Editor, no date, in *Richmond Planet*, November 11, 1899; see also Kansas City *American Citizen*, December 8, 1899.

90. P. C. Pogue to the Editor, November 24, 1899, in Gatewood, "*Smoked Yankees*," pp. 258–259.

lazy and idle and found service irksome," while the black soldier deserted "for the purpose of joining the insurgents," whose struggle he interpreted as the struggle of a colored people to free themselves from white domination. Black soldiers who joined the insurgents not only received high-ranking military commissions but also enjoyed the respect of their new colored comrades.[91] Not the least of their contributions to the insurgent army was the training they provided in the proper use of firearms. American troops who encountered insurgents trained by deserters were singularly impressed by the improvement in "the accuracy of their gunfire." [92]

Although four Negro deserters from the Ninth Cavalry attracted considerable attention for their activities in behalf of the insurgents' cause, the greatest publicity was lavished upon David Fagen of the Twenty-fourth Infantry. On November 28, 1899, Fagen deserted near San Isidro while his company was advancing into northern Luzon with the army of General Lawton. During this northward thrust the Twenty-fourth encountered Aguinaldo's placards addressed "To the Colored American Soldier." A white officer remembered Fagen as a "good-for-nothing whelp," but a black noncommissioned officer of his company recalled that he "had a pretty hard time" and had been "made to do all sorts of dirty jobs." The black sergeant concluded: "From the treatment he got I don't blame him for clearing out." Fagen accepted a commission in the insurgent army under General Lacuna and periodically issued appeals for other black soldiers to join him in taking up the cause of Filipino liberty. Although the *Manila Times* refused to consider him a source of danger, it nonetheless believed that he was "a vile traitor" who merited the most severe punishment.[93]

Once General Funston had engineered the capture of Aguinaldo, he turned his attention to Fagen. On two occasions Funston had received what he described as "impudent and badly spelled letters" from Fagen. When Lacuna surrendered his army to Funston in May, 1901, he refused to include Fagen because Amer-

91. Bonsal, "Negro Soldier in War and Peace," 326.
92. *Manila Times*, July 9, October 15, 1901.
93. *Ibid.*, September 8, 1901; see also "Record of Events," Regimental Returns, 24th Infantry, November, 1899; *New York Times*, October 29, 1900.

ican military authorities would not promise to treat him as a prisoner of war. Although the whereabouts of the Negro deserter remained a mystery, he continued to be the subject of rumors and false reports in Manila. Some claimed that he had joined the forces of Malvar in Batangas; the San Francisco *Chronicle* even printed a story explaining how he had escaped to California and had been arrested in Los Angeles. Convinced that Fagen was still in the Philippines and isolated from any insurgent force, General Funston laid plans for his capture. With the approval of military authorities in Manila, he posted "a reward of $600 for Fagen dead or alive." Proclamations in Spanish and Tagalog announcing the reward were posted in every town in Nueva Ecija. Funston let it be known that in his opinion the deserter was "entitled to the same treatment as a mad dog." Late in November, 1901, a party led by Anastacio Bartolome, a Filipino deer hunter and scout, found and beheaded Fagen in his camp at Dingalan Cove on the Pacific coast. Bartolome collected the reward after delivering Fagen's head in a basket at the American military station at Bongabong. Extraordinarily pleased with the results of his plan for offering a reward, Funston declared that Fagen was "at least one American traitor who got what was coming to him." [94] A Negro editor in Indianapolis who probably reflected the sentiments of many black Americans noted that "Fagen was a traitor and died a traitor's death, but he was a man no doubt prompted by honest motives to help a weaker side, and one with which he felt allied by ties that bind." [95]

The ideological and racial motives used by some observers to explain the actions of black soldiers such as Fagen provided the theme for a polemical novel by Robert L. Bridgman. In *Loyal Traitors*, which appeared less than two years after Fagen's capture, the principal character was Washington Douglas, a Negro who persuaded two friends to join him in volunteering for service in the insurgent army. The son of a slave, Douglas claimed to "have some idea of what freedom and liberty and duty mean." He was ashamed that Negro soldiers had gone to the Philippines "to

94. Funston, *Memories of Two Wars*, pp. 376, 380, 430–431; *Manila Times*, May 12, 14, December 7, 1901; Leon Wolff, *Little Brown Brother: How the United States Purchased and Pacified the Philippine Islands at the Century's Turn* (Garden City: Doubleday, 1961), pp. 249, 357–358.
95. Indianapolis *Freeman*, December 14, 1901.

help the white man conquer these brown men, killing them because they are fighting for their liberty and independence." As "a personal and race tribute to the memory of Abraham Lincoln whose Proclamation freed his mother," Douglas joined the Filipino insurgents, whom he believed "thoroughly right in their moral and political position"; he was killed in an engagement against American troops. According to Bridgman, Douglas's commitment to American ideals impelled him to resist what he considered to be the immoral course of his own country; a "higher patriotism" prompted him to commit treason.[96]

Despite the publicity which a dozen or so Negro deserters attracted, the overwhelming majority of black soldiers in the Philippines ignored the blandishments of the insurgents and hoped that their service would result in rewards commensurate with their record. The Negro regular still believed that he was entitled to "a commission from the ranks." [97] During the congressional consideration of the Army Reorganization Bill which passed in February, 1901, the black press in the United States pleaded not only for an increase in the number of Negro regiments in the regular army, but also for the appointment of black officers.[98] Their efforts were unsuccessful in both respects, although the four existing regiments of black regulars were expanded in order to accommodate men of the Forty-eighth and Forty-ninth Infantry who desired to enlist in the regular army upon the expiration of their tenure in the volunteer service. According to Adjutant General Henry C. Corbin, the increase in the size of the four black regiments meant that the new army under the Reorganization Act included "6000 colored men . . . which at its maximum of 100,000 probably exceeds the per centage of colored population." [99]

96. Gianakos, "Spanish-American War and Double Paradox," 48–49. For a short story which relates racial amalgamation to overseas expansion, see Pauline E. Hopkins, "Talma Gordon," Colored American Magazine, I (October, 1900), 271–290.

97. See the letters of Negro soldiers in Gatewood, "Smoked Yankees," pp. 248, 302; Solomon Johnson to the Editor, no date, in Army and Navy Journal, October 12, 1901, p. 141.

98. See Washington Colored American, February 9, 1901; Richmond Planet, March 23, 1901.

99. George K. Nash to William McKinley, March 23, 1901, H. C. Corbin to George K. Nash, March 30, 1901, #370613, Memorandum by H. C. Corbin, April 20, 1901, #374185, Adjutant General's Records.

Although the commissioning of Benjamin O. Davis of the Ninth Cavalry through competitive examination early in 1901 [100] offered a measure of hope that more black men would be represented in the officer corps, Negro regulars continued to feel that the army had drawn a color line against them. Reflecting this view, a Negro editor in Kansas City asked: "What's in a Negro being a soldier?" In his opinion there was "absolutely nothing at present for a Negro to hope for in facing bullets in defense of Uncle Sam," because there was a "line that Mr. Negro can get to—when once there—he reads: 'Thus far and no farther.'" [101] Negro soldiers also complained that they were denied commissions in the constabulary and scouts organized in the Philippines by the American army. Early in 1902 the *Independent,* a leading white periodical, agreed that black soldiers in the Philippines had been subjected to "real and unwise discrimination" in the distribution of both military and civilian appointments.[102]

Despite such discrimination, black soldiers throughout their service in the islands reported favorably on opportunities for enterprising black Americans. They described the soil and climate as conducive to productive agriculture and particularly emphasized the openings awaiting the Negro in business. F. H. Crumbley of the Forty-ninth Infantry urged black Americans "of Christian education" who desired to labor "among an appreciative people" to migrate to the Philippines at once. "They should not wait till the field is covered by others," he advised, "but should come in the front ranks and assist in developing these people." [103] Sharing Crumbley's enthusiasm, a black enlisted man of the Twenty-fourth wrote home: "I shall say to all industrious and energetic colored Americans . . . that they cannot do anything more beneficial to themselves than to come over here while the country is still in its infancy and help . . . reap the harvest which we shall

100. Washington *Colored American,* April 6, 1901; George W. Prioleau to the Editor, no date, in Gatewood, *"Smoked Yankees,"* pp. 302–303.

101. Kansas City *American Citizen,* September 6, 1901.

102. Washington *Colored American,* November 30, 1901, February 15, April 19, 1902; "Race Discrimination in the Philippines," *Independent,* LIV (February 13, 1902), 416–417.

103. F. H. Crumbley to the Editor, February 7, 1900, in Gatewood, *"Smoked Yankees,"* p. 271.

soon begin to gather in. In this country will be many fortunes made." [104] The soldiers believed that the friendly relations which they had established with the Filipinos would operate to the advantage of Negro Americans who sought their fortunes in the islands.[105]

On July 2, 1902, President Roosevelt issued a proclamation which, in effect, announced the end of the Filipino Insurrection. Even before his announcement American troops had begun to depart from the Philippines; beginning in May, the first black troops had shipped out of Manila for San Francisco. By mid-autumn all Negro soldiers, except those who chose to be mustered out in the Philippines, had taken stations in the United States.[106] Most of those taking up residence in the islands secured jobs in hotels and restaurants in Manila or appointments as clerks in the civil government. In addition, there were "several school teachers, one lawyer and one doctor of medicine." One black American to remain in Manila when his regiment left in 1902 was T. N. McKinney of Texas, who first served on the city's police force and later as a minor civil servant. Ultimately McKinney acquired considerable wealth as the proprietor of the Manila Commission House Company; he became the recognized leader of the "colored colony in the capital city." [107] Late in 1902 a black veteran of the Philippine campaign stationed at Fort Assiniboine, Montana, made public his views on the emigration of Negro Americans to the islands. Despite the fact that racial prejudice had "kept close in the wake of the flag" and was "keenly felt in that far-off land of eternal sunshine and roses," he was nonetheless convinced that the islands offered "our people the best opportunities of the century." [108]

104. William F. Blakeny to the Editor, January 24, 1902, *ibid.*, p. 311. For the expression of similar sentiments, *ibid.*, pp. 254–255, 290, 296, 316.

105. See Charles Steward, "Manila and Its Opportunities," *Colored American Magazine*, III (August, 1901), 248–256; Joseph H. Tucker to Booker T. Washington, March 19, 1900, Washington Papers.

106. Corbin to Chaffee, June 27, 1902, *Correspondence*, II, 1350; Glass, *History of the Tenth Cavalry*, p. 40; Nankivell, *Twenty-fifth Regiment*, p. 97; Muller, *Twenty-fourth Infantry*; Sexton, *Soldiers in the Sun*, pp. 284–285.

107. "In the Philippines," *The Crisis*, IV (April, 1918), 279; Indianapolis *Freeman*, October 27, 1906; E. B. Thompson, "Veterans Who Never Came Home," *Ebony*, XXVII (October, 1972), 104–106, 108–115.

108. T. Clay Smith to the Editor, no date, in Gatewood, *"Smoked Yankees,"* p. 316.

Eleven

Black Emigration and the New Pacific Empire

Now that the war is practically ended, the Philippines and other dependencies present inviting fields for negro exploitation, in which they can develop their possibilities without always running up against a dead wall of color discrimination.

If it is the intention of the Government to Americanize its new possessions, no class of citizens can serve better than college-trained Afro-Americans. Climate, temperament, racial affinity are all in their favor.

—A. R. Abbott, September, 1901

. . . the task at hand then is not to hunt a new home [for Negro Americans], but to make the present one more comfortable.

—Harry H. Pace, October, 1904

The return of Negro troops from the Philippines in 1902 attracted none of the publicity which had been bestowed upon black veterans of the Cuban campaign. More important, their military contribution had obviously failed to have a salutary effect upon the status of black civilians at home—in fact, their return coincided with what one observer described as the "renewed agitation" of the Negro Question. The agitation had been acute for some years, to be sure, but rarely if ever had the rhetoric and imagery of whites in discussing the issue been more blatantly racist. Indicative of the prevailing atmosphere was the concerted effort in the fall of 1902 by white leaders of the Spanish-American War Veterans Association to exclude black veterans from the organization.[1] During Emancipation Day ceremonies in Indianapolis earlier that year,

1. Indianapolis *Freeman,* September 27, 1902.

Bishop Alexander Walters had spoken about the plight of black Americans; although he counseled them not to be discouraged, his catalogue of assaults upon the dignity and personality of colored people provided little basis for anything but despair. "I observe," Walters concluded, "that the laws are growing more stringent and the lines tighter. There was many places in the North forbidding the colored man's entrance. Southern ideas are making their way northward." [2] A few months later an editorial in the *New York Times* seemed to corroborate the bishop's observation by proclaiming that "practically the whole country" had acquiesced in the "southern solution" to the race problem, since "there was no other possible settlement." [3] Such an admission deepened the disenchantment of those Negroes who had espoused the cause of the "white man's burden" abroad in the hope of obtaining a brighter future for their race at home.

By July, 1902, when President Roosevelt declared the Filipino Insurrection at an end, imperialism per se was no longer the subject of lively debate among Negro Americans. Those who continued to manifest interest in the extension of the nation's overseas possessions generally operated on the assumption that an American empire was an established fact, and they attempted to reconcile themselves to the nation's new status as a colonial power. Returning to an argument put forward by black expansionists earlier, T. Thomas Fortune's *New York Age* claimed that "the more dark peoples that we have under our flag the better it will be for those of us who came out of the forge and fire of American slavery." [4] Early in 1902 Edward E. Cooper's *Colored American* used a similar rationale to justify American acquisition of the Danish West Indies. "The more islands we annex and the more diverse our population becomes," Cooper declared, "the better it will be for the American Negro. The government becomes too great for petty prejudices when big issues are at stake." [5] Such arguments might have been useful to black Americans in accommodating them-

2. *Ibid.,* July 2, 1902.

3. *New York Times,* January 6, 1903.

4. Quoted in William S. Scarborough, "The Negro and Our New Possessions," *Forum,* XXXI (May, 1901), 344.

5. Washington *Colored American,* February 15, March 8, 1902; see also Indianapolis *Freeman,* February 8, 1902.

selves to the colonies already established in the Philippines, Puerto
Rico, and Hawaii, or to the possible annexation of the Danish West
Indies, but they obviously did not apply to Haiti and the Dominican Republic. Fortune, Cooper, and other editorial spokesmen
were quick to condemn any effort by the United States which they
viewed as threatening to the integrity and independence of the
two Caribbean black republics.[6]

In the opening years of the twentieth century the most urgent
concern of black Americans was not the fate of Haiti and the
Dominican Republic but their own future. Booker T. Washington, who reached "the plateau of his power and influence" about
1901, counseled patience and emphasized the opportunities open
to Negroes rather than the assaults upon their dignity and manhood; however, he clearly recognized the seriousness of the crisis
which confronted black people. The "present season," he observed
in 1903, was one of "anxiety, and almost of despair" among certain
segments of the colored population.[7] For some Negro spokesmen,
the burden of prejudice had become so heavy that blacks had no
alternative but to "begin life over" in a place where color did
not limit their opportunities. "Emigration or extermination" no
longer appeared to be merely an empty slogan voiced by the pe-
rennial emigrationists.[8]

Throughout the late nineteenth century the question of emigration, especially Bishop Henry M. Turner's back-to-Africa movement, had been the subject of debate within the black community.
By 1898 popular interest had shifted from Turner's scheme to
diverse proposals for the emigration of black citizens to Cuba.
Within two years, however, the image of Cuba as a place of refuge
had also lost most of its appeal. Although Africa, Puerto Rico,
Cuba, and even Haiti continued to be publicized as possible havens
for black Americans, the discussion of emigration between 1900
and 1903 focused on the nation's new possessions in the Pacific,
notably Hawaii and the Philippines.

As in the case of earlier emigration proposals, Negro spokesmen

6. Indianapolis *Freeman,* September 27, 1902.
7. Harlan, *Booker T. Washington,* p. x; Emma Lou Thornbrough, ed., *Booker T. Washington* (Englewood Cliffs, N.J.: Prentice-Hall, 1969), p. 64.
8. Harry H. Pace, "The Philippine Islands and the American Negro," *Voice of the Negro,* I (October, 1904), 482.

generally opposed any scheme involving the deportation of large numbers of blacks. In August, 1900, Congressman George H. White, himself a victim of the Democrats' white supremacy campaign in North Carolina, spoke out against efforts to colonize "the colored people in some separate state or territory." "What is good for the white man is good for the colored man," he declared. According to White, most of the trouble confronting black people stemmed from the fact that too many were concentrated in the South. Although he believed that conditions in the region would eventually cause some blacks to emigrate to Cuba, the Philippines, and other tropical islands, he preferred that they "scatter into the North and West," where the racial climate was more conducive to their rapid advancement.[9] At the expiration of his term in Congress in 1901, White followed his own counsel and settled in the North. Ironically, he established a separate, all-black town— Whitesboro, New Jersey.

Other black spokesmen, though more enthusiastic about the prospects of emigration to Hawaii and the Philippines, echoed White's hostility toward wholesale colonization. Edward E. Cooper continued to promote selective emigration and urged Negroes not "to lie asleep when the Anglo-Saxon is packing his grip" for the Pacific islands. Addressing himself to educated, enterprising black citizens, Cooper counseled: "Our pioneer instinct should not be stifled by superstition nor mawkish sentiment." [10] George L. Knox's Indianapolis *Freeman* had no objection to emigration by those Negroes who desired to seek their fortunes in the Pacific, but it warned that any government-sponsored colonization project would "meet with but small favor in the eyes of American Negroes." [11]

The most comprehensive statement on "the Negro and our new possessions" was provided by William S. Scarborough, a noted black scholar at Wilberforce University. As early as mid-1900 Scarborough argued that a certain amount of emigration would

9. Kansas City *American Citizen*, August 31, 1900.

10. Washington *Colored American*, January 13, 1900; March 22, 1902; see also Milwaukee *Wisconsin Weekly Advocate*, June 5, 1902; J. H. Morgan, "The Negro as a Businessman," in Culp, ed., *Twentieth Century Negro Literature*, p. 386.

11. Indianapolis *Freeman*, November 17, 1900; see also Cleveland *Gazette*, October 25, 1902.

not only contribute to the solution of the Negro Problem in the United States, but would also allow the black American to assist in the development and elevation of his "color kinsfolk" in the Orient. According to Scarborough, Negroes were in the midst of their darkest period since the Civil War, even darker than the era of Reconstruction, because then the Negro's friends "were many more than now." Emigration, he believed, afforded an escape especially for the "educated Negro, the capable Negro" who suffered "from the keen humiliation incident upon the stress of the [present] situation." The "higher classes of the race," rather than the black masses, should make up the majority of those emigrating to the Pacific islands. In Scarborough's opinion the emigrants ought to be black men "who can do something, manage something, create something." The United States should emulate Germany's experiment which employed "trained Negroes" from Tuskegee to promote cotton culture in its African colonies. To allow the "Negro to reach out individually" in the Pacific possessions would benefit "the present generation and may help on marvelously future generations," both in America and in its colonies.[12]

Whether they favored selective emigration or mass deportation, Negro and white advocates of black colonization maintained that Negro Americans would find the climate, society, and economy of the Pacific islands congenial to their welfare and prosperity. The notion that blacks thrived in tropical climates was a standard argument of most emigrationists. Others emphasized that the Pacific islands, especially the Philippines, were undeveloped countries with unlimited opportunities.[13] Scarborough, himself a linguist, claimed that the existence of foreign tongues in these lands should not deter black Americans because "the Negro has a natural aptitude for language." But most advocates of emigration, particularly those within the Negro community, considered color and racial considerations of primary importance. Citing evidence provided by black soldiers in the Philippines, Scarborough maintained that Filipinos viewed "the American colored man" as "a distant

12. W. S. Scarborough, "Our New Possessions—An Open Door," *Southern Workman,* XXIX (July, 1900), 422–427; see also Scarborough, "The Negro and Our New Possessions," 314–349.

13. Milwaukee *Wisconsin Weekly Advocate,* May 21, 1898, June 5, 1902; *Washington Bee,* December 20, 1902.

relative of theirs" and desired that Americanization "come through hands of a like complexion to theirs." Because of his color, therefore, the "thrifty, energetic Negro" possessed "a free passport without credentials" in America's Pacific possessions which gave him an advantage over all whites.[14] These views were echoed by Charles Steward, writing in the *Colored American Magazine* about the opportunities available to black Americans in Manila. According to Steward, Filipinos possessed "the full color sympathy" and appeared "to entertain a decided fondness for colored Americans." Because of this "affinity of complexion," the argument ran, the appointment of black citizens as "educators and pioneers of civilization" in the Pacific islands, especially in the Philippines, would make the dark-skinned natives "amenable and reconciled to American rule." [15]

By mid-summer, 1900, the emigration agent was "abroad in the land," especially representatives from Hawaiian planters who were signing up blacks to work on the islands' sugar plantations. Ten years earlier the inadequate labor force in Hawaii had prompted suggestions that black Americans be used there in the production of sugar,[16] but not until the turn of the century was there a serious attempt to implement the idea. In July, 1900, John Hind and J. B. Collins, agents of the Koloa Plantation, established themselves in New Orleans for the purpose of recruiting three hundred Negro laborers. During the next nine months other agents appeared in Tennessee, Alabama, and Texas. Those black laborers who went to Hawaii from the South signed contracts to remain there for two or three years. In addition to the cost of transportation, their employers usually provided free housing and medical attention. Wages ranged from fifteen to thirty dollars a month depending on the type of contract.[17]

The appearance of Hawaiian labor agents throughout the South

14. Scarborough, "The Negro and Our New Possessions," 344–346. See also opinions of Negro soldiers stationed in the Philippines in Gatewood, *"Smoked Yankees,"* pp. 269–271, 290, 311–312, 316, and William F. Blakeney to the Editor, May 31, 1902, Indianapolis *Freeman,* August 2, 1902.

15. Steward, "Manila and Its Opportunities," 248–256; A. R. Abbott, "The Employment of Negroes in the Philippines," *Anglo-American Magazine,* VI (September, 1901), 196–201.

16. Merze Tate, *Hawaii: Reciprocity or Annexation* (East Lansing: Michigan State University Press, 1968), p. 248.

17. Wichita *Searchlight,* July 14, 1900; Indianapolis *Recorder,* July 28, 1900; Indianapolis *Freeman,* July 28, 1900; Washington *Colored American,* January 12, 1901;

in 1900–1901 prompted widely disparate reactions within the Negro community. Calvin Chase of the *Washington Bee* was wary of their recruitment schemes and warned Negroes that, once in Hawaii, they would be treated as slaves and not allowed to return to the United States. If black people desired to leave the South, he argued, they should take advantage of the free lands in the West rather than settling in remote islands amidst an alien people.[18] W. N. Miller, a black attorney and editor in Wichita who took an opposing view of emigration to Hawaii, expressed pride in the fact that Hawaiian planters had chosen "colored laborers to supplant the two faced Japs." Such recognition, he exclaimed, only proved that "the whole world is becoming acquainted with the fact that the Negro is a man!" A year later, when Booker T. Washington's dinner at the White House set off an acrimonious controversy in the United States, Miller noted that the meal caused not the slightest ripple in Hawaii because the islands had "no color line." [19]

The absence of racial distinctions in Hawaii became a favorite theme of those who encouraged blacks to sign contracts with the islands' sugar planters. Returning from an inspection tour of Hawaiian plantations late in December, 1900, John Henry Cook, a black minister from Mississippi, gave a glowing account of the islands as a place where Negroes could find respite from oppression and poverty. According to Cook, Hawaii not only provided higher wages, shorter hours of work, and better health facilities; it also had a "good system of free public schools and an absence of race antagonism." [20] Echoing Cook's appeal, a black Texan, M. A. Majors, pointed out that Negroes who worked in the sugar fields of Louisiana could "do the same thing" in Hawaii without the ever-present threat of lynching, because "hemp stretching was never known in the Pacific Islands." Majors believed that if oppressed blacks settled in Hawaii, there was at least a glimmer of hope that they might have an opportunity "to amount to something." [21]

Kansas City *American Citizen*, March 22, 1901; "Report of the Commissioner of Labor of Hawaii," *Bulletin of the Department of Labor.* No. 47 (July, 1903), p. 701.

18. *Washington Bee*, January 19, 1901; see also Clarissa Olds-Keeler, "Negroes in Hawaii," *Voice of Missions*, VIII (February 1, 1900), 2.

19. Wichita *Searchlight*, July 14, 1900, December 14, 1901.

20. Washington *Colored American*, December 29, 1900.

21. Indianapolis *Freeman*, July 28, 1900.

Despite predictions that "hordes" of black Southerners would emigrate to Hawaii, the actual number of emigrants was small, perhaps no more than 500. The ordeal of leaving familiar surroundings to live among a strange people and culture in order to provide labor for white planters undoubtedly had little appeal for most Negroes in the South, regardless of their existing conditions. And the experience of those who did go to the islands was anything but happy. Their new environment proved considerably less congenial than had been depicted in the emigrationists' publicity. A white American resident of Hawaii may have hinted at the source of their discontent when he remarked: "Our native Hawaiians are a different race entirely, and are capable of becoming assimilated in all branches of modern civilization with Anglo-Saxons, but, with Negroes as a class, never." [22] Or perhaps, as a *New York Times* reporter observed, Negroes were unsuited to labor in the islands because they "had too long a taste of independence." The result was that they were "not as docile and abject as the coolie" who, in addition, did "not possess the boon of citizenship." [23] Whatever the causes of their unhappiness, few Negro emigrants wished to remain in Hawaii; by mid-1901 dozens lined the Honolulu waterfront in search of some means to return to the United States. [24] Their experience stood in sharp contrast to that of T. McCants Stewart, a Negro attorney in New York who had moved his family to Honolulu late in 1898. A respected member of the bar in that city, Stewart obviously had encountered few obstacles because of his race. His success in the islands seemed to support the views of those who contended that emigration should be limited to the "higher classes" of black Americans. [25]

Although the advocates of emigration between 1900 and 1903 usually mentioned Hawaii as a possible home for Negro Americans, they were primarily interested in the Philippines. Despite their references to the absence of color prejudice in Hawaii, emigrationists recognized that white Americans already dominated the

22. Quoted in Merze Tate, "Decadence of the Hawaiian Nation and Proposals to Import a Negro Labor Force," *Journal of Negro History*, XLVII (October, 1962), 248–263. See also "Report of the Commission of Labor of Hawaii," pp. 701–702.

23. *New York Times*, December 12, 1902.

24. *Manila Times*, May 12, 1901; "Report of the Commissioner of Labor of Hawaii," p. 701.

25. Thornbrough, *T. Thomas Fortune*, p. 236.

economy and government of the islands. Furthermore, as one observer noted, Hawaii was "a white man's country and coolie labor . . . [was] exactly what the white man wants. . . ." Any proposal for large-scale colonization of Negroes in the islands would therefore meet bitter opposition. On the contrary, the Philippines was "not a white man's country and some say it never will be." [26] Emigrationists argued that the Philippines as a sparsely settled, economically underdeveloped country inhabited by dark-skinned people offered the greatest opportunities for black Americans.

In fact, no sooner had Dewey sailed into Manila Bay in 1898 than the black press began to refer to the Philippines as "a paradise for colored men." Enterprising Negroes were encouraged to take advantage of the opportunities available in the islands before white men preempted them. A black editor in Kansas spoke for much of the emigration-minded black press when he declared that Negroes should settle in the Philippines primarily "for the purpose of making money." [27] After the landing of Negro troops in Manila in mid-1899, the discussion of the archipelago as a "new field" for emigration assumed more serious proportions. The letters of Negro soldiers described in detail the opportunities awaiting black men in the Philippines, also emphasizing that economic advancement could be achieved without having to combat race prejudice among the native inhabitants. The soldiers agreed that a man of color possessed "the vantage-ground over the white brother" in dealing with Filipinos.[28] Such assurances from first-hand observers at a time when negrophobia in the United States was assuming more ominous dimensions quickened the interest of black Americans in the islands as a place in which they could start life anew.

While Negroes debated the feasibility of emigration, the issue was taken up by Southern Democrats; their schemes for colonizing the Philippines with blacks were designed to "solve" the Negro Problem in the United States. As early as November, 1898, Senator Donalson Caffery of Louisiana proposed that the government underwrite a project for deporting 8,000,000 black Americans to

26. *New York Times*, December 12, 1902.

27. Milwaukee *Wisconsin Weekly Advocate*, May 21, 1898; *Parsons Weekly Blade*, May 20, 1898; Coffeyville *American*, May 28, 1898.

28. Scarborough, "The Negro and Our New Possessions," 344; Gatewood, "*Smoked Yankees*," pp. 271, 296, 303.

the archipelago. His plan met with loud opposition from both blacks and southern whites. Most Negroes were opposed to any scheme which involved involuntary emigration and which meant isolating the black population in a specific, separate territory. Such a course would be an assault upon their rights as citizens and, according to Scarborough, would also be "detrimental to any rapid development" of the race. Edward E. Cooper accused Senator Caffery of "talking through his hat" because white Southerners were too dependent upon Negro labor to allow such a proposal to be implemented.[29] Such a view found support in the attitude of the Memphis *Commercial Appeal,* which saw "no reasons why negroes should leave the country." The newspaper maintained that blacks were "doing well, and so long as they behave themselves they will be protected, and when they fail to behave themselves, they will be attended to." [30] Caffery's proposal failed to receive serious consideration; indeed, emigration projects similar to his were unlikely to attract much attention until the United States had put down the Filipino insurrection.

Nevertheless, the idea of solving the nation's Negro Problem by colonizing blacks in the Philippines continued to elicit sympathetic responses among whites. Early in 1900, for example, General A. G. Greenwood, a financier and former soldier, expounded favorably on the notion in an interview published in the *New York Times.* Invoking the standard arguments about the availability of fertile land in the islands and the black man's ability to thrive in tropical climates, Greenwood maintained that at least 5,000,000 Negro Americans could be accommodated in the archipelago. They would find ample opportunities for agricultural pursuits, he argued, and would also be relieved of contact with racial barriers. Since the South was becoming rapidly industrialized, Greenwood concluded, the removal of the black population from the region would open more factory jobs for whites.[31] In response, William C. Warmsley, a black army surgeon stationed in Luzon, maintained that Greenwood was actually proposing nothing more

29. Washington *Colored American,* December 17, 24, 1898; Scarborough, "The Negro and Our New Possessions," 343.

30. Memphis *Commercial Appeal,* November 27, 1898.

31. *New York Times,* February 25, 1900; Kansas City *American Citizen,* March 4, 1900.

than a thinly disguised scheme of forced deportation. Warmsley suggested that it would be far easier for Americans to solve their so-called Negro Problem simply by getting rid of "their silly race prejudice." [32] Later in the spring of 1900 when John Temple Graves, the race-baiting journalist from Atlanta, took up the cause of a black exodus in the Philippines, the Savannah *Tribune* pronounced all colonization schemes as wholly inappropriate and suggested that the race question would never be solved by such men as Graves. "The Negro is here to stay," the *Tribune* declared, "and the sooner all concerned understand this the better." [33]

Despite such opposition, public interest in colonizing the Philippines with Negro citizens substantially increased in 1901 as Filipino resistance to American rule diminished. At this juncture the principal advocate of the colonization idea was Senator John T. Morgan of Alabama, who had favored federal support for the back-to-Africa movement a decade earlier. An expansionist and ardent champion of a canal across Central America, the senator viewed the acquisition of colonies in the Orient in terms of their potential commercial relations with the South; he believed that the Pacific islands, especially the Philippines, offered his native region an extraordinary opportunity to dispose of its race problem.[34] In a communication to the press early in 1901 in which he endorsed the movement to disfranchise black citizens, Morgan raised the question of Negro emigration to the Philippines. Convinced that Negroes would be "happy and free there," he argued that their departure from the South would solve the race problem and allow "more room for white people" in the region.[35]

In December, 1901, Senator Morgan suggested to Secretary of War Elihu Root that black soldiers in the Philippines be encouraged to settle in paramilitary colonies "as a prelude to government-sponsored emigration" of Negro civilians. The senator also out-

32. *New York Times*, July 5, 1900. See also a communication from Warmsley in Washington *Colored American*, January 11, 1902; for a lengthy biographical sketch of Warmsley, see Washington *Colored American*, July 27, 1901.

33. Savannah *Tribune*, May 12, 1900.

34. For a study of Morgan, see August C. Radke, Jr., "John Tyler Morgan, An Expansionist Senator, 1877–1907" (Ph.D. dissertation, University of Washington, 1953).

35. Wichita *Searchlight*, March 30, 1901. A year earlier, in a speech to the Senate defending disfranchisement, Morgan had referred to the Philippines as a future home for black citizens. See *Congressional Record*, 56 Cong., 1 sess., 675.

lined a scheme by which the federal government would incorporate special steamship lines for transporting blacks to the islands, where each emigrant would be granted a twenty-acre homestead. After some prodding from Morgan, the secretary forwarded the colonization plan to General Adna R. Chaffee, the American military commander in the Philippines, who in turn requested General George W. Davis to respond to it. Davis, at the time in command of American forces in Mindanao, was described by Secretary Root as "one of the very ablest and broadest officers of the army . . . a man of very wide research and practical sagacity." By mid-April, 1902, just prior to the transfer of the black troops from the Philippines, Davis completed his detailed report which was forwarded through channels to Root.[36] Before receiving the document early in July, Morgan had apparently pressed the War Department in regard to his proposal to have the black veterans of the Philippine campaign establish paramilitary colonies in the islands upon the termination of their tour of duty there. It is not clear what effect, if any, his entreaties had, but some Negroes believed that the War Department's decision to allow black soldiers to be discharged in the islands was a direct result of Morgan's efforts.[37]

Davis's report began by noting the twofold purpose of what was termed Morgan's "scheme of a negro hegira from America to the Philippines": first, to cover the archipelago "with liberty-loving negro settlers whose religious independence would ever resist efforts of any priesthood to control their conscience," thereby solving the religious problem in the islands; second, "to relieve the existing congestion of negro population" in the South by "transferring large numbers of this race to the congenial soil of the Philippines, where they may aid in the development of the country." Morgan proposed to solve both the Negro Problem in the United States and the Religious Question in the Philippines by his colonization project. General Davis first addressed himself to Morgan's suggestion that the military forces in the islands hence-

36. Joseph O. Baylen and John H. Moore, "Senator John Tyler Morgan and Negro Colonization in the Philippines, 1901 to 1902," *Phylon*, XXIX (Spring, 1968), 65–67.

37. Elihu Root to John T. Morgan, July 8, 1902, Elihu Root Papers, Manuscript Division, Library of Congress; Savannah *Tribune*, January 10, 1903.

forth be made up of black soldiers under the command of white officers and that each black soldier, upon the expiration of his term of enlistment, be induced to settle permanently in the islands by offering him a land bounty. Davis agreed that Negro troops had rendered "efficient and useful" service and had associated with natives "as social equals," but he did not believe it possible to transform well-paid, "aristocratic colored soldiers into tropical laborers and farmers in competition with the natives." Few black soldiers entered agricultural pursuits upon being discharged from military service, and the long-term veteran had "no need to work as his retired pay will support him." Nor did Davis believe that conditions in the Philippines favored the large-scale importation of Negroes as proposed by Morgan. There was, he pointed out, "nothing grown in the Oriental tropics by methods known to our southern negroes," and most of the fertile areas in Luzon, Panay, Negros, and Ceba were already densely populated. The general rejected the idea that Negroes, on their own initiative, could develop the techniques necessary for the profitable cultivation of sugar, coffee, and rice. Indeed, he questioned whether blacks in the Philippines would "do better than any others of their race in the West Indies" where, in his opinion, Negroes had proved themselves to be "lazy, thriftless and unreliable." Davis, therefore, suggested that white sugar planters from Louisiana bring black laborers under contract to the islands and train them in the techniques of agricultural production peculiar to the "Oriental tropics." At the termination of their contracts some of the laborers would "launch out as small planters." Those who succeeded would "write home of their prosperity," inducing more Negroes to the islands either as contract laborers or as settlers.[38]

Early in 1902, before Davis's report reached Morgan, the feasibility of Negro emigration was discussed during congressional hearings on Philippine affairs. The question arose in connection with testimony regarding the labor problem in the islands. Those witnesses with a firsthand knowledge of conditions in the archipelago agreed that the introduction of white American labor was "out of the question," but only General Robert P. Hughes favored

---

38. For an edited version of General Davis's report, see Baylen and Moore, "John Tyler Morgan," 69–75.

the idea of encouraging blacks to emigrate there. Arguing that Negroes ought to be given opportunities in the insular possessions,
Hughes maintained that the cordial relations between black soldiers and the natives during the insurrection indicated that Filipinos would welcome Negro emigrants. General Elwell Otis, on
the contrary, believed that the labor force already in the Philippines was "sufficient for ordinary development." During an appearance before the House Committee on Insular Affairs, Governor William Howard Taft was asked by Congressman John
Sharp Williams of Mississippi whether Negroes from the United
States could be effectively used in railroad-building projects in the
Philippines. Without hesitation Taft replied that their employment would be "inexpedient." He opposed the importation of
blacks into the islands on the grounds that "the Filipino considered
himself superior to the negro." For different reasons Senator Fred
T. DuBois of Idaho also thought that Negroes offered no solution
to the Philippine labor problem because there was no way to entice them to leave the United States. And DuBois remarked: "We
can not deport the negro." In his opinion the only alternative for
solving the problem was through the introduction of Chinese and
Japanese workers.[39]

The negative tone of both the congressional hearings and the
report by General Davis did not cause Senator Morgan to abandon
his colonization scheme. He persisted in his efforts to win over
Root and Taft and attempted to persuade President Roosevelt and
his cabinet of the plan's feasibility.[40] His endeavors were not in
vain. In November, 1902, Roosevelt appointed T. Thomas Fortune of the *New York Age* as a special commissioner to Hawaii and
the Philippines for the purpose of studying labor and race conditions—"sociological questions"—in the islands. Although the object of Fortune's mission remained somewhat vague, it appears
certain that he was instructed to investigate and report on the
possibilities of colonizing black Americans in the Pacific possessions.[41] The *Colored American* denied that Fortune's appointment

39. *Hearings before the Committee on the Philippines,* Pt. I, pp. 646, 647, 845;
Savannah *Tribune,* March 8, 1902.
40. *Washington Post,* December 16, 1902; *The Independent,* LVI (December 25,
1902), 3047.
41. *Richmond Planet,* December 13, 1902; Indianapolis *Freeman,* November 29,
1902.

was in any way related to the various emigration schemes then under discussion, but the rival *Washington Bee* and other journals were certain that Fortune owed his appointment to the agitation by Senator Morgan. Calvin Chase of the *Bee* was also certain that Fortune would prepare "a long winded report describing the beauties of the yellow fever country" and recommending it as "just the country for American Negroes." [42]

The decision to appoint Fortune scarcely indicated that either Roosevelt or Root embraced Morgan's project. They probably welcomed the idea of a special mission in order to mollify the senator and at the same time to delay action of any kind. For Roosevelt, it provided a solution to a patronage muddle which had prevented him from rewarding Fortune for his services in the presidential campaign of 1900. Earlier attempts to take care of the controversial New York journalist had been unsuccessful largely because of opposition from his critics and rivals in the black community. For example, reports that he was to become American minister to Haiti prompted black Republicans in New Jersey, where Fortune had recently moved, to lodge vigorous protests, charging that he was "barely a resident of the state." [43] Failing to receive the Haitian post, Fortune conceived the idea of a special mission to the insular possessions in the Pacific. In view of the deteriorating racial situation in the United States, he had for some time urged the government to assist those Negroes who desired to emigrate to the Philippines. His proposal of a fact-finding mission to the Pacific islands won the endorsement of James S. Clarkson, one of Roosevelt's principal advisors on patronage matters. In fact, it was largely through Clarkson's efforts that Fortune was appointed a special agent of the Treasury Department for a period of six months to investigate conditions in Hawaii and the Philippines.[44]

The announcement of what some termed Fortune's "mysterious mission to the Orient" touched off a lively discussion of Negro

42. Washington *Colored American*, January 1, 1903; *Washington Bee*, December 20, 1902.

43. *New York Times*, November 30, 1902; see also Topeka *Kansas State Ledger*, January 25, 1902; *Washington Bee*, November 16, 1901; *Boston Guardian* quoted in Indianapolis *Freeman*, April 5, 1902.

44. Thornbrough, *T. Thomas Fortune*, pp. 234–235; James S. Clarkson to Theodore Roosevelt, December 27, 1902, Roosevelt Papers.

emigration, particularly of the Philippine project advocated by Morgan. The *New York Times* noted that in spite of the failure of efforts to colonize black Americans in Africa, there was reason to believe that an emigration movement to "our new possessions" would succeed. All the while Senator Morgan attempted to win support for his project; he assured whites that an exodus of blacks to the Philippines would solve the American race problem. In appealing to blacks, he extolled the economic opportunities, abundance of fertile land, and favorable climate of the islands, always insisting that his plan in no way involved compulsory emigration.[45] In a letter to a well-known black attorney, the senator wrote: "I have thought and am now satisfied that in the Philippine Islands, they [Negroes] can find localities for very large colonies, in a country well suited to their wants and tastes, where they will be free from the actual competition of the white race. It is a country in which they could do much good to other races who would welcome them." According to Morgan, the Philippines possessed an advantage which the black emigrant would not have in either Africa or Cuba—namely, the protection of the American flag. "All I have tried to do," he concluded, "is to assist in providing for the negro race an attractive home in the native countries of their race." [46]

In spite of Morgan's pleas, the response to his Philippine project was overwhelmingly negative. Senator Tillman likened it to the "forty acres and a mule scheme" of Reconstruction, finding it no less "chimerical." Senator Edmund W. Pettus, Morgan's colleague from Alabama, pronounced the project as too visionary and too costly. "We have no right," Pettus further maintained, "to move citizens out of the country without their consent." Senator Anslem J. McLaurin of Mississippi believed that colonization projects should include only mulattoes because he wanted to keep "our genuine black negroes here." McLaurin insisted that "our black negroes are all right," and that there "never was any trouble . . . until the inception of the mulatto breed." [47] The *Washington Post*

45. *New York Times*, December 12, 1902; Little Rock *Arkansas Gazette*, December 20, 1902.

46. John T. Morgan to Thomas L. Jones, no date, in *New York Times*, January 29, 1903.

47. Rienzi B. Lemus, "The Negro and the Philippines," *Colored American Magazine*, VI (February, 1903), 318; Savannah *Tribune*, January 10, 1903; Memphis *Com-*

voiced similar objections to the Philippine colonization scheme
and suggested that it might be more feasible if those shipped out
of the country included only "the ridiculous and tiresome negro
'leaders,' agitators, and incendiaries." [48] Leading white dailies in the
South which opposed Morgan's project generally agreed with the
Memphis *Commercial Appeal*'s description of it as "a Himalayan
absurdity" useful only "as a subject of polemical discussion." The
attitude of many white Southerners toward the colonization idea
was summed up in the question, "What'll we do fer cotton?" [49]
But their opposition invoked more than a fear of depleting the
supply of agricultural labor. *Dixie,* an editorial mouthpiece of
southern industry published in Atlanta, claimed that the presence
of the Negro was "a blessing to the South" because he provided
regional manufacturers with a source of labor free from the complications of unions. Southern whites, therefore, "would not consent to his removal" to the Philippines or anywhere else.[50]

Although Negroes might applaud the appointment of Fortune
as political recognition long overdue one of the most prominent
members of their race,[51] few displayed any sympathy for proposals
to colonize the Philippines with black citizens. To be sure, William S. Scarborough favored Negro emigration to the islands as a
means of overcoming the unrest in race relations in the United
States, but he always emphasized that such emigration should be
purely voluntary. Like others, Scarborough believed that Morgan's plan smacked too much of deportation.[52] Bishop Turner,
who in 1900 had organized the Colored National Emigration Association to promote his back-to-Africa movement, was quick to
condemn all schemes for sending black Americans anywhere but
to their "homeland." [53] In an address before the Bethel Literary

mercial Appeal, December 17, 1902. For an account of Tillman's views on Negro
colonization schemes in general, see Francis B. Simkins, *Pitchfork Ben Tillman:
South Carolinian* (Baton Rouge: Louisiana State University Press, 1944), pp. 402–403.

48. *Washington Post,* December 20, 1902.

49. Memphis *Commercial Appeal,* December 15, 1902; *Atlanta Constitution*
quoted in Savannah *Tribune,* January 24, 1903; New Orleans *Times Democrat*
quoted in *Washington Post,* December 20, 1902; Lemus, "The Negro and the
Philippines," 318.

50. *Dixie* quoted in the *Literary Digest,* XXVI (February 7, 1903), 176.

51. *Richmond Planet,* December 13, 1902; Indianapolis *Freeman,* November 29,
1902.

52. Scarborough, "The Negro and Our New Possessions," 343.

53. *New York Daily Tribune,* August 29, 1901, December 7, 1902.

and Historical Association in Washington on January 27, 1903, Thomas L. Jones, a Negro attorney, severely arraigned "Senator Morgan and the Deportation Fallacy." He accused the senator of hypocrisy and deception in posing as the friend of black people and reminded him that deportation was no substitute for justice to Negro citizens at home.[54] Booker T. Washington was more explicit in his opposition to emigration to Africa than to other places, but he consistently maintained that black Americans should seek to work out their destiny in the United States.[55]

The black press was almost solidly opposed to Morgan's Philippine colonization project. The *New Age,* a Negro weekly in Portland, Oregon, conceded that blacks who desired to emigrate to the islands should be allowed to do so, but assured its readers that any large-scale exodus such as that proposed by the senator from Alabama was wholly impracticable. Other Negro newspapers agreed that Morgan's project was little more than the old Liberia scheme in new clothes.[56] Calvin Chase's *Washington Bee* maintained that no matter what the findings of Fortune or any other investigator might be, the "United States was the place for the Negro." [57] The St. Louis *Palladium* refused to believe that "so good a friend of the Negro" as President Roosevelt would seriously entertain any proposal for solving the race question made by so blatant a racist as Morgan. Lest Negroes succumb to the enticements of emigrationists, the *Palladium* pointed out that if black citizens were unable to "stand the oppression here," they certainly would not "survive the struggle for existence in the Philippines." [58] Edward E. Cooper, who was usually eager to embrace anything that could be interpreted as the black man's share in the imperialistic harvest, refused to view the Philippine colonization project in such a light. His *Colored American* was profoundly skeptical of mass emigration schemes in general and those

54. *Washington Bee,* February 7, 1903. Speakers at the Ex-Slave Congress which met in Washington early in January, 1903, endorsed colonization as "the only salvation of the race" but opposed Morgan's Philippine project on the grounds that blacks should emigrate to their homeland in Africa. See *Washington Post,* January 7, 1903.
55. Booker T. Washington, *The Future of the American Negro* (New York: Negro Universities Press, 1969), pp. 157–163.
56. Portland *New Age,* January 9, 1903.
57. *Washington Bee,* January 10, 1903.
58. *The Palladium* (St. Louis), January 17, 1903.

advocated by white Southerners in particular. Dismissing Morgan's project as "out of the question," Cooper declared that "the children of the little band of slaves that began their experience in the banks of the James River two hundred and eighty three years ago intend to stay in what has become their native land." [59]

Undoubtedly one of the most comprehensive and authoritative reviews of Morgan's Philippine proposal by a black citizen appeared early in 1903 in the *Colored American Magazine*. The writer was Rienzi B. Lemus, a veteran of the Philippine campaign who had reported regularly to the black press on conditions in the islands. In exposing the "fallacies" of the senator's scheme, Lemus first discussed the racial composition of the Filipino, which was often described by both white and black Americans as closely akin to that of Negroes. He emphatically denied any racial kinship between Filipinos and Africans, despite the superficial similarity in the hue of their skin. Furthermore, clannishness was a strong trait of Filipinos; as Lemus put it, they were "nepotists," deeply suspicious of outsiders. And since Negroes were outsiders, they would not "have a ghost of a show in 'business advantages' . . . as blood is thicker than all the water they would cross to get" to the islands. The second fallacy in Morgan's scheme, Lemus pointed out, concerned the proposal to give twenty acres of land to each black emigrant. According to his calculations, such a proposal could not be implemented without depriving Filipinos of land which rightfully belonged to them. Like General Davis earlier, Lemus insisted that, contrary to popular notions, the amount of tillable land in the islands was not abundant. He predicted that any expropriation of lands for outsiders would lead the Filipinos to violence and "acts of lawlessness"—indeed, to a wholesale slaughter of Negro colonists. A third fallacy of the Morgan plan involved its cost. To transport millions of black Americans to the Philippines, Lemus argued, would require a tax burden which whites would not bear willingly. "I am positive," he observed, "that whites . . . would rather have the Negro taxpayer living among them as at present than to pay for him to live somewhere else."

Finally, Lemus pronounced as absurd Senator Morgan's asser-

59. Washington *Colored American*, January 1, 1903.

tion that blacks would be better off in the Philippines than in Africa or Cuba because in the islands they would be under "the protection of the Stars and Stripes." Fully aware of the kind of protection which the same flag afforded black people in the senator's own state, Lemus wondered why Morgan thought their rights and lives would be more secure in Asiatic isles than in Alabama. Sentiment rather than the Constitution had followed the planting of the flag in the archipelago, and "the sentiment of the Stars and Stripes now seems to be 'White Supremacy.'" Mass emigration to the Philippines would only complicate the black man's problems, as there was "nothing embodied in Senator Morgan's scheme to prevent whites from going there too." Like other critics of the Philippine colonization project, Lemus raised no objections to emigration by individual Negroes but promised that black Americans would "never leave in a body." He reminded Morgan that Negroes were at home in the United States as much as whites and "nothing but Divine Power can remove them." [60]

In the midst of much hostile criticism regarding Philippine colonization, T. Thomas Fortune began his tour of the nation's insular possessions in the Pacific. He arrived in Hawaii late in December, 1902, remaining for several weeks as the guest of his old friend T. McCants Stewart. Fortune collected information about race relations and labor conditions on the islands' sugar plantations; his observations prompted him to encourage southern Negroes to emigrate to Hawaii, not only because jobs were abundant, but also because race prejudice was absent. He attributed the racial harmony in the islands to the fact that many of the whites were descendants of New England missionaries "who had planted there a civilization based on the Christian virtues in which race prejudice had no part." [61]

Upon leaving Honolulu, Fortune stopped first in Japan, then in Hong Kong, before sailing for Manila. Arriving in the Philippine capital in February, 1903, he immediately encountered an atmosphere which contrasted sharply with that in Honolulu. The

60. Lemus, "The Negro and the Philippines," 314–318. For a similar view by a black veteran of the Philippine campaign, see G. Bradley Kelley to the Editor, Indianapolis *Freeman*, February 20, 1904.

61. T. Thomas Fortune, "Politics in the Philippine Islands," *The Independent*, LV (September 24, 1903), 2206–8; Thornbrough, *T. Thomas Fortune*, p. 236.

Manila press was overtly hostile to his mission; one newspaper
called upon American residents in the city to invite him to return to the United States immediately, as no Afro-American was
"needed or desired in the Philippine Islands." Fortune likened
the atmosphere to that which he might have encountered in Kentucky or Tennessee, where "race hatred and personal vitupera-
tion" dominated "the administration of civil and military affairs."
In fact, he attributed such conditions in Manila to the presence
of so many white Southerners—those volunteers from the South
who remained in the islands after being mustered out of military
service and "the abnormally large number of Southern white men
who were appointed to . . . high positions by President McKinley." Never one to acquiesce quietly in anything that smacked of
racial discrimination, Fortune himself had an encounter with the
police in Manila when his guide and interpreter, Robert Gordon
Woods, was arrested for a petty offense. The New York editor accompanied Woods to the police station, where an argument led to
a fist fight. As a result of the fracas Fortune was charged with resisting arrest. The incident created a stir in the Manila press, and
some white editors in the United States claimed that because of
his conduct Fortune was forced to return home. His critics in the
black community used the occasion to allude to his problem with
alcohol and to pronounce him "a dangerous leader." [62]

During his six weeks in the Philippines Fortune took a trip
across Luzon accompanied by Woods, formerly an officer in a
black volunteer regiment.[63] At Tarlac, Dugapan, Bayambang,
Rosales, Carranglan, Tuguegarao, and other towns he had an opportunity to talk with many of the black Americans already residing in the islands. Most of these residents were ex-soldiers employed as clerks and manual laborers by the civil government.
Among the self-employed blacks whom Fortune encountered was
Dr. W. C. Warmsley, a former military surgeon who at one time
had advised blacks to emigrate to Cuba. Warmsley had settled at

62. Fortune, "Politics in the Philippine Islands," 2206–7; T. Thomas Fortune,
"The Filipino," *Voice of the Negro*, I (May, 1904), 202; Thornbrough, *T. Thomas
Fortune*, pp. 239–240; *New York Daily Tribune*, May 15, 1903; St. Louis *Palladium*,
May 23, 1903; Chicago *Broad Ax*, June 6, 1903.
63. The following account of Fortune's observations is based upon three articles
which he published in the issues of the *Voice of the Negro* for March, May, and
June, 1904.

Tuguegarao in northern Luzon; he operated a drug store and "several large tobacco plantations" in conjunction with his lucrative medical practice and duties as president of the board of health of Cagayan Province. In describing a visit with an old black trooper in Carranglan, Fortune wrote:

> He had a native wife, kept a small store . . . and cultivated a large rice plantation. Like all the Negroes we had so far met in our journey, he was coal black and seemed to be perfectly at home. He was happy and making money, and never expected to return to the United States—and what black man out of it and doing well—should? [64]

Despite such occasional evidences of prosperity, Fortune also noted that many black Americans previously employed as manual laborers on government projects were out of work and "fearful of the future." [65]

The plight of these unemployed people might have caused others to be skeptical of migration to the Philippines, but Fortune was favorably impressed by the possibilities of the archipelago as a future home for oppressed, poverty-stricken black Americans. He insisted that opportunities in agriculture were virtually unlimited, because the soil was "the richest in the world, capable of producing indigenous crops in rotation all the year." More important was his discovery that Filipino natives were "not affected with this prejudice against the black man" and deeply resented the "social line" drawn against all colored people by white Americans in the islands. According to Fortune, the Filipino hated "the white man as the devil hated holy water and will never learn to love him," and the white man despised the native and his ways as much as he did the tropical climate of the islands. Convinced that the United States would never achieve peace and "get the best results out of the Filipinos" as long as prejudiced whites occupied all places of influence, he believed that the solution lay in the emigration of black Americans to the archipelago: "Indeed, all in all, the Afro-Americans in the Philippines stand the climate better and are on terms of better and more helpful understanding with the Filipinos than are the white Ameri-

64. Fortune, "The Filipino," 243.
65. Ibid., 242.

cans. . . ." Fortune called upon the Roosevelt administration to recognize the handwriting on the wall: if the American flag remained in the Philippines, "the Afro-American will have to be drafted to hold it up in civil and military establishments and in labor necessary to develop the resources of the country and put it on a paying basis." As a first step in this direction, the War Department should be forced to end its discrimination against Negroes in filling positions in the islands.[66]

From his observations in the Philippines Fortune concluded that "under proper arrangements" 5,000,000 Negroes could be located on the island of Luzon alone. A combination of circumstances prompted this suggestion: "the Negro and the Filipino get along splendidly together"; also, Filipinos had neither a knowledge of efficient agriculture nor an inclination to work the fertile soil of their homeland. Hence blacks from the farms of the South who had been "wronged and robbed" by whites could obtain respite from their oppression in the Philippines and at the same time assist the natives in developing the resources of the country. Large-scale emigration of blacks, therefore, would be "good for the Filipinos who badly need rejuvenation of blood," as well as "good for the United States . . . in solving the Filipino problem and the Negro problem, both of which promise to cost the Nation more blood and money in the future than in the past." Avoiding endorsement of Morgan's colonization scheme or any project which might imply forced emigration, Fortune urged the government to give the Negro American "a proper chance to enjoy life, liberty and the pursuit of happiness" in the Philippines "if he wants to go." [67]

The day following his return to the United States on June 24, 1903, Fortune was entertained at a New York reception at which he expounded on the Philippines as "the ideal place for the Negro." He also suggested that the appointment of a prominent Afro-American such as Booker T. Washington as governor of the islands would go far toward reconciling Filipinos to American rule and would encourage Negro emigration.[68] The *Washington Bee* scoffed at Fortune's glowing reports on the Philippines and

66. *Ibid.*, 96–98, 200–203.
67. *Ibid.*, 246.
68. *New York Daily Tribune*, June 26, 1903.

regretted "to see how rapidly an individual can change when he becomes intoxicated by official consideration." Although some Negro editors took up Fortune's suggestion about making Washington governor of the islands as a way to extend appropriate recognition to a "race leader," the *Bee* endorsed the idea for wholly different reasons. Its editor, Calvin Chase, welcomed Washington's removal to some distant island in the Pacific on the grounds that it would relieve black Americans of the burden of his baneful influence. Few Negro editors accepted Chase's ideas regarding Washington's leadership, but an overwhelming majority agreed with his view of Negro emigration to the Philippines.[69]

As in the case of emigration to Cuba, black Americans recognized that the ideal emigrant to the Philippines—the enterprising individual with education and capital—was precisely the type of individual least likely to leave the United States. Weary of all the discussion about "future homes" for black citizens, the Omaha *Progress* succinctly stated the position of the black press regarding emigration schemes when it declared: "Rest assured there are only two places to which the Negroes are going after they leave America—two-thirds of them to heaven and the other third to hell." [70] Or as a young black businessman named Harry H. Pace put it, "the task at hand then is not to hunt a new home, but to make the present one more comfortable." Reflecting the views of Booker T. Washington, Pace maintained that a majority of Negroes would remain in the South "for a long time to come," and it was "best that they should." Only by "casting down their buckets" in the South and working to achieve economic self-sufficiency could Negroes hope to make America "the home of the free." Least of all, Pace concluded, could black Americans afford to ally themselves with a people who, like the Filipinos, would "add to the already heavy burden of illiteracy and thriftlessness which the intelligent portion of the race has to bear today." [71]

Clearly, by the time Fortune returned to the United States the hostile reaction to the proposal for colonizing the Philippines with Negroes had reached such proportions that there was little prospect for its implementation. Senator Morgan lost interest in the

69. *Washington Bee*, July 4, 11, 1903.
70. Quoted in Indianapolis *Freeman*, January 24, 1903.
71. Pace, "Philippine Islands and American Negro," 482–485.

Philippine project and turned his attention to another scheme involving the emigration of black Americans to the Congo. Those still concerned about the labor problem in the Philippines tended to focus their attention on the solution which proposed the introduction of Chinese coolies into the islands, rather than the emigration of Negroes. Having never been enthusiastic about Morgan's scheme, the Roosevelt administration by mid-1903 seems to have abandoned the cause of Negro emigration altogether. In fact, the Treasury Department informed Fortune that his mission had terminated on May 16 and refused to pay his per diem expenses after that date;[72] nor was any official report of his mission ever made public. In 1904 the *Voice of the Negro,* a magazine then published in Atlanta, printed three articles which incorporated his basic findings and recommendations regarding emigration to the Philippines. But the publication of Fortune's observations in the same year that Luke E. Wright, an ex-Confederate soldier from Tennessee, succeeded Taft as governor of the Philippines scarcely enhanced the appeal of the islands as a paradise for the colored man.[73]

Although Philippine colonization proved no more successful than similar proposals for the emigration of blacks to Cuba, Hawaii, and other islands, the archipelago continued to attract occasional attention in the Negro community. The press took pride in those individuals "making good" in the islands. In 1906, for example, the Indianapolis *Freeman* called attention to the success of David J. Gilmer, Edward L. Baker, John E. Green, and other black veterans who had remained in the Philippines, as well as to the appointment of Mary F. Dickenson as a government school teacher and James H. Fitzbutler as an inspector of vessels.[74] The *Freeman* might also have included in its list the name of Carter G. Woodson, a black student from Berea College who served as a supervisor of schools in the islands from 1903 to 1905.[75] The return of the black infantrymen of the Twenty-fourth and Twenty-fifth Regiments to the Philippines, where they were em-

72. Thornbrough, *T. Thomas Fortune,* p. 240.
73. On Wright's inauguration, see *New York Times,* February 2, 1904.
74. Indianapolis *Freeman,* October 27, 1906.
75. Rayford W. Logan, "Carter G. Woodson," *Phylon,* VI (Fourth Quarter, 1945), 319–320.

ployed primarily in putting down a rebellion by the Moros in
Mindanao, serve to renew the interest of Negro Americans in the
archipelago during 1906 and 1907.[76]

During the Mindanao campaign Major John R. Lynch, who
had been commissioned a paymaster in the regular army following the disbandment of the volunteer forces, arrived in the Philippines for a two-year tour of duty. No less than other Negro
Americans, Lynch was impressed by the possibilities of such "a
rich and fertile country." Although the great majority of Filipinos still wanted "absolute independence and self-government,"
the major believed that it was in their best interest to remain under American authority "for at least one generation." Granting
that "all just governments derive their power from the consent
of the governed," he justified American control of the islands
"against the will of the people thereof" on the grounds that in the
United States thousands of colored Americans were not allowed
"a voice in making and enforcing the laws by which they are governed." [77] Then, in an obvious reference to emigration, Lynch
wrote:

> Notwithstanding these things, the colored American is much better
> off in his own country than it is possible for him to be in any
> other. He is aware of the fact that his own deficiencies, for which
> he is not wholly responsible, are among the alleged causes of the
> conditions of which he complains. He is therefore hopeful and
> confident, and he has a right to be, that the wrongs to which
> he is now subjected will eventually cease to exist.[78]

Similarly, according to Lynch, Filipinos had reason to believe that
they would ultimately achieve self-government. But like other
black Americans who sympathized with the aspirations of the
brown people of the Philippines, he was convinced that Negro
citizens were superior to Filipinos, especially in terms of fulfilling civic obligations. Although Lynch did not go as far as some
other black Americans in pointing up the backwardness of Filipinos, he did believe that "the colored American can and does ex-

76. Muller, *Twenty-fourth Infantry;* Nankivell, *Twenty-fifth Regiment,* pp. 120–
131.

77. Lynch, *Reminiscences of an Active Life,* p. 485.

78. *Ibid.,* p. 486.

ercise the elective franchise and discharge the duties and responsibilities of citizenship with much more intelligence, wisdom and
discretion than the average 'Filipino.' " [79]

If black citizens showed less inclination to identify with the
colored inhabitants of America's possessions in the Pacific, whites
scarcely gave emigration projects a hearing. The return of black
troops to the Philippines during 1906–9 prompted M. J. Menman, a candidate for Congress from Texas, to attempt to resur-
rect Morgan's Negro colonization project. If elected, he promised
to sponsor legislation "to get all Negroes sent to the Philippines."
The scheme was apparently even less popular in 1908 than it had
been a half-dozen years earlier, and it elicited little interest among
white Texans. Menman lost the election and was never in a position to sponsor such legislation.[80]

79. *Ibid.*
80. Indianapolis *Freeman,* July 11, 1908.

Conclusion

Although black Americans displayed no more consistency or unanimity of opinion regarding imperialism than other citizens, the context within which they viewed the issue was substantially different. Theirs was the perspective of a colored minority in a white-dominated society—a minority whose emergence from the "forge and fire of American slavery" had been followed by a generation of frustrated hopes and thwarted aspirations. The last decade of the nineteenth century in particular witnessed a dramatic increase in racial repression and legal discrimination. By the end of the decade, as an epidemic of negrophobia threatened to trap black citizens in a new form of slavery, a sense of mounting crisis pervaded the black community. Whether one of endorsement or opposition, Negro Americans' initial response to overseas expansion was prompted largely by their view of its effect upon the future of the race in the United States.

At one extreme were those blacks who from the outset maintained an anti-expansionist position principally on the grounds that a crusade abroad would divert attention from the racial crisis at home, thereby allowing what was left of the heritage of Reconstruction to be obliterated altogether. At the other were the champions of imperialism, a group made up primarily of black Republican officeholders, who argued that by participating in the acquisition of an empire Negroes would reap a rich and varied harvest, especially in terms of respect and recognition from the dominant element in American society. According to their rationale, contact with the colored peoples and colored cultures outside the United States would have a beneficent effect upon the racial attitudes of white citizens.

Few black Americans consistently embraced either view. In responding to the nation's imperialistic ventures, most Negroes pursued a tortuous course characterized by ambiguities, contradic-

tions, and dramatic reversals. Plagued by uncertainties and conflicting loyalties, they often appeared at sea on the question of
imperialism. Although the black citizen considered participation
in the military struggle for empire a civic duty and hoped that a
display of patriotism would dissipate anti-Negro prejudice, he
was suspicious of the humanitarian rhetoric employed by white
imperialists and persisted in the belief that charity ought to begin
at home.

Much of the ambivalence and vacillation which characterized
the black citizen's reaction to the quest for empire stemmed from
his anomalous position in American society. He was not merely
an American; he was an American Negro—a double personality
in one. As an American citizen, he felt obligated to do his full
duty, including military service in the Caribbean and Pacific.
Keenly aware of the tendency to equate criticism of the expansionist policy with disloyalty, he was hesitant, at least initially, to
jeopardize his precarious position by embracing the anti-imperialist cause. As a Negro, he recognized the similarity between his
predicament in the United States and that of the colored peoples
in Cuba, Puerto Rico, Hawaii, and the Philippines. Like them,
he longed for liberty and freedom from white oppression. Within
the context of his own experience the black American was led to
suspect that the policy of imperialism was but another manifestation of white supremacy likely to have frightful consequences for
colored people abroad as well as those at home. The alignment of
the two major political parties on expansion did little to help him
resolve the ideological conflicts posed by the issue. Despite their
objections to "McKinley imperialism," relatively few Negroes
were willing to abandon their traditional allegiance to the Republican party—the party of Lincoln and Emancipation—in order to
take up the cause of anti-imperialism espoused by the Democratic
party, the party of Tillman and other outspoken racists.

In the case of Cuba, Negro Americans encountered fewer ideological difficulties; military intervention there promised not only
to relieve the island of Spanish rule but also to assure its independence. That many of the islanders were of African descent made
it easy for Negroes in the United States to identify with the cause
of Cuba Libre. For some years prior to 1898 the black press fol-

lowed every development in the Cuban insurrection and heaped praise upon heroes such as Antonio Maceo and Quintin Banderas. Indeed, the role of Afro-Cubans in the struggle for freedom lent credence to their idea that Cuba would become another black republic in the Caribbean—"a paradise for colored men," especially from the United States. Even though the island was transformed into an independent republic, the result scarcely conformed to the expectations of Negro Americans. They believed that Afro-Cubans had been ignored in the establishment of the new government and that the American military regime had introduced prejudice in the island, establishing a color line in a society where it had not previously existed. Their disillusionment was only deepened when they discovered that the Afro-Cuban, having so thoroughly "made himself a part of Cuba in thought and action," [1] placed nationality above race and therefore did not reciprocate the racial identity of his cousin in the United States.

By 1899, even before the Senate approved the treaty ending the war with Spain, black Americans had begun to alter their views regarding the outward thrust of the United States. Few were misled by the praise bestowed upon Negro soldiers in the wake of the Cuban campaign, which proved both brief and illusory. Even fewer were able to detect any evidence of the rich harvest promised by black advocates of expansion. Instead, the war seemed to have multiplied the black citizens' grievances. In the South, where the presence of black soldiers aroused fear and resentment among whites, the reward for the Negro's demonstration of patriotism and valor was a tightening of racial lines. As an elderly black Georgian predicted late in 1898, the departure of the Negro soldier from camps in the South was followed by hard times for black residents of the region. And with the disbandment of the volunteer army after the Spanish-American War, one state after another eliminated the remaining Negro units from its militia. More ominous was the effect which the much-heralded sectional reunion accomplished by the war was likely to have upon race relations. Black spokesmen agreed that the dissipation of sectionalism actually meant northern acquiescence in the "southern solution" to the Negro Problem. The mob violence which erupted throughout the nation between 1899 and 1902 seemed to confirm

1. Washington, *Future of the American Negro*, p. 217.

the notion that the principal harvest of imperialism for black Americans was an abundance of negrophobia.

Against this background of frustrated hopes, the black man's original reservations about overseas expansion reemerged in 1899 in the form of forthright opposition to the war in the Philippines. Despite warnings about the dangers of making color an issue in the conflict, the black community in general established an affinity of complexion with the Filipinos and tended to take a sympathetic view of Aguinaldo's resistance to American rule. For some Negroes the insurrection in the Philippines was an aspect of the larger struggle of darker races throughout the world to combat oppression by white men. Black soldiers who served in the islands were aware of the irony and contradiction inherent in their role as instruments of empire for a nation which made color a badge of inferiority. For black Americans, in general, the ideological dilemmas raised by the Philippine Question prompted a welter of ambivalent attitudes, not only about their colored brothers in the Asiatic islands, but also about themselves and their status in the United States.

The acquisition of insular possessions inhabited by darker races spawned a variety of emigration schemes, all of which promised Negro Americans an escape from their yoke of prejudice and oppression. Cuba and the Philippines, in particular, were described as places where racial distinctions were virtually nonexistent and where wealth could be acquired by any enterprising black man with a little capital and a willingness to work. Individual Negroes did emigrate to the islands, and a few prospered. But there was never the large-scale exodus advocated by emigrationists. Not even the Philippines, which T. Thomas Fortune recommended so enthusiastically as a home for several million black citizens, attracted many emigrants. Fortune estimated that there were 300 to 400 Negro Americans in the islands in 1903, but by 1918 the census revealed that the number had shrunk to 185.[2] Convinced that color prejudice had accompanied the American flag to Cuba, the Philippines, and other islands, Negroes preferred to fight their battles

2. Fortune, "The Filipino," 97. The official census of 1903 listed 505 "foreign-born" blacks in the Philippines, while the census of 1918 listed only 185 "American Negroes" in the islands; see *Census of the Philippine Islands, 1903* (Washington: U.S. Bureau of Census, 1905), p. 246; *Statistical Bulletin of the Philippine Islands, 1923* (Manila: Bureau of Printing, 1924), p. 3.

in the familiar environment of their birth rather than to confront
the same enemy among alien civilizations thousands of miles away.

By the time the United States declared the Filipino insurrection at an end, black Americans were thoroughly disenchanted
with the expansionist policy and less inclined to identify with the
peoples of the insular possessions. Rather than viewing the islanders as colored cousins, they came to look upon them as inferior
aliens—a shift explained largely by the growing feeling that the
nation was less concerned with the welfare of its black citizens
than with that of the peoples in the colonies. "It seems," Edward E. Cooper observed in 1902, "that our white friends have a
habit of expending their sympathy upon the black man who is
farthest off." [3] In discussing the same issue, Kelly Miller posed
this question: "If the moral sense of the American people would
not leave the distant Filipino to his pitiable fate, but impelled
them to reach out a saving hand across the seas and snatch him
within the ennobling circle of benevolent assimilation, how much
more incumbent is it to elevate the Negro who is within our
gates, and is closely associated with our national destiny?" [4] Perhaps more graphically than anyone else George W. Prioleau, a
black captain who served in the Philippines, expressed the new
attitude of black Americans when he suggested that the generosity
of the United States might well enable the Filipino to "outstrip
the Negro." His fear was that the brown man in the Pacific would
become "America's 'china' baby," while the black citizen continued "to be the 'rag' baby of the republic." [5] By 1903 Negro
Americans might still sympathize with Filipino aspirations for independence and freedom, but they were convinced that the first
obligation of the American government was to its own colored
minority. The nation's saving hand was needed in taking up the
black man's burden at home, rather than in looking across the
seas for more "little brown brothers."

3. Washington *Colored American*, April 26, 1902.
4. Kelly Miller, "The Expansion of the Negro Population," *Forum*, XXXII
(February, 1902), 679.
5. George W. Prioleau in Washington *Colored American*, July 13, 1901. By 1906
John P. Green, an ardent advocate of imperialism during the McKinley years, had
come to view such a policy "as the great mistake of the McKinley-Roosevelt admin-
istrations." See John P. Green to Theodore Bliss, August 12, 1906, Green Papers.

Bibliography

MANUSCRIPTS

PERSONAL COLLECTIONS

Robert L. Bullard Papers. Manuscript Division, Library of Congress.

Asa Bushnell Papers. Ohio Historical Society, Columbus, Ohio.

Charles W. Fairbanks Papers. Lilly Library, Indiana University, Bloomington, Ind.

Christian A. Fleetwood Papers. Manuscript Division, Library of Congress.

John P. Green Papers. Western Reserve Historical Society, Cleveland, Ohio.

Francis R. Lassiter Papers. Duke University Library, Durham, N.C.

Samuel Powell Lyons Papers. United States Army Military History Collection, Carlisle Barracks, Pa.

William McKinley Papers. Manuscript Division, Library of Congress.

J. Sterling Morton Papers. Nebraska State Historical Society, Lincoln, Nebr.

James A. Mount Correspondence. Archives Division, Indiana State Library, Indianapolis, Ind.

George A. Myers Papers. Ohio Historical Society, Columbus, Ohio.

Theodore Roosevelt Papers. Manuscript Division, Library of Congress.

Elihu Root Papers. Manuscript Division, Library of Congress.

Daniel L. Russell Papers. Department of Archives and History, Raleigh, N.C.

Booker T. Washington Papers. Manuscript Division, Library of Congress.

RECORDS OF THE DEPARTMENT OF WAR, OFFICE OF THE ADJUTANT
GENERAL, RECORD GROUP 94, NATIONAL ARCHIVES

1. Document File, 1898–1902.
2. Regimental Returns, 9th Cavalry, 1898–1902.
3. ———, 10th Cavalry, 1898–1902.
4. ———, 24th Infantry, 1898–1902.
5. ———, 25th Infantry, 1898–1902.

6. Regimental Records, 7th Infantry, U.S.V., 1898–99.
7. ———, 8th Infantry, U.S.V., 1898–99.
8. ———, 9th Infantry, U.S.V., 1898–99.
9. ———, 10th Infantry, U.S.V., 1898–99.
10. ———, 3rd Alabama, U.S.V., 1898–99.
11. ———, 8th Illinois, U.S.V., 1898–99.
12. ———, A and B Companies, Indiana, U.S.V., 1898–99.
13. ———, 6th Massachusetts, U.S.V., 1898–99.
14. ———, 3rd North Carolina, U.S.V., 1898–99.
15. ———, 9th Battalion, Ohio, U.S.V., 1898–99.
16. ———, 6th Virginia, U.S.V., 1898–99.
17. ———, 48th Infantry, U.S.V., 1899–1901.
18. ———, 49th Infantry, U.S.V., 1899–1901.

OTHER UNPUBLISHED SOURCES

MATERIALS IN THE UNITED STATES ARMY MILITARY HISTORY
COLLECTION, CARLISLE BARRACKS, PA.

A. S. Allen, transcription of a taped interview, July, 1970.
John H. Allen, Questionnaire, January 15, 1969.
Army War College, "The Colored Soldier in the United States Army,"
    typescript.
Walter Ervin, Questionnaire, January 23, 1969.
John Hill, Questionnaire, December 14, 1968.
Richard Johnson, "My Life in the U. S. Army, 1899–1922," typescript
    copy.
George Rhodes, Questionnaire, January 13, 1969.
Samuel Waller, Questionnaire, January 11, 1969.

THESES AND DISSERTATIONS

Deacon, Marie. "Kansas as the 'Promised Land': The View of the
    Black Press, 1890–1900." M.A. thesis, University of Arkansas, 1972.
Early, Gerald H. "The Negro Soldier in the Spanish-American War."
    Master's thesis, Shippenburg State College, Pa., 1970.
Fletcher, Marvin E. "The Negro Soldier and the United States Army,
    1891–1917." Ph.D. dissertation, University of Wisconsin, 1968.
Gates, John M. "An Experiment in Benevolent Pacification: The U.S.
    Army in the Philippines, 1898–1902." Ph.D. dissertation, Duke Uni-
    versity, 1967.
Kennedy, Philip W. "The Concept of Racial Superiority and United

States Imperialism, 1890–1910." Ph.D. dissertation, St. Louis University, 1962.

Radke, August C. Jr. "John Tyler Morgan, An Expansionist Senator, 1877–1907." Ph.D. dissertation, University of Washington, 1953.

Roster of Officers, Alabama State Troops, Department of Archives and History, Montgomery, Ala.

Taylor, John R. M. "The Philippine Insurrection against the United States—A Compilation of Documents with Notes and Introduction." 5 volumes. Unpublished MS, microfilm, National Archives.

PUBLISHED AUTOBIOGRAPHIES, CORRESPONDENCE, AND MEMOIRS

Atkins, John B. *The War in Cuba: The Experiences of an Englishman with the United States Army.* London: Elder, Elder, 1899.

Bigalow, John, Jr. *Reminiscences of the Santiago Campaign.* New York: Harper and Brothers, 1899.

Crane, Charles J. *The Experiences of a Colonel of Infantry.* New York: Knickerbocker Press, 1923.

Daniels, Josephus. *Editor in Politics.* Chapel Hill: University of North Carolina Press, 1941.

Flipper, Henry O. *Negro Frontiersman: The Western Memoirs of Henry O. Flipper.* Ed. Theodore D. Harris. El Paso: Texas Western College Press, 1963.

Foner, Philip S. *The Life and Writings of Frederick Douglass.* 4 vols. New York: International Publishers, 1955.

Funston, Frederick. *Memories of Two Wars: Cuban and Philippine Experiences.* New York: Scribner's, 1914.

Gatewood, Willard B., Jr. *"Smoked Yankees" and the Struggle for Empire: Letters from Negro Soldiers, 1898–1902.* Urbana: University of Illinois Press, 1971.

Gibbs, Mifflin W. *Shadow and Light: An Autobiography.* Washington: n.p., 1902.

Green, John P. *Fact Stranger Than Fiction: Seventy-five Years of a Busy Life.* Cleveland: Riehl Printing, 1920.

Lynch, John Roy. *Reminiscences of an Active Life: The Autobiography of John Roy Lynch.* Ed. John Hope Franklin. Chicago: University of Chicago Press, 1970.

Morison, Elting, ed. *Letters of Theodore Roosevelt.* 8 vols. Cambridge: Harvard University Press, 1954–56.

Moss, James A. *Memories of the Campaign of Santiago.* San Francisco: Mysell and Rollins, 1899.

Payne, W. C. *The Cruise of the U.S.S. Dixie.* Washington: E. C. Jones, 1899.

Post, Charles Johnson. *The Little War of Private Post.* Boston: Little, Brown, 1960.

The Santiago Campaign: Reminiscences of the Operations for the Capture of Santiago de Cuba in the Spanish-American War, June and July, 1898. Richmond: Williams Printing, 1927.

Walters, Alexander. *My Life and Work.* New York: Fleming Revell, 1917.

Wells, Ida B. *Crusade for Justice: The Autobiography of Ida B. Wells,* ed. Alfreda M. Duster. Chicago: University of Chicago Press, 1970.

PUBLISHED DOCUMENTS AND PROCEEDINGS

Annual Report of the Adjutant General of North Carolina. 1899, 1901.

Annual Report of the Adjutant General of Ohio. 1891, 1896, 1897, 1899.

Annual Report of the Department of War. 1898, 1899, 1900, 1901, 1902.

Biennial Report of the Adjutant General of Alabama. 1896–98.

Biennial Report of the Adjutant General of Illinois. 1896–98, 1898–1900.

Census of the Philippine Islands, 1903. Washington: U.S. Bureau of Census, 1905.

Congressional Record. 55 Cong., 1 sess.—57 Cong., 1 sess.

Copies of Correspondence from the Adjutant General Relating to the Campaign in Cuba. Washington: Government Printing Office, 1898.

Correspondence Relating to the War with Spain and Conditions Growing out of the Same, Including the Insurrection in the Philippine Islands, and the China Relief Expedition. 2 vols. Washington: Government Printing Office, 1902.

Hearings before the Committee on the Philippines of the United States Senate. Senate Doc. 331, 57 Cong., 1 sess.

Official Proceedings of the Twelfth Republican National Convention Held in the City of Philadelphia, June 19, 20, 21, 1900. Philadelphia: Press of Dunlap Printing, 1900.

Papers Relating to the Foreign Relations of the United States, 1895. Washington: Government Printing Office, 1896.

Report of the Adjutant General of Georgia. 1899–1900, 1903.

Report of the Adjutant General of Virginia. 1897, 1898–99.

Report of the Commission Appointed by the President to Investigate the Conduct of the War Department in the War with Spain. 8 vols. Senate Doc. 221, 56 Cong., 1 sess.

"Report of the Commissioner of Labor of Hawaii." *Bulletin of the Department of Labor,* No. 47, July, 1903.

The State of the Union Messages of the Presidents, 1790–1966. 3 vols. Ed. Fred Israel. New York: Chelsea House–Robert Hector, 1966.

Statistical Bulletin of the Philippine Islands, 1923. Manila: Bureau of Printing, 1924.

NEWSPAPERS

The Afro-American, Baltimore, Md.

Afro-American Advance, St. Paul, Minn.

Afro-American Advocate, Coffeyville, Kans.

The Afro-American Sentinel, Omaha, Nebr.

The Age-Herald, Birmingham, Ala.

The American, Coffeyville, Kans.

American Citizen, Kansas City, Kans.

The Appeal, St. Paul, Minn.

Arkansas Democrat, Little Rock, Ark.

Arkansas Gazette, Little Rock, Ark.

Army and Navy Journal, New York, N.Y.

Atlanta Constitution, Atlanta, Ga.

Atlanta Journal, Atlanta, Ga.

Augusta Chronicle, Augusta, Ga.

The Boston Globe, Boston, Mass.

The Boston Transcript, Boston, Mass.

The Broad Ax, Salt Lake City, Utah, and Chicago, Ill.

The Broad-Axe, St. Paul, Minn.

Chicago Tribune, Chicago, Ill.

The Colored American, Washington, D.C.

Colored Citizen, Topeka, Kans.

Commercial Appeal, Memphis, Tenn.

The Commonwealth, Greenwood, Miss.

Daily American Citizen, Kansas City, Kans.

The Daily Picayune, New Orleans, La.

The Daily Register, Mobile, Ala.

The Daily Times, Chattanooga, Tenn.

The Defender, Philadelphia, Pa.

The Dispatch, Richmond, Va.

The Enquirer, Columbus, Ga.
The Enquirer, Richmond, Va.
The Enterprise, Omaha, Nebr.
The Evening Star, Washington, D.C.
The Florida Times-Union and Citizen, Jacksonville, Fla.
The Freeman, Indianapolis, Ind.
The Gazette, Cleveland, Ohio.
Huntsville Gazette, Huntsville, Ala.
Illinois Record, Springfield, Ill.
Iowa State Bystander, Des Moines, Iowa.
The Journal, Indianapolis, Ind.
The Journal and Tribune, Knoxville, Tenn.
Kansas State Ledger, Topeka, Kans.
The Ledger, Baltimore, Md.
Manila Times, Manila, Philippine Islands.
Morning News, Savannah, Ga.
Nashville American, Nashville, Tenn.
The National Pilot, Petersburg, Va.
The Negro World, St. Paul, Minn.
The New Age, Portland, Ore.
New York Age, New York, N.Y.
New York Daily Tribune, New York, N.Y.
New York Times, New York, N.Y.
The News and Observer, Raleigh, N.C.
Ohio State Journal, Columbus, Ohio.
The Palladium, St. Louis, Mo.
Parsons Weekly Blade, Parsons, Kans.
The Post-Dispatch, St. Louis, Mo.
The Recorder, Indianapolis, Ind.
The Reformer, Richmond, Va.
The Reporter, Helena, Ark.
Republican, Seattle, Wash.
Richmond Planet, Richmond, Va.
The Searchlight, Wichita, Kans.
The Southern Republican, New Orleans, La.
The State, Columbia, S.C.
State Capital, Springfield, Ill.
Tampa Morning Tribune, Tampa, Fla.
The Telegraph, Macon, Ga.
The Times, London, England.
The Tribune, Savannah, Ga.

The Tribune, Wichita, Kans.
Twin City American, Minneapolis–St. Paul, Minn.
Union Republican, Winston, N.C.
Voice of Missions, Atlanta, Ga.
Washington Bee, Washington, D.C.
Washington Post, Washington, D.C.
Weekly Call, Topeka, Kans.
Wide-Awake, Birmingham, Ala.
Wisconsin Weekly Advocate, Milwaukee, Wis.
The World, Indianapolis, Ind.
The World, Seattle, Wash.

ARTICLES

Abbott, A. R. "The Employment of Negroes in the Philippines." *Anglo-American Magazine,* VI (September, 1901), 196–201.
———. "Negro Soldiers for the Philippines." *Anglo-American Magazine* II (November, 1899), 453–457.
"Atkinson, McKinley, Expansion and the Negro." *A.M.E. Church Review,* V (October, 1899), 275–276.
Bailey, Thomas A. "The United States and Hawaii during the Spanish-American War." *American Historical Review,* XXXVI (April, 1931), 552–560.
Bassett, E. Don Carlos. "Should Haiti Be Annexed by the United States?" *Voice of the Negro,* I (May, 1904), 191–198.
Batten, J. Minton. "Henry M. Turner: Negro Bishop Extraordinary." *Church History,* VII (September, 1938), 231–246.
Baylen, Joseph O., and Moore, John H. "Senator John Tyler Morgan and Negro Colonization in the Philippines, 1901 to 1902." *Phylon,* XXIX (Spring, 1968), 65–75.
Bond, Horace Mann. "The Negro in the Armed Forces of the United States prior to World War I." *Journal of Negro Education,* XII (Summer, 1943), 263–287.
Bonsal, Stephen. "The Negro Soldier in War and Peace." *North American Review,* CLXXXVI (June, 1907), 321–327.
Braxton, George H. "Company 'L' in the Spanish-American War." *Colored American Magazine,* I (May, 1900), 19–25.
Bullard, Robert L. "The Cuban Negro." *North American Review,* CLXXXIV (March 15, 1907), 623–630.
———. "The Negro Volunteer: Some Characteristics." *Journal of the Military Service Institution,* XXIX (July, 1901), 29–39.

Campbell, Nicholas H. "The Negro in the Navy." *Colored American Magazine*, VI (May–June, 1903), 406–413.

Chafe, William H. "The Negro and Populism: A Kansas Case Study." *Journal of Southern History*, XXXIV (August, 1968), 402–418.

"Cuban Immigration." *Alexander's Magazine*, II (August 15, 1906), 14.

Durham, John S. "Confessions of a Man Who Did." *Southern Workman*, XXVIII (May, 1899), 168–172.

Fleming, Robert E. "Sutton E. Griggs: Militant Black Novelist." *Phylon*, XXXIV (March, 1973), 73–77.

Foreman, John. "The Americans in the Philippines." *Contemporary Review*, LXXXVI (September, 1904), 392–405.

Fortune, T. Thomas. "The Filipino: A Social Study in Three Parts." *Voice of the Negro*, I (March, 1904), 93–99; I (May, 1904), 199–203; I (June, 1904), 240–246.

———. "Haytian Revolutions." *Voice of the Negro*, I (April, 1904), 138–142.

———. "Politics in the Philippine Islands." *The Independent*, LV (September 24, 1903), 2206–8.

Gatewood, Willard B., Jr. "Alabama's 'Negro Soldier Experiment,' 1898–1899." *Journal of Negro History*, LVII (October, 1972), 333–351.

———. "An Experiment in Color: The Eighth Illinois Volunteers, 1898–1899." *Journal of the Illinois State Historical Society*, LXV (Autumn, 1972), 293–312.

———. "Indiana Negroes and the Spanish-American War." *Indiana Magazine of History*, LXIX (June, 1973), 115–139.

———. "Kansas Negroes and the Spanish-American War." *Kansas Historical Quarterly*, XXXVII (Autumn, 1971), 300–313.

———. "A Negro Editor on Imperialism: John Mitchell, 1898–1901." *Journalism Quarterly*, XLIX (Spring, 1972), 43–50.

———. "Negro Troops in Florida, 1898." *Florida Historical Quarterly*, XLIX (July, 1970), 1–15.

———. "North Carolina's Negro Regiment in the Spanish-American War." *North Carolina Historical Review*, XLVIII (October, 1971), 370–387.

———. "Ohio's Negro Battalion in the Spanish-American War." *Northwest Ohio Quarterly*, XLV (Spring, 1973), 55–66.

———. "Virginia's Negro Regiment in the Spanish-American War." *Virginia Magazine of History and Biography*, LXXX (April, 1971), 193–209.

"General Garcia and Cuban Conduct." *Literary Digest,* XVII (July 30, 1898), 121–123.

Gianakos, Perry E. "The Spanish-American War and the Double Paradox of the Negro American." *Phylon,* XXVI (Spring, 1965), 34–49.

Grimké, Archibald. "The Dominican Republic and Her Revolutions." *Voice of the Negro,* I (April, 1904), 133–138.

Hall, Charles W. "The Eighth Illinois, U.S.V." *Colored American Magazine,* I (June, 1900), 94–103.

———. "The Old or the New Faith, Which?" *Colored American Magazine,* I (August, 1900), 172–176.

Harlan, Louis R. "Booker T. Washington and the White Man's Burden." *American Historical Review,* LXXI (January, 1966), 441–467.

———. "Booker T. Washington in Biographical Perspective." *American Historical Review,* LXXV (October, 1970), 1581–99.

———. "The Secret Life of Booker T. Washington." *Journal of Southern History,* XXXVII (August, 1971), 393–416.

Harrington, Fred H. "The Anti Imperialist Movement in the United States, 1898–1900." *Mississippi Valley Historical Review,* XXII (September, 1935), 211–230.

Harroun, Gilbert. "The Cuban Educational Association of the United States." *Review of Reviews,* XX (September, 1899), 334–335.

Henderson, Tom Wells. "The Phoenix Election Riot." *Phylon,* XXXI (Spring, 1970), 58–69.

Himelhoch, Myra. "Frederick Douglass and Haiti's Môle St. Nicolas. *Journal of Negro History,* LVI (July, 1971), 161–180.

Hopkins, Pauline E. "Talma Gordon." *Colored American Magazine,* I (October, 1900), 271–290.

"In the Philippines." *The Crisis,* IV (April, 1918), 279.

Jackson, W. H. "From Our Friends in the Far East." *Colored American Magazine,* I (August, 1900), 145–149.

Kennedy, Philip W. "Race and American Expansion in Cuba and Puerto Rico, 1895–1905." *Journal of Black Studies,* I (March, 1971), 306–316.

———. "Racial Overtones of Imperialism as a Campaign Issue, 1900." *Mid-America,* XLVII (July, 1966), 196–205.

Lanier, Robert A., Jr. "Memphis Greets the War with Spain." *West Tennessee Historical Society Papers,* XVIII (1964), 39–58.

Lasch, Christopher. "The Anti-Imperialists, the Philippines and the

Inequality of Man." *Journal of Southern History,* XXIV (August, 1958), 319–331.

Lemus, Rienzi B. "The Enlisted Man in Action, or the Colored American Soldier in the Philippines." *Colored American Magazine,* V (May, 1902), 46–54.

———. "The Negro and the Philippines." *Colored American Magazine,* VI (February, 1903), 314–318.

LeRoy, James A. "Race Prejudice in the Philippines." *Atlantic Monthly,* XC (July, 1902), 100–112.

Lewis, Elsie M. "The Political Mind of the Negro, 1865–1900." *Journal of Southern History,* XXI (May, 1955), 189–202.

Lockhart, Milledge. "The Colored Soldier in the South." *New York Times Illustrated Magazine,* XLVII (August 14, 1898), 7, 14.

Logan, Rayford W. "Carter G. Woodson." *Phylon,* VI (Fourth Quarter, 1945), 315–321.

"Major Charles W. Fillmore: Promoter of the Economy Fire Insurance Company." *Colored American Magazine,* XII (April, 1907), 310–312.

Meier, August. "The Negro and the Democratic Party, 1875–1915." *Phylon,* XVII (Second Quarter, 1956), 182–191.

Members of the State Project of the Works Project Administration of the State of Illinois. "Camp Lincoln." *Journal of the Illinois State Historical Society,* XXXIV (September, 1941), 281–302.

Miller, Kelly. "The Expansion of the Negro Population." *Forum,* XXXII (February, 1902), 671–679.

Miller, Stuart C. "Our Mylai of 1900: Americans in the Philippine Insurrection." *Transaction,* VII (September, 1970), 17–29.

Moffett, Cleveland. "Stories of Camp Wikoff." *Leslie's Weekly,* LXXXVII (October 13, 1898), 286–287.

"The Negro as Soldier and Officer." *The Nation,* LXXIII (August 1, 1901), 85–86.

Nickles, Katheryn R. "The Case of John L. Waller." *Ozark Historical Review,* I (Spring, 1972), 21–30.

Olds-Keeler, Clarissa. "Negroes in Hawaii." *Voice of Missions,* VII (February 1, 1900), 2.

Pace, Harry H. "The Philippine Islands and the American Negro." *Voice of the Negro,* I (October, 1904), 482–485.

Padgett, James A. "Diplomats to Haiti and Their Diplomacy." *Journal of Negro History,* XXV (July, 1940), 265–330.

Palmer, Frederick. "The White Man and the Brown Man in the Philippines." *Scribner's Magazine,* XXVII (January, 1900), 76–86.

Putnam, Frank. "The Negro's Part in National Problems." *Colored American Magazine,* I (June, 1900), 69–79.

"Race Discrimination in the Philippines." *Independent,* LIV (February 13, 1902), 416–417.

Reddick, L. D. "The Negro Policy of the United States Army, 1775–1945." *Journal of Negro History,* XXXIV (January, 1949), 9–29.

Robinson, Albert Gardiner. "The Outlook in the Philippines." *The Independent,* LII (February 8, 1900), 349–351.

Roosevelt, Theodore. "Rough Riders." *Scribner's Magazine,* XXV (April, 1899), 420–440.

Rouse, W. J. "The United States Colored Regulars." *New York Times Magazine,* June 5, 1898, pp. 4–5.

Scarborough, William S. "Our New Possessions—An Open Door." *Southern Workman,* XXIX (July, 1900), 422–427.

———. "The Negro and Our New Possessions." *Forum,* XXXIX (May, 1901), 341–349.

Schellings, William J. "Key West and the Spanish-American War." *Tequesta,* XX (1960), 19–29.

Smith, Willard H. "William Jennings Bryan and Racism." *Journal of Negro History,* LIV (April, 1969), 127–147.

Steward, Charles. "Manila and Its Opportunities." *Colored American Magazine,* III (August, 1901), 248–256.

Steward, Theophilus. "Two Years in Luzon." *Colored American Magazine.* IV (November, 1901), 4–10.

Sweetser, William S. "Opportunities for Stock-Raising in Cuba and Puerto Rico." *Southern Workman,* XXIX (July, 1900), 407–413.

Tate, Merze. "Decadence of the Hawaiian Nation and Proposals to Import a Negro Labor Force." *Journal of Negro History,* XLVII (October, 1962), 248–263.

Thompson, E. B. "Veterans Who Never Came Home." *Ebony,* XXVII (October, 1972), 104–106, 108–115.

Villard, Oswald Garrison. "The Negro in the Regular Army." *Atlantic Monthly,* XCI (June, 1903), 721–729.

Washington, Booker T. "Industrial Education for Cuban Negroes." *Christian Register,* LVIII (August 18, 1898), 924–925.

Welch, Richard E. "Motives and Policy Objectives of the Anti-Imperialists, 1898." *Mid-America,* LI (April, 1969), 119–129.

Wheaton, F. H. "A Feast with the Filipinos." *Colored American Magazine,* III (June, 1901), 154–155.

Wood, Richard E. "The South and Reunion, 1898." *The Historian,* XXXI (May, 1969), 415–430.

BOOKS

Appleton's Annual Cyclopaedia and Register of Important Events of the Year 1897. New York: D. Appleton, 1898.

Aptheker, Herbert, ed. *Documentary History of the Negro People in the United States*. New York: Citadel Press, 1951.

Beale, Howard K. *Theodore Roosevelt and the Rise of America to World Power*. New York: Collier Books, 1968.

Beisner, Robert L. *Twelve against Empire: The Anti-Imperialists, 1898–1900*. New York: McGraw-Hill, 1968.

Blount, James H. *The American Occupation of the Philippines, 1898–1912*. New York: Putnam, 1912.

Bonsal, Stephen. *The Fight for Santiago*. New York: Doubleday and McClure, 1899.

Brawley, Benjamin. *A Social History of the American Negro*. New York: Macmillan, 1921.

Carlson, Lewis H., and Colburn, George A., eds. *In Their Place: White America Defines Her Minorities*. New York: John Wiley and Sons, 1972.

Carroll, John M. *The Black Miliary Experience in the American West*. New York: Liveright, 1971.

Cashin, Herschel V., et al. *Under Fire with the Tenth Cavalry*. New York: F. Tennyson Neely, 1899.

Chew, Abraham. *A Biography of Colonel Charles Young*. Washington: R. L. Pendleton, 1923.

Christopher, Maurine. *America's Black Congressmen*. New York: Thomas Y. Crowell, 1971.

Clanton, O. Gene. *Kansas Populism: Ideas and Men*. Lawrence: University Press of Kansas, 1969.

Coletta, Paolo. *William Jennings Bryan: Political Evangelist, 1860–1908*. Lincoln: University of Nebraska Press, 1964.

Coolidge, Archibald Cary. *The United States as a World Power*. New York: Macmillan, 1908.

Cosmas, Graham A. *An Army for Empire: The United States Army in the Spanish-American War*. Columbia: University of Missouri Press, 1971.

Coston, W. Hilary. *The Spanish-American War Volunteer*. Middletown, Pa.: Mount Pleasant Printery, 1899.

Croly, Herbert. *Marcus Alonzo Hanna: His Life and Work*. New York: Macmillan, 1912.

Cromwell, John W. *The Negro in American History*. Washington: American Negro Academy, 1914.

Cronin, Captain Marcus D. *Historical Sketch of the Twenty-fifth Infantry, United States Army*. Fort Bliss, Texas: n.p., 1907.

Culp, D. W. *Twentieth Century Negro Literature*. Atlanta: J. L. Nichols, 1902.

Curtis, Mary. *The Black Soldiers, or the Colored Boys of the United States Army*. Washington: Murray Brothers, 1915.

Dabney, Wendell P. *Cincinnati's Colored Citizens: Historical, Sociological and Biographical*. Cincinnati: Dabney Publishing, 1926.

Davis, Richard Harding. *The Cuban and Porto Rican Campaigns*. New York: Charles Scribner's Sons, 1904.

Draper, Andrew S. *The Rescue of Cuba: An Episode in the Growth of Free Government*. Boston: Silver Burnett, 1899.

Du Bois, W. E. B. *The Conservation of the Races*. Washington: American Negro Academy, 1897. Occasional Papers, No. 2.

———. *The Souls of Black Folk: Essays and Sketches*. Chicago: A. C. McClurg, 1931.

Dulles, Foster R. *America's Rise to World Power, 1898–1954*. New York: Harper and Row, 1963.

Edmonds, Helen. *The Negro and Fusion Politics in North Carolina, 1894–1901*. Chapel Hill: University of North Carolina Press, 1951.

Edwards, Frank E., *The '98 Campaign of the Sixth Massachusetts, U.S.V.* Boston: Little, Brown, 1899.

Floyd, Silas X. *Life of Charles T. Walker*. New York: Negro Universities Press, 1969.

Foner, Jack D. *The United States Soldier between Two Wars: Army Life and Reforms, 1865–1898*. New York: Humanities Press, 1970.

Foner, Philip S. *The Spanish-Cuban-American War and the Birth of American Imperialism*. 2 vols. New York: Monthly Review Press, 1972.

Fowler, Arlen L. *The Black Infantry in the West, 1869–1891*. Westport, Conn.: Greenwood Publishing, 1971.

Frederickson, George M. *The Black Image in the White Mind: The Debate on Afro-American Character and Destiny, 1817–1914*. New York: Harper and Row, 1971.

Freidel, Frank. *The Spendid Little War*. Boston: Little, Brown, 1958.

Friend, Theodore. *Between Two Empires: The Ordeal of the Philippines*. New Haven: Yale University Press, 1965.

Glass, E. N. *History of the Tenth Cavalry*. Tuscon: Acme Printing, 1921.

Gloster, Hugh M. *Negro Voices in American Fiction*. Chapel Hill: University of North Carolina Press, 1948.

Goode, W. T. *The "Eighth Illinois."* Chicago: Blakely Printing, 1899.

Green, Constance M. *The Secret City: Race Relations in the Nation's Capital*. Princeton: Princeton University Press, 1967.

Griggs, Sutton E. *Imperium in Imperio: A Study of the Negro Problem*. Cincinnati: Editor Publishing, 1899.

Grunder, Garel A., and Livezey, William E. *The Philippines and the United States*. Norman: University of Oklahoma Press, 1951.

Guthrie, James M. *Camp-Fires of the Afro-American: or, the Colored Man as a Patriot*. Philadelphia: Afro-American Publishing, 1899.

Hackney, Sheldon. *From Populism to Progressivism in Alabama*. Princeton University Press, 1969.

Harlan, Louis R. *Booker T. Washington: The Making of a Black Leader, 1856–1901*. New York: Oxford University Press, 1972.

Hawkins, Hugh, ed. *Booker T. Washington and His Critics: The Problem of Negro Leadership*. Boston: D. C. Heath, 1962.

Healy, David F. *The United States in Cuba, 1898–1902: Generals, Politicians, and the Search for Policy*. Madison: University of Wisconsin Press, 1963.

——. *U.S. Expansionism: The Imperialist Urge in the 1890's*. Madison: University of Wisconsin Press, 1970.

Hirshson, Stanley P. *Farewell to the Bloody Shirt: Northern Republicans and the Southern Negro, 1877–1893*. Bloomington: Indiana University Press, 1962.

Huggins, Nathan I.; Kelson, Martin; and Fox, Daniel M., eds. *Key Issues in the Afro-American Experience*. 2 vols. New York: Harcourt Brace Jovanovich, 1971.

Johnson, Edward A. *History of Negro Soldiers in the Spanish-American War and Other Items of Interest*. Raleigh: Capital Publishing, 1899.

——. *School History of the Negro Race in America from 1691 to 1890*. Chicago: W. B. Conkey, 1891.

Johnson, William Henry. *History of the Colored Volunteer Infantry in Virginia, 1871–1899*. Richmond: n.p., 1923.

Jordan, Philip D. *Ohio Comes of Age, 1873–1900*. Columbus: Ohio State Archeological and Historical Society, 1943.

Keller, Allan. *The Spanish-American War: A Compact History*. New York: Hawthorn Books, 1969.

Kletzing, Henry F., and Crogman, William. *Progress of a Race, or the Remarkable Advance of the Afro-American*. Atlanta: J. L. Nichols, 1897.

Koenig, Louis W. *Bryan: A Political Biography of William Jennings Bryan*. New York: G. P. Putnam's Sons, 1971.

Lee, Irvin H. *Negro Medal of Honor Men.* New York: Dodd, Mead, 1967.

LeRoy, James A. *The Americans in the Philippines.* 2 vols. Boston: Houghton Mifflin, 1914.

Logan, Frenise A. *The Negro in North Carolina, 1876–1894.* Chapel Hill: University of North Carolina Press, 1964.

Logan, Rayford W. *The Diplomatic Relations of the United States with Haiti, 1776–1891.* Chapel Hill: University of North Carolina Press, 1941.

———. *The Great Betrayal of the Negro from Rutherford B. Hayes to Woodrow Wilson.* New York: Collier Books, 1965.

Lynk, Miles V. *The Black Troopers, or the Daring Heroism of the Negro Soldiers in the Spanish-American War.* Jackson, Tenn.: Lynk Publishing House, 1899.

Mabry, William A. *The Negro in North Carolina Politics since Reconstruction.* Durham: Duke University Press, 1940.

Maddex, Jack P. *The Virginia Conservatives, 1867–1879: A Study in Reconstruction Politics.* Chapel Hill: University of North Carolina Press, 1970.

Marks, George P., ed. *The Black Press Views American Imperialism, 1898–1900.* New York: Arno Press, 1971.

Marshall, Harriet Gibbs. *The Story of Haiti.* Boston: Christopher Publishing, 1930.

Meier, August. *Negro Thought in America, 1880–1915: Racial Ideologies in the Age of Booker T. Washington.* Ann Arbor: University of Michigan Press, 1963.

———; Rudwick, Elliot; and Broderick, Frances L., eds. *Black Protest Thought in the Twentieth Century.* Indianapolis: Bobbs-Merrill, 1965.

Millis, Walter. *The Martial Spirit: A Study of Our War with Spain.* Boston: Houghton Mifflin, 1931.

Morgan, H. Wayne. *America's Road to Empire: The War with Spain and Overseas Expansion.* New York: John Wiley and Sons, 1965.

Muller, William G. *The Twenty-fourth Infantry: Past and Present.* N.p., 1923.

Murray, Pauli. *State Laws on Race and Color.* Cincinnati: Women's Division of Christian Service, Methodist Church, 1950.

Nankivell, John H. *History of the Twenty-fifth Regiment of the United States Infantry, 1869–1926.* Denver: Smith-Brooks, 1927.

Nugent, Walter T. K. *The Tolerant Populists: Kansas Populism and Nativism.* Chicago: University of Chicago Press, 1963.

O'Connor, Richard. *Black Jack Pershing*. Garden City: Doubleday, 1961.

Osofsky, Gilbert. *Harlem: The Making of a Ghetto, Negro New York, 1890–1930*. New York: Harper and Row, 1966.

Penn, I. Garland. *The Afro-American Press and Its Editors*. Springfield, Mass.: Willey, 1891.

Phillips, Clifton J. *Indiana in Transition: The Emergence of an Industrial Commonwealth, 1880–1920*. Indianapolis: Indiana Historical Bureau and Indiana Historical Society, 1968.

Quarles, Benjamin. *Frederick Douglass*. Washington: Associated Publishers, 1948.

————. *The Negro in the Making of America*. New York: Collier Books, 1969.

Redkey, Edwin S. *Black Exodus: Black Nationalist and Back to Africa Movements, 1890–1910*. New Haven: Yale University Press, 1969.

Roosevelt, Theodore, *The Rough Riders*. New York: Charles Scribner's Sons, 1899.

Rudwick, Elliot M. *W. E. B. Du Bois: Propagandist of Negro Protest*. New York: Atheneum, 1968.

Schiener, Seth M. *Negro Mecca: A History of the Negro in New York City, 1865–1920*. New York University Press, 1965.

Schirmer, Daniel B. *Republic or Empire: American Resistance to the Philippine War*. Cambridge: Schenkman Publishing, 1972.

Sexton, William T. *Soldiers in the Sun: An Adventure in Imperialism*. Harrisburg: Military Service Publishing Co., 1939.

Simkins, Francis B. *Pitchfork Ben Tillman: South Carolinian*. Baton Rouge: Louisiana State University Press, 1944.

Spencer, Samuel R. *Booker T. Washington and the Negro's Place in American Life*. Boston: Little, Brown, 1955.

Steelman, Joseph F., ed. *Essays in Southern History*. Greenville, N.C.: Department of History, East Carolina College, 1965.

Steward, Theophilus G. *The Colored Regulars in the United States Army*. Philadelphia. A. M. E. Book Concern, 1904.

Straker, D. Augustus. *A Trip to the Windward Isle, or Then and Now*. Detroit: Press of James H. Stone and Co., n.d.

Tate, Merze. *Hawaii: Reciprocity or Annexation*. East Lansing: Michigan State University Press, 1968.

Thornbrough, Emma Lou, ed. *Booker T. Washington*. Englewood Cliffs: Prentice-Hall, 1969.

————. *The Negro in Indiana: A Study of a Minority*. Indianapolis: Indiana Historical Bureau, 1957.

————. *T. Thomas Fortune: Militant Journalist*. Chicago: University of Chicago Press, 1972.

Thweatt, Hiram. *What the Newspapers Say of the Negro Soldier in the Spanish-American War*. Thomasville, Ga.: n.p., n.d.

Tindall, George B. *South Carolina Negroes, 1877–1900*. Columbia: University of South Carolina Press, 1952.

Titherington, Richard H. *A History of the Spanish-American War of 1898*. New York: D. Appleton, 1900.

Tompkins, E. Berkeley. *Anti-Imperialism in the United States: The Great Debate, 1890–1920*. Philadelphia: University of Pennsylvania Press, 1971.

Uya, Okon Edet, ed. *Black Brotherhood: Afro-Americans and Africa*. Lexington, Mass.: D. C. Heath, 1971.

Walters, Everett. *Joseph Benson Foraker: Uncompromising Republican*. Columbus: Ohio History Press, 1948.

Washington, Booker T. *A New Negro for a New Century*. Chicago: American Publishing House, 1900.

————. *The Future of the American Negro*. New York: Negro Universities Press, 1969.

Watterson, Henry. *The History of the Spanish-American War*. New York: n.p., 1898.

Weaver, John D. *The Brownsville Raid*. New York: W. W. Norton, 1970.

Welles, Sumner. *Naboth's Vineyard: The Dominican Republic, 1844–1924*. 2 vols. New York: Payton and Clarke, 1928.

Weston, Rubin. *Racism in U.S. Imperialism: The Influence of Racial Assumptions on American Foreign Policy, 1893–1946*. Columbia: University of South Carolina Press, 1972.

Whipple, James E. *The Story of the Forty-ninth*. Vinton, Iowa: n.p., 1903.

Willets, Gilson. *The Triumph of Yankee Doodle*. New York: F. Tennyson Neely, 1898.

Wolff, Leon. *Little Brown Brothers: How the United States Purchased and Pacified the Philippine Islands at the Century's Turn*. Garden City: Doubleday, 1961.

Index